The
REAL WITCHES
of
NEW ENGLAND

"*The Real Witches of New England* offers illuminating insight into contemporary witchcraft's place in New England's larger Pagan community. Following an introductory section tracing the devastating evolution of the Western cultural construct of conspiratorial 'witchcraft,' Hopman conducts two series of interviews that mirror the divide between the historical persecution of purported Satanic 'witches' and today's self-identified beneficent witches. This will appeal to both those who are simply curious about this widespread yet covert subculture and those who, having observed American Paganism from its youthful beginnings in the 'Occult Revival' of the 1970s, will see how adherents of today take up the cause now that the movement's pioneers are in retirement or have passed on."

JIM BAKER, AUTHOR OF *THE CUNNING MAN'S HANDBOOK*

"Hopman mixes a historian's curiosity with a journalist's zeal, resulting in a monumental achievement that bridges our own world with that of America's earliest witches."

THOMAS HATSIS, AUTHOR OF *THE WITCHES' OINTMENT* AND
PSYCHEDELIC MYSTERY TRADITIONS

"*The Real Witches of New England* is a truly fascinating and original approach to the subject. Hopman gives us a wide-ranging overview of the topic that covers not just historical witches but also their descendants, both actual family and some of the notables who practice Witchcraft in New England today. In someone else's hands this might have been a dry recital of facts, but instead it is a fun and entertaining read from start to finish."

DEBORAH BLAKE, AUTHOR OF *EVERYDAY WITCHCRAFT*

"A fascinating read and a brilliant and creative approach to American witchcraft—with moving portraits of America's first accused 'witches,' fascinating interviews with their descendants, and thoughtful insights from modern New England witches who redeem the label with dignity and spiritual depth. Who we remember will never die."

PHYLLIS CUROTT, ESQ., WICCAN PRIESTESS, AUTHOR OF
BOOK OF SHADOWS, WITCHCRAFTING, AND THE LOVE SPELL

"Ellen Evert Hopman took a discerning eye to accomplish this tome of knowledge. In our age of accountability this book is of its time, an account of the oppression of women and the incredible knowledge they so willingly shared. Witches all, we celebrate our heroes of the past."

LADY RHEA, AUTHOR AND CREATOR OF
THE ENCHANTED CANDLE AND COAUTHOR OF
THE ENCHANTED FORMULARY

"A detailed and very well researched book focusing on witches and witchcraft in New England. Primarily dealing with Salem, Massachusetts, and historical and present-day links thereto, Ellen Evert Hopman has opened a window into some of the occult practices in this part of the country. An excellent read!"

JANE T. SIBLEY, PH.D., AUTHOR OF
THE WAY OF THE WISE AND *THE DIVINE THUNDERBOLT*

The
REAL WITCHES
of
NEW ENGLAND

History, Lore & Modern Practices

ELLEN EVERT HOPMAN

Destiny Books
Rochester, Vermont

Destiny Books
One Park Street
Rochester, Vermont 05767
www.DestinyBooks.com

Destiny Books is a division of Inner Traditions International

Library of Congress Cataloging-in-Publication Data
Names: Hopman, Ellen Evert, author.
Title: The real witches of New England : history, lore, and modern practices
    / Ellen Evert Hopman.
Description: Rochester, Vermont : Destiny Books, 2018. | Includes
    bibliographical references and index.
Identifiers: LCCN 2018002259 (print) | LCCN 2018027995 (ebook) |
    ISBN 9781620557723 (pbk.) | ISBN 9781620557730 (ebook)
Subjects: LCSH: Witches—New England.
Classification: LCC BF1575 .H67 2018 (print) | LCC BF1575 (ebook) |
    DDC 133.4/30974—dc23
LC record available at https://lccn.loc.gov/2018002259

Printed and bound in the United States by P. A. Hutchison Company.

10 9 8 7 6 5 4 3 2 1

Text design by Priscilla H. Baker and layout by Virginia Scott Bowman
This book was typeset in Garamond Premier Pro with Heirloom Artcraft and
Futura used as display typefaces
Statue photo used for cover (left) and on page vii by Jennifer Marie Russo
Symbol used for cover (center) and chapter opening design courtesy of Uinen and
Yssion (Coven of Astraeos)

To send correspondence to the author of this book, mail a first-class letter to the
author c/o Inner Traditions • Bear & Company, One Park Street, Rochester, VT
05767, and we will forward the communication, or contact the author directly at
www.elleneverthopman.com.

*This book is dedicated to all minorities
who have experienced persecution.
May tolerance and understanding grow.*

A special thank-you is due to Judika Illes,
to Andrew Theitic, and to Christopher Penczak
for their help in finding the "hidden ones."

Contents

Modern Witches of New England   95

Foreword

By Judika Illes

"She's a *real* witch."

I hear that phrase frequently and have done so for about as long as I can remember. Rarely is it intended as a compliment. The person saying it is not praising someone for her potent spell casting or for her skills as a healer, herbalist, or clairvoyant. Neither is it meant as an acknowledgment of exceptional beauty, charisma, or even wisdom, despite the fact that the English word *witch* derives from similar etymological roots as the words *wisdom* and *wise*.

Instead the phrase is typically used as an insult for women in the public eye, often for women in politics or other prominent positions. These women span the entire political spectrum from one end to the other. I've seen the word *witch* directed at Hillary Rodham Clinton, Ann Coulter, and Condoleezza Rice as well as at assertive women in other fields. The synonym implied for this kind of "witch" is the word that it rhymes with—not *sorceress* or *enchantress*.

Even after decades of hearing and reading that phrase used in this way, I never fail to find it jarring. For me, *witch* is a positive word indicating a person possessing certain admirable qualities, such as independence, autonomy, and determination. *Witch* is a word to wear as a badge of pride, not an epithet that makes one cringe and flee.

Of course, historically, this has not been the case. As Ellen Evert Hopman recounts in these pages, the history of witchcraft is one of persecution, and it is not the witches who have been the persecutors, despite propaganda that says otherwise. Witches are too often described as evil and wicked, but across the board, they are the victims, not the victimizers.

And yet, despite thousands of years of persecution, the appeal of the witch survives. Whatever you think witches are—whether you see them as healers or practitioners of magic, repositories of ancient wisdom, persistent devotees of ancient deities or Satan's minions, disobedient women or the proud and unbowed—it is fair to say that witches consistently fascinate. All attempts to eradicate witchcraft and witches have failed, something that is acknowledged by the Old Testament, if you read between the lines.

Not long after the passage where Saul, first king of Israel, banishes and outlaws witches, we see him desperately searching for one himself.* In Saul's hour of need, he sends his minions out to find a bone-conjuring woman and seems to have little doubt that one will be found, despite his own laws to the contrary. Indeed, that woman is quickly found. In English, she is usually identified as the Witch of Endor or sometimes as the Medium of Endor or just the Woman of Endor.† According to the Bible, she does as the king commands effectively. She is depicted not as a fraud, but as a kind and professional practitioner, who comforts the king after delivering bad news.

So why the controversy? Why the insults? Why the attempts at eradication?

Here's my own theory: Authority of all kinds, secular as well as religious, fears a freethinker. Whatever else witches may be, they are people who think for themselves and who seek to define their own identities and carve out their own destinies, regardless of what those in power may desire. It is lack of obedience that is at the heart of antiwitchcraft efforts. (Remember, Pagan Rome was no friendlier to witches than Christian Rome, as the bacchantes can well attest.) Witches have his-

---

*First Book of Samuel 28:7–25.

†In the original Hebrew, she is identified as a *ba'alat ob*—the mistress of the now mysterious magical device known as an *ob*, which many contemporary scholars believe to be akin to Vodou govi jars, sacred receptacles that enable communication with the dead.

torically been canaries in the coal mine. The more brutal and oppressive the authority, the less tolerance there is for witchcraft or anything perceived or branded as witchcraft.

Of course, there's one huge exception: when analyzing the history of witch persecutions, it's always wise to follow the money trail. Although it may not be at the very root of what irritates authorities so much about witches, witchcraft accusations have long been an excuse to seize other people's wealth and property. Historically, one of the highest risk factors for being accused of witchcraft was being an independently wealthy woman. To be convicted of witchcraft was to forfeit lands and wealth; hence the refusal of Giles Corey, that indomitable man of Salem, to plead guilty or innocent to charges of witchcraft in order to save his property for his descendants. Likewise, the family of Countess Erzsébet Báthory, the so-called Blood Countess of Austria-Hungary, succeeded in having all charges of witchcraft dropped but did not fight the accusations of murder against her. To be convicted of murder meant being punished alone. To be convicted of witchcraft would impoverish one's entire family.

Giles Corey and Countess Báthory are well remembered, Giles for his bravery, the countess for her notoriety. Too many of the victims of the witch panics, however, lost their identities as well as their lives. Their names have been forgotten. Relatives hid family histories since it was dangerous to be a descendant or a relation of a convicted witch. What is remembered, though, lives. Ellen Evert Hopman documents those affected by the witch panics and then demonstrates how the repercussions of those panics affect the present. This is a valuable addition to the history of witchcraft and an important work.

For me, to be described as a "real witch" is praise indeed, regardless of how it's intended. Ellen and I are blessed to live in a place and era where there is freedom to practice as one pleases, to identify yourself publicly as a Druid or witch, and to discuss witchcraft without negative repercussions.

Sadly, that is not the case everywhere on Earth, even now in the twenty-first century. Depending where you are, especially in some regions of Africa and Asia, it is still dangerous and potentially a death sentence to be branded a witch. I hope during my lifetime this ceases to be true. I hope someone in those areas is documenting the individual cases and interviewing survivors and descendants in the same manner as Ellen has done here in *The Real Witches of New England*.

JUDIKA ILLES was born in New York City and has a degree in English and communications from Rutgers College. She is an aromatherapist and has been a professional card reader and spiritual advisor for over two decades. Judika is the author of numerous books devoted to traditional spirituality and the magical arts, including *Encyclopedia of Witchcraft, Encyclopedia of 5,000 Spells,* and *The Weiser Field Guide to Witches*.

Druids, Witches, and the Birth of This Book

I am not a Witch. I am a Druid. Witches and Druids are subsets of the larger religious umbrella called Paganism. I do have many friends and acquaintances who are Witches and they are all kind and decent folk. The following is a definition of Paganism from the Committee for the Pope's Millennium Apology:

> Paganism is, quite simply, Nature worship. It is also called "The Old Religion," "Ancient Ways," "Earth-Centered Spirituality," "Natural Religion," and "Nature-Based Religion."
>
> The early Christians, most of whom lived in cities, adopted the Roman word "Pagan" to refer to persons living in outlying areas who had not converted to Christianity. Paganism was pre-Christian. Over time the term came to be used to describe any non-Judeo-Christian religious minority, often in a negative way.
>
> Today, the word "Pagan," in its broadest sense, refers to persons following alternative spiritual paths, and who probably do not strictly adhere to the tenets of the world's largest religions, such as Hinduism, Islam, Buddhism, Judaism, and Christianity. Most modern Pagans feel a close connection to nature and the seasons, and

may look to early "Pagan" or indigenous cultures for guidance in strengthening this connection.

Modern Paganism (sometimes referred to as "Neopaganism" to distinguish it from original and indigenous pre-Christian folk traditions) is a revival and reconstruction of ancient Nature-based religions, adapted for the modern world.*

One of my personal mentors was Lord Theodore (Ted) Mills.† Ted was a Witch and a priest of the goddess Isis with whom I had tea about every two weeks for six years, until he made his transition to the Otherworld. Ted was a distant relation of Rebecca Towne Nurse of the Salem Witch trials, and his Coven could never figure out why he wanted to spend so much time with me. It turned out that he had vivid memories of his past life as a Druid, living in a cave. I myself have been a Druid since 1984, two years before I moved to New England.

I have always seen Druids and Witches as distinct, for a number of reasons. Druids were and still are polytheists, and the word Druid is a Celtic title bestowed on intellectual experts after many years of training. In ancient times it took twenty years to make a Druid, and Druids were lawyers, doctors, ambassadors, judges, historians, genealogists, poets, magicians, public ritualists, and political advisors to royalty. Witches were more often solitary commoners who operated in hamlets and rural areas as counselors, therapists, midwives, herbalists, veterinarians, and shamans, for farmers and the producers of goods.

In modern times the general public often thinks of Witches as "Wiccans," but Wicca is a religion that was created in the 1930s by Gerald Gardner. Modern Wiccans are duotheists who posit that "all the Gods are one God and all the Goddesses are one Goddess," so it hardly matters whom you call on. Wiccans will invoke "the Goddess" and "the God" in their rituals, to which a Druid must always ask, "Which god

---

*A definition of "Paganism" from the Committee for the Pope's Millennium Apology, www.lafond.us/pagans/Papal_Apology/FAQ.htm.

†Read more about Ted in my book *People of the Earth* and in this interview from *Fireheart* magazine at www.earthspirit.com/fireheart/fh4-ted.html.

do you mean?" and "Which goddess?" because we see them all as separate and distinct, from different cultures, with their own unique methods and personalities.

Witches like to cast circles and raise cones of power by dancing and chanting within a closed, prescribed ritual circle, an approach derived from medieval high ceremonial magic. Druids follow a more ancient pattern of leaving the ritual area open so that people, animals, and land spirits can wander in and out at will.

Modern Witches most often call upon the horizontal "four quarters" (north, south, east, and west), while Druids invoke the vertical "three worlds" of land, sea, and sky or nature spirits, ancestors, and gods. There are many other differences that are too numerous to cover here.

I have done a number of interview books in the past that studied Witches, generic Pagans, and Druids. I researched and then wrote each book in an effort to learn more about the ancient Pagan religion as it is expressed today, in the words of its adherents. For more about Druids, please see my books *A Legacy of Druids, A Druid's Herbal for the Sacred Earth Year, A Druid's Herbal of Sacred Tree Medicine,* and my trilogy of Iron Age Druid novels, which were specifically written to teach the Druid path, hidden inside a tale of religious conflict, war, and romance. For more about Wiccans, Witches, and Pagans, please see my book *Being a Pagan.*

I will tell you how this particular book came about. One day I happened to attend a poetry reading at the Deja Brew Café in Wendell, Massachusetts, and there I heard poet Michael Mauri read. We struck up a conversation and he gifted me with his little chapbook titled "Mary Webster, Witch of Hadley, 1683." I was amazed by the story of Mary, mainly because I have lived in this area of New England for thirty years and while I was vaguely aware of the goings-on in Salem, I had no idea that Witch persecutions and hangings had also happened here in western Massachusetts.

And so I began to research Mary Webster. I visited the local cemetery where she is buried, but being unable to locate her grave, I left a red rose under an old oak in the colonial-era section of the graveyard for her, asking the oak to convey my respects to her spirit. Soon the shadows of Mary and all the other, mostly female, persecuted "Witches" of New England began to haunt my thoughts and dreams and this book was born.

Here is an excerpt from Michael Mauri's poem that lit a small fire within me:

> **Mary Webster, you're poor,**
> **not rich,**
> *and so you stand, barefoot, accused,*
> *someone must be blamed—you are*
> > *a witch!*
>
> **You are a witch!**
> **in times like these,**
> *because, before your door,*
> *you make hay carts tip and tumble,*
> *of honest men on goodly errand*
> *on the long slog of mud road that never drains,*
> *through your dooryard, in the darkened bend*
> > *because you make*
> *their horses balk and oxen cease to draw*
> *and oxcarts shake, and drovers' cattle spook—you make*
> *milk curdle, and chimneys smoke, and soap-kettles*
> *boil over, and, generally, in wood or mowing, barnyard,*
> *hearth-side or high-way, you*
> *our Lord's good works suspend*
> > *upend!*
> *till good-wives, vexed, curse,*
> *and yeo-men,*
> *bedeviled,* hop, *in unholy rage*
> *from stone to stone with unchristian thought*
> *with rod or switch*
> *to beat or whip*

the fear—of Him
from whom all good things come!
back into you and break
your unkind mischief
Aye, Mary Webster, in the
Meeting House
you have not been seen,
this twelve-month, on many a Sabbath-Day,
to hear His wonder-working Word—you
have borne no witness, done no Christian Deed,
and now of witchcraft you're under strong suspicion.*

I empathize with Mary, buried just seventeen minutes by car from my house and deep within my psyche by sad arrows of feeling.

ELLEN EVERT HOPMAN,
UNDER THE OCTOBER FULL MOON

---

*Excerpt from "Mary Webster, Witch of Hadley, 1683," republished by permission of the author, Michael Mauri, Recession Editions Press, mikemaur@crocker.com. The Mary Webster poem was recorded with live music in 2012 and is available on *Yeoman*, a recording by Rob Skelton's Pitchfork & Mike Mauri (see www.cdbaby.com/cd/mike mauri) as well as in the MileLong listening lounge at https://soundcloud.com/milelong.

History
of Witch
Persecutions

Throughout history learned philosophers and thinkers have studied magic, alchemy, and other arcane arts. In Iron Age Europe it was the Druids (500 BCE to 500 CE) who kept the historical records and genealogies in their heads, taught the children of the nobility, practiced law and medicine, perfected the arts of magic, studied philosophy, performed religious rites, observed the motions of the stars and planets, were sacred singers and poets, and were the indispensable political and legal advisors to rulers.

The Greek magician and philosopher Pythagoras (570–495 BCE) and the poet, magician, and scientist Empedocles (490–430 BCE) were other examples of ancient magi (*magi* is Persian for "sorcerers"). Later Neoplatonist Italian Renaissance thinkers such as Marsilio Ficino (1433–1499) and Giovanni Pico della Mirandola (1463–1494) took on the mantles of magician and sage. In England John Dee (1527–1608), an advisor to Queen Elizabeth I and a mathematician, astronomer, astrologer, occult philosopher, alchemist, and Hermeticist, was an example of the learned wise man, and in France Éliphas Lévi (1810–1875) was an occult author and ceremonial magician.

But these kinds of educated mages were exceedingly rare. It was generally powerless, uneducated persons from the lower classes who were targeted in the witch persecutions and for a variety of reasons generally unrelated to witchcraft. Witch hunting, witch burnings, and executions continue in Tanzania and other areas of Africa to this day.

Because these people were mostly ordinary citizens wrongly accused of witchcraft, I use the lowercased *witch* to refer to them throughout this book and the uppercased *Witch* when speaking of the modern self-identified Witches of today.

WHO WAS TARGETED AND WHY

The typical victim of the witch persecutions was the wife or widow of a laborer or farmer, likely a woman with an assertive or quarrelsome nature. In fact, 75 to 85 percent of those executed were female because women were seen by the curia as more susceptible to lust than men and thus more likely to be swayed by temptations of the Devil. Women were also thought to be less intelligent than men, making them more likely to sin.

> *For Adam was formed first, then Eve. And it was*
> *not Adam who was deceived, but the woman who was*
> *deceived and fell into transgression.*
>
> Tim. 2:13–14*

The biblical myth of Adam and Eve taught that all women were inherently evil and the cause of the fall of mankind:

> *When the woman saw that the tree [of the knowledge*
> *of good and evil] was good for food, and that it was a*
> *delight to the eyes, and that the tree was desirable to*
> *make one wise, she took from its fruit and ate; and she*
> *gave also to her husband with her, and he ate.*
>
> Gen. 3:6

---

*All bible verses used in this book can be found at http://biblehub.com.

Then the Lord God said to the woman, "What is this you have done?" The woman said, "The serpent deceived me, and I ate."

So the Lord God said to the serpent, "Because you have done this, cursed are you above all livestock and all wild animals! You will crawl on your belly and you will eat dust all the days of your life.

And I will put enmity between you and the woman, and between your offspring and hers; he will crush your head, and you will strike his heel."

To the woman he said, "I will make your pains in childbearing very severe; with painful labor you will give birth to children. Your desire will be for your husband, and he will rule over you."

To Adam he said, "Because you listened to your wife and ate fruit from the tree about which I commanded you, 'You must not eat from it,' Cursed is the ground because of you; through painful toil you will eat food from it all the days of your life.

It will produce thorns and thistles for you, and you will eat the plants of the field.

By the sweat of your brow you will eat your food until you return to the ground, since from it you were taken; for dust you are and to dust you will return."

GEN. 3:13–19

Midwives and herbalists were targeted because they knew how to heal with herbs, which threatened the credibility of priests and their prayers. They also knew how to produce birth control and abortions at a time when Europe was recovering from the ravages of the Black Death, and nobles needed more workers to maintain their estates and kingdoms.

EXECUTION OF MRS. ANN HIBBINS.

Hanging of Ann Hibbins for witchcraft on Boston Common in 1656;
sketch by F. T. Merril, 1886. Ann was the inspiration
for Nathaniel Hawthorne's *The Scarlet Letter.*

Women with power over their own reproduction and bodies were less
amenable to control by their husbands and the male priesthood.

Lonely women such as widows who kept cats as pets were targeted,
especially in England. There, ownership of a cat was taken as proof of
witchcraft because the cat was seen as the witch's "familiar," an animal-
shaped demon that served the witch as servant, spy, and companion and
aided her in bewitching her enemies and divining their secrets. Most

of the cats in Tudor England were burned or killed so they would not spread evil. The killing of cats, of course, was an ignorant and cruel practice that aided the spread of rodent-borne diseases such as the plague.

In ancient times the aged had been treated with respect as the ones who carried the knowledge of how to survive. During the witch persecutions, the elderly, especially old crones with bad teeth, skin marks, and facial hair, were singled out as "evil" and marked for death, providing a convenient way for younger family members and neighbors to seize their property.

Men were seen as more valuable as workers so they were less likely to be accused. And while women with facial hair, especially if they were old, were automatically suspect, a man old enough to sport a beard was considered wise.

> *A hairy man's a geary [wealthy] man, but*
> *a hairy wife's a Witch.*
>
> OLD ENGLISH SAYING

Social causes for the witch persecutions included crop failures and famine. It was far more convenient to blame the old widow next door than to admit that an all-powerful God had allowed the crops to wither. Plague and other diseases were also blamed on witches and sorcerers. In areas where there was conflict between Roman Catholics and Protestants, torture, burnings, and executions for heresy were common (though more witches were killed in Catholic territories than in Protestant ones). The accused were often deprived of sleep for days, and many women were forced to sit on a red hot stool to keep them from having sex with the Devil. Thumb screws and leg irons heated over a fire were used on old women to extract confessions. Other punishments included whipping, fines, exile, banishment, burning at the stake, beheading, and hanging. Those who were able to endure torture and not confess were usually let go, but the use of torture often made the victim accuse themselves or others, leading to ever-wider panic.

The witch killings were a way to eliminate unpopular neighbors, antisocial loners, and aggressive people who simply did not get along well with others. The poor who were dependent on the community for support and those who cursed the better off were targeted, and the upper classes used the witch persecutions to control the lower classes, upon whose labor they depended. Church and state colluded to consolidate power using fear tactics, and hunting witches was a fine distraction from bad economic conditions.

Although most executed witches were female, in Germany, in 1629, about 60 percent were children. In Mora, Sweden, in the 1660s, fifteen boys were executed and forty children were whipped. In some areas men—primarily healers, elderly peasants, and sorcerers—were the targets. In Iceland 92 percent of those killed were men, as were 60 percent of those executed in Estonia and two-thirds of those executed in Moscow.

UNDERLYING REASONS FOR THE WITCH HYSTERIA

Much of the witch hysteria was engendered by the insecurity of the Christian establishment and its fear of those who might be in contact with the Devil. Christian authorities (and before them high temple Hebraic authorities) feared any threat to their own power and sovereignty. Evil "satanic" witches and Devil worshippers were said to participate in witches' Sabbats, which were a direct affront to authorized church Sabbaths. In Europe there was an intense competition between Catholics and Protestants that led to deadly confrontations and the torture and burning of those in the opposite camp, setting the scene for massacres and persecutions of anyone perceived as holding different beliefs.

In homogenous Catholic countries like Spain and Italy there was less violence against witches. The Holy Roman Empire and countries such as France, where sectarian conflict was at its worst, had more virulent witch persecutions, and in the Pyrenees, Languedoc, the Alpine areas, the northeast, Lorraine, and Franche-Comté there were numerous witch purges.

A witch and her familiars, from a 1579 publication
that dealt with witch trials in Windsor

Germany was also one of the most violent witch-hunting nations, but southern Bavaria and the Lower Rhine saw fewer executions than other regions. This was probably because Germany was a crazy quilt of over three hundred territories at that time and, being highly decentralized, was judicially impossible to control. The Basque region of Spain (near the Pyrenees) saw more violence against witches than other parts of Iberia.

Ireland had few witch trials and saw very little preoccupation with Satanism. In England the major concern was malevolent sorcery rather than demonic contact and there was a greater obsession with witches' familiars. Scottish trials led to far more executions, with numbers resembling those seen in France and Germany.

The difference between England and Scotland was likely that England had stronger laws and judicial centralization, which resulted in greater protection for persons. The English also had a jury system that exerted restraint on prosecutions, and there was less torture because only monarchs could authorize its use. Scotland's legal system was more locally based and thus harder to control.

TIMELINE OF PERSECUTIONS IN EUROPE

Thou shalt not suffer a witch to live.

Exod. 22:18

A man also or woman that hath a familiar spirit, or that is a wizard, shall surely be put to death: they shall stone them with stones, their blood shall be upon them.

Lev. 20:27

The total number of witches who were executed during the European persecutions appears to have been between forty thousand and three hundred thousand. The killing of just one "witch" in a given area would have been enough to spread terror in ripples across the entire community. The following is a timeline of the most significant events in the history of trials and executions of Europe's "witches" between 1400 BCE and 1945.

1400 BCE: Written by various authors and probably existing in the oral tradition before that, the Old Testament phrases shown above are the fountain from which the European and American witch persecutions sprang. The term "familiar spirit" also led to the torture and execution of cats and other animals.

The word *witch* in the Old Testament is an English translation and scholars disagree on the original meaning. The Hebrew word *kashaph,* meaning "to whisper," is one possible root word, as in "one who whispers a spell." *M'khashepah* is another word meaning "evil sorceress" or "a woman who uses spoken spells to harm others." A third translation posits *chaspah* or "poisoner."

While it's conceivable that there were terrifyingly powerful sorceresses and poisoners running rampant in the Hebrew tribes, there are other possibilities. Are these dire words describing actual practices or were they designed to warn devout Jews away from foreign gods, religions, and customs? Was it female and earth-centered goddesses that the male high temple priests were actually worried about, or were they simply using fear to mold polytheistic beliefs into a new monotheistic dogma?

The Hebrew high temple religion was different from the older earth-based folk religion. Canaanite religion, for example, was polytheistic, with gods and goddesses, the Elohim (plural), and ancestor worship. Near Eastern deities such as Baal, El, and the goddesses Asherah and Astarte were honored. Were the educated high priests of the temples trying to consolidate a new, male-centered, monotheistic religion's outlook? Their writings seem to describe a time when the Goddess was perceived as a threat to the sovereignty of God or Yahweh. The later book of Jeremiah, written between 630 and 580 BCE, records Yahweh's complaints:

> *The children gather wood, and the fathers kindle the*
> *fire, and the women knead their dough, to make cakes*
> *to the queen of heaven, and to pour out drink offerings*
> *unto other gods, that they may provoke me to anger.*
>
> JER. 7:18

> *"And," said the women, "when we were burning sacrifices*
> *to the queen of heaven, and were pouring out libations to*
> *her, was it without our husbands that we made for her*
> *sacrificial cakes in her image and poured out libations to*
> *her?"*
>
> JER. 44:19

First century CE: The monotheist Hebrew high temple religion had morphed into the new male-dominated monotheist Christian religion, and most other gods and goddesses were firmly banished (I say "most" because the Virgin Mary, Holy Spirit, and legions of male and female saints took over the roles once assigned to other divine personages and in some ways Christianity is actually polytheist, though it will never admit this of itself).

Fourth century CE: Saint Augustine of Hippo expressed his opinion that only the monotheist God was able to control the powers of nature, so it was impossible for a witch to have power. Since witches were deemed powerless, the church had no reason to persecute them at that time.

1000 CE: There was widespread panic and belief that the world was about to end. Those of us who remember the Y2K bug hysteria at the turn of the second millennium will recall the fear that computers would stop working, markets would crash, economies would burn, and nation states would collapse. Millions of people began hoarding food, building survival shelters, arming themselves, and preparing for societal collapse.

At the turn of the first millennium, the fear that the Devil would soon make an appearance was running rampant. At this time Satan began to take on his characteristic goat-like features as belief in demons amped up. People began reporting (or fantasizing about) having sex with male "incubi" and female "succubae." By the year 1200 the Devil was appearing in Christian art and clergy specialists in the field of demonology were sprouting up.

1208: Next began another episode where religious authorities sought to consolidate power. The church under Pope Innocent III started persecuting Gnostic Cathars as heretics for believing that God and Satan were in competition with each other. The Cathars were a protofeminist (they allowed women sacerdotal roles), duotheist Gnostic movement that believed the Devil created matter and the Old Testament "good God" created spirit. Catharism threatened the strictly monotheistic church dogma, and to frighten people away from it, the church spread the idea that Cathars were actually Satan worshippers. The public began to see satanic Cathars as a threat in their midst, and the massacre of Cathars commenced.

1273: Thomas Aquinas held that the world was full of evil demons and that those demons were determined to lead men into temptation with women in order to spread their seed. This was the first time sex and witchcraft were associated.

1300s: Witches were being depicted as malevolent Devil worshippers who had made a pact with Satan that gave them vast supernatural powers. At their death they would as a consequence go straight to Hell. Theologians were preoccupied with the idea that witches were in league with the Devil, the powerful adversary of the church, while peasants and common folk were more concerned about potential harm to their flocks and fields.

The Knights Templar, a powerful military and financial order to whom King Philip IV of France was in debt, were tortured and burned in France. Both Cathars and Knights Templar were accused of sodomy, Satanism, and sorcery. Other minorities such as Jews, Waldensians,* lepers, and homosexuals were persecuted, accused of conspiring to weaken or destroy Christianity.

1326: While early Christians had held the belief that it was a heresy to believe that witches had any real powers, Pope John XXII officially launched the Inquisition that authorized the prosecution of witchcraft as a type of heresy.

1348–1350: The Black Death happened, and Christians were led to believe that it was caused by a conspiracy of their enemies. Incest, orgies, and the spreading of disease, cannibalizing of children, and worshipping of Satan were crimes attributed to witches, heretics, and Jews. Anti-Semitism was conflated with demonic witchcraft practices.

1376: Nicholas Eymeric, an inquisitor in Aragon and Avignon, published his *Directorium Inquisitorum*, which was a manual for inquisitors that described how to conduct investigations, proper trial procedures, and definitions of different kinds of heresies.

1428: The Valais witch trials of the Western Alps region saw their first prosecution of demonic witches.

1431–1437: These years saw the convening of the Council of Basel, an antiwitch church council that standardized the satanic witch stereotype. Those attending would go on to spread their ideas throughout

---

*The Waldensian movement, founded by Peter Waldo, eschewed offices, dignities, and relics and believed in apostolic poverty, which put it at odds with the Catholic church.

Europe. The later invention of the printing press in 1440 speeded the transmission of their antiwitch ideas.

1437: An anonymous treatise called *Erorres Gazariorum* (*Error of the Cathars*) appeared. It described the witches' Sabbats, which included eating murdered children, kissing the Devil's behind, desecrating the host, and sex orgies, along with details of a pact between a witch and the Devil and elaborate recipes for magical potions. In this work witches were described as being predominately male.

1458: The inquisitor Nicholas Jacquier, who had attended the Council of Basel, wrote *Flagellum haereticorum fascinariorum* (*A Scourge for Heretical Witches*), which described witchcraft as an "abominable sect and heresy of wizards" and declared that the persecution of witches was justifiable.

Mid-1400s: The Cathars who had fled the Inquisition and moved to Germany were being tortured. They confessed to flying to meetings with Satan, kissing Satan's rear end, casting spells, raising storms, and having sex with animals. The stereotypical "witch" persona was created at this time.

1475: Johannes Nider published *Formicarius,* where for the first time witches were said to be primarily uneducated and female. His reasoning was that females were inferior physically, mentally, and morally and therefore more susceptible to the Devil. Previously witches were considered to be educated male mages.

1484: Pope Innocent VIII accused German "Satanists" of consorting with demons, ruining crops, and aborting babies. He issued a papal bull, *Summis desiderantes affectibus,* which affirmed the existence of witches and approved the Inquisition (it is also known as the witch bull of 1484). He charged the Inquisition to do everything necessary to eradicate witches, whom he blamed for causing abortions, making men impotent, and making women barren. He also commissioned friars Heinrich Kramer and Jacob Sprenger to pen a detailed report called

The *Obscene Kiss* by Francesco Maria Guazzo is a 1608 depiction of witches kissing Satan's rear end.

Malleus Maleficarum (*Hammer of Witches*), which became the new orthodoxy. Witches were to be hunted down and killed; female witches were accused of collecting penises and keeping them in boxes, of having sex with demons, and of killing babies. The *Hammer of Witches* gave instructions to strip suspects naked and to inspect them for "witch's marks" such as moles and flea bites.

1489: Ulrich Molitor published *De Lamiis et Pythonicis Mulieribus* (*Of Witches and Diviner Women*). He advocated execution for heretics and witches but also argued that witches' Sabbats were a satanic illusion with no basis in reality. He was considered a moderate at that time for stating that evidence obtained by torture was unreliable: "For the fear of punishments incites men to say what is contrary to the nature of the facts."*

---

*Rossell Hope Robbins, *The Encyclopedia of Witchcraft and Demonology* (New York: Crown Publishers, 1959).

Early to mid-1500s: Witch hysteria and mass executions took place in Catholic and Protestant areas of Switzerland, Italy, Germany, England, Ireland, and France. Torture and the testimony of children were used to entrap witches. Under torture witches would name others, which caused the witch panic to spread. About eighty thousand people were executed, and about 80 percent of those were women.

Two Dominican monks burned at the stake
by order of the Inquisition in Geneva, Switzerland,
in 1549 for allegedly signing pacts with the Devil

1531: In Germany a witch was charged with burning the town of Schiltach. A witch hunt spread out to northern Italy, Switzerland, and southern Germany.

1536: The Reformation of Denmark occurred, and Danish witch burnings increased.

1542: The English Witchcraft Act established official penalties for witchcraft. Also during this year the Italian Roman Inquisition restrained the secular courts from torture and executions. The official

Roman Catholic manual for the hunting of witches urged caution, the goal being to urge witches to renounce their sins and be reconciled back into Catholic society.

1561–1670: The worst witch hunts in Europe peaked in central and southern Germany.

A depiction from a popular print in Germany of witch trials in Derenburg, Germany, in 1555

1562: The Elizabethan Witchcraft Act was passed during the reign of Queen Elizabeth I. It was "agaynst Conjuracions Inchauntmentes and Witchecraftes."

1577: Protestants began to associate witchcraft with wild orgies, lewd naked dancing, cannibalism, and infanticide. Witchcraft was viewed as a heresy that violated the commandment "Thou shalt have no other God before me."

1581–1593: These years saw the height of the witch persecutions in Trier, Germany.

1590–1591: The North Berwick witch trials were held in Scotland. King James VI of Scotland became engaged to Princess Anne of Denmark. On the way to the wedding Anne's boat encountered a bad storm and she was forced to take refuge in Norway. James traveled there to meet her and they married, but on the way back to Scotland they encountered another terrible storm. Six Danish women confessed to having raised the storms, and James, now terrified of witches, began torturing and burning suspects.

James believed that Francis Stewart, the Fifth Earl of Bothwell, was a witch. Hearing this, Francis Stewart fled. The king then outlawed him as a traitor and created a royal commission to hunt down witches in Scotland.

1597: An advocate for the torture of witches, King James published *Daemonologie*, a dissertation on necromancy, demonology, black magic, divination, and the reasons witches should be persecuted under canonical law. This book was a major inspiration for Shakespeare's *Macbeth*.

Suspected witches kneeling before King James,
from *Daemonologie,* 1597

Witch burning in Amsterdam in 1571 by Jan Luyken

1600–1692: Witch persecutions and trials occurred in Norway.

1603–1606: The witch trials peaked in Fulda, Germany.

1606: Shakespeare wrote *Macbeth*, a play that featured witches in prominent roles. In act 4, scene 1, witches are depicted as strange old hags gathered around a cauldron chanting a rhymed spell: "Double, double, toil and trouble / Fire burn and cauldron bubble."

1609–1611: The witch trials peaked in the Basque region.

1612: The English Pendle witch trials took place when three generations of a single family were driven through the streets of Lancaster to be hung, by order of King James.

1613: The last witch execution in Holland took place.

1626–1631: The witch hysteria and trials were at their peak in Wurzburg and Bamberg, Germany.

1635: The Roman Inquisition admitted that it had found "scarcely one trial conducted legally."

1640s: Intense witch hunting continued in France and England, after which things began to gradually calm down.

1647: Englishman Mathew Hopkins, a failed lawyer who styled himself the "witch-finder general," wrote the book *The Discovery of Witches.* He and his accomplices killed nearly three hundred suspected witches using forced confessions, examinations for witch's marks such as warts, moles, and insect bites, and swimming tests where the accused witch would have her thumbs bound to her opposite big toes and be thrown in a river. If she sank or drowned she was pronounced innocent; if she floated it was proof of guilt.

He also pricked the skin of his victims with a "jabbering needle" to see if they were insensitive to pain. It was a retractable needle that guaranteed that the witch felt nothing, leading inevitably to her or his death. His book was brought to America and fueled the witch persecutions in the colonies.

1648: Holland declared an end to all punishments for witchcraft.

1650: Councilors of Rothenberg, Germany, begin treating witchcraft cases with caution.

1674: The witch trials in Scandinavia peaked. In the trials in Torsaker, Sweden, seventy-one witches were executed in just one day.

1675–1690: One hundred and thirty-nine people were executed for witchcraft in Salzburg, Austria.

1682: Some of the last gasps of the English witch panic occurred when Temperance Lloyd, a senile, elderly woman, and Susannah Edwards were executed for witchcraft in Exeter. The overall numbers of those killed were lower in England than in other countries, and only four witches were killed in Ireland, due to stronger laws and better legal protections. By now the Enlightenment had begun to set in with its emphasis on

MATTHEW HOPKINS,
OF MANNINGTREE, ESSEX,
THE CELEBRATED WITCH-FINDER.

Matthew Hopkins, "the witch finder, General,"
author of *The Discovery of Witches*

logic, reason, and humanitarianism. The idea that witches did no real harm and that seeking confessions through torture was cruel and inhumane had begun to spread.

1693: The last witch execution in Denmark occurred.

1712: Jane Wenham was tried in Walkern, Hertfordshire, England. She had won a defamation case after a farmer accused her of witchcraft and was awarded a shilling, but the same farmer then accused her of bewitching a servant, making his daughter ill, and killing his livestock. She was examined for witch's marks and when asked to recite the Lord's Prayer apparently stumbled, which was taken as evidence against her. She was convicted but was eventually secreted away by William Cowper, the First Earl of Cowper, and lived out her days in a cottage on his estate.

1715: Kate Nevin was hunted for three weeks in Scotland and then burned at Monzie, Perthshire.

1716: Mary Hickes and her nine-year-old daughter Elizabeth were condemned to death and hanged in Huntingdon, England, on July 28, accused of taking off their stockings in order to raise a rainstorm.

1727: Elderly and senile Janet Horne was executed in Dornoch, Scotland, and was the last person executed for witchcraft in Scotland.

1735: The English Witchcraft Act changed prosecutions from witchcraft to fraud once the fear of Satan began to diminish. Now fortunetellers and mediums became the new targets of harassment.

1750: Maria Theresa of Austria outlawed witch burning and torture.

1756: Fifteen-year-old Veronika Zeritschin was beheaded and burned in Landshut, Germany. She was the last witch executed in that country.

1775: The last witch execution took place in France, and the last witchcraft conviction in Germany took place.

1782: The last witch execution in Switzerland occurred.

1793: The last Polish witch execution took place.

1811: The last witch execution in Prussia took place.

1863: An accused male witch was drowned in a pond Hedingham, Essex, England.

1895: Bridget Cleary of Ireland was beaten and then burned to death by her husband because he suspected that the fairies had taken the real Bridget and left a witch in her place.

1945: An elderly farm hand was executed in Meon Hill, Warwickshire, England, accused of being a wizard.

1951: The English Witchcraft Act was finally repealed. It had been in force until the 1940s and in the twentieth century was mainly used to persecute Spiritualists and gypsies.

1997: Two Russian farmers killed a woman and injured her family members because they thought she had used folk magic against them.

WITCH PANIC COMES TO THE NEW WORLD

The witch trials in the English colonies were in many ways a continuation of the persecutions engendered by King James's terror of witches. The first witch accusation in Massachusetts happened in May 1649 in Springfield, when Mary Lewis Parsons accused Widow Marshfield of being a witch. Mary Parsons was found guilty of slander for the accusation, and her husband Hugh was forced to pay a fine in Indian corn. In 1651 Mary herself was accused of being a witch, and then she in turn accused her own spouse of witchcraft.

Thirty-five neighbors also turned out to accuse Hugh Parsons, who was not well liked due to his bad business dealings and foul temper. The accusations against Hugh included exploding sausages, missing knives and trowels, and making men fall from their horses. Mary had already endured the deaths of two of her children, which had left her mentally unhinged. During the trial a third child died, and Mary went insane, saying she was guilty of its death.

Hugh was acquitted, and Mary was found innocent of witchcraft but was sentenced to hang anyway for the murder of her child. Sick and mentally ill, Mary seems to have died in prison before the execution could take place.

From there the witch hysteria began to spread through New England. Once a person was accused, accomplices were sought out.

Colonial-era witch hysteria in the United States,
from *A History of the United States of America*, 1828

Herbalists, healers, and midwives were often suspects, and property disputes and other arguments between neighbors led to more accusations.
Ergot fungus poisoning from damp grain has been alluded to as a possible reason for the mass hallucinations about witches, but many other
societal forces were also at work, as we shall see below.

In 1669 Susannah North Martin had to post a hundred-pound bond
and appear in court for the charge of witchcraft in Salisbury, Massachusetts.
Susannah and her husband, George Martin, seem to have had a fractious
relationship with their neighbors, and according to reports Susannah was
a forthright, opinionated woman who spoke against authority. William
Sargent Jr. claimed that he saw Susannah give birth to and then stran-
gle an illegitimate child in a stable. Sargent also said that Susannah was
a witch and that one of Susannah's sons, George Martin, was a bastard
and the other, Richard Martin, was her "imp" (a witch's familiar). While
the court dropped the charges regarding the boys, it upheld the charge of
witchcraft, although it was later dismissed by a higher court.

A second witchcraft accusation was brought against Susannah in 1692, the year that the well-known Salem, Massachusetts, witch mania began. George Martin had died in 1686, leaving Susannah in an impoverished state, and as witchcraft hysteria gripped the area neighbors came forward to bring charges against her. Susannah was arrested in Amesbury on May 2 and brought to Salem Village (now known as Danvers), where residents began to claim that Susannah had tried to recruit them as witches, and accusations including anything from changing a dog into a cask to doing "great hurt and damage" to the bodies of a number of young women of Salem Village continued to pile up. Susannah pleaded not guilty but was not allowed to have legal counsel. After her conviction she was held in the Salem jail for two and a half months, and on July 19, 1692, she and several other accused women were driven in a cart to Gallows Hill. After they were hung, the bodies of the women were placed in a shallow grave.

Depiction of the Salem witch trials, from *Giles Cory, Yeoman*, a play by Mary E. Wilkins Freeman, 1893

Depiction of Tituba by John W. Ehninger, 1902

Tituba, who was either a Native South American or of mixed African and Caribbean descent, was captured as a child and taken into slavery, and in 1680 she was either bought by Samuel Parris or given to him to settle a debt. In 1688 Parris, his family, and his slaves moved to Salem.

Tituba's troubles started in 1692 when three girls in the Parris household began to throw fits, falling down and shaking and babbling incoherently. Although doctors made efforts to deal with the mysterious malady, the final diagnosis was witchcraft. The girls identified Tituba and two other women as the cause of the witchcraft against them, and on February 29, 1692, the women were arrested.

Symptoms began to spread throughout the community. Now others claimed to feel the effects of witchcraft against them, or claimed to have witnessed it years before. At first Tituba pled not guilty, but she soon realized that was not what her inquisitors wanted to hear. Tituba became the first accused witch to "confess" in Salem, and she was also the first to name other witches in an effort to avoid further punishment. By continuing to admit her guilt she managed to evade a trial and

THE SHERIFF BROUGHT THE WITCH UP THE BROAD AISLE, HER CHAINS
CLANKING AS SHE STEPPED.

A witch in chains, possibly a depiction of Rebecca Towne Nurse, by Freeland A. Carter, from *The Witch of Salem*, 1893

saved her own life. In May 1692 a grand jury found her not guilty due to lack of evidence.

Although the witch hysteria in Salem, Massachusetts, is perhaps the most famous, witch persecutions also occurred in other areas of the New World. In 1706 Grace Sherwood of Virginia, a healer and midwife, was accused of shape-shifting herself into a cat, ruining her neighbor's crops, killing livestock, and causing a woman to miscarry. She was tested by ducking, and unfortunately for her, she floated (if she had sunk and drowned she would have been deemed innocent). She spent eight years in jail before being released.

In the 1830s Joseph (or William) Stout of Fentress County,

One of the sisters in the Towne Sisters Statue in the Salem Wax Museum; photo by Jennifer Marie Russo

Tennessee, was the last person tried for witchcraft in the United States. The charge was for "damaging the health of a young woman," but since she failed to appear at the trial, the case was dismissed.

Altogether more than 200 men and women were accused of witchcraft in the New World. Of those, 35 were executed and 5 died in jail. In Salem alone, between 144 and 185 were accused, and out of this group, 28 were convicted, 19 were hanged, 1 was pressed to death, and 4 died in prison.

PRACTICES AND TRADITIONS OF REAL WITCHES

The Christian man who in any of this like is afflicted,
and he then will seek his health at unhallowed practices,
or at accursed enchantments, or at any witchcraft, then

will he be like to those heathen men, who offered to an
idol for their bodies' health, and so destroyed their souls.

ABBOT AELFRIC OF EYNSHAM,
THE HOMILIES OF THE ANGLO-SAXON CHURCH

Likewise some witless women go to cross-roads, and
draw their children through the earth, and thus commit
themselves and their children to the Devil.

ABBOT AELFRIC OF EYNSHAM, FROM WALTER W. SKEAT'S
AELFRIC'S LIVES OF SAINTS: BEING A SET OF SERMONS
ON SAINT'S DAY FORMERLY OBSERVED BY
THE ENGLISH CHURCH

What were the heinous folk practices that had clergy and legal experts so upset? We have now seen that most witches were uneducated laborers of the lower classes. Witchcraft, if it was practiced at all, was primarily a craft of the rural peasant.

The common people held on to their goddesses, such as Diana, Holda, Brigid, and Perchta, for centuries after they were supposedly "converted." A Strega (Italian Witch) once told me that to this day some of the old women dressed in black go to Italian churches to light a candle in honor of Diana (not Mary), while wearing the horns for luck and protection.

At the time of the witch persecutions, it was English "white Witches," "cunning men," and "cunning women" and earlier Anglo-Saxon "Wiccan" (possibly from *witega*, meaning "prophet" or "seer") who used their voices to chant magical charms, raised the spirits of the dead to consult with them, and operated as counselors, healers, midwives, veterinarians, and soothsayers in rural areas. The Scots had their "weird-women," "weird-wives," and "spaeing women." The Norse *spákona* was a woman of prophecy. Irish "fairy doctors" could cure diseases, protect against sorcery (also known as "black Witchcraft"), divine the future, identify enemies, and locate lost or stolen property and treasure. German witches had their *wunsciligerta*, a hazelwood divining rod or "wishing thorn" to find water, ores, and hidden objects. That practice is still known as "water witching," or dowsing, today.

All these practitioners could cast lots, read omens, predict the future, and cure ailments with herbs and spoken spells. Herbalists and healers were especially suspect. They sang over plants before they picked them, praising the plants and beseeching them to heal a sick person. They chanted prayers and spells over medicines and potions and asked a plant's permission before cutting it, leaving offerings of milk, cider, or honey on the earth in exchange.

An Old English penitential document describes the punishment for using healing herbs as follows: "If a woman should work wizardry and enchantment and poisonous drugs and it should so come about, let her fast for twelve months on bread and on water."*

Below is a chant from the "Nine Herbs Charm" in the Old English *Lacnunga* manuscript that honors the herb mugwort, a wound-healing herb that was also good for women's maladies. It would have been chanted or sung by healers as they gathered the herb or made a potion from it. These kinds of incantations were viewed as idolatry by the church because herbalists were honoring the divine spark within plants, a type of Creation Spirituality.

> *Remember, mugwort, what you revealed*
> *what you set out in mighty revelation*
> *una you are called, oldest of plants*
> *you have might against three and against thirty*
> *you have might against poison and against infection*
> *you have might against the evil that travels around the*
> *land.*
>
> STEPHEN POLLINGTON, *LEECHCRAFT*

---

*Stephen Pollington, *Leechcraft: Early English Charms, Plantlore, and Healing* (Norfolk, England: Anglo-Saxon Books, 2003), 55.

Here is a hymn of praise for "waybread" or plantain, which was also a powerful agent to pull infection from wounds and insect bites:

> *And you, waybread, mother of plants*
> *open to the east, mighty within,*
> *carts ran over you, ladies rode over you,*
> *brides cried over you, bulls snorted over you,*
> *you withstood all then, and you were crushed / so may*
> *you withstand poison and infection*
> *and the evil that travels round the land.*
>
> STEPHEN POLLINGTON, *LEECHCRAFT*

The Scottish *Carmina Gadelica* records a hymn to St. John's wort:

> *Saint John's wort, Saint John's wort,*
> *My envy whosoever has thee,*
> *I will pluck thee with my right hand,*
> *I will preserve thee with my left hand,*
> *Whoso findeth thee in the cattle fold,*
> *Shall never be without kine.*
>
> ALEXANDER CARMICHAEL, *CARMINA GADELICA:*
> *HYMNS & INCANTATIONS*

St. John's wort, known as *alla-bhi, alla-bhuide* (the noble yellow plant), was considered a magically protective herb that could shield a person from second sight, Witchcraft, spells, and death. It was said to bring peace to the home and growth and fertility to the fields and herds. Women would wear it secretly, hidden in their clothing, and men hid it in their vests. The magic only worked if the plant was found accidentally.

Shamrocks—the four- or five-leafed variety being the most magically significant—were supposed to be found by accident too. The hymn that follows is one of my favorites because the image of Mary "under the bank" is so clearly an allusion to an Earth goddess:

Thou shamrock of foliage,
Thou shamrock of power,
Thou shamrock of foliage,
Which Mary had under the bank . . .

ALEXANDER CARMICHAEL, *CARMINA GADELICA*

Pagan deities were still being called on for healing. Here is a Scottish charm for a sprain that is an invocation of Bride (Brigid):

Bride went out
In the morning early,
With a pair of horses;
One broke his leg,
With much ado,
That was apart,
She put bone to bone,
She put flesh to flesh,
She put sinew to sinew,
She put vein to vein;
As she healed that
May I heal this.

ALEXANDER CARMICHAEL,
CARMINA GADELICA

Compare this to the Pagan Old High German Merseburg incantation that was first written down in the tenth century by a Christian cleric:

Phol and Wodan rode into the woods,
There Balder's foal sprained its foot.
It was charmed by Sinthgunt, her sister Sunna;
It was charmed by Frija, her sister Volla;
It was charmed by Wodan, as he well knew how:
Bone-sprain, like blood-sprain,
Like limb-sprain:

Bone to bone; blood to blood;
Limb to limb—like they were glued.

D. L. ASHLIMAN,
MERSEBURG INCANTATIONS

Both this charm and the one before it start with a historical recounting of a culturally appropriate event involving the Old Gods, followed by a magically formulaic chant to cause healing.

The practice of singing over plants, sick persons, and remedies has very ancient Indo-European roots. Below is an excerpt from the Sanskrit hymn "Praise of Herbs" used by Vedic physicians and taken from the *Rig Veda*, possibly the oldest written book on the planet and composed roughly between 1500 and 1200 BCE:

6 *He who hath store of Herbs at hand like Kings amid a*
crowd of men,—
Physician is that sage's name, fiend-slayer, and chaser of
disease.

7 *Herbs rich in Soma, rich in steeds, in nourishments, in*
strengthening power,—
All these have I provided here, that this man may be
whole again.

8 *The healing virtues of the Plants stream forth like cattle*
from the stall,—
Plants that shall win me store of wealth, and save thy
vital breath, O man.

9 *Reliever is your mother's name, and hence Restorers are*
ye called.
Rivers are ye with wings that fly: keep far whatever
brings disease.

10 *Over all fences have they passed, as steals a thief into the*
fold.
The Plants have driven from the frame whatever malady
was there.

11 *When, bringing back the vanished strength, I hold these*
herbs within my hand,
The spirit of disease departs ere he can seize upon the
life.

12 *He through whose frame, O Plants, ye creep member by*
member, joint by joint,—
From him ye drive away disease like some strong arbiter
of strife.

13 *Fly, Spirit of Disease, be gone, with the blue jay and*
kingfisher.
Fly with the wind's impetuous speed, vanish together
with the storm.

"Hymn XCVII. Praise of Herbs," in *Rig Veda*,
translated by Ralph T. H. Griffith

There were other healing practices that church clerics frowned upon and for which they meted out punishment. For instance, a seven-year penance was required for "any woman who place[d] her daughter on a roof or in an oven for her recovery."*

What was this "blasphemous" practice all about? It had to do with fevers. Healers would place a feverish person on a roof to cool them and bring down a fever or place them in a warm oven to bring on a sweat so the body could cool itself. The Irish *teach allais* (sweat house) was used for this purpose, as were Native American "sweat lodges," which are still used to this day.

Another magical practice involved the tying of knots and the charming of thread (*eólas an t-snáithein* in Gaelic). Three threads colored red, white, and black (or blue) were wound around the affected part while a charm was recited. Here is an example:

I put my trust in the remedy
Which Dian Cécht left with his people,

---

*Pollington, *Leechcraft*, 55.

In order that whatever it goes upon may be healed.
Traditional Scottish charm

When a woman went into labor, her hair was combed loose and all the knots in her shoes and clothing were untied. Windows and locks in the birthing area were unlocked and unbolted. To cure warts, a length of string was rubbed over them and then as many knots as there were warts were tied in the string. The string was buried in the ground so that as it dissolved, so would the warts.*

Herbalists and healers used many other practices as well. They applied magical girdles and healing stones and draped healing cloths such as the Irish *brat* Bhride† over the sick. They hung special herbs, tree limbs, and charmed wreaths over doorways, tied herbs such as rowan (mountain ash) to the necks and tails of cattle to protect them from disease and the evil eye, tied ritually blessed strips of cloth on the sick to transfer illnesses from persons to trees, passed sick babies over a fire to ritually purify them, smudged houses with juniper, mugwort, and other sacred herbs, carried torches or lit coals around houses and the boundaries of land to purify the area, collected holy water from special streams and wells, and passed sick children through clefts in trees and holes in stones. All of these practices were described by church authorities as witchcraft and sorcery.

One can only imagine the lives that would have been saved if the village cunning women and herbalists had been allowed to use freely their knowledge of plants, clean water, and sweating. Herbalism is only now starting to recover from the centuries of suppression.

Pagan Folk Religion Was Suspect

At the time of the witch hunts the spiritual practices of Witches and other Pagans were seen as a direct threat to the hegemony of the

---

*Ellen Evert Hopman, *Scottish Herbs and Fairy Lore* (Los Angeles: Pendraig Publishing, 2010), 54.

†Brat Bhride is Gaelic for "Brigid's mantle," which was left out on Imbolc Eve each year so Brigid could bless it as she passed by.

Christian church. (It is worth remembering that most accused witches were actually Christians.) Witches and healers performed a shamanic role in rural communities: along with the healing of animals and people, they would be called upon to help make the land fertile.

One old Anglo-Saxon "field remedy" called "Æcerbot" involved rising before dawn and digging a chunk of turf from each of the four quarters of a farm. A bit of each tree and herb growing on the land was collected and then yeast, milk, honey, oil, and a sample of each plant found on the farm were mixed together and poured over the roots of the turf, and then the turf was put back in the ground.

Once the turf was replaced, the Witch or healer faced east toward the rising Sun, turned three times clockwise, and asked the Sun to fill the earth so the crops would grow. A plow was anointed with a paste of fennel, oil, and salt and plowing began with the following chant: "Erce, Erce, Erce, Eordan Modor. Hal wes thu Folde, fira moder."* (Erce, Erce, Erce, Earth Mother. Hale be thou Earth, mother of humanity.) "Erce" may be from the Old High German word *erchan* (meaning "genuine" or "true"), or it may refer to the name of an Earth goddess.*

A good way to understand the old Pagan spiritual life is to look at the writings of the church fathers who condemned it. By using reverse logic, we can appreciate what the actual beliefs and practices were.

The 1601 "Annual Report of the Society of Jesus" records the following about Lithuanian Pagans:

> Elsewhere they keep stones, not small ones, in their granaries, dug into the ground with the smooth surface uppermost, covered not with earth but with straw and they call them "Deyves" (gods). They religiously worship them as guardians of their corn and herds.†

---

*Jacob Grimm, *Teutonic Mythology,* vol. 1, 4th ed., trans. James Steven Stallybrass (London: W. Swan Sonnenschein & Allen, 1880), 254.
†Ken Dowden, *European Paganism: The Realities of Cult from Antiquity to the Middle Ages* (London: Routledge, 2000), 64.

The 1618 "Annals of the Wendish Residence of the Society of Jesus" states:

> They worship certain stones as sacred which they keep in their stores or granaries. . . . It is a terrible sin amongst them to profane such places or for them to be touched by anyone else except the person who has the right from the (power) above. They pour over such stones the blood of whatever animals they slaughter and they put there a small portion from any meal.*

These stones were obviously a focus for spiritual devotion and respect, a type of domestic altar. It is worth remembering that in those days most people were farmers who slaughtered their own animals for food and that every farmstead had fresh blood as a result. There was nothing lurid about the practice, which was intended as a kind of thanks offering.

Sacred trees were another focus of Pagan worship. Anglo-Saxon St. Boniface (675 CE–754 CE) was engaged in converting German Pagans in 723 CE. Willibald, an Anglo-Saxon priest, wrote in his *The Life of St. Boniface:*

> Some were sacrificing secretly to wood and springs, others again openly. Some were practicing haruspicy [examining the organs of sacrificed animals] and divination, portents and incantations in secret, others indeed blatantly. Some turned to augury and auspices and practiced various sacrificial rites; others again did none of this. Planning to deal with all this, St. Boniface attempted the chopping down of a particular oak tree of amazing size which was called the "Oak of Jupiter" in the former language of the pagans, at a place called Geismar [not far from Göttingen] with the servants of God standing beside him. When, finding strength through the constancy of his mind, he had cut down the tree, a large number of pagans

---

*Dowden, *European Paganism,* 64.

appeared and amongst themselves they vigorously cursed the enemy of their gods.*

And who can blame them?

The 1606 "Annual Report of the Society of Jesus" reports on tree worship in Lithuania:

> Some have two particular trees: one is an oak, the other a lime. They call the oak masculine and at fixed times put two eggs beneath it. They call the lime feminine and offer it butter, milk, cheese and fat, for the well-being and protection of them and their children. If any are taken ill, straightaway they send the Popus [priest] to the trees to demand of the trees why they are allowing them to be unwell in view of their having made the due gift to them. If they do not get well immediately, they bring the trees twice the said goods and are so freed. . . . They offer in the woods several barrels of beer, more beer or less beer in proportion to the help they have had from the god. . . . They offer these gifts in this way to the trees. The old Popus, together with the other old men, mumbles a fixed formula and presents and offers gifts. Then, some people run up and lift the barrel of beer on high. The Popus, before they begin to drink, takes a sprinkler [i.e., a branch] from a lime tree and sprinkles the bystanders. Afterwards, fires are prepared in many places and they throw part of the offerings, the fat, onto the fire. They think the gods will never hear them without beer. And in this way, well drunk, they begin to hold dances around the trees and to sing.†

St. Martin of Tours (316 or 336 CE–397 CE) was passionate about cutting down Pagans' sacred trees. In Sulpicius Severus's *Life of St. Martin of Tours* we read the following account:

---

*Dowden, *European Paganism,* 71.
†Dowden, *European Paganism,* 73.

When in a particular village he had demolished a very ancient temple and was moving on to fell the pine tree next to the shrine, this was the point at which the priest (antistes) of that place and the general mass of the pagans began to put up resistance. Though at the command of the Lord these same people had been quiet when the temple was being destroyed, they would not allow the tree to be chopped down. Martin painstakingly reminded them that there was nothing religious about a stump and that they should rather be following the God he himself served. This tree had to be chopped down because it was dedicated to a demon.[*]

By "demon" he presumably means one of the Old Gods.

Pope Gregory wrote to Brunnhilda, queen of the Franks, in 597:

We equally encourage you to do this also, namely to restrain your other subjects under the control of discipline so that they do not sacrifice to idols, so that worshippers of trees should not exist, so that in the matter of the heads of animals they should not exhibit sacrilegious sacrifices, because it has reached our ears that many of the Christians also meet at churches and—an evil thing to report—do not refrain from instances of worship of demons.[†]

Which brings us to sacred water. Martin Martin, who died on October 9, 1718, was the author of *A Description of the Western Isles of Scotland*. He visited the Western Isles at the close of the seventeenth century and described Pagan rites pertaining to sacred water. James Mackinlay paraphrases his findings:

A custom connected with ancient sea-worship had been popular among the inhabitants of Lewis till about thirty years before his visit, but had been suppressed by the Protestant clergy on account

---

[*]Dowden, *European Paganism*, 76.
[†]Dowden, *European Paganism*, 77.

of its pagan character. This was an annual sacrifice at Hallowtide to a sea god called Shony. Martin gives the following account of the ceremony: "The inhabitants round the island came to the church of St. Mulvay, having each man his provision along with him; every family furnished a peck of malt, and this was brewed into ale; one of their number was picked out to wade into the sea up to the middle, and, carrying a cup of ale in his hand, standing still in that posture, cried out with a loud voice, saying, "Shony, I give you this cup of ale, hoping that you'll be so kind as to send us plenty of sea-ware for enriching our ground the ensuing year," and so threw the cup of ale into the sea. This was performed in the night-time.*

Mackinlay also shares these Orkadian Witch charms of the seventeenth century:

The charm had to do with the churning of butter. Whoever wished to take advantage of it watched on the beach till nine waves rolled in. At the reflux of the last the charmer took three handfuls of water from the sea and carried them home in a pail. If this water was put into the churn there would be a plentiful supply of butter. Sea water was also used for curative purposes, the patient being dipped after sunset.†

Another Scottish water rite is described thusly:

Healing virtue was attributed to water taken from what was called a dead and living ford, i.e., a ford where the dead were carried (in coffins) and the living walked across. The same belief was entertained with regard to the water of a south-running stream. The patient had to go to the spot and drink the water and wash himself in it.

---

*James M. Mackinlay, section 4 of "Worship of Water" in *Folklore of Scottish Lochs and Springs* (Glasgow: William Hodge & Co., 1893), https://archive.org/stream/folkloreof scotti00mackuoft/folkloreofscotti00mackuoft_djvu.txt.
†Mackinlay, section 6 of "Worship of Water" in *Folklore*.

Sometimes his shirt was taken by another, and, after being dipped in the south-running stream, was brought back and put wet upon him.*

And here is an account of a healing ritual at a lake:

In the parish of Penpont, Dumfriesshire, about a mile to the south of Drumlanrig, is a small sheet of water called the Dow, or Dhu Loch, i.e., Black Loch. Till towards the end of last century the spot was much frequented for its healing water. A personal visit was not essential. When a deputy was sent he had to bring a portion of the invalid's clothing and throw it over his left shoulder into the loch. He then took up some water in a vessel which he carefully kept from touching the ground. After turning himself round Sun-ways he carried the water home. The charm would be broken if he looked back or spoke to anyone by the way.†

Historian and bishop St. Gregory of Tours (538 CE–594 CE) described Pagan water worship in Gaul in *Glory of the Confessors*:

There was a mountain in the land of the Gabali . . . called Helanus, with a big lake. Here, at a certain time, a large gathering of rustics, as though they were making offerings to that lake, threw in pieces of cloth, and material for the making of men's clothes. Some gave fleeces of wool, very many cheeses and wax, or bread, and all sorts of things, each one according to their resources, which I consider it would take too long to list. They came with wagons, bringing food and drink, slaughtering animals, and feasting for a period of three days. But on the fourth day, just before they had to go, there would be a storm with mighty thunder and lightning. And so huge a rainstorm would descend, with the force of stones that scarce any of them thought they would escape. So it happened every year and

---

*Mackinlay, section 6 of "Worship of Water" in *Folklore*.
†Mackinlay, section 12 of "Worship of Water" in *Folklore*.

the foolish people were engulfed by terror. A long time afterwards, a priest from the city . . . who had taken up the bishopric went to the place and preached to the crowd that they should desist from this to avoid being consumed by the anger of heaven, but his preaching had no effect on such basic rusticity. Then inspired by the Divinity, the priest of God built a basilica in honor of St Hilary of Poitiers . . . at a distance from the shore of the lake, in which he placed his relics, saying to the people, "Do not, my sons, do not sin before the Lord . . . there is no religious power in a lake. . . ." Then the people, touched to the heart, were converted and, leaving the lake, they took all the things they had been accustomed to throw in the lake and brought them to the basilica.*

However, the Christian attempt to eradicate Gaulish water worship was probably not as effective as St. Gregory thought. In 1897 Bertrand wrote the following:

As for the terror which the lake inspired in the peasants of the Gévaudan, one of my good friends who come from Lozére told me that it has not disappeared. Peasants do not pass along the shores of the lake without throwing coins into it; and it is not certain that people do not still go there individually on pilgrimage.†

These passages illustrate the policy of the church to take over or convert sites such as holy wells, special trees, lakes, and hills that were sacred to Pagans. Of course, to this day we still make offerings to water by throwing coins into fountains for "luck."

Sacred fire was another important aspect of Pagan worship. In Celtic areas the major festivals such as Imbolc (the festival of Brigid), Beltaine (May Day), Lughnasad (the festival of the first fruits of the harvest), and Samhain (Halloween) are still known as "fire festivals"

---

*Dowden, *European Paganism*, 50.
†Dowden, *European Paganism*, 51.

because a large bonfire was central to the observances of those days. Candles and burning incense filled Pagan temples, and offerings were made to sacred fires so that the flames could send the offerings skyward to the realm of the gods.

In conclusion, let's read an excerpt from *De Correctione Rusticorum (On the Instruction of Peasants)*, written by St. Martin of Braga (520 CE–580 CE):

Many demons, expelled from heaven, also preside either in the sea, or in rivers or springs or forests; men ignorant of God also worship them as gods and sacrifice to them. They call on Neptune in the sea, on Lamiae in the rivers, on Nymphs in the spring, on Diana in woods, who are all malignant demons and wicked spirits . . . the rustics . . . are so inconstant that they apply the very names of demons to each day and speak of the days of Mars, Mercury, Jove, Venus and Saturn. . . . And how can any of you, who has renounced the Devil and his angels and his evil works, now return again to the worship of the Devil? For to burn candles at stones and trees and springs, and where three roads meet, what is it but the worship of the Devil? To observe the days of Vulcan [August 23] and the first days of each month, to adorn tables and hang up laurels . . . to pour out fruit and wine over a log in the hearth, and to put bread in a spring, what is it but the worship of the Devil? For women to invoke Minerva in their weaving, to keep weddings for the day of Venus [Friday], to consider which day one should set out on a journey, what is it but the worship of the Devil? To mutter spells over herbs and invoke the names of demons in incantations, what is it but the worship of the Devil?*

St. Martin's castigation gives us a nice little overview of Pagan practices in southern Europe and shows the beliefs and actions that were used to persecute witches for centuries to come.

---

*Richard Fletcher, *The Barbarian Conversion: From Paganism to Christianity* (New York: Henry Holt and Company, 1997), 53.

Were Witches Evil?

All of this brings us to the thorny question of whether so-called Witches were actually "evil." Despite all the negative publicity about Witches, we can be sure that any mayhem they caused was miniscule when compared to the pain, torture, and murder of the witch hunts and the Inquisition.

As I said above, educated mages and sages such as the Druids worked closely with the nobility and were trusted, publicly recognized tribal functionaries. Queen Elizabeth had her own court astrologer and magician, John Dee, who was a trusted advisor. But Witches were often uneducated (in the sense of schooling) commoners and often loners. They worked in secret, which made them an unknown agent as far as the aristocracy was concerned. No one could be exactly sure what they might do or whose side they were really on, so the church and state felt threatened and conspired to wipe them out.

The moral and ethical perception of magic is very much in the eye of the beholder. We have ancient reports of battle magic performed on behalf of the tribe by Druids and Witches. In an account of the Irish *Cath Maige Tuired (The Battle of Moytura)* we read the following:

> And Figol, son of Marnos, the Druid, was asked then what he would do, and he said: "It is what I will do, I will cause three showers of fire to pour on the faces of the army of the Fomor, and I will take from them two-thirds of their bravery and their strength, and I will put sickness on their bodies, and on the bodies of their horses. But as to the men of Ireland," he said, "every breath they breathe will be an increase of strength and of bravery to them; and if they are seven years in the battle they will never be any way tired."
>
> Then Lugh asked his two witches, Bechulle and Dianan: "What power can you bring to the battle?" "It is easy to say that," they said. "We will put enchantment on the trees and the stones and the sods of the earth, till they become an armed host against the Fomor, and put terror on them and put them to the rout."

Then Lugh asked Carpre, the poet, son of Etain, what could he do. "It is not hard to say that," said Carpre. "I will make a satire on them at sunrise, and the wind from the north, and I on a hilltop and my back to a thorn tree, and a stone and a thorn in my hand. And with that satire," he said, "I will put shame on them and enchantment, the way they will not be able to stand against fighting men."*

"Evil" is, of course, in the eye of the beholder. For the tribe on whose behalf the Druids, poets, and Witches were working, such magic would have been seen as "good." For the opposing side it would have been seen as "evil." In modern times clergy are still expected to bless the troops and armaments to ensure victory as they head off to battle.

As another example of the relativity of "magic" (causing things to happen in ways that other people can't understand), we can look at the work of herbal healers. Herbalists who were Witches knew how to prevent conception and cause abortion. Some people find that idea repugnant. But women are not stupid and there are times when an abortion is truly necessary. If a woman has too many children to feed, if her life would be threatened by bearing another child, if she has been raped, if the fetus is nonviable due to death or deformity, it might make sense for her to get rid of an undesirable zygote. In times of famine, war, and migration, it is not always a good idea to be pregnant. Church authorities, who in the last few thousand years have overwhelmingly been men, have decided that a potential zygote is more valuable than a fully grown woman and that a "good" woman will bear a child no matter the cost to her own life or to the other dependent children she may already have.

The pre-Christian indigenous European Celtic religion teaches that life is eternal. That being so, the temporary interruption caused by death should not be seen as a lasting tragedy. Those who die in this

---

*Lady Gregory, "Part I Book III: The Great Battle of Magh Tuireadh" in *Gods and Fighting Men*, 1904, at sacred-texts.com, www.sacred-texts.com/neu/celt/gafm/gafm07.htm.

world are bound to return after a brief respite. As the ancient Druids taught:

> *According to your [the Druids'] authority, the shadows*
> *do not strive for the silent abodes of the underworld*
> *and for the pale realm of the deep sovereign of the*
> *dead: The same spirit directs the limbs in a different*
> *region (orbe alio). If you sing an approved truth,*
> *death is the center of a long life.*
>
> MARCUS ANNAEUS LUCANUS
> (FROM *BELLUM CIVILE*)

Witches were accused of raising storms that sank ships. Could they really do that, or was it simply a way to excuse commercial losses, poor seamanship, or just plain bad weather when ships sank? Witches and the evil eye were also blamed for crop failures, animal diseases, and rancid milk. It was said that a Witch could "steal a neighbor's luck" by taking dew from the neighbor's land and applying it to their own milking vessels, and that this would cause the cows next door to give less milk and the Witch's milk yield to increase.[*] Was that just a convenient excuse for poor husbandry?

I mentioned the use of healing threads above. Cursing threads were also employed by Witches. Threads of three colors (most often black, red, and white) were braided after three knots were tied into each thread and a curse muttered into each knot. A Witch could reportedly cause barrenness in a woman by hiding a ball of cursed black thread behind her loom.[†]

Other forms of curses included blackening stones in a fire and singing spells over them to cause harm or making a circle of the stones and chanting over them during the Waning Moon. A poppet of unfired clay could be made, given a name, pierced with thorns from a hawthorn tree,

---

[*]Hopman, *Scottish Herbs*, 191, 233.
[†]Hopman, *Scottish Herbs*, 236.

and placed in a river. As the clay figure melted, so would the victim wither away. And finally, the name of a person could be inscribed on a rock (or a lead tablet) and dropped into the water of a cursing well.*

I leave it to the reader to decide if such curses and spells would have been effective.

---

*Hopman, *Scottish Herbs*, 237.

# Accused Witches in New England and Interviews with Their Descendants

And now we turn to the modern descendants of the accused witches to learn who they are and how they feel and think in the twenty-first century. This chapter includes interviews with accused witches' descendants whom I discovered through online research. These interviews were conducted through an emailed question-and-response format rather than a verbal conversation, so each descendant was given a similar set of questions to answer that only differed slightly when I asked for a bit more information. Over two hundred persons were accused of witchcraft in North America. It would be impossible to cover all of them and their descendants in just one book. I hope that these few collected interviews will provide a glimpse into the kind of people these individuals have become due in part, perhaps, to their accused "witch" ancestors.

"HALF-HANGED MARY," THE WITCH OF HADLEY, MASSACHUSETTS

Mary (Reeve) Webster was born in England in around 1624. At the age of fifty-three she married William Webster of Hadley, Massachusetts, a second son with few prospects. Mary and William were poor, and the town was required to give them charity. According to reports, Mary had a temper, which was probably made worse by her straitened circumstances. Given to harsh words, she offended her neighbors, who began to taunt her with the name "witch."

Accusations and So-Called Evidence

It was said that cattle and horses being driven by Mary's door would unaccountably stall. The driver would then enter her house and beat her, after which the animals would easily move forward. One time she entered a house, and the baby within rose into the air from its cradle and fell back three times without anyone touching it. At another house a hen fell down the chimney and into the cooking pot, where it was scalded. Soon afterward Mary was found to be scalded also—clear evidence of witchcraft.

On March 27, 1683, Mary was brought to the county court in Northampton. She was determined to have entered into a covenant with the Devil and had familiarity with him while in the form of a fisher cat. It was said that the Devil's imps would suck on her, and that she had extra teats and marks on her body.

Mary was handed over for trial in Boston on May 22, 1683, where she pleaded not guilty, and the jury evidently agreed because they sent her back home to Hadley. The village was not pleased. Soon accusations that she was bent upon revenge began. According to Cotton Mather's *Magnalia*, Mary began to attack a certain Philip Smith, aged fifty, who was a deacon of the church, a member of the general court, a justice in the county court, a selectman, and a lieutenant of the troops.

Smith had set about "relieving the indigences" of a "wretched woman" in town who "expressed herself to him in such a manner" that he feared harm would come to him. In January 1684 Smith became ill and suspected that Mary had "made impressions with inchantments upon him."

Some young men of the village went to Mary's house to "give disturbance" to her, and it was said that these were the only times Smith could finally fall asleep. Medicine was provided for Smith that "unaccountably emptied." Scratching sounds were heard around his bed and fire was seen on his bed, which if any onlooker mentioned it would vanish. Something as big as a cat was seen to move around in the bed and the bed would sometimes shake violently.

When Smith eventually succumbed, noises were heard in the room like a clattering of stools and chairs. Cotton Mather declared that Smith was "murdered with a hideous Witchcraft," and when examined postmortem, Smith's body was found to be riddled with holes, as from awls.

Local boys took matters into their own hands while Smith was still alive and dragged Mary away from her house. They hung her by the neck, then took her down and buried her in the snow, leaving her for dead. But she did not die. Mary lived another eleven years and went to her grave at about age seventy, on June 3, 1698. She is buried in Old Hadley Cemetery in Hadley, Hampshire County, Massachusetts.

Outcome and Real Reasons behind the Accusations

Mary was the fourth Hampshire County resident sent to Boston to be tried as a witch. All four were acquitted and no Hampshire County person was ever executed for witchcraft. Through the years about thirty residents of Massachusetts and Connecticut were executed for witchcraft. In 1692 alone, twenty persons were killed in Salem Village due to a destructive and delusional witch-hunting frenzy. The local people were so ashamed of what they had done that less than a year later the mania stopped and persecutions of witches ended in New England.

Interview with Steven R. Dunn
Wilderness, Virginia

First, can you say a bit about who you are, where you live, and what you do for a living these days?

My family was from Kansas, but many of my ancestors were Separatists, Puritans, Quakers, etc., from Massachusetts and Connecticut. I moved to Tennessee from Virginia in October 2016. I am currently a material handler at a huge distribution center for a sports and outdoors retailer. I've previously worked in the technology and cabinetry manufacturing fields but have mostly worked with the special needs population in their residential environment.

I have several ancestors who were accused of witchcraft. Alse Young, the first person executed for witchcraft in America, was one of my mother's ancestors. She was hanged in Hartford on May 26, 1647. John and Joan Carrington were also my mother's ancestors and were hanged in 1651 in Connecticut. Ann Alcock-Foster was twice my tenth great-grandmother on my dad's side. She died in prison in Salem, Massachusetts, in 1692, awaiting execution during the witch trials.

Ann Alcock-Foster came from London on the ship *Abigail* in 1635. Her husband was Andrew Foster. They lived in Andover, Massachusetts, and had five children. Her daughter, Mary Foster-Lacey, and granddaughter Mary were accused of witchcraft along with Ann. Ann took the blame so that they would be exonerated. I honor Ann greatly for her sacrifice. The elder Mary has gotten a lot of bad press for turning on her mother and accusing her in order to save herself. I have a suspicion that Ann and Mary may have agreed to this beforehand, though.

Another daughter of Ann was Sarah, who married Samuel Kemp (or Kempe). Sarah's son, Zerubbabel, married the younger Mary, his first cousin. They were my seventh great-grandparents, so I'm twice descended from Ann and Andrew Foster.

There is a large obelisk monument in the Ancient Burying Ground cemetery in Hartford with the names of the original proprietors inscribed on it. Twenty-five of them were my direct ancestors on both my mom's and dad's sides. These families married into each other in England quite a bit pre-emigration, so I am related to most of them, even if I'm not a direct descendant. My sons and I visited this cemetery in June 2015. The execution site of Alse Young was not far at all from there.

As far as Mary Reeve Webster is concerned, Governor John Webster of Connecticut was my tenth great-grandfather. John's children were born into a successful family. Lexicographer Noah Webster was a relative on this line of my father's family. John's son Robert was my ancestor. Robert's brother William seems to have fallen into some hard circumstances and became poor. His wife, Mary Reeve Webster, from what I've read, seems to have been a fairly bitter and contemptuous woman. Apparently the couple was disliked by the townspeople of Hadley, Massachusetts.

Mary was accused of witchcraft in 1683 and was tried in Boston. She was acquitted of the charges and was allowed to return home to Hadley. The townspeople's disdain for her was probably exacerbated by her exoneration. They took it upon themselves to hang her. Mary was sixty-six years old at the time. According to the information I have, they stripped her naked, abused her, then hanged her from a tree, where they left her overnight. They came to cut her down the next day, unaware that she wasn't dead. I don't know if she was so near to death that they couldn't discern that she was still barely alive or if she did a great faking job, but they buried her regardless, thinking she was dead. Somehow, this tough old lady revived and survived to live many years longer after this.

You'd have thought that not dying after being hanged would have been deemed as proof that she was indeed a witch, but as far as I've read, no one took any further actions against her. The hanging was illegal, but nobody was charged for this crime.

As far as my thoughts on her go: I think she was an unhappy, bitter woman who was severely disliked by her community. They brought false charges of witchcraft against her to get rid of her. When this failed, they tried to kill her themselves (illegally), but this failed too. I think she was a very tough lady!

You are a descendant of a number of New England witches. Did your family carry the stories of these women or did you find out about it all recently?

No, my family did not carry any knowledge of the accused witches in our ancestry. I found out about them by working on my genealogy.

What do you make of the fact that those you are related to, who were accused, were mostly women?

I think it's really interesting to learn about my ancestors' lives—not just about the accused witches. I have twelve *Mayflower* ancestors, plus some of the founders of towns and cities, colonial governors of the early colonies, etc. The witchcraft hysteria that occurred in New England is a travesty, because none of those accused actually practiced witchcraft, and were falsely accused. It's also interesting to learn about the Puritan mind-set and what led them to these beliefs and actions. Most of the people accused were indeed women, but not all of them. As I mentioned, John Carrington was my mom's ancestor. Salem witch trial victim Giles Corey (not my ancestor) was a male—there are others as well.

Have you had any experiences with modern Witches, and if so, how did that make you feel?

I've known some people who were Wiccans, but I don't really think of them as the witches that the Puritans were afraid of. They're not evil Devil worshippers. I myself am an atheist, so it's just another silly religion to me, but some of them have been close coworkers, and I liked them a lot as people.

How do you personally define Witchcraft?

I don't believe in the supernatural, so I guess my definition of witchcraft fits the Puritan view of them as conjurers of magic spells and being in league with Satan. I don't believe in any of it, but it's fun for Hollywood and Halloween. I myself am a secular humanist/atheist. I don't believe in the supernatural, witchcraft, etc., but I do find it interesting. I've visited Salem on both of my visits to Massachusetts. I went to both of the old cemeteries in town.

Have you had any feelings of contact from any of these "witches"? Any past-life memories or dreams involving them?

No, I haven't had any supernatural experiences, dreams, etc., from my ancestors or anyone else.

Do you have strong impressions regarding any one of the witches you are descended from?

I feel really sorry for my ancestors who were accused of witchcraft. They were totally innocent of the charges leveled against them. Ann Foster took the blame for her daughter Mary and granddaughter (also named Mary), who were also accused, so that they could be exonerated. I'm sure she was tortured to death in prison, so I feel that her sacrifice for her daughter and granddaughter was totally selfless and courageous. I honor her a lot for her sacrifice.

Any other thoughts you care to add?

I did have one other noteworthy ancestor who supposedly was possessed by a demon. Her name was Elizabeth Knapp and she lived in Groton, Massachusetts. I don't believe she was really possessed, but that she was a teenage girl who was bored with her life as a servant. This was the only way she knew to call attention to herself and break the tedium of her life. The description of her supposed possession sounds a lot like *The Exorcist* movie. Pretty scary!

Elizabeth was my eighth great-grandmother on my dad's mother's side. It's interesting to imagine living in the circumstances and mind-set of the Puritan settlers of places like early Groton, Massachusetts. They were constantly under threat from Native American raids. As a matter of fact, Elizabeth's son-in-law (my seventh great-grandfather), Phineas Parker, was captured by the Abenaki during a raid on Groton in 1694 in which both of his parents, James Parker Jr. and Mary Parker, were slaughtered. Phineas was held captive for four years before he escaped. He had been maimed and walked with a limp for the rest of his life.

The early settlers faced an untamed wilderness, with some dangerous wild animals and a lot of very hard work clearing and settling the small villages that would later become towns and cities. Their new environment was completely foreign to them. England was nothing like this, so these very real dangers plus the fear of the supernatural that the

Puritans had made for a pretty scary existence. A teenage servant girl's life was boring on a day-to-day basis, though.

Teenagers generally tend to like excitement; Elizabeth's life was anything but exciting. Although she may consciously have believed that she was being possessed, subconsciously I think it was an outcry for attention and to break the tedium of her boring life. The real and imagined threats in these people's lives and minds made fertile ground for things like witch hunts, supposed demon possessions, etc. The Puritans were rarely ever boring people—lots of drama!

I'm kind of the "black sheep" in my family for being an atheist. Most of my family are still very deeply religious people, so we butt heads on some things. We love each other a lot despite that, though.

MARY BLISS PARSONS, THE WITCH OF NORTHAMPTON

Mary Bliss was born in England in 1628 and came to America at age eight. At about age eleven or twelve the family moved to Hartford, Connecticut. In 1646 she married Joseph Parsons and moved to Springfield, Massachusetts.

In 1654 the couple moved to Northampton, Massachusetts, where Mary bore eleven children, most of whom survived to adulthood. She was reportedly talented and beautiful but "not very amiable" and of "haughty manners." Joseph became a successful merchant and fur trader, making the Parsons among the wealthiest families in Northampton.

Accusations and So-Called Evidence

In 1656 Joseph Parsons accused one Sarah Bridgman of slander against his wife, Mary. Sarah had alleged that any time there was an argument between Mary and any member of the Bridgman family, a horse, cow, or pig belonging to the Bridgmans would contract a fatal disease.

One accusation involved the death of William Hannum's cow. Mary reportedly went to Hannum's house to inquire about some missing yarn. An argument ensued and the next morning a young cow lay near death in Hannum's yard. Hannum nursed the cow with care but she eventually succumbed. This was "proof" of Mary's witchcraft.

On another occasion the Bridgmans' eleven-year-old son was tending cows in a swamp when "something" came and "gave him a great blow." He stumbled and his knee went out of joint. After being set, the knee never properly healed, and the boy was in "grievous torture" for a month. During his convalescence he cried out that "Goody Parsons would pull off his knee" and that he could see her sitting on a shelf. Then he said she was running away with a black mouse following her.

During the same period the Bridgmans lost a young son. Sarah reported that while in bed with the baby in her lap, "something gave a great blow on the door," and at that instant the infant suddenly changed so much she was afraid he would die. Then, looking through a hole in the door, she saw two women wearing white cloth on their heads. She sent a girl to see who these women were, but they had disappeared.

Sarah accused Mary of being a witch, and many witnesses came to testify on Sarah's behalf, but the witnesses began to change their stories and blame gradually shifted to Sarah. The magistrates found Sarah guilty of slander, and she was sentenced to publicly acknowledge her guilt in both Springfield and Northampton or pay a fine. Sarah chose to pay the fine rather than recant her tales in public.

Now Mary Parsons's name was cleared, but the accusations of witchcraft continued. As the years went on Mary's husband grew wealthy and her children did well. In 1674 a female resident of Northampton named Mary Bartlett died suddenly at the age of twenty-two. Mary Bartlett was the mother of an infant and also the daughter of Sarah and James Bridgman. Her husband and her father suspected that witchcraft had caused her death, and they once again blamed Mary Parsons.

On September 29, 1674, Mary Parsons argued for her own defense in Hampshire County court. The court deferred further action on the case until November and on January 5, 1675, they met for a third time. Some new depositions were added, and Mary again defended herself, claiming innocence.

The magistrates decided that final jurisdiction in the case should go to the Court of Assistants in Boston, and they also appointed a group of women to examine Mary's body for "any marks of Witchcraft." John Parsons, age twenty-four, was Mary Parson's unmarried second son and he also had accusations against him, but the court did not find enough evidence to prosecute him for witchcraft.

On March 2, 1675, Mary was finally taken to Boston and indicted by a grand jury. She was sent to prison to await trial. Because they were a family of means, the Parsons family most likely purchased for her a larger cell, good food, and clean water. At the trial fresh accusations emerged. Before the Parsons had moved to Northampton another Mary (Lewis) Parsons had also been sentenced for witchcraft and was condemned to be executed but died in jail. This Mary was no relation, but it was reported that during Mary Lewis Parsons's trial Mary Bliss Parsons would go into fits and have to be confined in the house by her husband.

The court concluded that Mary Bliss Parsons had "entered into familiarity with the Devil" and had "committed several acts of Witchcraft on the person or persons of one or more." Mary pled not guilty and defended herself yet again. The jury found Mary not guilty and set her free with a full acquittal. Mary and Joseph left Northampton and moved back to Springfield.

Mary's son Ebenezer was killed in September 1675 while fighting Native Americans in Northfield. Locals said this was punishment for Mary's collusion with the Devil.

Joseph Parsons died in 1683, leaving a prosperous estate. Mary enjoyed a thirty-year widowhood, but rumors of witchcraft surrounded her for the rest of her days.

In 1711 Mary Bliss Parsons's granddaughter, Mary Parsons, married Ebenezer Bridgman, a grandson of Sarah Bridgman. Mary Bliss Parsons was a witness.

Outcome and Real Reasons behind the Accusations

Mary Bliss Parsons died in January 1712 at about age eighty-five after seeing her sons and grandsons assume prominent positions in local towns. The real basis for Sarah Bridgman's enmity toward Mary seems to have been that the Parsons had many healthy children while Sarah's children died, and that Sarah's family had financial troubles while the Parsons prospered.

Interview with Frances F. Denny
Brooklyn, New York

First, can you say a bit about who you are, where you live, and what you do for a living these days?

I am an artist and photographer living in Brooklyn, New York. I grew up just outside of Boston in Brookline, Massachusetts. Much of my work studies the development of female identity and the various factors that impact that development (such as familial influences and societal pressures). My 2016 monograph, *Let Virtue Be Your Guide*, is a series of thirty-six photographs about the women in my New England family and the particular femininity that they embody. In the process of researching my family's ancestry for that series, I discovered that I am the descendant of Chief Justice Samuel Sewall, who presided over the Salem witch trials. I also discovered that Mary Bliss Parsons is my tenth great-grandmother, and that realization sparked my initial interest in the word *witch*—what it meant historically and what it means now.

Mary is the inspiration for my current body of work, which explores the archetype of the Witch from a contemporary vantage point and involves a series of photographic portraits of women who practice or identify with Witchcraft in any incarnation, whether they are aligned with a specific spiritual belief system or are self-defined.

The portraits complicate prevailing notions of what a modern Witch is—they reveal a diversity of belief systems and personalized practices. Some Witches see themselves as part of the Pagan community, while some do not. Though my subjects' beliefs vary greatly from one person to the next, one common denominator is a deep, almost primal, connection to the natural world. Even this manifests in disparate ways—rituals performed during specific phases of the Moon, herbal medicine, environmental activism, astrology, and so on.

Did your family carry the stories of your ancestors or did you find out about it all recently?

When I was a teenager, my father compiled a document that catalogs my ancestry on both sides of my family. The Mary Bliss Parsons connection is from my father's side of the family.

What do you make of the fact that those you are related to, who were accused, were mostly women?

There's a tension for me about the fact that I am related to both an accuser and the accused (albeit from slightly different moments in history and in different Massachusetts towns). The fact that the accuser was male and the accused was female is also relevant to the work I am doing now.

Have you had any experiences with modern Witches, and if so, how did that make you feel?

In the past year since I began my current project, I have met many Witches, all of whom define Witchcraft differently for themselves. Some are members of circles or Covens, and some practice independently. Some have an eclectic, self-defined sense of spirituality that draws from various Pagan traditions, and some ascribe specifically to Wicca, Voudou, or other such religions. All of the women I have met have complicated and expanded my notion of who a Witch is.

How do you personally define Witchcraft?

I see Witchcraft as a way of perceiving the world and one's place in it. Witchcraft is about how a person reflects, heals, sets intention, and manifests change in her own life and often in the lives of others. This happens in many different ways and is distinct to each practitioner.

Are you a Witch?

I'm not sure yet if I can consider myself a Witch. Despite my ancestral connection to Mary Bliss Parsons and the Salem trials, my personal beliefs are still being sorted out. I find many aspects of Witchcraft compelling, particularly the connection to the natural world and the feminist leanings of some of the traditions I've encountered, but I think I am too new to all of it to have earned the identification of "Witch."

Interview with Kathy-Ann Becker
Wendell, Massachusetts

First, can you say a bit about who you are, where you live, and what you do for a living these days?

I am an appreciative and honest woman who has grown in amazement to the beginnings of the golden end of maturity. I live in a rural hill town on a dirt road in the woods in north-central Massachusetts with my husband and our obedient and enthusiastic English springer spaniel. We are happy, simple people who fish, hunt, mushroom and forage, camp, and kayak. We are also active in local town government and our community. We are called the grand-neighbors on our hill. We have another life with an informal "tribe" of bluegrass musician friends with whom we gather to play bluegrass music at picking parties and festivals. My husband is a respected musician who plays blues and bluegrass harmonica. I am learning clawhammer-style ukulele, a quiet instrument, in order to share music and to take flight in chords and melodies. My husband of over forty years, Myron, is a chef who creates all-natural and high-quality cooking sauces for our company, Myron's Fine Foods, Inc. I am a registered nurse whose specialty is working with adults who are challenged by intellectual and physical disabilities. My mission is to maintain their optimum health and facilitate their choice-making. I write and have written a historical biographical fiction novel about an ancestor who was accused of being a witch in the Pioneer Valley in the seventeenth century.

Which accused New England witch or witches are you descended from?

My ninth-generation great-grandmother on my father's side is the infamous Mary Bliss Parsons, the so-called Witch of Northampton. Her third son was also maliciously accused of witchcraft. I am descended from that son, John, and also her first daughter, Mary. One of John's sons and one of Mary's daughters (Mary) married. My line comes from that marriage of cousins.

Did your family carry the stories of your ancestors or did you find out about it all recently?

My ancestress was discovered by my family. In the mid-seventies, my father and mother, anticipating their future retirement from the dual professions of Universalist minister/minister's wife and teachers in public schools, took up the hobby of genealogy. My father soon discovered that he was directly, and my mother indirectly, descended from a "witch," Mary Bliss Parsons. He called me with that news. His declaration appalled me. I felt an instant kinship with her and a desire to defend this unknown ancestor in her struggle. Together, my parents and I began to search out her story.

What do you make of the fact that those you are related to, who were accused, were mostly women?

My research showed me how deeply in theology there runs an adverse gender bias against women, particularly in the New Testament. Women were expected to remain silent in the churches and to be obedient to their husbands. Any questions a woman had, as stated unequivocally in Corinthians, were to be asked of her husband at home; any other behavior demeaned the character of the head of the household. A man who could not control his wife was a cuckold, for his wife had betrayed him in the eyes of God. Women are trying to emerge from that legacy today.

My ancestors are an example of the vulnerability of women. Mary Bliss Parsons was married to Cornet Joseph Parsons, a man whose business prowess at trading with the natives and providing goods and services to his community resulted in his becoming the most prosperous man in the first settlement at Northampton. Any natural jealousy that his neighbors harbored could not be directed at a man, especially not one so powerful and well connected. His wife, on the other hand, was a different story. She was from a common family. Her excessive beauty and her proud, outspoken manner were too provocative for her community to tolerate. Fingers of jealousy and suspicion began to be pointed at her. The structure of a religiously dominated government imbued with gender politics discouraged a woman from speaking out, even to defend herself. In her lifetime, Mary Bliss Parsons is known to have been accused multiple times of being a witch. She was imprisoned for a prolonged period at the Boston jail waiting for trial before the highest court of the colony. Although she was found innocent, evidence shows that suspicions about her followed her to her death. Ironically, the final verdict came from her God, who graced her with a long life and many living progeny, a sign seen then of having found favor. Her descendants and all the descendants of this Puritan legacy of fear have at last reached a time when we can begin to hold out the possibility of community acceptance of those who do not follow the traditional prescribed norms, but the pathway is wet with a history of tears and blood.

Have you had any experiences with modern Witches, and if so, how did that make you feel?

I do know women friends and some men who have identified themselves to me as Witches. While this is not a common experience we share as a spiritual discipline, I see that their practice seems to bring them nearer to the Whole, nearer to the Great Mystery. I respect this path. My path is different.

How do you personally define Witchcraft?

It would appear that Witchcraft is loosely defined and is a personal experience of opening to the magic and mystery of the unknowable. When accepted with delight and appreciation, without the trappings of ego or attempts to dominate others, the practice of Witchcraft appears to be wholesome and healthy. That being said, in experimenting with Tarot cards, I have found that there is a dark veiled hole in the middle of the Tree of Life that holds allure, which a person might be drawn into, where negative energy boils. Some people go into that place. Those who choose to be "witches" from that dark place are people I would not wish to define or approach.

Have you had any feelings of contact with the accused "witch" in your family? Any past-life memories or dreams involving them?

Mary Bliss Parsons's blood beats in my pulse. She is one of those kinds of ancestors who want to be known. The energy of her prayers lives on in images that are accessible mind to mind. I now accept that her life has gifted me with strong impressions of her. I know I am not crazy because at least two other descendants have had this same feeling and have written about her, all of us in the same generation.

She entered my mind as a place memory when I was twenty, before I knew who she was. Having visions of another person's life threatened my perceptions of being. I tried to ignore the sensing of another person who was invading my thinking. Only in the last decade have I felt secure enough in myself to explore these memories from someone else.

I sought her through meditating upon the Psalms of David. I reasoned that everything else, the land and all physical things, have changed since her time. The commonality between us that exists now is the Psalms. They would have been the framework of a Puritan life. I practiced dropping the impressions of myself and allowing myself to float as a humble being, allowing the words of the Psalms of the ancient Hebrew Tehillim to flow like water through my mind. Vivid memories surfaced. I was not culturally competent to understand what I saw. I had to diligently study the Great Migration to the Massachusetts Bay Company from many different vantage points for many years before the images I was seeing and the emotional load they carried began to shape a personality so different from my own. When I tried to anticipate or infer her mind, a harsh sense of disapproval settled upon me. I had to wait and record her life at a pace as fast or slow as what came to me from an increasingly familiar source. "We" established an understanding, and I honored that undefinable rhythm.

I have never seen Mary Bliss Parsons; this is not a ghost story. I felt her life as if through her eyes and emotions. I did once perhaps "hear" her voice. I had been waiting patiently for more images of her life to come to me, but none came. I went to a high bluff overlooking the place where a favorite river goes to the sea. Looking over the vista, I begged in my heart for something from her. I heard a woman's voice speak, low and firm, seemingly real, with no person present. The voice said, "There. It is done." When I argued that the book, in fact, was not complete, the same words were repeated: "It is done!"

I rushed back to my little Newfoundland cabin and called my mother for advice about ending the book abruptly. My father's mind had wandered so far away from him that he could not help me in my dilemma, but my mother, Mary, was a loyal cheerleader and advisor in writing the adventure with Mary Bliss Parsons. When my mother heard where the story was to end, she was vehement that I owed something more to the story's readers. "Who are you writing for, Mary Bliss Parsons or your readers?"

My mother's opinion swayed me. Mary Bliss Parsons and I had to part ways. I had to finish her story without her. She remained stonily silent thereafter. I can only speculate that revisiting the indignity of the courtroom of her accusation was not a memory she could share with me or with her God. I did not revisit the courtroom, out of respect, but I did offer her, and the reader, an ending of grace.

Mary Bliss Parsons has left me now. My book about her was completed in 2013. Since then she has given me only one last vision of explanation about the meaning of a particular event. I was surprised to "meet" her again and felt mixed about her reappearance. I am rather glad to be alone in my mind these days. Should she "visit" me again, I am at peace with her. I love her.

Any other thoughts you care to add?

Because you [Ellen] are compiling this book about Witches and accused witches, perhaps you will permit a segue to a related vignette about a living Witch who impacted my story. My mother had a premonition that she and my dad would not live to see my book published and suddenly urged me to hurry, to self-publish instead of waiting for the verdict of the established publisher that was considering my manuscript. My mother was correct about the need to hurry. Soon she called to say that she and my dad "were finished." We wept together. I was not sure what she was worried about, but she said something was to happen the next day. She had a plan how to avoid it and she kept promising, "I will not take your dad for his ride tomorrow." She was not able to carry out her avoidance plan. The next morning, within minutes of her fateful decision to go against her plan, she and my father had a freak car accident. My mother was killed at the scene instantly; my father passed two days later from his injuries. It has been difficult to reach a resolution about the meaning of her premonition coming true.

A year and a half later, I was attending a music festival and was walking down an aisle of vendors toward the stage. A woman called out to me from a booth. I hesitated to go up to her because her sign indicated that she was a medium. We locked eyes. I thought about it and, on impulse, went under her little pop-up tent and sat down. She started to explain what she offered. Before she could finish, her eyes fluttered and she said, "Oh, there is someone here who wants to talk to you."

"Yeah, right," I thought.

The woman's eyes closed. She began to speak. The voice was my mother's.

"I want you to know that we rose together like butterflies," my mother said, through someone else's mouth.

I was shocked and upset, skeptical yet yearning toward that familiar voice. I wondered how and why this medium was inflicting this cruel sham upon me. How could she know my mother's unusual inflections of a blended Massachusetts North Shore/Ohio accent, or that my mother loved butterflies?

"No!" I shouted at the strange woman with her eyes closed, who talked like my mother. "No, Dad died two days later!"

My mother's voice came again, gently, calm and definite. "We rose together like butterflies. We went together. Your dad is here with me. We are happy."

The medium opened her eyes and said the person was gone. My mother's voice was gone. I could hardly breathe or keep from crying. I croaked a thank-you to the stranger and pulled out the money to pay her. She extended back some bills because I did not get the fifteen minutes she would have set on her timer.

Then she said, "Wait. Someone else is here. He is asking permission to speak."

It was my father. He said, "I know you wrote the book. I am proud of you. But paper is fragile. You throw it on the ground and it melts." Then he, too, was gone.

I paid the Witch medium lady the $15 and left a different person. I do not understand what it is to be a Witch, but there is more to know than what can be seen.

If you are interested in reaching out to the mind of an accused witch, you can read about my ancestor in *Silencing the Women: The Witch Trials of Mary Bliss Parsons* by Kathy-Ann Becker, published by BookLocker.com, Inc., 2013.

Thank you.

MARY TOWNE ESTEY, DAUGHTER OF A WITCH

Mary Towne was born on August 24, 1634, in Great Yarmouth, Norfolk, England, to William Towne and Joanna Blessing. She married Isaac Estey Sr., a well-to-do farmer and barrel maker in Topsfield, Massachusetts, in 1656. The Estey farm was one of the largest in Salem Village.

Accusations and So-Called Evidence
Mary was accused of witchcraft in 1692 at the age of fifty-eight, along with her sisters Rebecca Nurse and Sarah Cloyce. She was initially

examined on April 22, 1692. During the examination Mercy Lewis, a local girl, would clasp her hands each time Mary did, unclenching her hands only when Mary did so. When Mary bowed her head, local girls screamed for her to straighten her neck because their necks were "being broken."

A magistrate took all this as proof of witchcraft and asked Mary, "How far have you complied with Satan?" Mary refused to admit any guilt and was sent to prison. After two months she was released for good behavior, but two days later Mercy Lewis went into fits, claiming she was being strangled.

Margaret Reddington, aged seventy, reported that three years prior she had gone to the Estey home to discuss an illness with Mary and afterward fell ill. She said that Mary's specter had appeared to her and offered her fresh meat that was "not fit for the dogs." When Margaret refused the meat, Mary disappeared.

Samuel Smith of Boxford, aged twenty-five, said that five years prior he had been rude to Isaac Estey, and Mary had warned him not to be rude again or he would regret it. Riding home he felt a blow on his shoulder and a stone wall made a noise that frightened his horse.

On May 23, 1692, Abigail Williams and Ann Putnam testified that when Abigail went to visit Mercy, who was ill with fits, Mary's specter had appeared and said she was torturing Mercy because she refused to clear Mary's name. They said Abigail was being similarly afflicted.

On August 4, 1692, Elizabeth Hubbard, Edward Putnam, Mary Walcott, Mary Warren, and Ann Putnam reported being tortured and choked by Mary Estey during her examination. That same day another warrant went out for Mary's arrest, and Mary was pulled from her bed at midnight to be imprisoned and chained. As soon as Mary was imprisoned, Mercy Lewis immediately stopped having fits.

Reports were given that Mary was well behaved, civil, and sober while in prison. At her trial, she essentially shamed the court with impeccable logic. Before her death she pled eloquently on behalf of other accused witches: "I petition to your honours not for my own life for I know I must die and my appointed time is set but the Lord he knows it is that if it be possible no more innocent blood may be shed."*

Estey also asked that all confessing witches as well as those confessing innocence be brought to trial and that all accusers be kept apart to see if they would report the same experiences. Her logic cast doubt on the witch hunts and may have led to their eventual end.

Outcome and Real Reasons behind the Accusations

Mary was tried and condemned on September 9, 1692, and hung on September 22, 1692. Her sister Rebecca Towne Nurse was also hung. Sarah Cloyce was jailed for witchcraft, but she had petitioned the court for an opportunity to defend her innocence and to exclude spectral evidence and was eventually set free for lack of proof. Mary's family was granted twenty pounds in 1711, as compensation for her wrongful execution.

The reasons for Mary's persecution as a "witch" were many. Mary's mother, Joanna Blessing Towne, had also been accused of witchcraft in 1670 at age seventy-five, after being a widow for two years. Local belief held that witchcraft was a hereditary trait, passed down from mother to child, and while Joanna was never officially charged, she was the subject of gossip and rumor all her life.

Joanna Blessing Towne had also defended Reverend Thomas Gilbert, a Scotsman accused of "intemperance" by the Gould family. The Goulds accused Joanna of being a witch after she defended Reverend Gilbert in court. At the time Joanna was living with her daughter-in-law, Phebe Perkins Towne, who was a Gould relation.

The Goulds were close friends of the Putnams, the main accusers of Mary Estey, Rebecca Nurse, and Sarah Cloyce. Isaac Estey and other Towne family members had once testified against John Putnam and his sons and cousins for illegally cutting trees on other people's properties within the Topsfield boundary. The court had found Putnam guilty of the charges.

---

*Rebecca Beatrice Brooks, "Mary Easty: The Witch's Daughter," *History of Massachusetts* (blog), Dec. 15, 2015, http://historyofmassachusetts.org/mary-easty-salem.

In 1639 the General Court of Massachusetts had granted Salem Village permission to expand to the north but four years later gave an authorization for villagers from Ipswich to found a settlement in the same area, to be named Topsfield, and as a result boundary disputes went on for a century. The Putnams of Salem Village quarreled with the Nurse family into which Mary Estey's sister Rebecca had married.

Rebecca Nurse, Sarah Cloyce, and Mary Estey were all daughters or wives of Topsfield men. The charges against Mary Estey seem to have resulted from ire between her family and the Putnams and from being a blood relative of another accused witch. The afflicted girls may have been suffering from ergot poisoning,* as some have theorized, or they may simply have been coached by their parents as an act of revenge against their neighbors.

Interview with Jennifer Marie Russo
Bellingham, Massachusetts

First, can you say a bit about who you are, where you live, and what you do for a living these days?

I live in the little town of Bellingham, Massachusetts, and I am a senior marketing program manager, a role that I just began in October of last year. I hold a master's in integrated marketing communications and a bachelor's in English literature. In addition to my full-time job, I have a photography business (concerts, events, fine art) and write entertainment and lifestyle articles for a magazine in Worcester, Massachusetts. I practice yoga regularly, and I have a beautiful six-year-old son.

Which accused New England witch or witches are you descended from?

---

*See "Causes and Effects of the Salem Witch Hysteria" at the end of this chapter.

I am directly descended from Mary Estey (also spelled Easty), who is my ninth great-grandmother on my mother's side. Mary's sisters, Rebecca Nurse and Sara Cloyce, my ninth great-grandaunts, were also accused, as was their mother Joanna (Johanna) Blessing Towne (my tenth great-grandmother).

Did your family carry the stories of your ancestors or did you find out about it all recently?

It is actually pretty interesting. I remember very vaguely going to Salem with my grandmother when I was perhaps eight or nine years old. I remember her saying something about me being related to an accused witch as we passed the old cemetery on the way to a shop. I never thought about it again. Then, when I was researching my family lines, which I have been doing for around twenty years, I uncovered Mary (this was in 2011, I believe) and my first thought was "Oh, well there she is," recalling my grandmother's comment from years before.

Coming from a Catholic family, I am not surprised that this was never mentioned by anyone who perhaps knew about it. My grandmother was different, practicing with crystals and Tarot as I recall, and more open to other ideas.

What do you make of the fact that those you are related to, who were accused, were mostly women?

It is not really that surprising. At the time women were considered inferior and more susceptible to spiritual evil, as women traditionally are more emotional creatures. They also were encouraged to follow their husbands and stay silent in political and religious matters, not really able to voice their own opinions on things. Additionally, women who did have a measure of power were often considered to be outside the circle of piety.

Women who owned land, like Bridget Bishop, or women who had a reputation for being able to heal with natural tinctures or who simply stood up for things they believed in were generally frowned upon. The women in my family were strong-minded, with Joanna voicing her opinion over land disputes that her husband William was having with the Putnam family as well as in religious matters. Joanna was accused of being a witch shortly after this. Her daughters were likely accused not because of anything they did personally, but because the belief was that witchcraft ran in families.

Have you had any experiences with modern Witches, and if so, how did that make you feel?

I have had both good and bad experiences with modern "Witches." I had a woman who was a Witch whom I did not know once come right up to me with a frantic look in her eyes and say, "Why are you here? Don't you know who you are?" which rather bothered me, and there was a woman sitting next to me at a bar once, who turned to me suddenly and told me that I should embrace who I am and what I can do instead of running from it.

In general I do not have a problem with anyone's religion or beliefs, as all are entitled to their own way of expression. I have plenty of friends who are Wiccan and plenty of friends who are Christians, friends who are Muslim, friends who are Buddhist . . . I think it is a personal choice what or whom you believe in or how you choose to follow those beliefs.

How do you personally define Witchcraft?

This is an interesting question. I think there are many different interpretations of what Witchcraft is. If I were alive in the 1600s, I am well aware that I would have been considered a Witch. I personally consider myself to be not a Witch, but an empath. It is not something I wanted for myself and not something I would wish upon anyone, as it can be scary and negative at times. It took me a long time to allow myself to be okay with that and understand how to live with it in a constructive way. I am guessing you already know what an empath is, but if you need further description I can provide that. The basic idea of it is that I am able to feel (and sometimes absorb) the energies, emotions, and moods that are around me very intensely, whether it be from other people, nature, animals, places, or things unseen. For example, I can walk into a place and start talking to a complete stranger and know exactly what they are feeling and what kind of person they are within minutes.

There are times when I will feel the need to sit next to someone, and that person will pour their heart out to me and what I tell them is a guidance that I know doesn't come from me alone, often bringing up details that only that person could understand. There is a certain tree, which for reasons I do not understand, draws me to it. When I touch it, I feel emotional pain. I have a very hard time leaving the vicinity of it, as if I am pulled in. I cannot explain it and the idea is as insane to me as it probably sounds to you, but nonetheless it is what happens. Is it "Witchcraft"? I don't think so, but these things would have surely gotten me hanged in 1692.

What I do believe, and many may disagree, is that some people are simply born with abilities. These cannot be learned or acquired because someone wants to have them. People who claim they are Witches, psychics, seers, etc., because they can pull out a Tarot deck or pendulum or go through the motions of casting a spell from a book are not genuine. There is a lot of that out there. People who "become" a Witch because they want power are completely missing the point. Power is fleeting and no one really owns it—it is not a personal trait, but something lent to them by the universe or whatever God you choose to believe in. A true Witch, in my mind, is humble, realizing that we are all one with everyone else, all the nature and elements around us, and that there is a responsibility to honor all of that and care for it, not be above it or use it for personal gain.

Have you had any feelings of contact with the accused "witch" in your family? Any past-life memories or dreams involving them?

Yes. For years before I found my ancestral connection to Mary, I would walk through Salem, which I just loved to visit anyway since it is a beautiful place with a lot to do, and have moments where I would get inexplicable chills up my spine. A sense of sudden emotion (both positive and negative) that seemed to come from the place I was standing. I remember telling my fiancé once, when he asked me what was wrong, if he had felt what I just felt. Of course, he thought I was out of my mind.

I have only had one dream of Mary. In it, she was telling me that she was not at rest and that something had to be done. It was very disturbing to me, mostly as I don't feel I have any way to help her if that is really the case.

Do you have strong impressions regarding the accused witch you are descended from?

I do. I feel pride. Not to have a person in my line who has a notable name, because honestly, I couldn't care less about that, but more because I am proud to be descended from a woman who had such courage and strength in the face of enormous terror. Her petition to the court is one of the most inspiring things I have ever read. To be sitting in a horrible prison as an older woman who was ripped from her family . . . twice, refusing to admit to something that she did not do when it would have been so easy to concede, and instead writing a letter telling those in power that they were wrong. That she knew she was going to die because of their blindness and refusal to do what was right. That even though she was going to die, they should consider what they were doing so that others would not have to die as a result of their stupidity.

What is most fascinating to me is that she wrote all of this in a respectful way and told them that the day would come when they would see their error. She remained true to herself until the very end, which is simply beautiful to me. Though the petition was ignored by the courts, it lives on to encourage and inspire people today.

REBECCA STEELE GREENSMITH, WITCH OF HARTFORD

Rebecca Steele was born in 1629 in Fairstead, Essex, England. She had three husbands: the first was Abraham Elsen, the second was Jarvis Mudge, and the third was Nathaniel Greensmith.

When Rebecca's first husband, Abraham Elsen of Wethersfield, Connecticut, died, the court left his entire estate to her. When she married her second husband, Jarvis Mudge, the local magistrates sequestered the Elsen house and land, making them a rental property for the benefit of Rebecca's two daughters.

Jarvis Mudge and Rebecca moved to New London, Connecticut, with the children, but Jarvis died in 1652. This time the court decreed that Rebecca could sell the Jarvis land to pay off her debts and support her children. Then Rebecca took the children to Hartford. Rebecca married Nathaniel Greensmith in 1660 and shortly thereafter the Hartford witch hysteria began.

Accusations and So-Called Evidence

In the spring of 1662, eight-year-old Elizabeth Kelly was "possessed" with fits during which she named Goodwife Ayres as the cause. Elizabeth eventually died and her parents concluded that the cause must have been witchcraft. Mary and Andrew Sanford were brought up for examination. Then Goodwife Ayres's husband named Rebecca Greensmith as the real culprit. Rebecca promptly implicated her own husband and other Hartford residents and over time the entire area gradually became rife with a witch terror, leading to charges against at least thirteen people.

During the witch panic another woman, Ann Cole, became "possessed." Increase Mather, Puritan minister and father of Cotton Mather, reported that Ann was "taken with very strange fits, wherein her Tongue was improved by a Daemon to express things which she herself knew nothing of." The demons said through her that "such and such persons [some of the already accused] . . . were consulting on how they might carry on mischievous designs against her and several others."

This only intensified the community's desire to hunt witches. Rebecca Greensmith, who was already languishing in jail awaiting trial, was also named. When brought before the ministers and magistrates, Rebecca admitted to "familiarity with the Devil" but denied any "covenant" with him. She also said she planned to meet with the Devil at Christmas and that the Devil had frequent "carnal knowledge of her body." She added that she and the other accused had their meetings near her house.

Rebecca said that the Devil came to her in the form of a deer so that she would not be frightened of him and that this had caused her to gradually begin conversations with him. Other spirits came in different forms, including a crow, foxes, and a cat.

Her husband Nathaniel pleaded his innocence, but he and Rebecca were ultimately hung, along with a Farmington, Connecticut, woman named Mary Barnes. The hangings took place on Gallows Hill, a spot just north of where Trinity College now sits, on January 25, 1663. The site was chosen because it offered a good view to crowds of witnesses who seem to have regarded these proceedings as almost a form of entertainment.

Ann Cole regained her health after the executions, and after the hangings, Rebecca's daughters Sarah and Hannah Elsen claimed their inheritance from which they were required to pay Rebecca and Nathaniel's jail fees. The year between 1662 and 1663 was the last year in which any witches were executed in Connecticut, thirty years before the tragic witch hysteria of Salem, Massachusetts.

Outcome and Real Reasons behind the Accusations

The idea that a person could enter into a covenant with the Devil was born in the witch hunts of England and imported to the American colonies, but other causes for these executions can be surmised from the Greensmiths' story.

One reason was probably because Puritans had a deep suspicion of the Christmas holiday. Thomas Mockett, rector of Gilston in Hertfordshire, in his work *Christmas: The Christians Grand Feast,* wrote that Christmas was just another version of the Roman Saturnalia and that it brought "all the heathenish customs and pagan rites and ceremonies that the idolatrous heathens used, as riotous drinking, health drinking, gluttony, luxury, wantonness, dancing, dicing, stage-plays, interludes, masks, mummeries, with all other pagan sports and profane practices into the Church of God."*

---

*Diane Purkiss, *The English Civil War: Papists, Gentlewomen, Soldiers, and Witchfinders in the Birth of Modern Britain* (New York: Basic Books, 2009), 240.

When Rebecca declared that she had agreed to meet with the Devil at Christmas, her confession had particularly lewd connotations to Puritan listeners.

Rebecca seems to have insisted upon implicating Nathaniel for the good of his soul, despite his claims of innocence, which implies a kind of religious mania on her part. There was also the unfortunate fact that Rebecca, Nathaniel, and their friends appear to have been particularly irritating and obnoxious neighbors in a small colony where everyone knew everyone else. Reverend John Whiting said of Rebecca that she was a "lewd, ignorant, and considerably aged woman" (apparently being old and a woman was offensive, at least to him).

Those who were caught up in the scandal were all local acquaintances with somewhat shady reputations. Nathaniel had previously been convicted of battery, stealing one and a half bushels of wheat and a hoe, and lying to the court. Despite this, he had also managed to accumulate quite a bit of property, which probably led to jealousy among his neighbors. A further irritant to the community was that he had allegedly built his barn on common land.

Rebecca, Nathaniel, and their friends seem to have been loud and fond of having a good time. Unfortunately, they liked to party out of doors, where they could be seen and heard. One night they made merry under a tree near the Greensmiths' house, where they danced and laughed and drank a bottle of sack. These nocturnal revels were repeated several times with James Walkley, Judith Varlett, William and Goodwife Ayres, Goody Seager, and the wives of Peter Grant and Henry Palmer taking part, much to the annoyance of neighbors.

Elizabeth (Goody) Seager was charged with blasphemy and adultery following these revels, but unlike Rebecca, she mounted an articulate and spirited self-defense and never admitted guilt. Because of this, and because no adulterous partner was ever named, her case was eventually dismissed.

Interview with Arielle Crawley
McCloud, California

First, can you say a bit about who you are, where you live, and what you do for a living these days?

I am currently living in McCloud, California, but I grew up on the Mendocino coast. I have an online business, which allows me to stay at home and raise my three children.

Which accused New England witch or witches are you descended from?

I am a descendant of Rebecca Greensmith. She is my twelfth great-grandmother. Her maiden name is believed to be Steele. She was married three times, with Greensmith being her third and final surname.

Did your family carry the stories of your ancestors or did you find out about it all recently?

I am a bit of a genealogy buff and have been working on my family tree for ten years. No one in my immediate family knew the story of Rebecca Greensmith until recently. I was not even aware that there were witch trials in Connecticut. I was only aware of the later, and much portrayed, Salem witch trials.

What do you make of the fact that those you are related to, who were accused, were mostly women?

To be honest, I am not very surprised. I do have some foreknowledge of the male-dominated medical profession looking for ways to eradicate the use of midwives. Men have been notoriously intimidated by women's inherent talents for natural healing and birth. It also seems that these fundamentalist Puritans were very nervous that the women in their communities might forget their expected roles. They wanted to remind these women that although they were in the "New World," the men still had the control, and they chose to implement this through fear.

Have you had any experiences with modern Witches, and if so, how did that make you feel?

Yes, I grew up in a place where there are quite a few Witches, and I myself have dabbled with white magic. I think it all feels very natural to me. I come from a mixed ethnic background of Irish, African, and Romani, and I often imagine that many of the women in my family practiced magic in their own ways.

How do you personally define Witchcraft?

To me, Witchcraft is the use of natural and supernatural elements, both seen and unseen, for the purpose of healing and creating the reality that you want.

Have you had any feelings of contact with the accused "witch" in your family? Any past-life memories or dreams involving them?

Yes, I have thought about her quite often since I found her in my family line. I have felt that she is crying out for justice and asking that I don't forget her. I don't remember images, but I have most definitely felt her presence in dreams.

Do you have strong impressions regarding the accused witch you are descended from?

I feel a very deep sadness emanating from her. One of the things I find the most upsetting is the thought that she is not able to tell the whole story in her own words. I am only able to guess at how this happened, and how she must have felt through it all. I would say that is the strongest impression I get from her—it is that eternal need for the truth to be told.

Any other thoughts you care to add?

When I first began working on my family tree, finding an accused witch was not something I had even considered. I know now that I will never forget her, and I hope that eventually she will be able to rest in peace.

REBECCA TOWNE NURSE, ACCUSED WITCH OF SALEM

Rebecca Towne was the daughter of William and Joanna Blessing Towne. She was born in 1620 or 1621 in Great Yarmouth, Norfolk, England, and married Francis Nurse on August 24, 1644, in Great Yarmouth. Francis was a woodworker who became the constable for Salem Village in 1672.

Rebecca appears to have been a deeply devout, religious Christian who raised her eight children to be pious. She was respected and well liked by her neighbors. Unfortunately, she grew almost deaf in her old age and when she couldn't hear others well would sometimes grow irritated.

Accusations and So-Called Evidence

On March 24, 1692, at the age of seventy, Rebecca was suddenly taken from her sickbed, arrested, and accused of witchcraft. When she was arrested Rebecca exclaimed: "I am innocent as the child unborn, but surely, what sin has God found out in me, unrepented, he should lay such an affliction on me in my old age?"*

The court was convened by Governor Phips at the request of Lt. Governor Stoughton. Stoughton was then appointed chief magistrate by Phips, an action that violated the system of checks and balances that was supposed to maintain fairness in governance. To make matters worse, none of the magistrates had any legal training.

Rebecca's sisters, Mary Towne Estey and Sarah Towne Cloyce, were similarly charged. Several years before, Rebecca's mother had also been accused of witchcraft but was never tried. A belief at that time was that witchcraft was hereditary and passed down from mother to child, which made the sisters more vulnerable to suspicion.

---

*Mary Jane Alexander, "Family History Proves Bewitching to Descendants of Salem 'Witches': Colonial America; Three Presidents, Clara Barton, Walt Disney, Joan Kennedy and One Unborn Child Are among Those Whose Ancestors Were Accused of Consorting with the Devil 300 Years Ago," *Los Angeles Times*, August 29, 1993, http://articles.latimes.com/1993-08-29/news/mn-29128_1_family-history.

The trial, when it came, was a sham. Ann Putnam testified that the ghosts of Benjamin Houlton, Rebecca Houlton, John Fuller, Ann's sister Baker's six children, and her other sister Bayley and her three children had all appeared in winding sheets crying for justice after being murdered by Rebecca.

John Putnam and his wife refuted the charge that their daughter Rebecca Shepard and their son-in-law John Fuller had been murdered by Rebecca Nurse, but Rebecca's daughter Sarah testified that she saw Goodwife Bibber pulling pins from her clothing, crying, "Goody Nurse pricked me."[*]

On June 2, 1692, midwives searched Rebecca's body twice for witch's marks (moles, scars, blemishes, birthmarks, and skin tags that were firm evidence that a woman had sealed a pact with the Devil or was suckling imps and familiars). On June 28, 1692, Rebecca petitioned for a third exam based on the contradictory conclusions of the first two: some of the midwives claimed they saw marks of the Devil, while others said the marks were just natural blemishes.

At the trial, forty of her neighbors testified as to Rebecca's Christian faith and behavior and her good care and education of her children. The jury was convinced and pronounced her innocent. Then Stoughton ordered them to retire and "reconsider" the verdict.

1692, July 3—After sacrament, the elders propounded to the church, and it was, by unanimous vote, consented to, that our sister Nurse, being a convicted witch by the court, and condemned to die, should be excommunicated; which was accordingly done in the afternoon, she being present.[†]

And the next day the jury changed their verdict to guilty.

---

[*]Dana A. Wildes, "Rebecca Towne Nurse," RootsWeb, accessed 8/27/2016, www.roots web.ancestry.com/~nwa/nurse.html.
[†]From *The Salem Witch Trials: A Reference Guide,* as quoted in Rebecca Beatrice Brooks, History of Massachusetts Blog, The Trial of Rebecca Nurse, November 5, 2012, http://historyofmassachusetts.org/the-trial-of-rebecca-nurse.

On July 3, 1692, Reverend Nicholas Noyes brought Rebecca from her cell to the church, forced her to listen to a blistering tirade from the ministers, and then excommunicated her in front of the entire congregation. A petition was signed by prominent members of the community and sent to Governor Phips, who granted a temporary reprieve, but when the reprieve expired Rebecca and four others were hanged on July 19, 1692.

Rebecca's grave was so shallowly dug that parts of her body remained exposed. Her family came in the dark of night and removed her body for reburial on family property.

Rebecca's son Samuel fought to clear her name and on March 2, 1712, the case was rescinded. In 1957 the General Court of Massachusetts resolved that "no disgrace or cause for distress be borne by descendants of Witch-trial victims."

Outcome and Real Reasons behind the Accusations

So what actually happened to Rebecca? The factors leading to her death were many. First, Francis Nurse, her husband, had been in conflict with the town of Topsfield over land on the border between Topsfield and Salem Town (the Putnam family estate). Second, Rebecca was a member of the Salem Town church, and Francis was on a church committee that believed that the church's Reverend Parris was not hired properly and should be removed. The Putnams held the opposite view and were pro-Parris. A third reason was likely that the whole business was a power play by the Putnams, who hoped that by bringing down a respected pillar of the community they would gain the political power to control others. A fourth reason was that Rebecca never actually admitted to wrongdoing. Those who claimed innocence were deemed especially dangerous, while those who admitted guilt, especially if they were willing to point out other "witches," were less likely to suffer. And finally, Rebecca was simply an old woman who was hard of hearing, which sometimes made her ill-tempered. Perhaps that was reason enough for the magistrates to want to purge her from their village.

Interview with Krystle Drenning (Towne)
West Virginia

First, can you say a bit about who you are, where you live, and what you do for a living these days?

I am a stay-at-home mother of three, all girls—a ten-year-old, a three-year-old, and a three-month-old—which keeps me very busy. I was born in Oakland, Maryland, and moved to Davis, West Virginia, about six years ago.

Which accused New England witch or witches are you descended from?

I'm directly descended from the Towne sisters, who were accused of witchcraft and tried during the Salem witch trials. The relation is through their father, William Towne. My maiden name is Towne, and my father was born in Maine, though I was born in Maryland. Their names were Sarah Cloyce, Mary Estey, and Rebecca Nurse. I'm directly descended from Rebecca Nurse.

Did your family carry the stories of your ancestors or did you find out about it all recently?

My aunts discovered our ancestry while doing genealogical research several years ago. I didn't find out about it until after I graduated from high school.

What do you make of the fact that those you are related to, who were accused, were mostly women?

I think it just shows the views and thoughts of society in general at that time. Women had no rights and were mostly seen as possessions. If a man disliked his wife, he could simply just say she was a witch, and it would generally be his word over hers, and the man would win nearly every time. Witches are also typically viewed as being female, but again, this could be because men were afraid of a woman with intelligence who could outwit them. This was unacceptable at the time, and anything that would "demean" the man had to be dealt with so they could avenge their hurt pride.

Have you had any experiences with modern Witches, and if so, how did that make you feel?

My husband and I spent a Halloween in Salem, Massachusetts. The town is now a mecca for modern-day Witchcraft. I must say every modern Witch that I came across was very personable and kind. They were also very open and told things as they were. They weren't afraid to express their views. It really changed my view of what I thought a practitioner would seem like.

How do you personally define Witchcraft?

I now define Witchcraft as more of a practice than a religion. It's not only something that you believe in, but something that you DO. I know the practitioners whom I've spoken to see it as being a more proactive way of life. Instead of waiting for things to come along or change, you take matters into your own hands via the use spells, herbs, or whatever their favored method may be. It's also very nature centered. Most techniques revolve around the elements.

Have you had any feelings of contact with the accused "witch" in your family? Any past-life memories or dreams involving them?

I do feel a very strong connection to my ancestor. Though I believe that Rebecca was wrongly accused and not a witch in any manner.

Do you have strong impressions regarding the accused witch you are descended from?

I believe that Rebecca's intelligence and unrelenting faith must have intimidated some people, which led to her demise. Even in the end she stayed strong. Even though she was an elderly woman and had to endure much, she never gave up on her faith. One particular quote of hers that stood out from the trials was: "I can say before my Eternal Father I am innocent and God will clear my innocency. . . . The Lord knows I have not hurt them. I am an innocent person."

Any other thoughts you care to add?

The main thing that I've always found odd was that from a very young age I was fascinated with the concept of Witches. Even as an elementary school student I would check out books from the library on Witches. I don't mean just children's books either. I mean adult books, some of which were even about the Salem witch trials. This was years before I had any clue I was related at all to anyone involved, as I didn't find out about that until after graduating from high school. Even then I was fascinated when I found out but also not surprised for some reason. It's very strange and hard to describe the feeling. I feel very connected to them, though at the same time I believe them to be innocent. Why I feel such a strong connection even long before I found out about my ancestry I cannot explain.

I have recurring dreams involving a woman with long black hair whom I always feel is a Witch and a relative. These are very elaborate dreams. But as I said, I don't believe that Rebecca was even a witch. I definitely am more open to paranormal experiences as well. As a matter of fact, my husband and I were recently on an episode of the SyFy network show *Paranormal Witness*, talking about experiences that we've had over the past decade and that still continue to this day. I've often wondered if these experiences were due to my ancestry. Am I more sensitive to the unknown due to this? Is this something my ancestors experienced? Though it's not typical witchcraft, is it possible that it played a small role in them being labeled "witches"? As you can see, I have many questions concerning all of this. I harbor no doubts that if I were alive at that time I would be labeled a "witch."

I've have always been curious as to whether or not anyone else related to those tried for witchcraft has had similar feelings or experiences.

Interview with Richard Sutherland
Greater New Orleans, Louisiana

First, can you say a bit about who you are, where you live, and what you do for a living these days?

I'm a Grammy-nominated musician and published author. I've played piano and organ in hundreds of venues, from the Hollywood Palladium to Madison Square Garden, and written an autobiography that is available on Amazon titled, *F 'n' A! My Crazy Life in Rock and Blues* (by Rick Allen, my stage and pen name). My wife and I live near Bayou Lacombe, on the north shore of Lake Pontchartrain, across from New Orleans.

Which accused New England witch or witches are you descended from?

Although I'm not a "genealogy addict," I had questions about my father's heritage. After his death, my mother told me that his ancestors had come to America from Ireland during the Great Famine, but that was all she knew.

I have many cousins on my mother's side, and one of them is a Mormon named Eloise with whom I'd been in contact via email. She has access to the vast genealogical records of the LDS Church in Salt Lake City and began researching my father about five years ago. Not much was discovered about him, but she learned that through my maternal grandfather, Don Sawyer Huntzinger, she and I were direct descendants of Rebecca Nurse and John Proctor, both hanged for witchcraft in Salem and immortalized in Arthur Miller's play *The Crucible*.

In Miller's play, John Proctor is depicted as a young man in his thirties, when in fact he was about sixty years old when he was tried for witchcraft. He was a wealthy farmer, with a seven-hundred-acre farm near Ipswich, Massachusetts, and a tavern on Ipswich Road. He was well known and respected in the community but fought against "spectral evidence" in witch trials—evidence supposedly received by others through their dreams or visions, rather than eye-witness testimony. This opinion caused a great deal of conflict with the courts and was a factor in his conviction in 1692. John Proctor maintained his innocence until his hanging.

Did your family carry the stories of your ancestors or did you find out about it all recently?

My immediate family had no knowledge of our ancestors' involvement in the Salem witch trials until recently. I feel that being the seventh great-grandson of Rebecca Nurse and John Proctor (not husband and wife; their grandchildren Sarah Nurse and my ancestor Henry Sawyer were married) is not only interesting, but very cool.

My maternal grandmother, Cora Lucas (Weaver) Huntzinger, came from a great line of ancestors, dating back to the early 1600s in colonial America. Her genealogy included many kings of Wales as well as English lords. She was a fine and sophisticated lady, but my maternal grandfather, Don, whose ancestry also went back to the early 1600s in the colonies, was impish in nature, always with a joke up his sleeve. It seemed appropriate that the witch's DNA would run through his veins, and had he lived to learn about Nurse and Proctor, I'm sure he'd have had a smile on his face and would have made some sort of witty remark.

What do you make of the fact that those you are related to, who were accused, were mostly women?

Women are much more in tune with nature and more apt to have psychic abilities than men. I think that's why most of the people accused of witchcraft were female. My Scottish wife is no exception. Automatic writing and even verbal communications used to emit from her when we were younger and "playing" with a Ouija board.

Have you had any experiences with modern Witches, and if so, how did that make you feel?

I have an incredibly intelligent and highly educated lifelong friend named Jeanne Coats who is a Witch, a good Witch with all sorts of healing methods and magical abilities, including healing a somewhat skeptical person like me. A little over a year ago, after a CAT scan, two nodules were detected in my lungs and my oncologist thought they might be malignant. Naturally, my wife and I were extremely concerned, and I thought that my days might be numbered. When I told Jeanne about my lungs, she burned a healing candle for me every day, accompanied with healing thoughts and mantras. One year later, I underwent another CAT scan to see if the nodules had grown. I can't deny that I was afraid to learn the results. When the report arrived, my wife and I were overjoyed to see that one of the nodules hadn't grown at all, and the other nodule had disappeared completely. My doctor's prognosis: no cancer! And now, Jeanne is working to make the other nodule disappear. I'll bet she can accomplish this!

How do you personally define Witchcraft?

I've studied Oriental philosophy for many years, especially Hinduism and Mahayana Buddhism, and consider this universe to be a super-magical event. Therefore, I'm not shocked or frightened by the magical aspects of Witchcraft. In fact, being of mostly Scots-Irish descent, I have three pebbles from a Scottish burn that I keep in a little wooden pot atop my piano. When one of my loved ones becomes ill, I place their picture in that little pot and hope for some Scottish magic to heal them!

Have you had any feelings of contact with the accused "witch" in your family? Any past-life memories or dreams involving them?

I wish I could answer yes to this question, because some sort of contact with Rebecca and John would be fun. Sadly, the answer is no.

Do you have strong impressions regarding the accused witch you are descended from?

When I watch Arthur Miller's play, I feel outraged at what was done to my ancestors in Salem. Of course, Miller used a great deal of poetic license, but it makes me realize the extreme insanity of the so-called

Christians who were my ancestors. It depicts such stupidity and superstition that my Celtic blood almost boils. Is this my heritage? When those "God-fearing" people found anyone practicing the rich and meaningful Celtic traditions or people with psychic abilities, they deemed them to be evil. If my Scottish wife had lived in Salem in those days, she would surely have been hanged. This would have included my good-Witch friend, Jeanne Coats, and, for that matter, myself for my Hindu-Buddhist views.

What we witness in today's tumultuous America is but an extension of the fundamentalist and fanatical Christian religion, now fully acceptable with the title of "Evangelical"—ignorant people who take the Bible literally and are devoid of the ability to decipher the real meanings from fictional events. Witchcraft may be a reality, but at least in my experience, it is used for good, not evil, and certainly not governed by some entity named "Satan," who is but the left hand of the Godhead. Good cannot exist without its opposite. The only Witch I know is as good and nourishing as a sweet mountain stream to a thirsty man.

WEALTHIAN LORING RICHARDS, ACCUSED WITCH OF DORCHESTER, WEYMOUTH, AND BOSTON

Wealthian Loring was born in Dorchester, England, in about 1602. She married Thomas Richards in 1620. They came to the American colonies in 1633 and were residents of Dorchester, Massachusetts, and later Weymouth, where Thomas was a successful merchant.

Each time Thomas made a trip to England he left his business affairs in the hands of his wife Wealthian, who must have been an intelligent and competent spouse. After Thomas's death, Wealthian's children petitioned the court to let her be executor of Thomas's will, which was further proof of her abilities.

Accusations and So-Called Evidence
When Wealthian moved to Boston, her behavior began to cause controversy. One complaint was that in 1640 she called Henry and William

Waltham "cozeners and cheaters." Henry Waltham wrote in a letter to John Winthrop, a leading founder of the Massachusetts Bay Colony, that she behaved in a fashion "unbeseeming a modest woman's carriage."

In 1653 or 1654 Wealthian was finally accused of witchcraft, nearly forty years before the Salem witch hysteria. It was alleged that in anger she threatened people who later suffered serious fates. One Thomas Thatcher wrote in her defense that she had taken care of her children well and that "God had so blessed them five or six of them have approved themselves to one church or another, and been readily entertained in their fellowship."

Outcome and Real Reasons behind the Accusations

Wealthian died on November 4, 1679, in Boston, Massachusetts. In her will she left property for her sons and daughters, for the poor of Boston, for the First Church of Boston, and for Harvard College. Wealthian was never prosecuted and seems to be yet another example of an intelligent, capable, and wealthy woman who simply expressed herself too freely.

Interview with Cairril Adaire
Bloomington, Indiana

First, can you say a bit about who you are, where you live, and what you do for a living these days?

I am a solitary Celtic Witch and priestess of the goddess Brigid. My paid job is in graphic design and web development, and I sing with Kaia, a world-music vocal and percussion ensemble. My passions include the performing arts, historic Paganism, feminism, the environment, history, my Goddess daughters and friends, and experimental baking! I blog at irishsparks.com.

I am a descendant of Wealthian Loring (1602–1679), an English immigrant to the Massachusetts Bay Colony. I am a direct descendant, a great, great, great, on and on granddaughter. My family isn't as interested in genealogy as I am, so I found her and celebrate her on my own.

In 1641 she was accused by a neighbor of behaving in a fashion "unbeseeming a modest woman's carriage," and in 1653 or 1654 she was threatened with the charge of witchcraft. It does not appear that her case was brought forward. So while I proudly call myself her descendant, I believe she was a Christian with an attitude rather than a witch. Her story is recounted in Robert Charles Anderson's *The Great Migration Begins: Immigrants to New England 1620–33.*

What do you make of the fact that those who were accused were mostly women?

The Burning Times actually had three phases and not all of them targeted women. The contemporary Pagan movement has a narrative that millions of innocent women were burned at the stake, but evidence simply does not bear this out. In Wealthian's case, I think we see how a strong woman could be accused, but also how the accusation could be retracted as cooler heads prevailed.

How do you personally define Witchcraft?

My definition of Witchcraft comes from the collective effort of over thirty leaders of national Pagan organizations in the 1990s when we successfully got dictionary definitions changed to the following: "a Pagan religion, loosely organized in autonomous traditions, honoring masculine and/or feminine divinities and practicing magic and folk traditions for benevolent ends, such as healing and the mystical development of the self."*

Witchcraft is more than what I do; it's who I am. When I go deep inside myself and access my core self, the self that has been with me always and that makes me unique, I find singing and Witchcraft rising

---

*This was done by the "Dictionary Project," when members of what would become the Our Freedom Coalition urged major dictionary publishers to augment their definitions of "Witchcraft" and "Paganism"; see www.ourfreedomcoalition.org/projects/pr_dictionary .html. —Ellen

up in a gold, glowing double helix. It is my every breath. I like heavy ritual, trance work, ecstatic dancing, and magic, but I also will take a bite of my sandwich and toss it in the grass, saying, "Back at ya, Goddess." Witchcraft has rescued me from a trauma-filled Catholic upbringing that denigrated women and kept them from their power. Now I have a deep feeling of the Sacred that accompanies every beat of my heart.

Have you had any feelings of contact from any of the old "witches"? Any past-life memories or dreams involving them?

I commune with the spirits of ancestors and historical Witches in depth each year during my Oidhche Shamhna (Samhain) celebrations. I invite the Witches in from the East, and they come swooping in cackling, full of power and life and danger. I love having them in my Circle! They teach me how to look life in the eye and how to come into my power. I celebrate light, dark, and shadow—all aspects of the human experience—in an ethical framework that works to transform evil into compassion and activism. My Witches love the freedom of being dead and enjoy playing tricks on me to bring me closer to my truest self and raw power.

I invite Wealthian as an ancestor, in the North Quarter [of the Circle]. I was speaking more broadly about my experiences with old Witches. I respect Wealthian's Christianity. One of my favorite Oidhche Shamhna memories is seeing Mark Twain, Boudicca, and two screeching Witches all chatting together over cakes and ale. When the Witches enter my Circle it's always in a rush, and I just open myself to their exuberance. I have called on nameless ones when I needed to do work with my shadow self, and they are very hard-core. They don't stop pushing past mind games to get me to Truth. They are all about facing life and death head-on and stepping into my power.

Do you have strong impressions regarding the witch you are descended from?

I have worked with Wealthian several times in Circle and named a tough, thorny tree on my land for her. She was/is a strong character who is not afraid to face life and death fully. I come from a long line of incredibly tough women who struggled against very steep odds to create a life for themselves and their families. I seek to walk in their footsteps, being ever mindful of the special obstacles they faced because of their gender. I seek to broaden their work beyond mere survival to the struggle for social and environmental justice as well as living with honor.

You are the founder of the Pagan Educational Network (PEN), which has done some amazing work with dictionaries and other issues. Can you please talk about that?

I founded PEN in 1993 to educate the community about Paganism and to build community. I had become frustrated with the political actions of national Pagan organizations, which at the time were totally reactive. A case of discrimination would occur, and the organizations would respond. I wanted to build a community of goodwill with non-Pagans to create a world where discrimination wouldn't happen. I also felt strongly that Pagans who were closeted for safety's sake could still feel part of a larger community by volunteering for nonprofits in their own neighborhoods, towns, and cities.

Paganism is a broad term that encompasses a wide variety of religious and magical paths, such as Witchcraft, Druidism, Church of All Worlds, Goddess worship, and much more. Pagans self-identify, so not all will agree with this construct. But it's a useful one for dealing with the non-Pagan community. For instance, Christianity encompasses Roman Catholics, Baptists, Episcopalians, and Mormons. Each path is different, but they share a common starting point. For Pagans, it's most often a view of the Earth as sacred. It is a positive, life-affirming religion. It does not include "evil" deities and does not even recognize the existence of Satan. Satan is an Abrahamic construct, and Paganism is completely different from those traditions.

Members of PEN have written letters to the editor about Pagan-related and non-Pagan topics, participated in Pagan Pride events, worked on behalf of Pagans in prison, taken part in national campaigns to support victims of discrimination, and contributed untold volunteer hours in their own communities. We provided our members with an orientation packet that explained how doing good in the community could eventually build a place where they'd be safe to come out. If you've been working alongside people of many religious faiths on a Habitat build, for instance, and they know you're a good person, they're going to be curious, not threatened, if the issue of religion comes up. We never went after the extremists who insisted that Pagans were devil worshippers; our philosophy was to build from the middle out. It was extremely effective.

The 1990s saw almost constant physical and legal attacks on Pagans, in the home, in businesses, in courts, you name it. Thanks to a large cultural shift brought about in part by Pagans coming out of the closet and educating the public in positive ways, discrimination happens only occasionally now. We continue our work to build a world where it never happens.

As the national coordinator of PEN, I was in contact with the leaders of numerous Pagan organizations across the United States. I saw that we could be much more effective if we coordinated our efforts and took action in the national sphere. Our first project was to try to get the Associated Press (AP) to include Pagan religions in its stylebook. While the AP people we talked with were kind and helpful, they made it clear that they took their lead from standard dictionaries. That led to my coordinating a massive national effort to change dictionary definitions for "Paganism" and "Witchcraft."

At that time there was a history of bickering and splintering in the Pagan movement. My job was to build a coalition of national leaders who organized around a shared goal rather than shared beliefs. Over thirty organizations and individuals participated, which was unheard of at that time. We eventually produced suggested definitions and a very thick book of citations to back up our claim. To our complete delight, all the major dictionaries did eventually change their definitions. While they didn't remove negative definitions, each included a neutral definition that reflected contemporary Pagan practice. This was a major victory for Pagan civil rights, as it impacted all spheres of society, from the Library of Congress to a schoolchild looking up a word in a dictionary.

We continued to coordinate successfully over the next few years. I found myself running into organizational issues with PEN and wanted to brainstorm with other leaders to see if we could collectively address issues common to us all. To that end, I organized the Pagan Summit in 2001. It was an invitation-only event for leaders of national organizations and a few people (magazine editors and freelance writers) who had significant impact on the Pagan movement.

I'll be honest: at first all these people who had held grudges for years were very hesitant to come together! But the late Isaac Bonewits wrote a clear exhortation to invitees that inspired all of us. We eventually ended up with nearly forty participants. Over the course of a weekend we focused on issues of organizing, financial management, personnel recruitment, etc. We did *not* discuss beliefs. We were never interested in organizing around shared beliefs—we organized around shared values and goals.

We emerged from the summit with tremendous momentum and goodwill and got to work. Unfortunately, the terrorist attacks of September 11 totally derailed our collective agenda, and national organizations instead turned to interfaith organizing, which they focus on to this day. While we weren't able to manifest all the goals we laid out for ourselves, the summit had two significant outcomes: it inspired regional summits that led to more effective regional leadership, and it engendered deep trust among summit participants. That trust led to more national projects and eventually to the foundation of Our Freedom: A Pagan Civil Rights Organization.

As a cofounder of Our Freedom Coalition: A Pagan Civil Rights Organization (OFC), can you please discuss some of the things that group has accomplished?

After the success of the 2001 Pagan Summit, leaders of national organizations saw the value of our continuing to work together. No one wanted to create a bureaucracy, but I was able to get buy-in to found OFC in late 2001. It has a sadly neglected website (someday, I promise myself, someday!), but it mainly functions as a closed email list that acts as a hotline for all the major national Pagan organizations. If a Pagan shop is fire-bombed in the South, within twenty-four hours we can provide a coordinated response.

Since we are a private group with strict membership guidelines, we are able to be open with one another about cases that come to our attention. For instance, while we may be thinking a coordinated media response is appropriate, an OFC member on the ground can let us know that face-to-face talks are proving more productive. This has led to a more effective use of resources and definitely better results!

Because OFC is consensus-based, we often can't issue press releases within twenty-four hours of an event happening. I regret this lack of nimbleness, but I respect that we are an extremely diverse group of people who want to make sure we don't sign anything that hasn't been fully vetted. After all, we are representing our organizations, not just ourselves personally. We've devised a process whereby members can propose joint action, and over the course of three or more weeks, the whole group can come to a consensus on whether or not to take it up. When we do take up projects, members feel a sense of ownership and are more willing to contribute more than just their name and affiliation at the end of a public statement.

OFC is the only organization of its kind in the United States. While I am very glad to see Pagans in all spheres get more active in their communities, it also heartens me to know that OFC members are able to lead their organizations more effectively and eventually pass them on to the next generation. See www.ourfreedomcoalition.org for information on the organization and "Past Projects" for a link to the Pagan Summit site.

CAUSES AND EFFECTS OF THE SALEM WITCH HYSTERIA

A theory has been offered in the past few years that the symptoms running rife in the Salem area were actually caused by ergot poisoning.

Ergot is a type of fungus found on grain, especially rye, which was a staple in the Salem area. There were also many underlying class prejudices at work, and to this day, Massachusetts, in particular, strives to be a liberal, fair-minded, and progressive state that bends over backward to ensure human rights are respected. In my mind the shock of the witch persecutions probably had a hand in that. When the people of the commonwealth overcame the fog of hysteria and realized what they had wrought, they were acutely embarrassed and apologetic, and the guilt over the Salem witch murders seems to linger in the collective unconscious of many Massachusetts residents today.

Modern Witches of New England

In nine hundred years of time and space, I've never met anyone who wasn't important.

DOCTOR WHO

Every person's life is worth a novel.

CARL ROGERS

Deciding who to include in this section was not easy, first because I am not a Witch and so the territory is new to me, and second, because the worthiest magical teachers and guides are often hidden. Of necessity, then, the public and vocal Witches were the ones that first came to mind. Thankfully these kind people recommended others and some new names cropped up. I hope they will surprise you as they did me. New England folklorist Peter Muise generously offered to pen an introduction to this chapter.

Please note that, as in the last section, these interviews were conducted through an emailed question-and-response format rather than in a verbal conversation, so each Witch was given a similar set of questions to answer that only differed when I asked for more information on a particular point.

WITCHCRAFT NEVER DIED
By Peter Muise

Back in the 1700s, a woman named Judith Howard lived in Harpswell, Maine. Judith worked as a healer, treating her neighbors' illnesses with herbs and homemade remedies. The people of Harpswell appreciated her skills but were always a little wary of Judith. The neighbors whispered that she was a witch. After all, no one could be so effective at healing without super-natural help, could they?

Judith was kind and caring all of her life, but when she was on her deathbed she made one demand of her neighbors. "Don't bury me in the graveyard near the harbor," she said. A man who had wronged her was buried there, and she didn't want to spend eternity next to him. Shortly after making this request, she expired.

The neighbors breathed a sigh of relief. Although they would miss her herbal remedies, they were quite happy to be rid of a suspected witch. They put her body in a simple pine coffin and, in spite of her dying request, buried it in the graveyard near the harbor, which was the closest to her house. Judith's grave was right next to the man who wronged her.

That night after her burial no one in Harpswell could sleep; every barn door in town blew open and shut all night long, even though there was no wind. The next night was worse. The barn doors made their racket again and were joined by the doors inside people's houses, which were endlessly slammed by invisible hands. The following night was even worse. The town's cats added to the door-slamming cacophony as they roamed through the town howling and screeching at unseen sights. No one slept a wink.

After three sleepless nights the people of Harpswell had learned their lesson. They unearthed Judith's coffin and carried her body across town for burial in another cemetery. The supernatural disturbances ceased, and Harpswell once again knew peace after sunset.

New England folklore is full of many such stories. Hannah Cranna, a Connecticut witch, demanded on her deathbed that her coffin be carried by hand to the graveyard. After she died her neighbors tried several times to transport it by wagon or sleigh but failed in every attempt until they at last honored her dying wish. Other stories describe how a witch's curse lingers long after her death. For example, on Cape Cod a dying witch named Aunt Rachel cursed the men who had killed her family. As the murderers sailed away, a rock suddenly erupted from the harbor floor and sank their ship. The rock was named "Aunt Rachel's Curse."

Unwilling to move on after their physical deaths, ghostly witches haunt many other New England towns. Moll Cramer's ghost is said to wander the woods of Woodbury, Connecticut, while the old graveyard in York, Maine, is haunted by the spirit of Mary Nasson, a suspected witch who died in 1774. The ghost of Giles Corey, crushed to death while being interrogated during the Salem witch trials, allegedly lurks in the field where he died, which is now the Howard Street Cemetery. Corey's ghost also supposedly appears in Salem to warn the city of impending disasters.

These stories have one thing in common: the witches in them don't die easily. They're probably all just legends, but they're also a metaphor for a basic truth: Witchcraft never died out in New England. That basic truth can explain how Salem went from being a town where accused witches were killed to one where modern witches are now celebrated—and help drive the economy. It can explain how witches went from being dangerous people in league with Satan to being people who can purify your home, tell your future, and help you find love. Witches were once social outcasts; now they're your neighbors, your coworkers, or your college roommates. Witches used to be scary, but now they are nice.

How did this happen? Legends claim that witches can change their shape, transforming themselves into animals, balls of light, or even other people. Well, witchcraft itself can change its shape too. Witchcraft was not limited just to Salem or to the 1600s. It was widespread and enduring. It never died. Over the centuries it has simply transmogrified itself into a new form.

Witchcraft has been in New England since the first English settlers set foot on these shores and was here even before that, when the Native Americans practiced shamanism in secluded forests and hidden swamps. It is still here today. The 1692 Salem witch trials are the most famous manifestation of witch belief in New England, but the belief has continued uninterrupted in different ways up until the modern era. After all, the Salem trials were shut down because the government realized witchcraft couldn't be proven in court, not because people stopped believing in it.

Of course, no one accused in the Salem trials was really a witch. Let's be clear. They were just ordinary citizens caught up in a sinister web of gossip who were forced to confess under threat of death. Their terrified neighbors projected the fearful attributes of the archetypal legendary witch onto them. But even though there were no real witches in the courtroom, the documents from Salem and other New England witchcraft trials do illuminate the landscape of witchcraft belief. The judges, the accused, and their alleged victims were all in agreement about what witches supposedly could do. For example, they could leave their body and fly through the night, they could transform into animals, and they could inflict harm on humans and livestock. Some sources also state that witches were in thrall to Satan, but this was a belief held mainly by the Puritan leaders and a few devout churchgoers. To the average New England settler, witches were problematic in the same way as wolves or disease. They were an unpleasant part of the natural world that just had to be dealt with.

You fight fire with fire, and you fight magic with magic. The English colonists used a wide variety of magic to fight witchcraft. For example, they created "witch bottles" by putting the urine of an allegedly bewitched person into a bottle full of sharp nails, believing these would harm the attacking witch. They hung horseshoes over doorways to prevent witches from entering their homes and put shoes by the fireplace to entrap any malevolent spirit that might find its way down. They hid metal items like harpoons in the walls and etched protective patterns on the beams of their houses to keep out witches. Bay leaves on the windowsill and around the doorway were also considered effective as protective magic.

Witchcraft and antiwitchcraft magic go hand in hand. Both are a vital part of witchcraft belief and are two sides of the same coin. To a modern reader this defensive magic looks indistinguishable from witchcraft itself, and the seventeenth-century Puritan elites agreed, claiming that all magic, even the defensive kind, came from the Devil and was forbidden. However, paradoxically, they practiced their own forms of magic. John Winthrop Jr., the son of Massachusetts's first governor, was so adept at alchemy that he was nicknamed the Christian Hermes (after the Greek god of magic), and divinity students attending Yale or Harvard often studied alchemy and astrology. According to one legend, in the 1640s Harvard's first president, Henry Dunster, even had to banish Satan back to hell after some experimenting students couldn't do it themselves. Students at Harvard and Yale studied these esoteric topics well into the 1800s, so alchemy and astrology weren't just seventeenth-century superstition. For many years they were an integral part of a New England minister's education.

Magical practices continued after the 1600s among the less educated as well. For example, in the 1770s Simeon Smith of Wentworth, New Hampshire, supposedly bewitched the son of neighbors who supported the British in the American Revolution. The neighbors put the bewitched boy's blood in a bottle, corked it, and for good measure stuck a knife through the cork. They then heated the bottle in a fire. Simeon Smith died, and the boy was cured. That's not a story about the Revolution you'll learn in American History class, but it shows how belief in witchcraft continued into the eighteenth century.

Fortune-telling also remained popular, whether among sea captains determining auspicious dates to set sail or single young women looking for husbands. New Englanders read tea leaves or each other's palms to divine the futures. Girls interpreted egg yolks or poured lead into water to learn about their future fiancés. Sometimes these practices were frowned upon, but sometimes they were used as party games.

New Englanders continued to believe in witchcraft even after the Enlightenment and the Industrial Revolution transformed the region. In the nineteenth century folklorists working in New England found abundant proof that people still believed in witches. A blacksmith in New Hampshire claimed he trapped a witch in his smithy by nailing a horseshoe over the door while the witch was inside. People across the region wore necklaces of mountain ash beads or carried twigs of that tree in their pockets to repel witches. A physician in Shaftsbury, Vermont, and his family ritually harvested the root of the bittersweet plant, which they believed offered protection against witchcraft. A woman in New Hampshire told folklorist John McNab Currier that she had heard witches flying overhead one night, laughing as they flew to dance and celebrate in a nearby abandoned building.

These accounts show that long after the Salem trials ended belief in witches remained strong across the New England states. Witchcraft even made its way back into the courtroom a few times. In October of 1787, John Estes and his wife Eleanor of Harpswell, Maine, sued Alcut Stover for slander after Stover said Eleanor was a witch. The Esteses won the case, but the verdict was later overturned. In 1878, Lucretia Brown of Ipswich, Massachusetts, took a Christian Science practitioner to court, claiming he had bewitched her. The case was to be heard in nearby Salem, but happily the judge threw the case out. The town did not want another witch trial.

Belief in witchcraft continued into the twentieth century. The writer Theda Kenyon reported that in 1923 a man in Chelsea, Massachusetts, believed he was bewitched and was only cured when a Boston "witch doctor" made a potion from cemetery grass. Eva Speare's 1932 book *New Hampshire Folk Tales* contains several allegedly true stories about witches and magic. They include many familiar elements, such as bewitched animals and various forms of defensive magic.

Witchcraft was always a popular theme for New England authors. Writers like Nathaniel Hawthorne, Henry Wadsworth Longfellow, and John Greenleaf Whittier incorporated witches and magic into their novels, plays, and poems. But in the twentieth century witchcraft began to escape from works of art and appear in the actual lives of artists and authors. For example, the British painter and occultist Austin Osman Spare (1886–1956) claimed he was taught magic by one Mrs. Paterson, a "colonial woman" descended from New England witches who had escaped the Puritan witch hunt. Spare alleged that Mrs. Paterson could change her appearance at will, externalize her thoughts in physical form, and foretell the future. He even said that Mrs. Paterson took him with her to the witches' Sabbath, which occurred outside the boundaries of time and space.

That last part sounds like something from a story by the Rhode Island horror writer H. P. Lovecraft (1890–1937). Lovecraft wrote many tales featuring witchcraft and the occult but was not a practitioner himself. However, apparently some of his fans were. Lovecraft reported that he once received a letter from a woman claiming she was a descendant of the Salem witches. She offered to share her knowledge of witchcraft if he would share his occult secrets. Unfortunately, Lovecraft never replied to her, so we'll never know what magic she practiced.

The writer Shirley Jackson (1916–1965) spent most of her adult life in New England, and witchcraft played an important role in both her life and her fiction. Magic and the occult figure prominently in many of her works (e.g., *The Haunting of Hill House* and *We Have Always Lived in the Castle*), but she was also a serious student of witchcraft. She owned hundreds of books on the topic and authored a children's book about the Salem witch trials. She was also a practitioner of the magical arts. When she was in college Jackson used magic to prevent pregnancy (before turning to modern contraception) and participated in a ritual intended to summon the Devil. Throughout her life she also read Tarot cards and created various charms and amulets.

Jackson described herself as an "amateur witch" in her publicity materials. Her publisher encouraged this, hoping that it would sell books, but Jackson felt some ambivalence about the label. Very few New Englanders before the twentieth century would have dared to identify themselves as witches in any way. Most people in the past who practiced magic did not consider themselves witches and usually focused on defensive, antiwitch-craft magic. However, there were a few who did dare to name themselves witches, despite the risks associated with that label.

For example, in the early 1800s a group of elderly widows and other single women living in the decrepit Massachusetts village of Dogtown seem to have declared themselves witches. Some of these women, like Daffy Archer, made their living selling herbal remedies, while others like Rachel Rich and her daughter Becky told fortunes using tea leaves and coffee grounds. Not all the Dogtown witches were quite so benevolent. Molly Jacobs was also a fortune-teller, but she threatened to curse any passerby who did not give her money. The most feared witch in the village was Tammy Younger, who lived in a half-collapsed house on the main road through Dogtown. From her front window she glared at travelers, who, fearing her malevolent powers, paid her for safe passage.

In the nearby town of Marblehead, a man named Edward Dimond earned the affectionate nickname "Wizard Dimond" in the late 1600s and early 1700s. Dimond claimed that magical abilities ran in his family, which had produced many notable astrologers. According to legends, Wizard Dimond used his powers to guide ships safely to harbor during storms and to punish thieves. His granddaughter Mary "Moll" Pitcher inherited the family powers and developed a reputation as the foremost fortune-teller in New England. Sailors and merchants sought her advice on when to sail, and young lovers asked her when to marry. Her reputation lingered for many years. In 1939 a *Boston Globe* article even claimed she had predicted everything from the American victory in the Revolution to the invention of the radio.

Like Shirley Jackson after them, these New Englanders took the pejorative term "witch" and used it to their own benefit. This would have been impossible during the Puritan witch hunts, but as time went on New England's attitude about witches had changed. It helped that Edward Dimond and many of the Dogtown witches focused on helpful magic, but overall feelings about witchcraft were changing in the region. Although some people still feared witchcraft, to others it had become a charming survival of the region's preindustrial past. It was a distinguishing aspect of New England culture. The West had its cowboys and rodeos, the South had blues music and soul food, and New England had its witches. It became a point of pride for people to trace their ancestry to someone accused of witchcraft. What was once a source of shame was now a sign of deep American roots.

In 1971, Laurie Cabot opened the first witchcraft shop in Salem, Massachusetts. Governor Michael Dukakis declared Cabot the "Official Witch of Salem" a few years later. Today Salem is home to many Witchcraft stores and has a sizable population of practicing Witches. In the weeks leading up to Halloween the streets are filled with revelers clad in black cloaks and pointed hats. The terrifying half-mythical figures of old legend are now made of flesh and blood. Less terrifying, of course, but no less magical.

The staff in Salem's stores will tell your fortune. They can help you find a lover or tell you how to protect your home from baleful spirits. They focus on the positive side of Witchcraft. Some of the techniques may be different and some of the magical ingredients might be new, but underneath the surface the magic is the same. Witches don't die easily, and Witchcraft in New England never died; it just took on a new shape for our modern era.

ADAM SARTWELL
Salem, New Hampshire

First, can you say a bit about who you are, where you live, and what you do for a living these days?

 I'm Adam Sartwell, cofounder of the Temple of Witchcraft and award-winning author of *Twenty-One Days of Reiki*. I live in New Hampshire now but was born in Vermont. I am a self-employed writer, teacher, healer, tarot reader, priest, and incense maker, so basically a full-time Witch.

Which religion were you raised in?

My parents went to a Methodist church before I was born. They had a disagreement with the local church when some of the parishioners asked them to remove a derelict drunk man from their street by scaring him off. My dad, being a marine just back from the Vietnam War, could definitely scare him off. He refused, though, because he thought that was not what Jesus intended churchgoers to do. They were supposed to be helping the poor and lost instead of running them out of town. So my parents didn't go back to church after that. My father refused. My brothers and I were not even baptized because of it. My parents moved to the next town before I was born.

I did go to a Methodist preschool, and one of my babysitters read to me from a picture Bible. Most of the stories of the Bible that I remember come from this time. As I grew older my parents ascribed to the belief that if any of their kids really wanted to have religion they could decide on their own. Yet strangely enough when I came out of the broom closet it took them years to become comfortable with it. I guess like most rural people they expected that if I were to find religion it would have been some brand of Christianity.

When I was a kid I was fascinated by *D'Aulaires' Book of Greek Myths*. I got it out from the library multiple times, and I believe we had a few fines on it. My older brothers had the same fascination and propensity to make this particular library book late, much to my mother's dismay. This started my education in Paganism.

How and when did you decide you were a Witch?

When I was little they used to have reruns of *Bewitched* on television. After my brothers left for school, I could control the TV until it was time for my mom to leave for work, and then I would go to my babysitter's. I would watch *Bewitched* at this time. One day I went to the stairwell and saw my mom getting her hair ready for work in the bathroom. I said to my mom I want to be a Witch. She said, I think that you would be a warlock because you're a boy. I told her in all my infinite child wisdom that this was not the case, and I would be a Witch. I believe my mom rolled her eyes skyward and kept on with her preparations. I remember it as clear as day and laugh to myself a bit about how I don't use the word *warlock* to describe myself now. I know some who have reclaimed the word, but I have never felt comfortable with it, thinking *Witch* is a gender-neutral word.

It was later when I was in my teens that I came back to this decision of being a Witch. I had always had magical experiences as a kid, but when I hit my teens I started to have a lot more of them. I started to dream of future events, say exactly what my friends were thinking, see auras, know things I couldn't have known, and more. It was my psychic experiences that brought me back to my earlier declaration.

I had begun to have a startling recurring dream that got clearer and clearer over time. A red blur hitting me, and me floating free of my body at first, then waking up with the knowledge that I would die before my fifteenth birthday. The dream would shock me awake and make me sit up in bed. Having had dreams of the future before, I was scared, and I began to think that this must just be my fate. I started to prepare like some do before a suicide attempt. I gave things away and made a list of who to give things to if I should die. I became fascinated with where people went after death. I researched different religions.

I even went to a Catholic priest with a friend of mine. I asked him about my dreams. Told him how they had predicted things before. He told me that I should pray for them to go away because they were from the Devil. I asked him why, when people in the Bible were guided by God they were called prophets, yet when I dreamed of the future he was so sure it was the Devil. The only religion I could find that accepted, encouraged, and trained me on how to use my psychic gifts was Witchcraft.

When I discovered this, I shared it with my good friend. She had also found Witchcraft and had her own psychic gifts. I told her about my vision and my "deadline," so to speak.

We were walking home from school on the day before my birthday. We walked home randomly when the weather was nice instead of riding the bus. As we came to the spot where you had to cross the street to stay on the sidewalk, I stepped out into the street. My friend grabbed the back of my shirt and pulled me out of the road just in time for me to see a red car blur past. The car stopped at a point that if I had been in the road I would have been dead. My friend told me that she had been worried about me all week because of my dream.

I spent a lot of time after this event not knowing what to do with myself. I felt as though I had cheated death or fate. It was because of Witchcraft and our shared love of it that I had shared my experiences with her at all. I have been a Witch ever since.

How do you personally define Witchcraft?

Witchcraft is the art, science, and religion of a Witch. The art is the craft of the Witch: spells, psychic arts, shamanic journeys, and esoteric workings. The science is the ability of the Witch to examine and experience the world around them and the spiritual truths of nature. The religion is the practice of connecting to the tides and times of nature and honoring deity in all forms.

Which tradition of Witchcraft do you follow? How did you find that tradition?

For years I was eclectic. My Witchcraft was a mix of things I had learned and tested by experience. I would read a book and then test to see if it worked for me, whether I thought it worked, or had an experience. This sort of haphazard absorption gave me freedom to practice as I willed, yet it didn't give me a solid foundation in the work of the Witch. The more I practiced, the better I got at it and figured out what it was I needed to make my approach less haphazard. I was proud at the time that I was not bound by tradition and that I had gotten as far as I did without a teacher.

Then I met my loves, Christopher Penczak and Steve Kenson. Christopher talked so lovingly about what it was to have a teacher, to not have to rely only on your wits alone to help you but to have guidance from a teacher. He observed me and knew that I had taught myself well. I asked if I could join his classes, and I went through the five-year course of study. I adopted a beginner's mind and tried to only use what I had learned from the Mystery School for those five years. I am glad I did because it opened up doors to experience things I thought I knew all over again. The process made me a better Witch. Through that process my partners—Christopher and Steve—and I founded the Temple of Witchcraft, a federal 501(c)(3) religious nonprofit, to give our graduates the ability to take their ministry out into the world. We based our tradition on the techniques and the personal connection with deity, not dogma.

What makes your approach or tradition unique from any others out there?

The Temple of Witchcraft is different because it doesn't ask you to forsake all other traditions. It is focused on technique and our own experience of deity and spirits, and it is based on having your own experiences instead of blindly following what someone says.

Would you say that Witchcraft is a "craft" or a "religion"? And can you talk about the difference?

I've always thought of it as both. If you want to separate them, I feel the craft is the practice of Witches. This is where we get into spells, meditations, divinations, and our act of creating the lives we choose. The religion is our connection to the divine and our work to become better people. It is kind of like the difference between theurgy and thaumaturgy. Theurgy is the work of connecting to the divine both within and without, so we become more like the divine. This is what I feel the religion of Witchcraft is. Thaumaturgy is using magic to effect change and create our circumstances. This is the craft. It is when you combine theurgy with thaumaturgy that our lives become divine magic.

Whom do Witches worship?

Witches worship that which they find divine. It changes from Witch to Witch. I've met Witches who work with Mary, Kali, Hecate, and practically all of the deities of the world's religions. I have even met some who worship deities or spirits you can't find in our world religions, with only their own unverified personal gnosis to go by. I have seen Witches who don't think there is a divine at all, just energy and consciousness. Personally, I have experienced the vision of the divine in all of creation, so I am able to see the divine both in specific things and also in everything. I feel that when there is paradox and seemingly contrary belief, we find the Great Mystery that is the divine. The divine is too big to hold within our mortal heads, so we worship that which "holds" more of the divine within it, like the gods.

When Witches meet, what do they usually do?

There are a multitude of things that Witches do when they come together. We take classes on enhancing our craft or going deeper with our spiritual knowledge. We have meet-ups where we discuss our lives and talk about our own experiences and beliefs. We gather to celebrate magical times and rites of passage. We come to festivals to share our knowledge, celebrate, and connect to nature and each other. We come together to support each other's great work.

Do Witches really do "spells" or can they do "magic"?

Many people look at the Hollywood "magic" on TV and think that is how magic works. Magic is natural and works with the nature of our universe. It follows a path of least resistance to make things happen. Many see the effect of spells and say that it is just coincidence. Witches know it isn't because they see the consistent results of their spells. I think the most potent mark of the Witch is when they—through the practice of spells and magic—begin to become magic. When they begin to have manifestation without even trying, because their lives have become an act of spellcraft, and they are magic.

If you do any spells, can you give examples?

Yes, I cast spells. When I lived in Vermont and was going to college, I went to an Introduction to Reiki class. I was so taken with the idea of using energy to heal that I wanted to take Reiki 1 with the presenter. At the time I only worked in the summer and saved all my money so I wouldn't have to work during the school year. When I found out how much the class was, I knew I couldn't fit it into my budget and get through the rest of the year, so I decided I would cast a spell to get the money for the class.

Near my parents' house there was a field with a little rise across the street where I had dowsed for ley lines and knew where they crossed near the top of the rise. Under the Full Moon's light I cast my circle and called in Brigid, goddess of healing. I cast my spell and raised a cone of power. As I sent out my spell, I felt burning warmth spread over my hands. I took this as a sign that I would have the money to take the class. Later that week I suddenly became obsessed with cleaning out my car. I remember I did it in the parking lot of the college. As I was searching through my car's refuse, I found a check I had not cashed from my summer job that was still good. It was for the exact amount of the class.

Spells aren't always huge affairs where you go to the top of a hill on a moonlit night. Sometimes they are just about finding your keys before you're late for work. One of the spells I use calls on fairy spirits to bring back a lost item. You make an offering to the fairies, outside in the wildest place of your yard. The offering can be some milk, a piece of bread, or anything you think your fairies would like. Visualize the object you have lost and say the following chant:

> *Fairy spirits, I am in a bind,*
> *what I seek, help me find.*
> *Where it is make it clear.*
> *What is lost now reappear!*

When the object comes back, I make a second small offering. What I have lost usually shows up in minutes, if not by the end of the day.

Are you a hereditary Witch?

I am not a hereditary Witch. No one in my blood family identifies as a Witch but me, as far as I know. Still, my family had talents I have incorporated into my Witchcraft. My family could all dowse but never talked about it because it was something you just did and didn't talk about. My grandmother and I had great conversations about how she, like me, dreamed the future at times, though she didn't think of herself as a psychic. With her pendulum made from my deceased grandfather's ring she predicted the sex and number of children my brother would have with his new wife. We spoke of my great-grandmother, who was a Spiritualist and made a pact with her husband to give her a sign after his death. A physical sign of a handprint appeared above her husband's desk after he died. We also had all sorts of superstitions, like not setting the table with an extra place setting because it invited spirits into the house. I think there is a little bit of Witch in everyone and the potential for more. My family doesn't seem that interested.

Did your family carry stories about Witches or did you find out about it all recently?

No stories about Witches that I know of, more psychic experiences. I remember one day driving with my grandmother after I had revealed myself as psychic. I was having fun changing traffic lights with my will and a gesture, and I remember my grandmother exclaiming, "Not only 'the sight' but 'the power' too!" She never went any deeper into explaining what that meant since my mother was in the backseat giving her a disapproving look. Does this mean there were people with "the power" that my grandmother had met in our family? I know some of them had "the sight" at certain times.

Have you had relationships or friendships with other New England Witches? If so, with whom? And what were the most significant experiences or learnings you had from those encounters?

I have met private and public Witches in New England. Some of the most potent were when I was just getting into the craft. Since I know some of them are still in the broom closet or have left the craft behind, I won't name them. We practiced a wild craft when I was in Vermont. We would form our circles in the stones by the river and dance around the fire. We would raise cones of power and meditate in the light of the Moon; we woould go hiking and get out in nature and connect to the power of the elements. I miss those days.

I remember one night when my friend and I went out into a public park near us under a cloudy, rainy sky. We cast our circle in the dark under the trees. We called to the Goddess and God. We were trying a new way to raise energy and send it out that I had read about: standing in the star position and letting the energy rise within us and within the circle until we released it up into the sky. I remember looking up and hearing my friend exclaim, "Holy crap." The clouds had parted around the forest we were in, and the Moon's light shined down all around us. We giggled and laughed and danced to see the effects of our power manifest.

Do you have any interactions with Witches in the Salem, Massachusetts, area? What is your impression of the current interest in Witchcraft in Salem, centuries after the witch hysteria of Puritan times?

I have had some interactions with some of the Witches in Salem, Massachusetts. It is hard not to when you're in this area. Anyone who visits from far away wants to go down to Salem to shop or meet some of the Witches there. It is interesting to me how much interest there is in Witchcraft there, after the hysteria of Puritan times. It reminds me of the saint shrines around the world in that the place of martyrdom becomes a holy place of pilgrimage. Many Witches from a distance see it like a Mecca. The only place I have seen like it is Glastonbury, England, but it has a totally different vibration.

Have you experienced any difficulties—any problems, persecution, or prejudice—as a result of being a Witch? Can you describe a time or times when that happened?

I have been pretty open about my Witchcraft for the past few years. It is hard to be a founder of the Temple of Witchcraft and not be out. I spent many years trying to get time to go to festivals or even to have a Sabbat off from work. I have had many times where I had to jump through figurative flaming hoops to get unpaid leave for my holidays, when more mainstream religions just got the day off without even asking. Every year to get unpaid leave I would have to produce a letter from our organization that I was necessary to the event.

I have had people ridicule me for my beliefs. Even my own brother for years would ask me if I had sacrificed a chicken to make something happen. It took multiple times for me to get through to him that that is not what Witches do. I've been told I will burn in hell or that people are praying for me. Usually this doesn't come from anyone who really knows me.

When I worked with special needs children in a collaborative, I was out to all my coworkers. I made sure that in every new class I joined I would come out of the broom and gay closets. I would answer any questions they had, and they got a chance to observe me doing my best every day. Once they get to know you, they begin to be more comfortable with who you are as a Witch. Sometimes I would get comments like, "You're so good, I can totally believe you meditate every day" or "What is your secret, how do you deal with this every day?" I know it is different in other parts of the United States and abroad, and I hope that one day we all can all live in peace.

What are special holy days for Witches? Can you please describe what Witches do on their holy days? How do you celebrate?

Every day is sacred when a Witch does their daily practice. Nature, the elements, and the gods are always there. There are times we consider more special. Usually these are the liminal, folkloric, or climactic natural times. The liminal times are when the seasons change at the equinox and solstice. Folkloric days are those mythic or natural events celebrated by our ancestors like Samhain, Imbolc, Beltane, and Lammas. The last is climactic, like the Full Moon or the New Moon, where magical energies reach their climax.

As someone who helps put on large events with the Temple of Witchcraft of up to a hundred or more people coming together, it is my own personal practice of celebration that feeds me, so I can do this greater work with the community. I try to always observe the holidays with a simple ritual that fills my spiritual cup. Usually I will cast a circle and call the quarters to consecrate my space as sacred. I call the gods to be present with me. In my own personal rituals I like to do something symbolic of the season. It could be eating an orange to take in the light of the Sun at the Summer Solstice, carving my jack-o'-lantern and laying out food and candles at my ancestral altar for when the veil is thin at Samhain, or lighting a candle in a bowl of snow at Imbolc to encourage the Goddess to wake and the Sun to return. Simple things remind me of the power of the season. Sometimes it is more complex, but I feel that when one is putting on or helping with large public rituals, it is a lot to have a complex personal practice as well. So I keep it simple. I always meditate to commune with the divine. Sometimes I cast a spell or do a divination if I need it.

AMORIC

New Haven, Connecticut

First, can you say a bit about who you are, where you live, and what you do for a living these days?

 I am a New Englander, a Connecticut Yankee born and raised except for a few journeys outside of Connecticut for academic study, which at times required living abroad for extended periods. My father's ancestry comes from the Galloway District of Scotland via the Canadian Maritime Provinces

to finally settle in the Green Mountains of northern Vermont. Those on my mother's side of the family are more recent arrivals to the United States. They originate from the northwest mountains of the Iberian Peninsula, arriving in the United States just before the start of World War II. Both sides of my family come from hardworking, mountain farming folk who lived in their respective areas for generations.

I was the first member from either side of my family to graduate from college and the first to receive an advanced college degree. I am a licensed clinical therapist with twenty-six years of experience working with patients and families in the field of terminal illnesses and hospice care. At present my hospice work continues in a part-time capacity. Currently my full-time position is as the administrative manager for a research department within an acute care medical hospital setting affiliated with the school of medicine for a local major academic institution. I have been performing these administrative duties for the past seven years.

How and when did you decide you were a Witch?

I have been involved in various aspects of the Witch community in southern New England for a very long time. During all this time I have never stood in front of a mirror, pointed at myself, and said, "I'm a Witch." The only time I have had to deal with the issue has been on the few occasions when someone from outside the Witch community has made the comment, "Oh, he is a Witch." For me becoming a Witch was an evolution. I had an interest in Witchcraft from when I was young. As I became more independent, mature, and financially secure, I simply pursued my interest. I guess I can't say there was one single event when I self-identified as a Witch.

How do you personally define Witchcraft?

Witchcraft is knowledge. What you do with the knowledge is up to you. However, remember and consider that just because you can do something does not mean you should always do it.

Which tradition of Witchcraft do you follow? How did you find that tradition?

If you were to look it up I believe you would find it under the title of British Traditional Witchcraft, or BTW for short. In other words, it is a tradition that descends from Gerald Gardner through Alex Sanders. Some may call the branch Alexandrian Wicca while others may more specifically use the term Algard Wicca. This is to identify that although my tradition comes down from Gerald Gardner through Alex Sanders, the founding High Priestess of my line, Lady Mary Nesnick, had been initiated into both Gardnerian and Alexandrian Wicca. Lady Nesnick used elements of both traditions in her practice.

I became involved with my group many years ago when I met the High Priestess at a book signing event. Shortly thereafter I met her again when she was speaking at a presentation on BTW and oath-bound traditions. While speaking with her at the reception following the presentation, I learned of her study group and made arrangements to participate in the group.

What makes your approach or tradition unique from any others out there?

We teach. This is not to say that other groups don't teach also, but with my group we expect commitment and dedication. The first step is to participate in study for a year and a day. During this time the other members of the group get to know the student's abilities and personality. This helps the group to determine if the student is a good match for the group and the student to determine if they are a good match for the group. After the year and a day, the study period may be extended or the question of initiation may be discussed, along with the requirements for further advancement.

Would you say that Witchcraft is a "craft" or a "religion"? And can you talk about the difference?

A craft for me is a skill for which you may demonstrate a talent, aptitude, or ability and perhaps perform the activity to gain your livelihood. In history early crafters were shoemakers, bakers, basket weavers, potters, coopers, shipbuilders, apothecaries, and even lawyers, teachers, and physicians. Someone who is skilled in Witchcraft develops and performs spells and or magic.

Religion for me has certain characteristics including but not limited to (1) a belief in a higher power or powers, (2) a system of philosophy and beliefs, (3) a hierarchy of ritual practitioners, and (4) a ritual calendar. My tradition has all of these: we believe in the high powers of the Goddess and God, we have a system of philosophy that includes the Law of Three, we have a hierarchy of ritual practitioners—Initiates, High Priest and High Priestess, Witch Queens, Witch Elders, and lineage groups—and we have a ritual calendar of thirteen Moons and eight holidays.

Although some may not want Wicca to be a religion, when the Department of Veterans Affairs recognized Wicca and decided to allow the pentagram as an engraving option for veterans to select for their grave markers, I think Wicca became a recognized religion.

Whom do Witches worship?

I believe Witches worship Goddess and God. In my tradition we have specific names that we use for Goddess and the God that we teach to our Initiates and use in our rituals. However, personally I believe Witches worship Goddess and God in all their many forms and interpretations. It is up to each individual Witch to understand the form of the deity in the context or ritual where it is being presented. No matter whether it is invoking Shiva by pouring ghee or Guanyin by lighting incense, you need to know who it is, why you are doing it, the object of the action, and the desired outcome.

When Witches meet, what do they usually do?

We talk. There are times we gather to plan an event, hold a class and teach, share of cup of tea, or go to a movie, and there are times when we gather for a ritual, for quiet meditation and contemplation, or with other groups for various purposes. We do what everyone else does in all those aspects for the support and continuation of their tradition or belief, no matter what you choose to call it.

Do Witches really do "spells" or can they do "magic"?

First I will define *spell* and *magic*. A spell for me is the collecting and assembling of materials—including the written word—needed to conduct or execute a step-by-step process to achieve a desired end. Conducting a spell for me also requires the right state of mind. A spell can be complex, with several elements such as candles, incense, herbal ingredients, time of day, etc., or it can be simple, such as using your pendulum to find a misplaced item in your home.

Magic is the manipulation of forces and energies that exist in nature to achieve an immediate end. Magic, however, for me has been tainted by modern media and perception. I think the term *magic* has been too sensationalized by modern film.

In the end a Witch in their craft should strive for proficiency in both spells and magic. However, proficiency varies and any Witch may be better at one than the other. A truly gifted Witch is someone who executes both spells and magic well. A truly wise Witch recognizes their deficiency in either area or both. To become good at both may take a lot of time, effort, study, and practice.

If you do any spells, can you give examples?

In reality I execute very few spells for myself. If someone wants me to construct a spell for them, I will put it together and provide the requestor with instructions on how to execute and activate the spell. Of course, I always counsel the requestor on the possible consequences of casting the spell, especially if the spell is initiated and not carried through. I have the requestor initiate and activate the spell because the requestor needs to be responsible for his or her own actions.

Some spells I have cast for myself include a cat protection spell, a bountiful garden spell, a safe travels spell, and a car protection spell.

Are you a hereditary Witch?

Both sides of my family come with folk belief systems that place strong emphasis on the observation of natural phenomena (e.g., the Sun, Moon, stars, wind, clouds, and changing tides, when the trees bud, when the leaves fall, how high the river is running, and how strong the current is flowing) as well as how to identify, process, use, and store wild and cultivated plants. Would this type of knowledge have placed my ancestors at risk of being called a Witch in the past? I don't know, but there is nothing in my collective family history of an ancestor on either side of the family being hung or burned as a Witch.

Did your family carry stories about Witches or did you find out about it all recently?

Both sides of my family have stories about people with special knowledge or abilities regarding the forest, the weather, the sea, and plants and animals. The types of stories varied. On one side of the family the stories were of people who had the gift of special sight through the third eye, someone who could throw the evil eye, and someone who could read the omens and tell you what type of child a pregnant woman would have as well as the baby's future. On the other side of the family it was all stories of magical creatures or beings and how they came to travel to the Americas. These stories included what we must do to successfully live with them.

Have you had relationships or friendships with other New England Witches? If so, with whom? And what were the most significant experiences or learnings you had from those encounters?

Over the years I have had the honor of meeting, getting to know, and working with Witches of other Alexandrian lineages as well as Witches of four additional oath-bound lineage traditions. In some cases, I have been granted the ability to work with an Alexandrian Witch Queen or Elder. This could have been either participating in a Circle conducted by another lineage or having the opportunity to participate in one-on-one training sessions with an honored Alexandrian Elder. Being invited into an honored Elder's home to be allowed to read and copy from their journals can be very profound.

However, as special as those times have been, I would like to add that some of the most profound "a-ha" moments have occurred while participating in ritual with my own Coven. My Coven is like family. Many of the members have been with us for long periods of time and some of us have been there from the beginning. Some of us have been in prior iterations of our Coven as the reigning High Priestess retires and passes her authority on to the new High Priestess. We have history together. We know and are comfortable with each other's energies. It can be a very profound thing when you know you are returning to work with the same people time after time. It is a dependable community that offers the environment in which to have the opportunity for spiritual growth.

Do you have any interactions with Witches in the Salem, Massachusetts, area? What is your impression of the current interest in Witchcraft in Salem, centuries after the witch hysteria of Puritan times?

To this day I am acquainted with and on friendly terms with members of the Witch community in Salem, Massachusetts. It was through these connections that I made some significant contacts, which led to my meeting and working with Alexandrian Elders, both here in the United States and internationally. I feel the Witch community is alive and well in the Salem area, and this is due to the continued dedicated work of several individuals in the Salem vicinity.

Any other thoughts you care to add?

Current considerations: How do we (meaning the BTW) remain viable for the present and in the future? In this modern age of secularism, with the decline of involvement in organized belief systems and religions, what are the challenges facing BTW that need to be addressed to ensure our continued growth into the future? I feel that these questions apply to all belief systems at present. However, it is even more difficult for us in BTW or other craft traditions frequently due to the negative connotations of Witchcraft beliefs and the frequent association of Witchcraft groups as "cults."

In my tradition we generally do not actively advertise or seek members. If "Seekers" happen to find their way to us, we are willing to consider all aspirants. From the Seekers we select our Initiates. Once initiated, we then pass along our knowledge from Elder to student in a relationship that can last years. This system has worked well for us since our beginning. The question is, will this system continue to work for us into the future? For the time being the Seekers appear to still be coming, but what if they stop coming? Our system does not work at the speed of the modern cell phone, and there are no applications for us that you can download. Can we continue to exist in the modern, high-speed, immediate-gratification society? Do we adapt or perish? How do we navigate the future?

Have you experienced any difficulties—any problems, persecution, or prejudice—as a result of being a Witch? Can you describe a time or times when that happened?

In my life I do not make my beliefs public information. My feelings are that if my beliefs became public knowledge, it would be detrimental to my positions as a therapist and as an administrator for a well-respected academic program. In modern medical terms some aspects of Wicca can be considered "magical thinking," which is often associated with psychiatric disorders. I do not feel my supervisors would be able to reconcile my beliefs with my continued involvement in medical programs that daily see and treat patients with psychiatric conditions, many of which have these symptoms. Although my supervisors by law would not be able to terminate me due to my beliefs, I think it would be very uncomfortable for them with me on staff. Publicly perceived reputation and excellence is very important in the medical and academic worlds. The aspects of good character and credentials are still very much part of these worlds.

What are special holy days for Witches? Can you please describe what Witches do on their holy days? How do you celebrate?

In review there are the thirteen Full Moons, the thirteen Dark Moons, the Spring Equinox, the Summer Solstice, the Fall Equinox, the Winter Solstice, and the four additional cross quarter days between the equinox-solstice-equinox-solstice cycle. Many of the days mentioned above are known to the general public by different names. In March at the Spring Equinox we celebrate with colored eggs and perform divination for the future. In May at the cross quarter day we put up and dance around the May pole while sharing food in the fresh air with our friends. In October at another cross quarter day we honor the spirits of deceased ancestors and visit their graves. In December at the Winter Solstice we celebrate the returning of the light (a.k.a. the Sun), share food, and give gifts. In order, the Spring Equinox occurs near Easter, the May cross quarter day is Beltane or May Day, in October is Samhain or Halloween, and in December is Yule, which falls near Christmas. This, of course, is a general and brief overview of the Wheel of the Year. If you want to learn more specifics of what we do and how we observe these various holidays, drop me a line in care of the publisher.

ANDREW THEITIC
Providence, Rhode Island

First, can you say a bit about who you are, where you live, and what you do for a living these days?

In this lifetime, I was born a Libra in 1956 in Providence, Rhode Island. I began studying Witchcraft in 1968, coming into contact with my first Coven in 1974—the year I met Gwen Thompson. I received initiation in 1976 into the New England Covens of Traditionalist Witches (NECTW) tradition. Continuing with study, I eventually became a

High Priest and consequently established a Coven in 1978. In the following year, in step with the studies that I pursued, I founded the Center for Exoteric Research and Esoteric Studies (CERES) in Providence. While continuously practicing the Craft from 1976 through the present, I also worked with a ceremonial magic tradition. Bringing my love of Witchcraft and magic into my mundane life, I opened a metaphysical and occult store called The Flaming Cauldron in 1974. During the 1980s and 1990s, I sought to broaden my horizons, taking initiations in Palo Mayombe, Santeria, and traditional Nigerian spiritual practices.

Currently, I am an active High Priest of three Covens of NECTW: Coven of Minerva, established and continuously active since 1987; Coven of the Crossroads, since 2009; and Coven Sidera, since 2007. Additionally, I am the historian for the NECTW tradition. After I went through the initiations and degrees of the Alexandrian Tradition (through the Mary Nesnick and Hans Holzer line), Morganna Davies and I established the Phoenix Rising Coven in 1995. Phoenix Rising was active for approximately ten years, seeding a number of Covens in the Northeast.

In the mid-1990s, I was trained in the Minoan Brotherhood, an all-male tradition of Witchcraft with practices based on an Aegean calendar. I established Magical Zominthos Grove (a Grove is the same as a Coven in the Brotherhood) in Providence some seven years ago. I also have taken degrees in Gardnerian Witchcraft, of which I am a High Priest. Although I am not running a Gardnerian Coven, I do maintain a close affiliation with my initiation Coven as well as with other Elders in the Northeast. To finish up on my esoteric endeavors, I am a thirty-second-degree Freemason-Scottish Rite member and have taken most of the York Rite degrees.

In my Craft business world, I am running two small publishing companies: Olympian Press and The Witches' Almanac Ltd. (www .thewitchesalmanac.com). I became the owner of The Witches' Almanac on the passing of my very close friend of thirty years, Elizabeth Pepper. Through Olympian Press, I coauthored with Robert Mathiesen *The Rede of the Wiccae,* a book examining the Rede and the family of the late Gwen Thompson (Healy).

Throughout my adult life, I have chosen to keep charity and giving as a guiding light. I am the executive director of Acts of Kindness (www.a-o-k.org)—a Pagan-run charity—Sacred Ground (www.sacred -ground.org), and the Society of the Evening Star (SOTES) (www.sotes .org), all 501(c)(3) nonprofit organizations.

In my non-Craft business life, I manage real estate and I consult for various other businesses. Currently, I live in Providence, Rhode Island, with my husband, Thor, and our beloved dogs Dana and Samson.

How and when did you decide you were a Witch?

I cannot say that there is actually a time when I decided I was a Witch. To me, Witchcraft is a process of unveiling. Personal qualities unfold over time—times when you are exposed to nature, confronting birth and death, facing fears, and so many more challenging experiences. All of these contribute to the process of becoming aware of the Witch within. Of course, the practices develop over the years as well. The learning process begins with the basics—meditation, candle burning, or spells—leaving inner work and invocation until the basics have had a chance to take root.

At some point, I just happened to look over my shoulder at my past and notice that I was now living the life of a Witch. It didn't just happen from an initiation or from the success of a spell. It didn't even come from the acceptance from other Witches. At some point, I just knew that I was a Witch.

How do you personally define Witchcraft?

Witchcraft is a way of life that incorporates the magic of our world. Witchcraft involves the interface between the world of the ordinary with the world of spirit and magic. All things that are veiled are part of the experience of Witchcraft. Learning to work with these powers and weave them through natural laws is a skill that the Witch learns and practices. Magic is in everything—every action, every word, every emotion. When emotions ride high, magic is apparent, and the person who recognizes this and knows how to work with the energy is practicing

Witchcraft. Developing your Craft skills or harnessing the natural powers comes over time.

Which tradition of Witchcraft do you follow? How did you find that tradition?

I am a priest of four Craft traditions. I also honor family practices that I learned as a child. I came to N.E.C.T.W. in 1974 and enjoyed the privilege of studying directly with Gwen Thompson very early on and continuing through the years, until she crossed over to the Summerland. Because of my training and affinity, I would say that the NECTW tradition and my personal family practice have always been and will always be my main focus.

The other traditions of Wicca in which I am initiated—Alexandrian, Gardnerian, and Minoan Brotherhood—came later in life and were a result of work done with other magicians and Witches. They have helped me to further my understanding of what many public Craft people practice today as well as add to my personal practice.

I came into contact with the NECTW tradition by placing an ad in a very early issue of *Gnostic News* (early 1970s). The ad was answered by a local priest of the only NECTW Coven in Rhode Island at the time. I continued to learn from the members of this Coven until I was of age and was able to receive initiation in 1976. I also had the extreme good fortune of training under Gwen Thompson, founder of the public version of her family's Craft tradition. Through the past four-plus decades, the tradition has grown slowly. Now, having Covens on both coasts of the United States, in Canada, and in Europe, NECTW has become a firmly rooted hereditary practice, with the largest number of Covens being in New England.

My family practices were all around me as a child—mostly sorcery, herbalism, and ancestor communication. Divination and the evil eye (casting and warding) were also taught to me. My grandmother and great-aunts were at the center of the action, with my maternal grandfather being the more psychic of my relatives. He was clairaudient and would receive messages from previously deceased relatives—on numerous occasions from his mother. We also have had card readers on both sides of my family. My father's aunt Rose and my mother's aunt Irene were both competent readers, but Rose had the following. Irene only read for her immediate family.

I am happy to say that I also see the spirit of the Witch in our youngest generation.

What makes your approach or tradition unique from any others out there?

Personally, I think that the mix of NECTW traditional practices with my family folklore, magic, and ancestor veneration works very well. In fact, even the family practices of Elizabeth Pepper folded in nicely to my personal work and practices. There are common threads that run through all three of these systems of practice—honoring the ancestors, myth and legend, simple sorcery, folklore, and herbalism, to name a few.

I grew up in an environment that provided respect for my ancestors and shared folklore and sorcery that I know goes back at least three generations in my family. The ever-present family folklore is the blood of my life—involving superstitions and communing with ancestors on a regular basis, it is shared with my blood family.

I share my NECTW practice with my Craft family. While my Craft studies were certainly more organized and holistic than my family's practices, both shared so very much and it all came to me very naturally.

In addition to my Craft practices, in the background I also adhere to Buddhist practices. These philosophies and observances are practices that I pursue exclusively by myself. Of course, it goes without saying that it does influence my occult practices, even if only in a limited way. Involving these three disciplines in my daily life brings a completeness to my spiritually.

Would you say that Witchcraft is a "craft" or a "religion"? And can you talk about the difference?

Wicca is a religion, with a liturgy, acts of faith, prayers, belief in deity, holy relics, religious attire, and ritual objects used in regular services. Witchcraft is the practice of a Craft—sometimes associated with religion, but more often associated with magic and the forces of nature.

Whom do Witches worship?

Witches who practice Wicca frequently worship a solar god and a lunar goddess. The dual nature of Wicca can also be viewed in other ways—nature's life and death, winter/summer, seasons, earth/sky, etc.

For those Witches who do not practice Wicca, defining what they practice as "Witchcraft" might be thought of as worshipping nature or natural forces. Many will say that they are not really practicing a religion at all. They are *acknowledging* forces or powers that are beyond what is commonly noticed in everyday life. By recognizing these forces and working with them, they practice their form of Witchcraft.

When Witches meet, what do they usually do?

Witches can have as many activities as there are grains of sand on a beach. The practices that I do along with my Coven members include magic, worship, healing, divination, connecting with ancestors and the dead, and consecrations. Working in a group builds my abilities via comaraderie and likeness of thought. Of course, many available books on the market today detail the activities of Witches. Often, these books hint to actual practices. Since each Coven is unique, how these practices are performed will be unique to each and is often a closely guarded secret and different from what is presented in books. In addition, every Coven has its own set of undertakings—usually having to do more with location, members of the Coven, or needs of the Craft and its practitioners.

Do Witches really do "spells" or can they do "magic"?

Yes, Witches do cast spells. Spells are a form of magic—low magic, or sorcery. A spell is an extremely focused and unified energy pattern, or stream, directed at an end. The construction of the spell is meant to raise raw energy, refine that energy, and link it to a recipient. When performed properly, the desired result is a natural occurrence. In some instances, "spells" and "magic" are considered to be the same thing. In actuality, spells are just a small portion of magic, which is a much broader subject.

If you do any spells, can you give examples?

Yes, I do. But no, I can't. For me, the fourth power of the pyramid prevails—"To keep silent."

Are you a hereditary Witch?

My family, entirely of Italian descent, never called what we did "Witchcraft." They only spoke of it as "things we do." As I mentioned, as a child, I was always surrounded by ancestor veneration, sorcery, and herbalism. Protection and warding were a big part of what we did as well. There was never a shortage of garlic in the house (or in our pockets!). Mint, basil, malva, chamomile, and rosemary were ever present, as were other garden herbs. Statues of saints, vases of flowers, a glass of water, a vial of holy water, and pictures of dead ancestors were to be found on an altar in my grandparents' home as well as in the homes of many older relatives—great-aunts and great-uncles.

My family's practices are not by any means a complete system. The children of each new generation learned the family's wisdom and folklore through a story format. My mother continued that practice with my nephew. Some of the more-than-simple family traditions were taught in a more unorthodox way. In fact, some of what my sister and I practice today came from my grandmother's recipe book.

Did your family carry stories about Witches or did you find out about it all recently?

There were always stories about Witches in my family, and they usually portrayed the Witches as those to be feared and shunned. We learned magic to keep Witches away! My grandmother said Witches were *cattivo*, or evil. She had practices and spells to keep a Witch's powers from troubling us. Most often, this involved a pair of scissors, a knife, garlic, and olive oil. She would cast her warding spell to keep

Witches away. Elder women on both sides of my family performed this practice—usually done when the men went outside "for a smoke."

Have you had relationships or friendships with other New England Witches? If so, with whom? And what were the most significant experiences or learnings you had from those encounters?

Although there were many friendships with New England Witches—family aside—I feel that the following three Witches had the most influence on me and my current practices. Do understand, Witches never talk about who else is a Witch without their permission or until they have passed over. I am comfortable talking about these three very dear friends, as they all were publicly known as Witches, and all of them have since passed over to the Summerland.

Theodore Mills

Theodore was a dear friend and a frequent visitor at my metaphysical store (The Flaming Cauldron, East Greenwich, RI), while on his way to visit Elizabeth Pepper. Theo was a big fan of the Egyptian pantheon, with Isis being his favorite goddess. On one of his trips to Newport, he stopped by my shop to purchase a present for Elizabeth. It was a dreary day—cloudy, cold, windy, with light rain. Ted and I did a chant and meditation to the Egyptian Sun god, Ra, for good weather and in minutes the sky was bright and sunny and the temperature went up to a comfortable level and remained so all day. He called me when he got home to say that he and Elizabeth had a lovely day—of course, thanks to our meditation on Ra!

On another occasion, I was visiting Theo in Massachusetts. It was in his later years, when he was on oxygen and unable to move about very easily. However, this didn't stop him from being the center of attention. He sat in his living room chair, with students sitting on the floor all around him, each patiently listening to his every word. Often, he would add some humor to his conversation—always the showman, as most Leos are.

Theo was the leader of the Parker Coven. Although he and I never shared Circle together, he told me on several occasions that the Parker Coven's practices were passed down to him through his family. He also said that Rebecca Towne Nurse of Danvers, Massachusetts, who was involved in the famous Witch trials, was one of his ancestors. He never said whether she was truly a Witch or not. I suspect he did not really know.

Ted used to love his gemstones. He had rings and other jewelry that he wore both magically and socially. He loved his "jewels" and would talk about them in great detail—where they came from, how they were gifted to him or where he bought them, and, of course, how much each one would shine!

Ted's goddess was Isis, and when he passed over in 1996, he was mourned by many and greeted by his Mother Goddess.*

Elizabeth Pepper

One day, Elizabeth came home from school and asked her mother, "Mother, are we Witches?" Her mother replied with a smile, "We study metaphysics, dear." Elizabeth never heard the word "Witch" being used to describe anyone in the family or any of their practices; however, they did indeed practice Witchcraft.

I met Elizabeth in 1975. At the time, I owned and operated The Flaming Cauldron. Elizabeth owned and operated a small company (Images) in New York State. I wrote to her asking to buy some of her printed cards. Elizabeth, having closed the mail order business earlier, offered to sell me the remains of her print overruns. And this is how we met. Over the thirty years that I knew Elizabeth, we shared many stories over a cup of tea. Here are a couple of those stories.

A Walk along the Beach: It was often a Sunday afternoon when I would visit Elizabeth and her family of five cats and two dogs at her

---

*For more information about Lord Theodore (Ted) Mills, please see his interview in my book *People of the Earth: The New Pagans Speak Out.* —Ellen home in Newport, Rhode Island. On one particular afternoon, we sat drinking tea for several hours. As always, our conversation would not be simply small talk. After the niceties, we would settle down to an earnest conversation, solving the problems of the metaphysical universe. On this particular afternoon, while enjoying our tea, Elizabeth suddenly said to me, "Let's take a walk along the beach." Knowing Elizabeth as I did, I knew there was a plan involved.

We drove to Crescent Beach in Newport. On arriving, we got out of the car and she immediately began telling me about how her aunt—I believe this was Mable—would instruct her to pick up three items at the beach, after which you would hand them to a gifted friend to psychically "read" them for you. She further elaborated that you could always put an item back and choose another, but after the walk was completed, you needed to have just three items in your hand.

We walked the beach, or should I say Elizabeth very briskly walked the beach, with me behind her trying to keep pace. Fortunately for me, she was already in her seventies, or I would not have been able to catch up to her. Elizabeth was an enthusiastic walker. Conquering varied terrain immediately, she went over the bordering rocks and across the beach sand. It was after about one hour of walking, picking up, putting down, and picking up again . . . we both had three items that we were satisfied with and were ready to go home to read for each other. As I recall, I had one shell and two pebbles.

We got to Elizabeth's home, and she began preparing the tea cart. We had tea, honey, sugar, cream, and a plate of lemon cookies. Once we settled down, we each held our own three objects, focused our desire for clarity into them, and concentrated. After that, we traded objects, and I began first. I gave her impressions as they came to me. Calling off objects, describing situations, repeating the words that came to me, and recounting everything I saw. Elizabeth was pleased. She used to frequently call me her "young apprentice." This brought her joy. After I was done with my prophecy, Elizabeth began. She went on to describe many things happening in my future. Most of these came to pass over the next couple of years.

Aunt Kitty's Love Spells: Elizabeth carried one family trait forward from her mother's sister, Kitty. Elizabeth was a meddler! She loved to match folks up. On more than one occasion, I found her doing it with me. There were times when I would go to visit, usually on a Sunday, and she would have someone there for me to meet. After the person left, she would pepper me with questions—did I like them, wasn't so-and-so funny, did I know that this person was not married, etc. Aunt Kitty's magic played an important part in Elizabeth's life. Much of what we would call a "Book of Shadows," in Elizabeth's case, was a book of love spells handed down from her aunt. Many of these appear in Elizabeth's book, *Love Spells.*

> *A true Witch loves animals . . . and it doesn't hurt to have a garden either.*

ELIZABETH PEPPER

Gwen Thompson

I was fortunate enough to have known and studied with Lady Gwen Thompson from 1974 until her death in 1988. It was during that time that I was afforded the opportunity to study with her every weekend for a continuous two and a half years. To say that Gwen was a remarkable woman does not do justice to her abilities. Her acute awareness and sensitivity to all things magical was the driving force and fabric of her life. Gwen, like most of us, faced the complications and obstacles that affect all our lives. She tackled all of these while maintaining her practices, never turning away from the Craft. Instead of giving in, she relied on her true convictions as a source of strength to overcome the hardships of life.

Gwen was politically natured and a powerfully principled woman. Occasionally described as a formidable force, she was not someone to be trifled with. Gwen was deeply loved by her friends and equally feared by her enemies—for good reason. Magic came naturally to her. She worshipped the old Pagan gods, but she always had one hand on a nearby box of candles. Gwen was magic, and it flowed through her blood.

During the 1970s, Gwen was an authority to many members of the Craft. She was a prolific writer and her teachings, transmitted through her letters and other writings, managed to influence other prominent American trailblazers such as George Patterson, Bonnie Sherlock, Kitty Lessing, Leo Martello, Roy Diamond, and Jill Johns. She also had a "pen pal" relationship with Theos and Phoenix, Ray Buckland, Leo Martello, Gavin and Yvonne Frost, Tim and Morning Glory Zell, and other popular Witches from the 1970s. In fact, it was during a phone call I had with Morning Glory some years later that she warmly referred to Gwen as "the grandmother of East Coast Witchcraft."

Gwen's heritage stretched back to the *Mayflower*. She was in the habit of talking about her ancestors, early New England, and, on occasion, the Salem trials. She was heard saying, "The real Witches in Salem were never caught or arrested because they were busy sleeping with the judges!" And as *The Rede of the Wiccae* states: "Her [Gwen Thompson's] ancient relatives—the Putnams, the Trasks, the Hales, and the Porters—included the accusers and those who worked behind the scenes to oppose the accusers, but not one of the accused."

Gwen Thompson established the New England Coven of Traditionalist Witches as her first "out of family" Coven. She boasted of having well-known Witches as members or frequent guests. The title New England Coven of Traditionalist Witches was passed down by Gwen through two generations of initiates to myself, and the center for her family's Tradition of Craft is currently based in Providence, Rhode Island.

Gwen became enamored with Wicca, like many other hereditary Witches of her generation. As a tradition, her practices were certainly a complete system of magic and cosmology. However, over time she would alter her handed-down material to come in line with contemporary Craft practices and beliefs of the times—then the 1960s and 1970s. In the public's mind, Wicca was a legitimate religion, whereas some forms of traditional or hereditary Craft were perceived as just a hoax, thought to be made up by thrill seekers. In the 1960s, Gwen's tradition was handed down to others, outside of her family, as a traditional system of Witchcraft and magic with a veneer of Wicca and Paganism.

The Rede of the Wiccae: There is almost no way of talking about Gwen Thompson without talking about the "Rede of the Wiccae." This poem was left to her by her paternal grandmother, Adriana Porter. A great deal of research went into the book of the same title that I wrote with Robert Mathiesen. Robert, a scholar and professor emeritus of Brown University, did most of the research and drew some fascinating conclusions regarding the Rede poem. Here, I have chosen to reprint an excerpt from an article by Gwen Thompson, which is the first time the Rede was put into print for the public. This article debuted in *Green Egg* magazine.

A Fundamentalist Christian recently said to me: "Satan rules this planet!" I replied: "I know it." My answer was unnerving to the person making the statement due to the fact that Fundamentalists, along with numerous other Christian demon-inations, firmly believe that Witches and Pagans are "devil-worshippers." I did not elaborate upon the fact that we do not believe in a "devil" as such, but we do believe in a CONTROLLING FORCE that is anathema to our way of life as we would like to live it, and should be able to live it, upon this planet. Our ancient lore tells us that thousands of Years ago there were two forces seeking control of the mode of life upon this planet; one group wishing to teach mankind the "facts of life" and the other to exploit mankind. There were many names applied to these beings: Gods, angels, Watchers, sons of God, etc. The leaders of these two opposing forces, for want of a better term or name, were referred to as The Lord of Light and The Lord of Darkness. There is no need to be specific about which of them wanted what. Oh yes, and lest we forget, their "hosts" (in modern terminology, armies).

The Christian Bible, garbled as it currently is, speaks of a battle in the "heavens." Well, we know there was one, although the Christians have their time-space continuum a bit mixed up, to the point where it is all done and over with, according to them. But, we know that as it was in the beginning so it will be in the end, giving us the Alpha and Omega of history. When Christians speak of "fallen angels" and "salvation," I merely reply: "Ummm . . . of course." Then they are gently (?) felled with the statement, "If the Lord of Light lost the battle for control of Earth, who won?" They were taught that the Lord of Light was Lucifer, a very naughty angel who went against God and got his. Along with his followers, naturally it is clear that a large number of the followers of the Lord of Light were confined to Earth, bred with Earth people and produced what we now have as a breed of "different" beings, classified as people who "have the POWER" or "KNOWING ONES." Thus, we have an admixture upon this planet of Light and Darkness. The demarcation line becomes more obvious daily. Shall we call it "The Omega Caper?"

When it comes down to the nitty gritty of hassles and bickering and the rest of the fertilizer, consider the fact that antagonistic elements of Darkness infiltrate for the express purpose of dimming the LIGHT. The sad tales of recorded history are replete with data on thousands of enlightened ones who brought forth progress upon the Earth as new inventions and new ways of Thought in order to ADVANCE mankind. Were they not all ridiculed at one time or another? Was there not an element among mankind that continually sought to prevent progress? We have had our "Mighty Ones" who overcame the opposing and controlling forces to progress our people in spite of any obstacle, often at great personal sacrifice.

We are all well aware of the people who have been continually opposed to our space program . . . they give various and sundry reasons: "expensive" (so what?); "we need the money for the poor and needy;" or "we should not mess around with God's Universe," etc. etc., blah, blah, blah. The numerous wars, inspired by Darkness, were also "expensive," very expensive. The "poor and needy" wouldn't be about to get any of the lucre, and as for "God's Universe" . . . it belongs to everyone to share equally. There is no need to be imprisoned upon the giant spaceship Earth if one wishes to go elsewhere. For those who are not already well aware of it, the battle is once more raging. This time, however, the thumb-screws are on the other pinkies.

Old Religionists who allow themselves to be photographed by the news media in the "altogether" (sky-clad), and often in positions that suggest obscene practices, aren't doing the Old Religion any service whatsoever, but rather giving it a very black eye. Worship in such a case, if it is worship, should be sacred to the Goddess and God alone and not for the eyes of cowans to see and misinterpret. We live in a clothed society which is not all that ready to accept what some Witches or Pagans do. If we wish to get across the message that we are intelligent, dignified and worthy of respect just as much as the controlling religions of Earth . . . then we should not use back-door tactics, but utilize some of the Wisdom our forebears bestowed upon us to give the proper impression of what and who we really are. Many Witches ignore the age-old counsel of the Wise Ones as given in the Rede.

Many different traditions have different redes. That is understandable, considering the time involved from Alpha to Omega. Our own particular form of the Wiccan Rede is that which was passed on to her heirs by Adriana Porter, who was well into her nineties when she crossed over into the Summerland in the year 1946. This Rede in its original form is as follows:

Rede of the Wiccae
(Being knowne as the counsel of the Wise Ones)
1. Bide the Wiccan laws ye must in perfect love an perfect trust.
2. Live an let live—fairly take an fairly give.
3. Cast the Circle thrice about to keep all evil spirits out.
4. To bind the spell every time, let the spell be spake in rhyme.
5. Soft of eye an light of touch—speak little, listen much.
6. Deosil go by the waxing Moon—sing an dance the Wiccan rune.

7. Widdershins go when the Moon doth wane, an' the Werewolf howls by the dread Wolfsbane.
8. When the Lady's Moon is new, kiss the hand to her times two.
9. When the Moon rides at her peak, then your heart's desire seek.
10. Heed the North wind's mighty gale—lock the door and drop the sail.
11. When the wind comes from the South, love will kiss thee on the mouth.
12. When the wind blows from the East, expect the new and set the feast.
13. When the West wind blows o'er thee, departed spirits restless be.
14. Nine woods in the Cauldron go—burn them quick an burn them slow.
15. Elder be ye Lady's tree—burn it not or cursed ye'll be.
16. When the Wheel begins to turn—let the Beltane fires burn.
17. When the Wheel has turned a Yule, light the Log an let Pan rule.
18. Heed ye flower, bush an tree—by the Lady blessed be.
19. Where the rippling waters go, cast a stone an truth ye'll know.
20. When ye have need, hearken not to other's greed.
21. With the fool no season spend or be counted as his friend.
22. Merry meet an merry part—bright the cheeks an warm the heart.
23. Mind the Threefold Law ye should—three times bad an three times good.
24. When misfortune is enow, wear the blue star on thy brow.
25. True in love ever be unless thy lover's false to thee.
26. Eight words the Wiccan Rede fulfill—an' it harm none, do what ye will.

The foregoing is explained fully to the initiated Witch. The contents of the Book of Shadows (our public name for it) must be orally taught as well as copied. All wording has its special meaning which the Wise can often quickly discern. Meditation is a most important adjunct to the learning of the Mysteries of the Old Religion. The number of Old Religionists currently abiding by counsel of the Wise can be counted on fingers of one hand and the thumb would be left over.

Food for thought: I don't care what anyone does just so long as they do not interfere with Life, this planet, or me. Surprising how limiting that can be. "As you sow so shall you reap" is not a Christian original . . . it is the Threefold Law simply expressed in farm language. Disharmony begets disharmony and time travels in a CIRCLE, not a straight line. The Serpent eating his own tail. Perversions of ancient Traditions often bring ancient curses as well. The invisible becomes manifest. Twin Earths exchanging bric-a-brac. The insatiable guru-chasers; Book collectors; Coven hoppers; name-droppers; and ego-trippers. We've all had our share of them. Monsters roam the planet in various guises. People who seldom make anyone happy, feigning Wisdom. Nobody can hear a whisper while they're talking. Wiccan-Pagan teachings are not for everyone.

Andrew, do you have any interactions with Witches in the Salem, Massachusetts, area? What is your impression of the current interest in Witchcraft in Salem, centuries after the Witch hysteria of Puritan times?

It may seem strange to many readers, but Rhode Islanders do not generally travel outside of Rhode Island. We seem to have our own little world here. Nevertheless, like most tourists, I travel to Salem from time to time. I have friends there and you can always find wonderful Craft gifts in the shops. However, Rhode Islanders rarely get involved in Salem Witchcraft. One thing is for sure—"What happens in Salem, *doesn't* stay in Salem!"

You are the editor of *The Witches' Almanac,* which is an important publication for Witches, and it is New England based. Can you talk a bit about the history of that publication?

The Witches' Almanac was Elizabeth's lifelong project and love. She began the *Almanac* in 1971 as a small private publication, but soon after, she looked for a distributor to make the *Almanac* available to the public. In a short time, the book was making a name for itself and was being printed by Grosset & Dunlap publishers/distributors. The *Almanac* was an immediate success and sold ninety-three thousand copies that year.

Elizabeth wanted to put out a handsome book that gave the reader just enough information on a subject to inspire. She had no motivation to tell the whole story but rather wished to tease the reader into doing more research. The short and teasing articles became a hit with our readership. *The Witches' Almanac* was published annually by Elizabeth, skipping just a few years in the 1980s, until she passed away in 2005, when she left the legacy to me. I have continued its publication each year since, knowing that she is behind me watching my every move.

Over the past ten years, the *Almanac* has doubled in size, is now printed on recycled paper, has a larger format and a stronger and sturdier cover, and is perfect bound. In addition to the improvements on the *Almanac's* format, we now have a stylish web presence, which can be found at www.thewitchesalmanac.com. Our website features all of the books that Elizabeth published as well as our newest *Almanac* and reprints of timeless classics (e.g., *Aradia* by Charles Leland and *Magic: An Occult Primer* by David Conway). Recently, we also published *The Witches' Almanac Coloring Book.*

Over the past few years, we have had requests for T-shirts, postcards, book bags, and other items. We have tried to accommodate these requests. For readers from our past, we will continue to grow our line of books and gifts and promise to publish the most interesting *Witches' Almanac* available today. For new readers, or those who are not familiar with our publication, please check us out—you will be pleasantly surprised.

Have you experienced any difficulties—any problems, persecution, or prejudice—as a result of being a Witch? Can you describe a time or times when that happened?

Yes, I have experienced difficulties in my mundane business life as a result of being a Witch. However, I have also sometimes experienced these difficulties as a result of being gay, practicing Buddhism, driving a Prius, and not wearing a suit and tie to business meetings. Our society is filled with prejudice. I feel compelled to stand up for my beliefs and to support those others who are persecuted for their beliefs that do not conform to society's norms. In many ways, this is the path of a Witch. We do not conform, and we do not sit in judgment of others.

What are special holy days for Witches? Can you please describe what Witches do on their holy days? How do you celebrate?

In addition to the recognized seasonal Sabbats, most Witches have specific days when they honor their ancestors, patron goddess or god, totem animals, or other special association to the world of spirit. During these times, we worship deity, honor the dead, commune with spirits, and practice magic—all in a sacred space. Again, these are performed in a way more secret than can be found in a book. The experience is necessary to fully understand what Witches do.

Any other thoughts you care to add?

The Craft takes on many different forms, and it is not for everyone. If you have received a calling or find yourself drawn to the mystical, then follow your heart, learn the old ways, practice magic, and honor the ancestors and the natural world. If you have not received the call, then Witchcraft is probably not for you.

If you would like more information, you can contact me at theitic@ thewitchesalmanac.com or theitic@nectw.org.

CHRISTIAN DAY
New Orleans, Louisiana

First, can you say a bit about who you are, where you live, and what you do for a living these days?

I am a modern-day Warlock living with my husband, Alexandrian High Priest Brian Cain, in New Orleans, Louisiana. New Orleans is a tapestry of magic that reaches back centuries, blending Old World European folklore with African spiritual traditions. Together, we are the copresidents of Warlocks, Inc., which is the umbrella corporation for our retail shops, events, and web-based brands.

In Salem, Massachusetts, we own Hex: Old World Witchery, an edgy Witchcraft shop with a continental European-meets-hoodoo-and-root-work vibe, and Omen: Psychic Parlor and Witchcraft Emporium, a psychic reading center and Witch shop featuring a softer, more feminine feel with an emphasis on healing and psychic development. We also have a Hex shop in New Orleans and are planning to open an Omen there this year.

Each October in Salem, we host the Festival of the Dead, featuring a monthlong psychic fair, the Official Salem Witches' Halloween Ball, a Dumb Supper, and a number of magical workshops. Every August in New Orleans, we host HexFest, which is geared to practitioners looking to deepen their connection to magic and features teachers from across the occult spectrum.

Online, we've got SalemTarot.com, in its twenty-second year, as well as PsychicsForHire.com, a website that allows clients to connect to their psychics by phone through a web application. Hex and Omen also have e-commerce sites at HexWitch.com and OmenSalem.com, respectively. These various projects keep us very busy, and we have a staff of magically gifted employees and readers who help us offer guidance to visitors from around the globe.

How and when did you decide you were a Witch?

I started reading Tarot cards when I was seventeen years old and then later, when I was eighteen, my mother had a friend over to the house one night who claimed she was a Witch. I found the whole idea of this fascinating and, on the woman's recommendation, visited a metaphysical bookstore in Salem. My first book was Marion Weinstein's *Earth Magic: A Dianic Book of Shadows*. I performed a dedication ritual on the night of a pretty crazy thunderstorm, and it was my first true connection to the magic of nature. A couple of years later, I took Witchcraft classes with Salem's "official witch," Laurie Cabot. Laurie's Witchcraft 1 class, a primer on psychic development, was my most life-changing event. I went into that class as a card reader and Witch but not sure how I could ever actually be psychic. I came out of that class understanding that each of has a wellspring of hidden abilities just waiting to be discovered, and I remain forever grateful to Laurie for introducing me to that power.

How do you personally define Witchcraft?

Defining Witchcraft is difficult for me because I think so much of the Craft is mired in the mystery of history, folklore, archaeology, etymology, and, of course, public opinion. I tend to identify Witches by criteria. To me, Witches find their roots in European folk magic and earth religion. They are typically outcasts because their authority had been stripped long before and given to the priesthoods—something I believe happened even before Christianity, as the Romans and Greeks had laws against Witchcraft and sorcery even before Christianization. I see the Craft as both a cult of fertility and life and a cult of necromancy and chthonic exploration. And, more than anything, I see Witchcraft as a religion that is intrinsically magical and cannot be separated from our powers and abilities.

I do not see the Craft as something that can truly be mainstreamed because I believe that the mainstream is typically concerned with mundane matters and wants religion to be something easy that they can integrate into their lives. Witchcraft is neither mundane nor easy. It is a doorway that, once entered, turns us into creatures of magic and power. We have always been the "other," and I'm okay with that because the world has always known to seek us out when all else fails. This story can be seen throughout myth and folklore in tales about Erictho, Canidia and Sagana, Circe, the Witch of Endor, and countless other Witches existing at the edge of society, ready to dispense their wisdom to those daring enough to seek it.

Which tradition of Witchcraft do you follow? How did you find that tradition?

It's hard to pigeonhole myself into a tradition, but I did receive training in the Cabot Tradition, and those are the psychic and magical techniques I most often fall back on. However, I did not pursue initiation into the religion of the tradition because my path took me in other directions. My husband, Brian, likes to say that I reside at the "dark fringe of Cabot society." I was also trained by my late best friend and business partner Shawn Poirier in his Salem Tradition of Witchcraft— which was essentially a collection of his ideas and practices, all of which veered heavily into spell casting and necromantic arts. It is from Shawn that I developed a deep interest in working with the spirits of the dead, and this has influenced my work considerably ever since.

What makes your approach or tradition unique from any others out there?

When I published my book, *Witches' Book of the Dead*, in 2011, I did so because I felt that many in the Craft had turned their backs on the dead or would only truck them out at Samhain. If there's anything I've brought to the table of the Craft, I think it's a reminder that if you honor and remember the dead, they will honor and remember you. Since the book came out, I feel we've seen a renaissance in the Craft of those whose focus is work with the departed, though I don't take all the credit for this. I think the popularity of paranormal television shows has probably had the biggest influence on this resurgence, and while I think that such shows can often lead people to show great disrespect to the dead, they have definitely brought the idea of engaging with spirits into the mainstream again.

Would you say that Witchcraft is a "craft" or a "religion"? And can you talk about the difference?

Laurie Cabot's description of Witchcraft as a "science, art, and religion" is by far my favorite description. I believe that the Craft involves not only the actual physical and spiritual craft of working magic, but it is also a religion where our interaction with deity and spirit actually manifests change in the world. And finally, I think it's important to seek an underpinning of science because it gives us the knowledge that what Witches do is real. We are not simply fantasists muttering over pots of smoke. The magic we do has real impact in the world around us, and it is always my hope that more Witches will embrace the accountability that goes along with such responsibility.

Whom do Witches worship?

I believe that the religion of the Witch is often malleable and personal. While I don't feel that Witchcraft is necessarily compatible with every religion that is out there, there have been those who have embraced the pantheons of religions such as Christianity and woven them into the European folk magic and earth-centered spirituality that defines Witchcraft. I personally believe in a universal mind—the "All" written of in books such as *The Kybalion*. My views are somewhat cabalistic in the sense that I see this spirit manifesting in ways we can relate to it. And so come the gods and goddesses of old: Hekate and Isis are both goddesses I've long been drawn to, while I recently developed a connection to Brigid while visiting Ireland earlier this year. Of course Herne of the Wild Hunt is a favorite, as are Hermes, Hades, and Anubis. I also have a particular affinity for the Voodoo queen Marie Laveau and the spirit Pazuzu—a somewhat visceral spirit that has come through for me more than once.

All this being said, I do not see what I do so much as worship but rather interaction and engagement with spirit. I do not believe in supplicating to the divine but dancing with it.

When Witches meet, what do they usually do?

When I meet with other Witches, it is to celebrate the mysteries and the magicks with people whose power, abilities, and will can join with my own to create even greater influence over the challenges and changes of life. Witches can raise great power, and together, they are a reminder to the gods of old that they have not been forgotten and remain relevant in the world today.

Do Witches really do "spells" or can they do "magic"?

Spells and magic are, in my opinion, inseparable from Witchcraft. While Witchcraft is not simply a synonym for magic, it is utterly steeped in it. To be a Witch is not only to embrace the deities of old and the spirits of the dead, but to unlock the full spectrum of abilities within oneself. To ignore this aspect of the Craft, in my opinion, is a great travesty, and it concerns me that some groups are so eager to mainstream us that they would water down our power.

If you do any spells, can you give examples?

My spells tend to be very mind focused and simple. I don't typically go in for excessive complexity, and often, magic for me can be as simple as visualizing a parking space at the mall or trying to psychically influence those around me to fulfill my various agendas. I do love candles, oils, and incense, though, and often focus on the planetary correspondences, so a success spell might involve a golden yellow candle for the Sun, anointed with a good frankincense oil, and burning a bit of frankincense, benzoin, and copal. Any words I use are created in the moment and on the fly. I've never been much for writing anything down.

Are you a hereditary Witch?

I am not a hereditary Witch. I think such Witches are rare, and I think most of the claims of those who say they are hereditary are false. That said, I do believe that folk magic and, perhaps, sometimes even the religion of Witchcraft itself have been passed down in families.

Did your family carry stories about Witches or did you find out about it all recently?

When I was a child, I was taught that Witches were hideous hags who flew on brooms and marauded the land on Halloween night. I still very much love the myths and stories of Halloween because I do believe that Witches have a connection to the dark and chthonic, so I embrace both the spiritual and the whimsical aspects of that magical time of year.

You have been quite influential in the development of Salem as a commercial and tourist attraction for Witches and the nonmagical public. Can you talk about what brought you to Salem and your experiences there?

It is often assumed that I came to Salem since so many Witches over the years have done so. Even our mayor—whom I adore—once told a television interviewer that when I came to town, it was like a "champagne cork unpopping." However, most don't know that I was born in Beverly, one town north of Salem, on Christmas Day of 1969. My single mom and I moved to Salem when I was four years old, and while we moved about the North Shore of Boston more than I care to admit, we were often in Salem, and I moved there more permanently in 1991 when I was twenty-one years old. Outside of a brief stint in nearby Marblehead, I lived in Salem right up until my move to New Orleans in 2012.

Salem is truly fascinating in so many ways. It has suffered an identity crisis going back all the way to the infamous trials of 1692. It could be argued that the trials were the result of an underlying war between those in Salem Village (now Danvers) who wanted to be a farming community and those who wanted ties to the emerging mercantile center of Salem Town. When I first entered the business of Witchcraft in 2002, I ran up against a massive wall that represented Salem's modern-day split personality. There were a number of groups desperate to define Salem as solely one thing. You had your maritime history people—whose claim is quite valid, as Salem was the greatest American port of the 1700s. There were the architectural history folks—who also had a claim, as our architecture is among the most celebrated in history. And, of course, Nathaniel Hawthorne gave us a literary connection to be celebrated. There are the 1692 Witch trials history folks who have despised being confused with real Witches in the past. And finally, there was my greatest nemesis at the time—the "arts and culture" crowd, who hoped to turn Salem into a museum town appropriately anchored by our admittedly wonderful Peabody Essex Museum, one of the twenty largest museums in America.

Into all of this, I walked as a Warlock with a background in advertising agencies and web marketing firms, and I set about teaching the powers that be that all of these supposedly disparate interests could be married. We were not allowed to join Salem's office of tourism in 2003 because we didn't fit the mission statement of arts and culture that they were solely pushing at the time. We got a new mayor in 2005 (Kim Driscoll, who is thankfully still in office), and I sat with her for two hours one afternoon to explain why modern Witchcraft matters in the scheme of Salem's marketing. I later became the first Witchcraft practitioner to sit on the board of directors of the same office of tourism that wouldn't let me join only a few years prior. I began to be respected by the powers that be, though I am guessing that has less to do with my religion and far more to do with my business sense and that they realized that they could make more money if they listened to me.

Later, in 2014, the chief marketing officer of the Peabody Essex Museum was at my wedding with his wife. I have great relationships with many of the power players in Salem because they finally understand that what we do is a legitimate part of the tapestry. It wasn't easy to get there, and there are still occasional challenges. There are landlords in Salem who refuse to rent to Witchcraft shops, and others who have evicted such shops upon purchasing buildings. I do not believe it is because they are bigoted against our religion but rather that they do not want to see Salem's identity so thoroughly impacted by our presence because it gets in the way of their vision of Salem as a generic arts and culture destination.

There are still people today who come to Salem not realizing our impact, and then they aggressively seek to change it. I've never understood this attitude. I've always said that if I didn't like the smell of Chinese food, I wouldn't move to Chinatown. Salem and Witchcraft are forever linked in the public mind-set, and this brand identity is reinforced by schools, universities, television shows, publications, and books throughout the world.

Salem can be very challenging in that there is a mind-set within certain corners of the Witchcraft community that one's shop, tradition, or practices must be the template for all others to follow. It has led to so many conflicts over the years, and even before Witchcraft was my career, I avoided such doctrinal and business disputes like the plague. Of course, as a businessperson who is in the spotlight, I've realized that it's sometimes hard to avoid such things. In my nearly thirty years in the Craft, I've watched so many come to Salem seeking to "replace Laurie Cabot" (and now me!), as though you can just step into someone else's shoes. I never became anything in my career as a Witch until I stopped trying to be Laurie Cabot. There will never be another Laurie Cabot. There will never be another me. Each of us is our own star, and if we focus on what matters, we'll continue shining our own light.

I've certainly been sucked into a drama or two over the years, but I've gotten much better at seeing the motivations behind these attempts to derail my work and that it's all about them and their baggage and has little to do with me or what I'm doing. I am encouraged that recent years have seen a willingness of groups and shops to work together. A number of us shops in town have great relationships and work to lift one another up. It took a while for folks to get to the point where they could see that the rising tide lifts all boats, but I'm happy to say that this is becoming the prevailing mind-set for the Witch City.

What is your impression of the current interest in Witchcraft in Salem, centuries after the Witch hysteria of Puritan times?

I think it's fantastic that so many see Salem as a Witchcraft mecca. One of the questions I am most asked by the media is, "If there were no

Witches in Salem in 1692, why are you all here now?" As rude a question as this is, I try not to assume bad motives on the part of journalists because few of them really understand who we are, and so I always answer it. First off, Mohammed never made a pilgrimage site in Dearborn, Michigan, Jesus never walked on water in Virginia Beach, and there's no Temple Mount in Brooklyn. What difference does it make to anyone if Witches choose Salem or any other town to make a community in which to live? Maybe we just like the charm of the place.

But in this case, it's more than that. Salem is more associated with Witchcraft than anyplace else in the entire world, so there is no greater platform in the world from which to educate hundreds of thousands of visitors about our beliefs and practices. And those visitors go back to wherever they live and say, "I met a Witch and she was so magical and really helped me!" What better way to reach across the globe to let people know that we aren't evildoers worshipping devils and sacrificing babies? And, finally, what do we really know about what they did in Salem anyway? It is doubtful that the accused were Witches, but there is no place that Europeans ever settled where some remnants of folk magic and religion can't be found—even among the Puritans.

Have you had relationships or friendships with other New England Witches? If so, with whom? And what were the most significant experiences or learnings you had from those encounters?

Being from New England, I count many New England Witches among my friends. The most notable New England Witch, of course, is my first teacher, Laurie Cabot. Her Witchcraft classes were truly life changing for me and helped me realize my true abilities. My departed best friend, Shawn Poirier, was also an incredibly magical teacher and powerful practitioner who taught me much about working with spirits. My more well-known regional Witch friends include Penny Cabot, Raven and Stephanie Grimassi, Christopher Penczak, Lorelei Stathopolous, Leanne Marrama, Sandra Mariah Wright, Jimahl di Fiosa, and Karagan Griffith. Each and every one of these people has influenced me and my path for the better.

Have you experienced any difficulties—any problems, persecution, or prejudice—as a result of being a Witch? Can you describe a time or times when that happened?

Many years ago, I heard Wren Walker of the Witches' Voice give a talk where she said, "We do not anticipate prejudice, and so we rarely experience it." This has been a guiding principle for me for years. No person can automatically avoid the harm of discrimination, but our attitude about ourselves has so much to do with it. That being said, in 2015, I experienced my first real case of discrimination: the steamboat on which our first HexFest opening ritual was to be held cancelled us less than two weeks before the festival after the owner had discovered that we were Witches. Luckily, we got a spot on the other local river-boat, but it was a devastating experience for everyone involved. They employed technicalities in the contract to get away with it, but they made it quite clear to our store manager and myself over the phone what the real reason was. We came very close to suing over it, but it would have been far too monumental a battle at the time, and so I resolved to infuse myself into local tourism more so that they'd be forced to look at me.

Now, while I have experienced relatively little discrimination outside of the Craft, inside the Craft is a different story. We are a faith movement in its relatively nascent stages and there are many fighting tooth and nail to define who we are rather than simply being who we are. Given that my public identity and my personal practices don't always fit into the norm of what people consider Witchcraft, I have sometimes felt a bit of an outcast because I do things a little differently. I do not let it bring me down, though, because I know that our ultimate lesson is to find our own inner Witch and let her shine. Each of us is our own rock star, and we don't need to rely on either the denigration or the elevation of another in order to be our best magical self.

What are special holy days for Witches? Can you please describe what Witches do on their holy days? How do you celebrate?

I'm pretty traditional about my magical days. I follow the Witches' Wheel of the Year and honor the eight Sabbats, with special emphasis for me on Beltane and Samhain—especially Samhain. I love the Full Moons and sometimes the New Moons when I can find the time. Because of my career, however, every day is magical for me, as I'm always finding some way to interact with spirit in my work and in my daily life.

CHRISTOPHER GIROUX
Mount Desert Island, Maine

First, can you say a bit about who you are, where you live, and what you do for a living these days?

My name is Chris Giroux. I was born, raised, and educated in Boston, Massachusetts. My partner and I began vacationing on Mount Desert Island, Maine, about twenty-four years ago and decided that we really wanted to live here, so we bought a little place and relocated in the summer of 2013. At the moment, I work as a regional compliance coordinator for a national property management company but soon plan to change careers. I have extensive experience managing metaphysical and spiritual retail stores and resource centers (I managed Arsenic and Old Lace, once of Cambridge, Massachusetts, and Unicorn Books, once of Arlington, Massachusetts) and would like to open a store on the island or in the vicinity of the island, but I haven't quite figured out the market just yet.

Which religion were you raised in?

I was raised Catholic. My mother is Irish Catholic, and my father is Italian Catholic, and although I realize that they are technically both Roman Catholic, anyone raised in such a household knows how radically different they are. Fortunately, for me, both of my maternal and paternal grandmothers were pre–Vatican II Catholics, so the Blessed Mother and the rosary were huge parts of my religious education.

How and when did you decide you were a Witch?

I was confirmed when I was twelve years old and had some pretty amazing spiritual experiences during my confirmation process. I was always drawn to religion and liked being Catholic, not really knowing any better, so, when I was about fourteen years old, I came to the conclusion that these experiences were a very strong calling to be a priest. Truth be known, I really wanted to be a nun, but I was dissuaded from the idea because I was a boy, and boys couldn't be nuns, so I settled for priest.

I made an appointment to meet with our local parish priest, Father Welch, to talk to him about some, what I thought were basic, questions that I still had about Christianity. I met with him one fateful day and had two questions to ask: (1) if God is all good, where did the bad stuff come from, and (2) if God is a man, how did he conceive of woman? In response to my first question, Fr. Welch explained to me that God was in fact all powerful, all loving, and all good, but that he gave us free will with which we could choose a bad option. This made no sense to me: someone or something that is all good couldn't create a "bad" option. I remember saying to him, "If I'm a human and you are a human, we can't make a monkey, a goat, or a dog, right? We can only make another human, right?" He responded, "Right."

I questioned again: "How could God, who is all good, create a bad option?" Logically, he could only create good options. Fr. Welch debated unsuccessfully with me for about fifteen minutes, at which point we had to agree that this might be a topic for another day. But it was when I asked my second question that it got really interesting for me. He told me that God wasn't technically male, but that we referred to him as our father out of respect. Well, this made no sense to me. Why would we use a masculine pronoun to describe someone or something that wasn't male? So I asked, "Why don't we say 'it,' instead of 'he'?" Fr. Welch said that this would be disrespectful, so I asked, "Then why don't we say 'she'?" To which he responded, "That would be even more disrespectful." And that's when the Catholic church lost me.

Having been nurtured by two grandmothers who taught me the importance of the Blessed Mother, despite Vatican II's attempt to lessen and practically eradicate her authority in the church, women were way more important to me than men. Jesus was a transcendent figure: "there" but not there. Whereas Mary was immanent for me; I found her everywhere. I found her in the world—in nature, at home, in school, at work, everywhere. But more importantly, I found her in me. And that just couldn't be wrong, even to a fourteen-year-old boy.

So, I started looking at other religions to find one that would affirm the presence of the female divine. I looked at other variations of Christianity, but the Protestant traditions I found seemed even more male oriented. I looked at Judaism and Islam, but the boys were the only ones who seemed to be affirmed. I looked at Buddhism, but that seemed very pessimistic to a fourteen-year-old: we are born to die. I looked at Hinduism but couldn't find anything that could really define the multitude of gods and goddesses I kept encountering.

Then one Saturday afternoon, I was perusing the shelves of an amazing bookstore in Harvard Square, now long since gone, called Wordsworth Books, and behind the stairwell I found a section called "Occult." I remember that there were about half a dozen books there, including Starhawk's *The Spiral Dance*, Margot Adler's *Drawing Down the Moon*, Paul Huson's *Mastering Witchcraft*, Linda Goodman's *Sun Signs*, and a book by Richard Cavendish called *The Black Arts*—and I bought all of them. I picked up and started reading *The Black Arts* and within the first few pages of the first chapter, Cavendish wrote something about God being the sum of everything—good/bad, male/female, black/white—and it was this marriage of opposites that drew me to Witchcraft.

So, I would have to say that was the day I officially claimed the word *Witch* as my own, although I would not publicly refer to myself as a Witch for another twenty years, not because of any fear of other people's reactions to the word, but because the word, the identity itself, meant a great deal to me, and I did not feel that I had the maturity to really use it outside of myself until later.

How do you personally define Witchcraft?

I feel that being a Witch is not something I believe. Being a Witch is something I am. Personally, I believe that you can be a Catholic Witch or a Buddhist Witch or a Pagan Witch. But what makes me a Witch, what I feel deeply makes any of us Witches, is that we are consciously working with four critical questions:

1. Am I living my truth, that truth that is self-evident to me and that others may or may not see?
2. Am I challenging myself to remain open to another person, place, or thing's way of being in the world even when, and especially when, it runs contrary to my way of being in the world?
3. Am I taking responsibility for my participation in the creation of the world and willing to be accountable for that participation?
4. Am I being compassionate and expressing that compassion in a healthy way for myself and others?

Being a Witch and practicing Witchcraft is a way of being, a philosophy if you will, that informs my journey and encourages and affirms my choices.

Which tradition of Witchcraft do you follow? How did you find that tradition?

I have really been a solitary practitioner for most of my life. I received training in, and so borrowed from, many traditions to create a spiritual path that "feeds" me personally. Initially I read everything I could get my hands on regarding Witchcraft and Wicca. I extensively studied Ifa, the spiritual tradition of the Yoruba people of West Africa that became Lucumi, Santeria, and Candomblé in the New World, with an Olokun Priestess in Boston and received multiple initiations.

I studied First Nations traditions with a Mohawk Elder in Concord,

Massachusetts, and underwent a vision quest and sweat lodge ceremonies. I studied meditation with Buddhists, the contemplative meditation of Thomas Merton, and feminist liberation "theology" of Barbara Walker and Mary Daly. I did puja with Hindus. About fifteen years ago I became very close friends with Christopher Penczak and then, by default, his partners Steve Kenson and Adam Sartwell, who collectively founded the Temple of Witchcraft (TOW) in Salem, New Hampshire, and so I have been celebrating the Sabbats with the temple for a while now. I teach at the temple, and I enjoy the community because all traditions are honored and welcome.

What makes your approach or tradition unique from any others out there?

I believe that there are as many spiritual paths as there are folks who choose to walk a spiritual path. Even when you are raised within a strictly dogmatic tradition, if you choose to develop a personal relationship with the divine, you have stepped onto a new, never-before-seen path because you bring to your path all the joys and sorrows, challenges, and wounds of you, and that colors how you relate to the divine and how you allow the divine to manifest in your life. I bring together for myself, and encourage others to bring together for themselves, a tradition rich in affirming my right to be here. I try to challenge myself daily to be honorable, honest, compassionate, responsible, and accountable to myself and the beings (human and otherwise) that I encounter on my personal journey.

Would you say that Witchcraft is a "craft" or a "religion"? And can you talk about the difference?

Obviously, I would say it's a craft or philosophy. I think Wicca, whether it is Gardnerian, Alexandrian, or Traditional British Witchcraft, is an attempt to give the spirituality of Witchcraft some form and validity for people who are interested in walking away from the religion they were raised with. However, as I have said, being a Witch is something I am, not something I believe.

Whom do Witches worship?

I believe that, traditionally, and this is of course what drew me to Witchcraft in the first place, Witches worship both female and male manifestations of the divine. As a Witch, I feel strongly that you are welcome to worship any number of deities from around the world, and we have certainly borrowed, confiscated, and outright stolen many of the deities that we work with. What I think is most important, though, is that we try to understand the roots and cultural backgrounds of these various deities, whether it be Ganesha or Eshu, Tara, Kuan Yin or Mary, so that when we enter into a conversation with a person who actually practices the particular faith we have borrowed our chosen deity from, we can engage in intelligent conversation and/or debate without making ourselves look foolish or alienating a person with our opinions.

When Witches meet, what do they usually do?

Quarrel. (Laughs.) Seriously, what we in the TOW do when we come together is try to create a safe and welcoming space where everyone's experience and everyone's relationship with the divine can be honored. We celebrate the Sabbats by creating sacred space and calling into that sacred space the energy of the Goddess and the God, and although we may give those manifestations of the divine specific names, we try to encourage everyone to bring their relationship into that circle as well. The Sabbats are designed to celebrate specific aspects of the natural world that we are experiencing and how those aspects of the natural world are played out in our conscious and unconscious minds. Through sacred drama we witness the change of the seasons through the changes in the Goddess and God, from the birth of the Child of Light at Yule onto the blessing of the fertility at Imbolc and Beltane, through the blessings and ripening crops in summer and the first harvest at Litha and Lughnasa, on through the decline of the year at Mabon and the descent of the Goddess at Samhain until we arrive again at Yule and the rebirth of the Divine Child of Light. I realize that this is pretty vague, but each Sabbat is unique and would take way too long to explain in any depth.

Do Witches really do "spells" or can they do "magic"?

This question confuses me a little. I understand spells to be a means of doing magic. Magic is about affecting the probability and outcome of a situation. Magic is about bringing reality into alignment with what we need or want. A spell is a prayer, or curse in some cases, that focuses our intention and speaks into the world an aspiration of what we would like to come to pass. I say aspiration as opposed to affirmation because I feel that an affirmation is the act of constantly telling ourselves and the universe something that we don't or might not necessarily believe in an attempt to convince ourselves that that something is true. But if I need to tell myself, "I am a good person who deserves x, y, or z," then maybe I need to look more closely at the "good person" part and why I need to convince myself of that. Whereas an aspiration takes into account exactly where I am and what I have done thus far in creating my world and then says, "This is where I am because of x, y, or z, but I want better and this is how I need 'better' to manifest."

Magic will take the path of least resistance, so "crafting" the spell with language that specifically identifies our needs and/or wants is important, regardless of the language the spell is spoken in. Often spells also require some sacrifice on our part, whether that is sacrificing the money to buy a jar of honey to offer to the river and remind ourselves of the sweetness of life and the ever-flowing energy of generosity or giving a homeless person on the street our coat for the same reason. It is up to our awareness and acknowledgment of our participation in the web of the universe to decide what the appropriate sacrifice will be.

If you do any spells, can you give examples?

I have done spells. I have done spells for healing myself and others physically and spiritually, and I have done spells to bring about changes in myself and the world around me. Most recently I did a spell so that the right circumstances would present themselves to help my partner feel comfortable giving up the security we had built in our home and careers in the Greater Boston area and moving to Maine, where both of us feel more at home and relaxed.

Are you a hereditary Witch?

No. My grandmothers both practiced what I now understand is a form of "folk magic" specific to their upbringings, but God and all the saints in heaven help you if you implied either was anything but a good Catholic. I personally have some issues with the idea of "hereditary Witchcraft." At this stage of things, hereditary Witches might claim something because Witchcraft's revival has been around for almost a hundred years. So if someone were to say to me that in the past twenty years or so they inherited a branch of Traditional British Witchcraft through so-and-so, I could get behind that. However, and I realize I risk pissing some folks off, I can't get behind the idea that anyone has inherited something, either through a family lineage or because they were tripping on some mushrooms and stumbled across an old Coven of Witches in the forest somewhere.

I think our desire to give authenticity to our belief systems causes people to create "traditions," but I also think that we are now at a stage of development, individually and as a species, where we need to just own that we are in the process of creating, or have created, something, and if other people are interested in participating in what we have found to be life affirming, then the more the merrier.

Have you had relationships or friendships with other New England Witches? If so, with whom? And what were the most significant experiences or learnings you had from those encounters?

Having worked in the metaphysical and spiritual retail world, I have had the honor, and horror, of meeting many Witches. As I mentioned earlier, my closest friend is Christopher Penczak and watching him create the TOW in order to create community was a most surreal experience. I say this carefully and with great respect, but knowing Christopher, I realize that his need for community did not stem from a desire to find an affirming voice in the world but to create that voice for others.

Like me, I think that being a Witch is who Christopher is, not something he "believes," although he has certainly put down in writing precisely what he believes and why. But oftentimes when we are out there trying to find a like-minded individual who affirms for us that we aren't completely "coo coo ca choo," it's good to see that in writing. Even if it isn't exactly our experience, it holds a certain truth that speaks to those deepest parts of ourselves and affirms what we have always known: we are Witches.

Do you have any interactions with Witches in the Salem, Massachusetts, area? What is your impression of the current interest in Witchcraft in Salem, centuries after the Witch hysteria of Puritan times?

Outside of the Witches from Salem who attend TOW events, I don't think I personally know or am close to anyone who identifies as a "Salem Witch." When I was a lot younger I thought it was odd that folks fought over being the Official Witch of Salem—with no disrespect meant to Laurie Cabot, whom we all know of and adore or, at the very least, should admire for her courage (or insanity) at putting herself out there so many years ago. Being the official Witch of the town known for putting so-called Witches to death was like being the Official Jew of Auschwitz (again, no offense meant to either Witches or Jews). But as I matured and reclaimed many things and words, I now understand the importance of taking back such a tragic period and putting our stamp on it in order to keep such insanity from manifesting again.

Have you experienced any difficulties—any problems, persecution, or prejudice—as a result of being a Witch? Can you describe a time or times when that happened?

I haven't experienced as much prejudice as a Witch as I have as an openly queer man, but then I don't have the word *Witch* tattooed on my forehead, and I think most people just assume that everyone follows a monotheistic, Middle Eastern tradition. In those cases where I have actually talked with someone, they are generally a little perplexed by it but rarely offended or offensive. There was one time I remember when I was in my late teens and I told a female friend that I was a Witch, because she wanted to know why she never saw me in church. For some unknown reason, she told her boyfriend, who told two friends who told two friends and so on. One of those friends was also someone who disliked me because he thought I was gay. One afternoon at work (I was a front-end clerk at a local grocery store), he decided to tease me about it. He seemed to start off with sincere enough questions, but then his bullying nature came to the forefront, and he asked me if he should be concerned about me turning him into a toad. Having grown up pretty obviously gay, I had developed a quick mind and razor-sharp wit and tongue as a defense mechanism, so I simply asked him why I should do something so redundant. It shut him up.

I think part of the reason I haven't suffered greatly at the hands of religious prejudice is that I was raised in the Greater Boston area, where there is a strong diversity of people represented. It is also heavily populated by college- and university-educated people who seem to be more open to diversity. Then there is the fact that I'm 6'7" tall and weigh in at about two hundred and seventy-five pounds. I also know my own mind, and I come across as intelligent and self-assured. All of these things tend to discourage stupid behavior in others.

What are special holy days for Witches? Can you please describe what Witches do on their holy days? How do you celebrate?

Most Witches celebrate the Wheel of the Year, eight holidays that span the year and include the two solstices and equinoxes plus four more key days that mark specific dates important to our agrarian ancestors. Beginning with Samhain on October 31, which marks the end of one growing cycle and the beginning of a new one, through Yule on December 21, celebrating the rebirth of the Sun and the lengthening of days, on to Imbolc on February 2, when the first lambs are born, to Ostara, around March 21, when the Earth begins to put forth her first hues of gold and green, on to Beltane on May 1, when we celebrate the awakening sexual energy within ourselves and the Earth that encourages life, to the Summer Solstice on June 21, when we celebrate the turning of the year and mark the beginning of the shortening of days, on to Lammas, or Lughnasadh, depending on your preference, where we mark the first harvest, through September 21 and the Vernal Equinox, marking the change in energy from the deities of spring, summer, and growth to the deities of autumn, winter, and rest. And then we're back at Samhain.

Prior to becoming a member of the TOW, I celebrated these by simply lighting an appropriately colored candle and contemplating the previous period—the good and bad choices and the decisions and experiences and how I was using them to grow—and thanking my personal deities and the deities of my place for their support and encouragement. Now, as a part of the TOW, we tend to have some ritual drama that plays out an expression of the holiday and the time to come, giving folks something to "chew on" throughout the upcoming season.

Personally, my own practice has been to work with the Full and New Moons of the fixed quarters (Scorpio and Taurus in the spring, Aquarius and Leo in the summer, Taurus and Scorpio in the autumn, and Aquarius and Leo in the winter). These are the strongest parts of the year for me, and I use these times to work out prayers and spells to encourage and challenge my own personal growth.

CHRISTOPHER LaFOND
Western Massachusetts

First, can you say a bit about who you are, where you live, and what you do for a living these days?

I live with my wife in the hill towns of western Massachusetts. A few years ago, we bought a home with five acres of land, bordered by one hundred acres of woods with a brook, the town cemetery, and multiple farms. Two acres of our property is the yard, and the rest is part of the woods, but two acres is enough for the small homestead that we have established. We grow most of our own vegetables, and we have laying hens for eggs. We also raise much of our own meat: chickens, ducks, turkeys, and rabbits.

My wife and I both went through periods in our youth (separately) when we were vegetarians for a number of years, and we both discovered that the journey was essentially one of coming to terms with the fact that things have to die for us to live. Years later, we have the honor of raising and butchering much of our own meat. This allows us to raise our animals the way we want to, with space to roam around, plenty of sunshine and air, good food, and the best life possible.

For over twenty years, I was on the faculty of Boston College, where I taught a number of levels of Spanish language courses. For most of that time, I was also one of the coordinators of the language program, and in addition to teaching, I trained graduate students to be teachers. A few years ago, I moved farther west and got married, so I left Boston College. I taught for a couple of years at Mt. Holyoke College in South Hadley and St. Joseph's University in West Hartford, Connecticut. Eventually, I got back into editing foreign-language learning materials for college-level courses, which I had done for a number of years when I was a graduate student. I now do that full-time. Technically, I am a subject matter expert, and I edit and create interactive digital tools for the online versions of textbooks in Spanish, French, Italian, and a bit of German. It's perfect for me, since it combines my being a techie with my language skills. It also allows me to work from home and do the housework, the cooking, and the caring for the animals.

How and when did you decide you were a Witch?

This is sort of a long-and-winding story. When I was a teenager, I spent three years in a diocesan seminary studying to be a Catholic priest. When I left, I almost joined the Franciscans, in great part because of their traditional connection to nature and the natural world. But I changed direction and ended up studying my other love, languages, at Boston College. During my time there, I became ever more troubled about the Catholic church's treatment of women, in particular. I started to look around for a new church, still Christian, which was a lot more liberal and egalitarian. But when I graduated from college, I was accepted to go to Ecuador for two and a half years as a volunteer teacher. I was aware that I was heading to the most Catholic continent in the world and so temporarily postponed the search.

While in Ecuador, I taught music, mostly in Quito, for two years and then in the jungle for about six months. Quito is at an altitude of almost two miles and sits in a valley. Ecuador has a very high indigenous and mestizo population, and I had a number of indigenous friends who came from families outside the city, and I would visit them sometimes. It was these visits, completely outside the city, with no electricity, no telephones, and sometimes no running water, where I was first aware of being in touch with nature in a really aware way. Ironically, I was working with the Catholic, Episcopal, and Lutheran churches as a teacher and musician during this time. To their credit, the people with whom I worked were also very in touch with nature, indigenous traditions, and indigenous spirituality, and I never had a conflict, even as I moved my own identification away from Christian to Pagan.

Eventually I returned to the States to begin my graduate studies, and when I returned, I knew that there were two possible paths to follow: Witchcraft or Native American spirituality. I decided pretty quickly that I would not pursue the Native American direction, even though I have a lot of Native in my family, most of whom are French Canadians, many of whom married Natives. I was aware that I would likely be seen as another white person who wanted to take something that was not mine. In addition to not having investigated the specifics of my Native background at the time, I wasn't in a position to find a Native community from my family background and go to be with them and make that sort of commitment, even supposing that they would have me.

So, I started to seek out opportunities to learn Witchcraft. In those days, Witchcraft was sort of being publicized as a Celtic thing, and the rest of my family is of Celtic origins. The French from Canada go back to Brittany, and one grandmother was Irish and Scottish. So it made sense at the time. This was, of course, before the internet was a real thing, so my options were somewhat limited. They had just built the commuter train that went from Boston, where I was in school, to Salem, Massachusetts. So I found classes there and started to study.

Which tradition of Witchcraft do you follow? How did you find that tradition?

I don't follow a particular tradition, though I find most of my inspiration in traditional Celtic culture. For many years I studied traditional Druidism, so my ties to Celtic tradition are strong. But I also don't try to reconstruct or rebuild any particular time period in their long history. I guess my tradition can best be labeled as "animistic Paganism." It's really where my heart has been for a very long time, but I would say that I first "found" it while participating in the EarthSpirit Community of Massachusetts, where I live. During the course of many years, I went from attending EarthSpirit events to presenting at them to volunteering to help run them, and I continue to do so. The folks at the center of EarthSpirit take their inspiration from Celtic (mostly Scottish Highland) animism, and I found that we "fit" together really well.

What makes your approach or tradition unique from any others out there?

One thing that differentiates what I do from what many modern Pagans do is that animism has a noticeable lack of deities. There is a central *anam*, or "soul," that is recognized as running through everything on various levels. But we tend not to invoke many god or goddess figures.

At the same time, I am an astrological priest. I make invocations and devotions and conduct rituals to and for the beings at the heart of stars and planets. I guess that's probably the most unique part of what I do.

Would you say that Witchcraft is a "craft" or a "religion"? And can you talk about the difference?

I think that it can be either or both. Some believe that people are born Witches and that you can't learn it as a craft later. I don't agree. I think that we are all born with some level of magical ability—some with much more than others, admittedly—and that we can either ignore it or practice it as a craft. For some, this craft can be interwoven with many different belief systems, even if the guardians of that belief system itself would not recognize the legitimacy of doing that. For others, exploring how to "do" magic and how magic works can lead to a much deeper level that really takes over one's worldview and spirituality. I think that this can border on religion.

Whom do Witches worship?

I think it depends on which Witch you ask. I also think that it depends on what you mean by "worship." While I engage in devotions, I wouldn't say that I worship any particular being, with the possible exception of Nature. And even then, I think that by "worship," I mean that whatever decision is at hand, I have to take into account how the pieces of that decision may impact any particular piece of the web of Nature. It may not be possible to always know or make the absolute best decision, but for me, taking that into account is imperative.

When Witches meet, what do they usually do?

Again, this depends on which Witch you ask. Many don't even meet up to do any sort of ritual. Years ago, when I was studying in Salem, Massachusetts, I used to joke that the only thing we can answer for certain about what Witches do when we meet is that we eat. There is always some sort of food and fellowship, either during or after a ritual or both.

As an animistic Pagan, when I meet with like-minded others, we usually open ourselves to all that is around us (rather than invoking elements, as many others do). We recognize that all these beings are already here, and we are among them. They are always with us, so we don't really "create" sacred space, but rather, we recognize that we are always in sacred space.

Do Witches really do "spells" or can they do "magic"?

Sure we do. Everything we do affects all others in the web—sometimes in small ways, sometimes in big ways. One way of looking at magic is that by manipulating certain things here in front of me, and by asking the aid of certain beings (in my case, these would be planetary or star beings), we can affect the unseen realm, which in turn reflects back to the world of what we see. This is where the maxim "As above, so below" comes from. We work to change a piece of the web from here "below," and it resonates up "above" the material world, but in the process, it then reflects back down "below" again to the physical plane.

If you do any spells, can you give examples?

I use many talismanic spells from books like the *Picatrix*, the *Key of Solomon*, and other astrological texts. They tend to be medieval because that's when more magicians were actually working astrological magic. But there are also modern versions of many of these, some of which are composed by my astrological magical acquaintances or by me.

Are you a hereditary Witch?

Not at all. I like to joke that it's all my parents' fault, since they were married on Beltane (May 1), and I was a honeymoon baby. But that's as far as that goes. My father is a Roman Catholic deacon, and one of my brothers is a convert to Greek Orthodoxy. So, we are a very multi-religious family. For the record, we all get along very well.

Have you had relationships or friendships with other New England Witches? If so, with whom? And what were the most significant experiences or learnings you had from those encounters?

I have had many relationships with other Witches and Pagans in the area. As I mentioned earlier, I've been an active member of the EarthSpirit Community for many years, and, of course, I worked and studied with you, Ellen, for about seven years. I have also been a member of the Western Massachusetts Pagan Pride committee for a number of years. I'm taking over as the director this year. All of these things afford me a lot of contact with other Witches, Pagans, Druids, Asatru, and many others.

I think that one of the most important things I've learned about community is something that I realized long ago when working with different Christian groups, and it holds true for Pagans as well: if you are looking for community, then you should focus on your actual local community folks rather than looking for a name like "Witch," "Pagan," "Catholic," "Protestant," and so forth. People live out their ideals on the local level independent of what any creed or dogma might say from above.

You have been instrumental in directing a choir of Witches as well as recording some lovely Celtic harp music. Can you talk about the Pagan music scene in New England?

There are a number of really good Pagan musicians in the area. Your question refers to my direction of MotherTongue, EarthSpirit's ritual performance group. My wife and I also perform at Pagan Pride Days and other events; while we don't always present ourselves as Pagan (it depends on the event), we are almost always presenting traditional Celtic or American folk music.

Right here in Massachusetts, we have Kellianna, Jenna Greene, Brian Willowfire, and other wonderful musicians. New Hampshire has Mike Dolan. Right next door in New York, we have Alyssa Yeager (as Rhiannon's Lark). And of course, we were all saddened at the unexpected loss of Jeff Martell last January. Jeff was active in the folk and Pagan music scene.

You have traveled to Barcelona, Spain, as an American Pagan representative to the Parliament of the World's Religions—can you talk about that a bit? How were you chosen for that role, and who did you go with?

In 2004, I went to Barcelona as part of the EarthSpirit delegation. At the time, EarthSpirit's founder and spiritual director, Andras Corban-Arthen, was a trustee of the board of the Parliament of World's Religions. Currently Andras is the vice chair of the Parliament, as well as the president of the European Congress of Ethnic Religions, and he serves on the board of advisors of the Ecospirituality Foundation.

MotherTongue presented and performed there. I also served as a real-time translator for some of the Pagan panel presentations, translating back and forth from English to Spanish. I also attended the Parliament of the World's Religions with EarthSpirit and MotherTongue in Melbourne, Australia, in 2009.

The Parliaments have been amazing experiences. My strongest memories and experiences are connected to the Parliament in Barcelona. What struck me about many of the local attendees was how open they were to Paganism in general, and how they wanted to learn more about it. After performing or translating, I would often have people recognize me on the streets and reach out to talk more about it, especially some of the older attendees. They seemed to value what we were presenting and representing in terms of being a part of the Earth and acting in ways that respect that connection.

One of my favorite experiences from Melbourne is that of an Anglican woman loaning me a Celtic harp so that I didn't have to take one of mine around the world. She presented a fantastic morning observance and really walks a fine line between Anglicanism and Pagan spirituality in a Celtic tradition. She just showed up and gave me a harp to haul around Melbourne for a week—talk about trust! I was thrilled to be able to return the favor to her a few years later when she was invited to present and perform near Boston.

Do you have any interactions with Witches in the Salem, Massachusetts, area? What is your impression of the current interest in Witchcraft in Salem, centuries after the Witch hysteria of Puritan times?

I studied in Salem for a few years, mainly because I didn't know where else to go. I had just returned from being in South America, and it was before the internet was really a thing. So, finding resources was challenging. I was working on my master's degree in Boston, and they had just built a commuter rail right to Salem, so I took advantage of the opportunity to head up there.

I haven't really had a connection with Salem in a long time. I think that while it's nice that Salem is sort of an icon for folks to maybe find out more about Witchcraft, most Witches and Pagans live outside of Salem and its surrounding area. So, Salem for me, as well as for many others, has served as a welcome "gateway" of sorts.

Have you experienced any difficulties—any problems, persecution, or prejudice—as a result of being a Witch? Can you describe a time or times when that happened?

Not really. I was spoiled in my now-former career as an academic. I was surrounded by people I had known since I was an undergraduate, most of whom were very open-minded and liberal when it came to civil liberties and freedoms.

There is one story that's more funny than anything. I directed music and liturgy at a Catholic church where I grew up. I agreed to do it for a couple of years, but that turned into five. The pastor was not the same as the one that was there when I was a child, but he was one of those old socially progressive 1960s lefty priests, so I was happy to work with him. He was leading the parish in doing really great things in the inner city where they were located, especially in the area of interfaith work. While they knew that I was no longer an active Catholic, no one knew that I was a Pagan or asked. Eventually, some of my choir members figured things out, but it was never a big deal. Many of them were older than me, had known me since I was very young, and trusted me. So, when the label "Pagan" was applied, it wasn't terribly shocking for anyone, and some were quietly curious. But I never talked about it there; I saw my role as one of doing quiet interfaith work, giving back to the place where I grew up, and supporting them as they were working in the city for the rights of poor people and combating racism.

After I finished there, they invited me back every Christmas and Easter to direct the choir for special services, since they didn't have a director after me. Eventually, the pastor moved on, and a new one was assigned. That's when the phone call came. I was at home, reading one of the Harry Potter books under a big maple tree in my yard, when the new pastor called to inquire about my Paganism. Somehow, he found out and saw some things online about my involvement. After grilling me for a while about whether it was just a passing curiosity or not, and explaining how they couldn't have a non-Catholic in the role of cantor and choir director, I politely pointed out that the organist was Jewish, and we never asked for the religious credentials of the special musicians that we sometimes employed for holiday services. I also drew his attention to the fact that it was the previous pastor who invited me to do the job (I had not applied for it); that I was paid what amounted to pennies for conducting rehearsals, having meetings, and directing the group; that it was the parish who continued to invite me back every year, even though I had long ago been ready to finish; that I considered my role there to be that of interfaith work; that the choir and liturgy had been more alive during my years there than they had in a long time; and that just a little appreciation might be in order. Of course, it was not forthcoming. I remember finishing the conversation by asking, "Are you done? Because I'd really like to get back to Harry Potter."

What are special holy days for Witches? Can you please describe what Witches do on their holy days? How do you celebrate?

While many celebrate the Wheel of the Year, I think that's a pretty modern, systematic way of looking at Pagans' and Witches' holidays. Many Witches historically would have celebrated holidays that were native to their local cultures and agricultural cycles. I try to do the same, though as an astrologer, I do tend to mark all eight of the "spokes" on the Wheel of the Year in some manner.

We celebrate the Celtic cross quarter days: Beltane, Lughnasad, Samhain, and Imbolc. We also mark the Summer and Winter Solstices in an important way. Our celebrations usually involve gathering with others outdoors somewhere, regardless of the weather, and opening to the season and the beings and elements that are present in a strong way at that time. Some of these are pretty low key, and some involve singing, gift giving, and making invocations or spells for the coming season.

Any other thoughts you care to add?

Readers can reach me at celticharper.net for CD and concert information and at lafond.us for astrology consultations and classes.

CHRISTOPHER PENCZAK
Salem, New Hampshire

First, can you say a bit about who you are, where you live, and what you do for living these days?

My vocation since 1998 has been a full-time Witch, doing healing work, psychic readings, consultations, and teaching. At the start of my full-time work, I began writing articles, put out a local newsletter called *The Second Road*, and eventually became an author, publishing books for Weiser and Llewellyn and eventually cofounding Copper Cauldron Publishing. While any one aspect of my vocation isn't a career, they all add up to my full-time work.

My particular focus right now is the development of the Temple of Witchcraft as a nonprofit. We purchased land, a house, a barn, and a cottage in Salem, New Hampshire, and are in the process of building deeper community and education through it. I was actually raised in Salem, New Hampshire, and lived there for most of my life—since I was a baby until after I graduated from college, when I moved to Merrimack, New Hampshire, with my partner and fellow Temple cofounder Steve Kenson. I moved back to Salem just five minutes away from my childhood home to create a permanent physical home for the Temple. Many people think we chose Salem, New Hampshire, because of the infamous Salem, Massachusetts, and its longstanding connection with traditional and modern Witches, but honestly, we loved the land, and it was fitting to return to where I began. I like to kid people and say that I'm the Witch of the "other Salem" and tell them that we have a Stone Age site in America's Stonehenge, which was called Mystery Hill when I was a kid. There's a lot of magick here. The lake, old graveyards, and land itself are wonderful. You don't have to be in Salem, Massachusetts, to be a Witch.

How and when did you decide you were a Witch?

I think I was nineteen. From the age of seven to about sixteen, I had conversations with my family, friends, and my art teacher, who gave me my first job in her studio as a part-time assistant. I was in a Catholic high school when I took the job, and those were the days when you didn't just tell people—particularly a minor—you were a Witch. Witch families were not open. My art teacher dropped hints in conversations about art, music, philosophy, and history and finally said, "You figured it out, right? I'm a Witch." I was shocked and thought she was crazy. I learned all I could to try to get her out of what I thought was a cult and soon realized it wasn't, and she was fine. I wanted to learn more. So, she started my training, but I was still pretty skeptical. It was not until she took me to her own teacher, Laurie Cabot, and I completed the first-degree training in the Cabot Tradition of Witchcraft that I officially became a Witch, at least in my mind. A profound psychic experience in the class made me realize how "real" it all was, and I wanted to dedicate myself to being a Witch and continue my training.

How do you personally define Witchcraft?

I learned that Witchcraft is a science, art, and religion, and I still use that definition, as you can approach it from those perspectives. I'm an occultist, and I think of that as being a metaphysical scientist. I create art, poetry, and ritual based upon the techniques, and I serve as a teacher and priest to a community. So those three work well for me. I think of being a Witch as a vocation, a calling, and an orientation to the world. Though I know a lot of people would disagree, I think being a Witch is like being queer. Either you are or you aren't. You wake up to it or hide from it, coming out a potential closet. You can experiment with and explore it and never commit to it, but at your heart, you are either called to be a Witch on some level, or you are not.

I like the view of the vocational Witch being much like another form of the medicine person, serving the spirits and gods and people in the community. I think modern Witches are still trying to figure out the best mechanisms to fulfill this vocation in a community. That's part of why I established our Temple of Witchcraft.

Which tradition of Witchcraft do you follow? How did you find that tradition?

I started in the Cabot Tradition of Witchcraft, where the science, art, and religion are emphasized, one in each of their three degrees, just as the main forms of Wicca have three degrees. My current focus is on the Temple of Witchcraft Tradition, or Temple Tradition for short, that I helped to cofound and create. It started through the material I was teaching. I got into teaching when people wanted to learn a bit of what I was doing in a Full Moon study group. I tried to send them to Laurie Cabot, but at that time, she was not teaching publicly, so they asked me.

I started with a simple Witchcraft 1 curriculum, honestly deeply based on what she taught. Then the same for Witchcraft 2. I wanted to stop, but they didn't, so I taught them what I was currently studying, and that became levels 3, 4, and 5. I didn't plan on making it a tradition. It was self-dedication and solitary initiation with mentorship and aid, but it worked in a pattern that over the years evolved into thick books and yearlong courses.

The graduates started us gathering at Sabbats. First, they started at my parents' house for Samhain and Beltane. Then the original groups of students formed a Coven of sorts, and we began hosting events. That grew into public circles in the Boston area with Unicorn Books as our host. Then a few people seeking belonging started referring to themselves as Christopherians or Penczakians, in reference to Gardnerian or Alexandrian Wiccans. One even said she was a fifth-degree Penczakian in the Cabot lineage. I never used those terms but realized people would seek an identity, with or without my approval, so the teachings that turned into a community became a tradition, and in an effort to depersonalize it, we called it the "Temple of Witchcraft Tradition," since it was a common phrase in the books and classes. In an effort to realize shared goals and to share power and responsibility, we established it as a 501(c)(3) religious nonprofit church, and it's the focus of my life right now.

What makes your approach or tradition unique from any others out there?

Well, we are a strange mix of the ecstatic and intuitive with the ceremonial and disciplined. We are not Coven based but describe ourselves as a magickal order offering service to community. People within the Temple can organize in any groups they wish for personal practices—Coven groups, partnerships, triads, and solitary. The training is done in classes, in person, or online and not in the traditional Coven setting of High Priest and High Priestess pairs. We have five degrees of training, describing what we see as five mysteries—oracular, fertility, ecstatic, gnostic, and the mystery of resurrection. Through the last mystery we seek service and have established twelve different ministries—based upon the twelve zodiac signs and the magical archetypes we associate with them—within our community for people who might not want to lead a Coven or do formal teaching to serve. The ministries each have a wide range of focus for both service and spiritual work. For example, our Gemini Ministry is based around the idea of the Trickster. Responsibilities include basic online communication, computers, networks, websites, and social media, as well as LGBTQA mysteries and a need to challenge assumptions and decisions and playing the role of the Trickster with the leadership, much like the court jester forces those in leadership to look at things from all sides. Areas covered by our twelve zodiac mysteries include healing, environmental action, martial arts, military support, prison ministry, public ritual, art, social services such as a food pantry, a shawl ministry, mediation, sacred sexuality, grief support, networking, queer mysteries, men's mysteries, women's mysteries, and community building.

We are open to all mythologies from all cultures, and people are welcome to worship the gods they come with, though our mythos is anchored in an ostensibly Western-mystery, Witchcraft-cult image.

We are occultists who are more concerned with technique than belief or formal religion, and with creativity in guidelines and parameters than doctrine. We believe experience from technique leads to some general conclusions, but no belief is required. We are fluid and flexible in things like element/direction orientation, teaching several different ways to align the elements and directions, but in the end an understanding of *why* one chooses to do it is more important than following the teacher.

Our philosophies draw not only from Wicca and more folkloric forms of Witchcraft, but from the ancient Pagan temple traditions of Greece and Rome, alchemy, Theosophy, Neoplatonism, and aspects of Hindu and Buddhist philosophy that have seeped into popular New Age lore. As occultists, if someone has a better description or idea of a phenomenon, we will be happy to use it, while referencing the original teaching or the culture from which it originated, but how we use it could be different from the original cultural context. In the end, our Craft is a scavenger religion—our magick is synthesized out of what we find, since we did not inherit a specific tradition. I think Witchcraft can be found, in essence, all over the world.

Our emphasis in the Temple is not on polarity and gender, but that is an aspect of our work. We honor the Sun and Moon but eventually see our group as a mystery of the Earth and stars. Our true focus is a triad of powers described as the Three Rays of Witchcraft, using the ceremonial teachings of love, power, and wisdom emanating from the Divine Heart, Divine Will, and Divine Mind. We tend to be very friendly to and embracing of the LGBTQA community, but despite the founders identifying as gay, that is not a requirement. Most members identify as heterosexual but are welcoming of all people.

A big part of our approach is on the development of trance techniques as a gateway to magickal experience, including inhibitory and exhibitory techniques. We learn to listen to the powers through psychic development and divination and how to speak to the powers through journey work, spirit contact, and spellcraft. The faeries, angels, and animal powers, along with the mighty dead and the enlightened ancestors of magick, factor deeply into our rituals, along with the more traditional gods and spirits.

I know that you initially learned Witchcraft from the Cabot Tradition and the Temple of Nine Wells. From what I know of that system, it greatly resembles the old Silva Mind Control techniques developed in the 1960s. Can you talk about that?

Well, I would say I initially learned from the Cabot Tradition and took Sabbats at the Temple of Nine Wells when Laurie, along with Richard and Gypsy Ravish, were putting them on. I never actually did any formal training with Richard and Gypsy but considered them honored elders of Salem. My first mentor introduced me to them soon after I met Laurie, and I saw them all together at many events. Many people assume that since I have a bit of a ceremonial side, many Alexandrian friends, and a relationship with Maxine Sanders, cofounder of the Alexandrian Tradition, that I have that British Traditional Alexandrian pedigree and that perhaps I got it through the Ravishes, so I want to make sure that it's clear that I don't and that it was not my background. The rumors and assumptions people make or the things half-remembered for which we fill in the blanks can be funny. I've had several people say that I worked in a few of the shops in Salem, Massachusetts, such as Crow Haven Corner or Nu Aeon, but I never did.

As for the Cabot Tradition, each of the three degrees had a different focus. Laurie often defined it as the science, art, and religion within these three degrees. The first degree material really had four basic parts to it, from what I could see. The first degree was trying to bridge the gap between the modern mind and the experience of the magickal and psychic. This was so important to me, as I entered into the path as a skeptic. I needed some understanding, some philosophy, and acknowledgment that to the modern mind, this all sounded quite crazy.

The real core of first level was entering into a trance state and developing psychic skills in altered consciousness. It was the material that had the most resemblance to the Silva Mind Control Method, though the countdown technique was different, focusing on the spectrum of light and making some reference to the Greek mystery teachings found in her first book, *Power of the Witch*. In conversations, Laurie also referenced research from Duke University on the science of alpha and experiments in what we might call "psychism," or "parapsychology," which she studied when she was trying to understand her psychic ability from a scientific view before she became so public, and which she wanted to use when she was first asked to teach publicly. That was the basis of much of her understanding of the alpha brain-wave state. If she had further exposure to the Silva Method, I'm not aware of it, though I know there is a lot of interplay between many of the occult and self-help books of the early 1970s. I only came across it much later in my own exploration, and I've had friends and even my partner, Adam Sartwell, take the Silva Method and have good results. I tend to recommend it to people who could certainly use the techniques but have no interest in Witchcraft specifically.

The second piece of the first degree included a huge emphasis on modern scientific theories on reality, including what was, at the time, cutting-edge thought on quantum physics, popularized in books like *Stalking the Wild Pendulum* by Itzhak Bentov and *The Tao of Physics* by Fritjof Capra. Laurie wanted to give us a scientific perspective on how this all could be possible, and we got into speculations of time and dimensional travel and kundalini awakenings.

She counterbalanced it with the third part: the summation of Hermetic philosophy found in *The Kybalion* by Three Initiates. The two streams of wisdom said much the same thing, but one was from a modern perspective and one was from a more archaic viewpoint. A lot of students went on to read the *Corpus Hermeticum* to get a broader understanding, but that wasn't required.

While *The Kybalion* lent an air of the occult to the teachings, the final piece of the first degree was the aesthetic of the Witch, with stories and exercises on Avalon as the Island of Apples and a focus for the Silva-style exercise on the conjuration of an apple, from somewhere in space and time. She would discuss her relationship with the gods, particularly Isis, the role of the Witch as an intermediary in speaking with the dead, the nature of the soul, and the journey to the Summerland. We'd balance the polarity of energies and scry into a Hermetic tablet. A psychic travel gateway was sometimes referred to as the "Druid's door." Each class group in the first degree would be different but involved Laurie teaching about her life as a Witch and incorporating stories that illustrated the techniques of psychic work, science, Hermeticism, and the aesthetic of Witchcraft lore and culture.

While the first degree had a much more open and available vibe on the science of the Craft, the second degree was more about the art and culture. I almost didn't take it because it was honestly too "Witchy" for me. I was running away from the Catholic religion. I didn't want to replace it, and I wasn't really into rituals at the time. It was my mother who said, "Yes, it's like being a priest, but you get to be your own priest. You don't need an intermediary. You should do it." Here my skeptical mother, who thought I was joining a cult, was encouraging me to be a Witchcraft priest, to be independent of the traditional priesthoods. I agreed, but only if she joined me, so she did, and we embarked further on our Witchcraft adventure.

In the Cabot second degree we focused on material manifestation and the tools found in nature. Here we got into more of the path of the Witch as ritualist and spell caster, learning about the magick circle and furthering our psychic development through psychometry and scrying. We learned altar building and how to perform candle magick and make charms. In particular Laurie emphasized her version of the Witch's cord as a full talisman for the household. When I first learned it, there was a *Drawing Down the Moon*–style sacrament with the athame and chalice, though in later times it transformed into the tradition of Cerridwen's cauldron, taking three drops of sacrament in the style of the brew of inspiration. We also learned about Witchcraft culture, including things like ritual robes, jewelry, the role of magickal tattoos, living as a Witch, and using Witchcraft as we look at and act in the world.

The third degree in the tradition focused on the religion and the role of the Witch as High Priestess or High Priest and minister. The study of the Wheel of the Year and seasonal celebration, the nature of the soul, death, fear, theosophical root races, and the healing quest found in the Arthurian mysteries as well as deeper counseling and healing work were the core themes. Laurie drew upon a lot of the British occultists and their interpretations of the Arthurian quests in modern light, and the inspiration of fiction on the Priestess of Avalon. Initiates were called to service in a very public way, much like Laurie was called. Some took on ritual tattoos of initiation. And while we were public, not all of us opened shops or did public classes and readings. I know many Cabot Priestesses and Priests quietly served.

One of the fascinating things about my relationship with Laurie and working with her on her own spell book, *Laurie Cabot's Book of Shadows,* and now a memoir, is getting to hear all the stories of her own training. She claims initiation into an enigmatic group by her teacher, a British librarian from Kent, England, named Felicity, who simply called her lineage "the Witches of Kent." I've done a lot of research to try to track down more about her and prove her existence but have only been able to find a ship manifest from Liverpool that possibly refers to her, since she changed her last name when she married an American with the last name of Bumgarner. We had the opportunity to correspond with Michael Howard, author and publisher of *The Cauldron,* before his death, seeking to verify that the Witchcraft information seemed authentic to England from the time and place it was said to come, which he did. Michael was an expert in all of the old and secret lines of Witches in the United Kingdom. While he was fascinated with the folkloric system that she presented, we could find no verifiable roots, but I documented the teachings and my search in an article on the Witches of Kent for *The Cauldron* newsletter.

What Felicity taught Laurie was primarily about psychic power and spell casting, in the days before New Age shops. Stone magick used river stones. Candle magick used all white candles with paper beneath them, as there were few colored candles. Her incense was obtained at church supply shops, and she carried a British army sword for rituals and a little wooden box with a hunk of dragon's blood resin, most likely from a violin maker. While I would hesitate to call it Traditional Craft in the way people often refer to it today, it certainly wasn't Wicca, but it also wasn't a complete system, or if it was, they only gave a part of it to Laurie as a young girl. The mythos focused on Arthur, the light of Excalibur, a flower-faced Goddess, and a forest God, but there were no visionary path workings or meditations as we do today. Faeries were mentioned, but nothing specific was done with them, and all the herbcraft was magickal, not medicinal.

All in all, I find Laurie's talks on Felicity, including her initiation by sword, quite fascinating. As she found more public material from the work of Gardner, and as articles about Sanders, Raymond Buckland, and other magickal practitioners came out of the closet, she incorporated a lot of ideas for a time, refining her systems and doing what worked best for her. While her heart is with the Celtic traditions in a very modern, pan-Celtic view based on the occultism she learned early on, rooted in similar myths found in books like *The White Goddess* and *The Golden Bough,* she also has a great love of Isis and the Egyptian mythos and studied for a time with a Rosicrucian master. All of it informed the ever-evolving Cabot Tradition of Witchcraft. It was a wonderful foundation and really the teachings I needed for when and where I was in my life when I found the Craft. I think anything else would have driven me away from it. I try to keep the best as our own Temple of Witchcraft teachings evolve in similar but branching directions.

Would you say that Witchcraft is a "craft" or a "religion"? And can you talk about the difference?

It's really both. We tend to think of it as a craft in terms of making things—potions, medicines, charms, talismans, candles, and other tools. We think of it as a religion in terms of rituals involving goddesses and gods, seasons, and rites of passage. But to the Witch, I think the two can't be divided. Our spirituality is in the material world and all that we do as well as being transcendent and in dreams and visions. The true craft is the transformation of the self, of the soul. We are crafting ourselves, and rituals, tools, projects, spells, and such are the means and mechanism through which we change ourselves and get to know ourselves better. We believe everything has an animating spirit, so the wood of the wand is not just a tool but an ally and can speak its wisdom. Its very presence in conscious engagement changes us, even if we don't have clear "communication" from the spirit of the wood or tree. We are artists of consciousness, and through our hands and our minds, through our actions and our hearts, we craft the art of our life. Our whole life, from birth to death, is one big ritual. Our whole life is an act of art. Religion is simply a way of thinking about connection.

Whom do Witches worship?

Worship is such a hard word. We often say honor, respect, venerate, or work with, so that we do not imply the same sense of subservience that many have when coming from a religion that worships a monotheistic God. I think Witches venerate the primordial spirits of creation and all their subsequent manifestations. My own personal practices recognize a Goddess and God stemming from the Divine Heart, Mind, and Will of a nongendered creative source—a Great Spirit, if you will. The Goddess and God have many cultural manifestations and guises. I tend to see the Goddess as threefold, as the fates of past, present, and future and of the heavens, Earth, and underworld. In those forms, she is the queen of Witches, but I could just as easily see her manifest in the Star Goddess and Earth Goddess. I see the God as the two-faced God, divine twins who are sometimes conjoined as the Lord of Light and Life and the Lord of Darkness and Death.

In my personal relationships, the goddess Macha, an Irish goddess associated with the Morrígan triune, is a matron and ally. She directed me to start teaching and doing healing work professionally and promised me I would be provided for as long as I did.

So, who a Witch works with directly and how that Witch sees divinity I think depends on the Witch.

When Witches meet, what do they usually do?

We could meet for a class, social group, or ritual. In the context of a ritual, we usually discuss the intent of the rite. We set up the altar with all the tools we need for the ritual. Then we cleanse ourselves in incense or with salt and water. We create sacred space through the casting of the magick circle and call to the powers of the four elements and directions. Once the temple is set in this manner, we evoke the goddesses and gods we wish to commune with through incantations and offerings. The work, the purpose of the rite, is enacted, often involving song, dance, meditation, drumming, or trance. It could be as simple as a candle spell or as big as an intricate celebration play. Once the work is done, the space is released much as it was created. We thank the divinities and spirits. We release the four directional powers and then release the circle, casting it out into the universe as a sign of our work.

Do Witches really do "spells" or can they do "magic"?

Yes, most definitely. I live a life of magick. I think everyone does. Magick is in every thought we think, every word we speak, and every action we take. The only difference between Witches and most people is that hopefully Witches know this! We are constantly casting spells of blessing or curses, often upon ourselves, and never know it.

A specific ritual act of magick is a spell, and we do spells all the time. When you first learn Witchcraft you do a lot of Waxing Moon magick, a type of magick to gain things. You realize that it works and do a lot of it, trying to gain all the things you think you lack. Then you grow a bit wiser and start doing Waning Moon magick to banish and dismiss all the forces that block you, to get rid of all that you don't want or need anymore, like a spiritual house cleaning of your life. Only then can you be open for real blessings. Hopefully, you reach a point of balance, manifesting and banishing as needed, for yourself and, when called upon, often for others.

If you do any spells, can you give examples?

A very simple spell to disperse and absorb unwanted, harmful energies from a home, particularly a place that has had violence or a lot of verbal arguments that are not dispelled by the more traditional methods of smudging with sage or incense, is to get a large bowl and place half of an onion inside it. Fill the bowl with vinegar and add a few tablespoons of salt. Leave it out overnight. This will absorb harmful energy. Dispose of it all off your property. Don't leave it in the kitchen trash, and unless you have a garbage disposal, do not put it down the drain. Ideally, if you can put it into a sewer off your property, all the better. It's simple and easy as folk spells go but works for almost anyone. No religious or ritual knowledge is needed to make it work. The esoteric properties of the natural substances work in your favor.

Are you a hereditary Witch?

By the technical definition of the term, no, I'm not, but I hear a lot of rumors about how I am. I do think spiritually that everyone called to be a Witch has it in their blood. I'm not necessarily talking about an elitist lineage or any racial superiority, as I see Witchcraft in all cultures as an orientation and vocation, but something deep within our blood and bones that calls us to the path. My friend Orion Foxwood, another notable Witch and author, teaches that if you are a Witch, you weren't the first one in your family, even if you don't know them. Somewhere, sometime, someone in your lineage was also called to the path, and you are carrying it forward. I agree with that wholeheartedly.

But when I started studying Witchcraft with Laurie Cabot, my mother thought I was joining a cult. She was friends with my first teacher and I think chalked it up to harmless fun in her backyard when I first started studying. But when my teacher took me to her teacher, Laurie Cabot, my mom got worried. She decided, rather than forbid me from study, as I was eighteen at the time while still living at home and going to college, she would feign interest. Either I would no longer think it was cool, or if I stuck with it, she would know exactly what I was doing and if it was dangerous or illegal. Later, she got so involved and enchanted with the idea of being her own priestess—without the need for a Catholic priest to act as intermediary—and of seeing the kitchen and the garden and woods as sacred churches that she gave up Catholicism for Witchcraft, and we formed our first Coven of three together with a good friend who is like a spiritual sister to me and daughter to my mom.

While my surname is Polish, my mother's family is decidedly Italian, and I later heard people talk about how lucky I was, being raised in a Strega (Italian Witch) household in a family of Witches. They assumed that since my mother was a Witch, she always had been and had taught me a family lineage. We didn't hear the word *Strega* until years later, and while she adopted it as an identity, she was never formally initiated into any Strega traditions. She borrowed and incorporated their folk practices, though, particularly things from the books of Raven Grimassi, and some of it became a part of our Coven.

Did your family carry stories about Witches or did you find out about it all recently?

While there were no family Witches, we did have folk healers and what I now see as magickal traditions. My great-aunt Mary read tea leaves, but just for fun. She never took it seriously, but people would come to her from the neighborhood to get answers. She was really devoted to Mother Mary and had a bit of a shrine in her bedroom, which I guess was not uncommon for devout Italian Catholics, but looking back on it, it all seems rather goddess-oriented and Witchy to me now.

My mother's godmother taught my grandmother and mother how to break the evil eye using a needle, pot, boiling water, and extra-virgin olive oil. It was a tradition passed on during Christmas Eve, and before my mother passed, she taught it to me. I think she and I made some Witchy variations, no longer being Catholic, but the essential ritual is the same.

One of the most striking Witch stories from my family was of a woman in the Italian neighborhood in Lawrence, Massachusetts, where my mother's family raised her, being the local Witch. She lived alone at the end of the street and had long white hair. The other kids called her a Witch and their parents did too. My mother said that everyone was afraid of her, but she felt a bit sorry for her. She seemed lonely. But if you had a big problem and removing the evil eye didn't work, you could go to her at night, and she would help you. As an adult looking back, my mom didn't know how real those stories were, but that was what she was told as a child. She saw the Witch several times but never really talked to her. It was something the kids were told not to do. So that always stuck with me about Witches being real on some level.

My father's family really had no interest as far as I can tell in the esoteric and occult. They divorced themselves from the Polish and Lithuanian culture pretty readily, and I never had the food or heard the stories or really much of anything from that side of the family. I found it ironic and fun that Lithuania was the last country of Europe to convert to Christianity, being one-quarter Lithuanian, but never learned any folklore from that side of the family.

Have you had relationships or friendships with other New England Witches? If so, with whom? And what were the most significant experiences or learnings you had from those encounters?

Of course, since so many of my closest friends are Witches. Some are famous and well known in and out of the community and some are not. Obviously, there is a connection with Laurie Cabot. While it was strictly teacher-student in my twenties, we have since forged a good friendship, and I'm so honored to have her in my life. She invited me as an author to do a book signing at her shop in Salem, the Cat, the Crow & the Crown, and soon I was teaching there regularly. I had never officially completed my third degree in the Cabot Tradition. When my group was studying, Laurie was going through some difficult changes and had left Crow Haven Corner, so she invited me back as an independent study to complete it, as I couldn't make classes with my own professional schedule. We also began working on some of her legacy: a spell book, a book of shadows, and now a memoir. It's been quite fun to work with her on this level too, and we can get into great talks about magick, faeries, and life. Through her I've gotten to know her daughter Penny Cabot quite well and love hanging out with her. She's an amazing artist and has been such a help with the books we have done together, filling in details and asking questions I wouldn't think to ask.

Also, through Laurie I've had a longtime relationship with Christian Day, an often infamous author and owner of the stores Hex and Omen in Salem, Massachusetts. We have a kinship since we are two of Laurie's students from the same generation who really went off to do our own thing, find our own success, and return and really honor her influence and legacy in our own lives. In some ways I've focused on her teaching and religious work, and he's focused on reaching out to the non-Witchcraft community through the retail world in Salem and, now, New Orleans.

I've been delighted to know many community leaders, teachers, Coven organizers, healers, store owners, and simple practitioners. Many are a part of the Temple of Witchcraft community, like life partners Steve Kenson and Adam Sartwell, fellow founders of the Temple, who are New England residents and were Witches before I met them. Steve is really responsible for so much of the curriculum of the Temple, though he doesn't like to take credit for it. His studies in Qabalah and chaos magick influenced both the topics and the attitude of the Temple as it evolved. He is also the voice of reason and clear communication in my life. Before I send an email I can ask him, "Is this too bitch?" and he honestly answers, often with a yes. Adam is a great intuitive, deeply connected to the faery world, and lives in a state of betweenness yet functions so well; he's taught me how to stand between quite a bit better than I did. His background in working with kids who are often themselves quite traumatized or disabled has kept him with a childlike sense of wonder, which I think is vital to the Witch. He reminds me to be more playful.

Alix Wright has become my longtime magickal partner and confidant. When I was leading rituals in the Wheel of the Year series in the Boston area for Unicorn Books and later Lap of the Goddess productions, she was my partner through it all, and if I couldn't make an event, she took over. Now she runs all the rituals for the Temple of Witchcraft. Christopher Giroux, the longtime manager of Unicorn, and later Seven Stars Books in Cambridge, is also an amazing friend and spiritual brother. He is the person I go to when I need advice or have a problem. He will tell you how it is with the motto, "Don't shake the tree if you don't want the fruit." I adore that about him.

Robbi Packard, owner of the metaphysical shop Robin's Nest, has also become an amazing Witch friend. We have a mutual love of gardens and do a lot of gardening projects together with Witchy herbs. She's taught me a lot about the nitty-gritty planning of landscaping, just charging forward and figuring it out, and how to build community in a public setting. Her shop community does a wonderful job of connecting people. One person who was incredibly supportive of me, whom I don't think is still in New England, was Shelly, the owner of the Wishful Witch in Deerfield, New Hampshire. She supported by newsletter and classes and was just an all-around amazing person, so openly available in her very public Witch shop. I often wonder how she is doing and where she ended up after she closed the store. She taught me that you could be out and proud and not be in Salem, Massachusetts.

Though they are recent additions to New England, I have a very close relationship with Raven Grimassi and Stephanie Taylor Grimassi. They have both been elders, teachers, and mentors to me in the Craft and in life. Not having a traditional High Priestess and High Priest Coven structure in my life, they are like the spiritual parents I never had, and have been great friends and supporters to me. Even our most mundane time hanging out, eating, or sharing a drink has been filled with magic and wisdom. When they lived in California, I stayed at their house on my first book tour. We had only met a few months before that, but they generously opened their house to me, and it was my last stop before flying back home. Since then we've done numerous events and festivals together and had many fun and crazy things happen. That's life on the road. Witches can get into some bizarre situations. I was so excited to have them move closer to me. We make an effort to visit quite often, and anytime they can come to the Temple teach, I'll have them.

Do you have any interactions with Witches in the Salem, Massachusetts, area? What is your impression of the current interest in Witchcraft in Salem, centuries after the Witch hysteria of Puritan times?

I honestly love it, simply because it makes it all so accessible to the seeker but also distracts the nonserious seeker with the glitz and glam of it. It's where I started, and it was a lot of fun. Samhain on Gallow's Hill is a trip. I've done it a few times, and while I prefer more intense and private experiences, it was well worth it. I have a lot of friends in Salem and applaud the stores and groups being open and visible to the public, to further the cause of the Witch.

I got my start with Gypsy and Richard Ravish, along with Laurie Cabot, and the Temple of Nine Wells on Gallow's Hill. When I can, I attend the Cabot-Kent Hermetic Temple Sabbats, though I'm often busy running my own in New Hampshire. I've shopped and taught at quite a few of the stores in Salem. The good ones have some staying power, even if they have to make compromises to keep financially solvent. You can find good books and deep practitioners if you know where to look. Three of my favorite readers hold office hours in Salem still. But a lot of people get trapped in the sense of drama, the sense of self and ego, and being important in Salem. While they can cause a lot of difficulties, it's a good filter for those of us wanting to teach things more deeply. There are some amazing groups, shops, and teachers in Salem, and you can get in with them eventually too, but those who are enamored of the idea of being a Salem Witch usually don't last long in my classes and groups, and it's good they have found something that they feel makes them happy. The desire for the fame filters them out and reveals where they are in their own process, which I find quite helpful as a teacher.

Have you experienced any difficulties—any problems, persecution, or prejudice—as a result of being a Witch? Can you describe a time or times when that happened?

Thankfully I haven't had a lot of problems or persecution as a Witch. Even before being a full-time Priest and author, I worked in many creative spaces, particularly the music industry. There people thought I was eccentric and didn't necessarily believe that anything I was talking about was real, though at times people came to me for readings and help without wanting others to know. Such is the classic experience of the Witch, I think!

My dad first thought it was amusing that my mother and I were Witches. At one point I think he felt we had devoted enough time, space, and money to it, and he became a bit passive-aggressive about it in small ways. Then we offered to do a spell for him when he was having difficulty at work, and it was so successful, creating a win-win circumstance for everyone involved, that he started to both believe and value. Since that time, he's been a huge supporter of my work in the Craft, and even after the passing of my mother, he still comes to all our public Sabbats and keeps relationships with people in the Temple of Witchcraft.

I think the worst of it was when we bought property for the Temple in Salem, New Hampshire, which, as I mentioned, is my hometown. I truly thought that it would be no big deal. New Hampshire is fiscally conservative, not religiously. Just as we were preparing to present to the town planning board a proposal to open the house as a classroom and religious worship space, a neighbor who likes us "warned" us that another neighbor was circulating what I felt was a very mean, fear-based letter to all the rest of the neighbors. I went over to speak with him, and he slammed the door in my face when he realized who I was and called me a liar before we could even talk. The fervor he stirred up truly shocked me, and I was glad we had a lawyer at our side when he tried to turn the planning board meeting into a hearing on the legitimacy of Witchcraft as a religion, after we had our 501(c)(3) from the federal government. We passed with five out of five votes in our favor, as we were in accordance with the state and local law for our plans.

What are special holy days for Witches? Can you please describe what Witches do on their holy days? How do you celebrate?

I think we celebrate all the "normal" Witch holidays—the eight Sabbats of the modern Wheel of the Year and Full Moon Esbats for the community. We reserve Dark Moon Esbats for ministers, High Priestesses, and High Priests, as a place for support, sharing, and advanced teaching. Rituals have traditions but are also artistic expressions, so they are different each time, and styles change depending on the team leading them and the size of the ritual. They involve drumming, dancing, ceremony, meditation, shamanic journeying, and song.

Our biggest difference in the Temple of Witchcraft Tradition is the added "ninth" holiday of the Wheel of the Year, the Feast of Hecate on August 13. We usually do a public oracular rite, with three Priestesses overshadowed, or lightly possessed, by an aspect of Hecate, the Goddess Queen of Witches and the Soul of the World. She speaks to individuals, answering their questions, through the three Priestesses and then gives a collective triple message to the community. It's quite a wonderful experience.

In teaching the fluidity of gender, I've actually been, in a pinch, one of the oracles overshadowed by Hecate, but usually I'm the attendant helper to our High Priestess in charge of the public rites, Alix Wright, and maintain her health and well-being while she is overshadowed by Hecate. I've noticed that many of the more modern yet seriously occult traditions of Witchcraft have been adding similar rituals to their schedules, which is really wonderful. We need to make deeper work more available to the public.

GAULTHERIA
Central Massachusetts

First, can you say a bit about who you are, where you live, and what you do for a living these days?

I'm a woman in my early sixties who lives in central Massachusetts. By day, I'm a writer in a corporate environment.

How and when did you decide you were a Witch?

I didn't decide I was a Witch. I decided I wanted to be one, sought out teachers, and trained to be one. I wish I had had one of those childhood awakenings where I knew instinctively who I was, but, alas, no. I was raised as a Catholic, so my knowledge of ancient Pagan cultures was very sparse and very biased.

How do you personally define Witchcraft?

My definition has changed over the years as the public face of Witchcraft has changed. Is Witchcraft the spell-working path, while Wicca is the nature worship? Or is Paganism the nature worship and Wicca the blend of Witchcraft and Paganism? I don't know what to call it; I worship nature, but I also believe in spells and superstition.

Which tradition of Witchcraft do you follow? How did you find that tradition?

Though I've settled into a solitary path these days, I started out in the Alexandrian tradition, which is more Coven based. It was the only Coven I could find at the time. I hadn't been looking for a tradition but had been looking for Witches. Someone I knew had heard about a Coven and eventually I ferreted out the contact information. The person I connected with seemed rational and it sounded like a serious group. I was invited to meet the rest of the group and eventually invited to join.

What makes your approach or tradition unique from any others out there?

I think that all solitary paths are, by nature, unique. How we incorporate our belief systems into our daily lives differs because all of our lives are different. Maybe what's most different about my path is that I'm very private about what I believe. With very few exceptions, I don't disclose my beliefs to coworkers, neighbors, or friends who aren't also Witches. Unless I'm hanging out with other Witches, you won't see me wearing occult jewelry. (That doesn't mean I'm not wearing it; it just means it's tucked away discreetly.)

Although I worship gods and goddesses, this is only part of my belief system. I'm probably more likely to do a spell for good luck than to pray to the gods. Part of that is my belief that they don't want to be bothered with trivial requests, so if, for example, I'm looking for a job, I'm going to pay attention to all the mundane details like writing a good résumé, dressing for the interview, and researching the company. But I might also try to schedule the interview when the planets are favorable, and I might create a good luck charm and tuck it in a private place. Before entering the building for the interview, I'll do a mental dusting off of all negative energies and will positive energy into the encounter. It's only if the situation is dire that I will petition the gods. I think that probably differs from the usual practice today, but I'm not sure. For healing, though, especially if it's someone close or a critical situation, I will definitely petition the gods in addition to sending healing energy from myself and lighting a candle with intention.

Would you say that Witchcraft is a "craft" or a "religion"? And can you talk about the difference?

I've tried to pick the right words over the years, but as I said, the definition keeps changing.

So let's say that path A is the craft. You apprentice to a teacher and learn hard skills like scrying, tarot card reading, astrology, magical herbalism, and spells. In 2004, I read about the opening of the Grey School of Wizardry and wondered if this was an example of what I considered the craft aspect. In the beginning, it seemed that people were saying it was something to cash in on Harry Potter, but reading the Grey School's web pages now, it seems more like what I visualize as the occult arts.

Let's say path B is the nature worship where you worship the gods and nature and interact and protect their realm. Examples of this are generic Pagan groups, including the Covenant of Unitarian Universalist Pagans.

Although there are people who will practice only the craft side and people who worship the gods but do not do spells, many people at this time, in this part of the country, combine the two. But what should we call that combination?

Whom do Witches worship?

I'm going to assume we mean someone who may or may not perform spells or do divination but worships the gods of nature, the Old Ones.

There are some who worship only the Goddess, and some who worship both God and Goddess. Some worship in a metaphorical way. For example, when they invoke the Goddess, they invoke an energy that is visualized in the form of the woman, but they aren't worshipping one particular goddess. Others, though, are dedicated to a named goddess and know her legends, her likes, and her dislikes.

When Witches meet, what do they usually do?

It varies so much from one group to another and has changed over the years. My experience has been that they greet with a hug and socialize a bit, catching up with each other. If it's a Coven celebrating a Sabbat, they bring food for the feast. They hurry to the kitchen, refrigerating it or warming it as needed, and when everyone has arrived, the group changes into ritual clothes and goes over the ritual. Some groups don't change clothing but instead wear street clothes. Some don't go over the ritual first but instead provide directions as the ritual unfolds. After the ritual, they feast, socialize a bit more, and then part.

Some groups won't perform healings as part of the Sabbat; others prefer to do so, riding on the wave of Sabbat energy.

Do Witches really do "spells" or can they do "magic"?

There's a very good example of a spell to prevent someone from harming another in the novel *The Old Power Returns* by Morven Westfield. The Witches create a wax poppet representing the person doing harm. They name the figure and then bind it while chanting their desire (to bind him from harming them).

In real life, a group might instead place a picture on the altar and invoke the gods and beg them to restrain him. And in other faiths, they might also have the picture, but instead would pray to their god.

So, can Witches do magic? Do the gods of other faiths answer prayers? Or is it all just coincidence? I have witnessed many successes—and many failures—in both scenarios.

If you do any spells, can you give examples?

I do spells of protection when I'm alone or when I'm traveling. At home, I'll visualize a circle surrounding me. When traveling, I'll carry a token that I've imbued with protective energy. It's often a stone or metal circle with protective runes engraved on it. For healings, I'll anoint a candle with healing oil and send energy to the person in need.

Are you a hereditary Witch?

No.

Did your family carry stories about Witches or did you find out about it all recently?

Not specifically Witchcraft, but folklore and superstition. I remember avoiding walking on a sidewalk crack ("Walk on a crack, break your mother's back") and looking for lucky four-leaf clovers. I remember that someone in the family had a rabbit's foot—I don't know if it was real or not—on a keychain.

Have you had relationships or friendships with other New England Witches? If so, with whom? And what were the most significant experiences or learnings you had from those encounters?

Oh, yes, many over the years. I met the owners of shops, the local tarot readers, and eventually Coven leaders and members. I feel awkward naming them; many are well known and I'd feel like I was namedropping. Many, though, are unknown, and I would fear compromising their privacy. Also, I'd be mortified if I forgot to mention someone who has been a major influence.

So I'll mention just a few of the local people I was fortunate enough to meet before they passed through the veil: Michael, founder of the Order of Ganymede; Morganna Davies, High Priestess and author of *Keepers of the Flame*; and Richard Ravish, High Priest of the Coven of Akhelarre and Magus of the Temple of Nine Wells ATC in Salem, Massachusetts.

Do you have any interactions with Witches in the Salem, Massachusetts, area? What is your impression of the current interest in Witchcraft in Salem, centuries after the Witch hysteria of Puritan times?

When I first became interested, I wasn't well-off financially, and the cars I owned were too unreliable to go there often. Then the gas crisis hit, and it became too expensive. Once there, I was too shy to really get to know people and didn't know where to go to meet the genuine Witches, so I didn't make the trip very often. Eventually, though, I met and became friends with many from the Salem area.

Have you experienced any difficulties—any problems, persecution, or prejudice—as a result of being a Witch? Can you describe a time or times when that happened?

As I said, I'm very private about my beliefs, but in the beginning, I was more open about it. I got the usual "You shouldn't get involved with that! It's dangerous!" and "You know this is all the work of the devil, right?" It also made my dating life difficult because people in the suburbs were particularly wary of anything out of the norm. Men dropped me because they thought I was weird, or I dropped them when they responded with a sneer and a condescending tone. I never suffered job problems because I didn't talk about witchcraft at work.

My hiding in the closet, though, has cost me too, especially in the heady days of the surge in interest. I remember one Witch who told me she thought I was being ridiculous being afraid of persecution. I remember another expressing sadness that I didn't have the courage to fight for my beliefs—and those of others. We all make our choices. I knew people who lost jobs and custody battles. I knew others whose parents broke all contact with them. Maybe that's all changed now, but it had a big impact on me and my willingness to be too public.

What are special holy days for Witches? Can you please describe what Witches do on their holy days? How do you celebrate?

The Alexandrian tradition and my personal solitary practice both follow the Wheel of the Year, which starts with Samhain in October. It's considered a Greater Sabbat, along with Imbolc (also called Candlemas), Beltaine, and Lughnasad (Lammas). Interspersed are the four Lesser Sabbats, which correspond to astronomical/astrological events: the Winter Solstice, the Vernal Equinox, the Summer Solstice, and the Autumnal Equinox.

What Witches do depends on their tradition, their Coven's pantheon, and geographical location. Whereas English Witches might celebrate Yule and Imbolc outdoors, many northern New England witches take the celebrations indoors then.

The Witches with whom I've celebrated the holy days usually focus on the agricultural aspects of the season (e.g., at the Vernal Equinox you focus on growing things and bringing new projects to fruition, and at Lughnasad and Autumnal Equinox you concentrate on the stages of the harvest.) Others, those who follow a specific pantheon (for example, Greek or Egyptian), may celebrate a deity associated with a specific time.

My solitary practice is sometimes as simple as a meditation on the Sabbat or a visualization of past Sabbats or even just the lighting of a candle. Sometimes I'm invited to Sabbats with people I worked with in the past, and the Sabbat celebration varies based on their practices.

Any other thoughts you care to add?

I worked with Covens from the mid-1970s to the mid-1990s. I saw a lot of practices change in that time. If you want more examples of how some Covens in the New England area worked around the late 1970s and early 1980s, I recommend that you read Margot Adler's excellent *Drawing Down the Moon*. If you prefer something less scholarly, check out Morven Westfield's two novels, *Darksome Thirst* and *The Old Power Returns*. In the novels, Coven members brainstorm, support each other, and explore the unknown together. Though they're not 100 percent consensus-based, they practice mutual respect. Even though the books are set in the past, I think they still provide an accurate picture.

GWEN OWEN
Biddeford, Maine

First, can you say a bit about who you are, where you live, and what you do for a living these days?

I am a fifty-four-year-old female who lives with her partner of eighteen years. I have his two wonderful children in my life and one five-year-old grandson. Time really flies! I enjoy being outdoors at the beach or in the woods, where I can be alone and find my source of strength, which is nature. I am an artist who does oil painting and works with natural objects that I make jewelry with. I have worked as a psychotherapist for the past fifteen years.

Which religion were you raised in?

I was raised in the Spiritualist church and am third generation. I grew up in Buffalo, New York, close to Lily Dale, which is the hub for Spiritualists.

This is interesting—can you please give more details on any mystical experiences and how these led to your Witch path ultimately?

Well, I was raised in a home where Eastern thought was "normal" and seeing/hearing spirit was too. All my life I have been able to talk with those who have moved on to the other side. I have been in mediumship groups and have two master-level degrees in Reiki. During my adult years I was drawn to Witchcraft because of a need to go deeper into the mystery of life, the desire to know more. As a twenty-year-old, I read the Bible cover to cover, but that didn't seem to do it for me (too much guilt and sin).

I took a comparative religion course and a philosophy course when I was an undergrad. I was getting closer, but it was not enough. I met a friend after college who was a Witch, and she and I talked about the tenets of Witchcraft and how it worked. It intrigued me and seemed to resonate with me. Then one day my partner, Tom, and I were in a local metaphysical shop were Christopher Penczak was holding a class. Tom offered to pay for it, so I went and fell in love with the practice and completed Christopher's Temple Tradition.

How and when did you decide you were a Witch?

I decided to become a Witch after I took the class with Christopher around 2004. He made me feel very comfortable during the class. I had had an interest for many years but had an approach avoidance issue with it prior.

How do you personally define Witchcraft?

I define the Craft as the ability to understand the mystery of life, to heal the self and then others, and to understand and then develop one's true will through meditation and spell work.

Which tradition of Witchcraft do you follow? How did you find that tradition?

At the present I would say that I follow the Temple Tradition, but I do still fall back on Spiritualism. The Temple Tradition is a study of the philosophy and science of Witchcraft. To me the approach is a well-researched, grounded look at what Witchcraft is and how it works. It incorporates quantum physics into the philosophy of Witchcraft. In other words, if one can understand how the world works on the micro level and see how everything is connected on that level, then they can see how that works on the macro level. "As above, so below."

What makes your approach or tradition unique from any others out there?

My approach is unique because of my upbringing in the Spiritualist church and my scientific interest in quantum theory. I like quantum theory because it really works well with each tradition. So, for me, if I look at the first law of thermodynamics, which states that energy cannot be destroyed but only transformed into something else, that tells me that the energy that animates me will never die. The energy I put out in a spell will never die. I know from physics that nothing is really solid—not me, not the table. This tells me that I have the ability to affect my life and my world. I'm a "prove it to me" kind of girl, and that's what does it for me.

Would you say that Witchcraft is a "craft" or a "religion"? And can you talk about the difference?

I think it is a craft, a religion, and a science. It's a craft such as that needed when one is an artist: you learn the basics of spell work and then use it to create your own spells. It's a religion in that we worship different gods, goddesses, and the Earth, and, for me, a science in that one can see various methods that work over time. In other words, the scientific method does seem to hold true. Also if someone studies quantum theory, they will see how it all works, how it makes sense.

Whom do Witches worship?

Some, but not all, worship various pantheons of gods, goddesses, and of course, the Earth. It's really up to the person.

Which deities do you worship? Are you devoted to a particular one?

I work with the Celtic pantheon such as the goddess Macha, Manannan, and Brigid. My devotion is to Macha, as I believe being able to look at and incorporate one's dark side is very important in order to have a complete and healthy psyche.

When Witches meet, what do they usually do?

Sometimes they have lunch and bitch about their jobs. Many times talk turns to the nature of the universe. They also can have ritual together, although I'm a solitary.

Do Witches really do "spells" or can they do "magic"?

Of course they can! Spells and magic are in a way like prayers but with the added magic of natural objects to enhance the "prayer" or thought. Or as many folks say, "I'm putting it out to the universe."

If you do any spells, can you give examples?

Yes, I do spells. I have several ongoing spells for myself and my family and then add ones when I see places they might be needed, such as Syria during the crisis.

Can you please explain what you mean here? What does a spell for the Syrian crisis look like?

I began a spell that I asked the Temple to do with me for the safety of the Syrian refugees. It involved lighting a candle each day and asking for help for safe travel, and it lasted for a month.

Are you a hereditary Witch?

While I can't be sure, I don't think so.

Did your family carry stories about Witches or did you find out about it all recently?

Sorry, boring in that area.

Have you had relationships or friendships with other New England Witches? If so, with whom? And what were the most significant experiences or learnings you had from those encounters?

My other Witch friends include one Witch and one woman who is into shamanism and whom I've known for twenty years. This woman and I devised a wonderful spell to get rid of a terrible neighbor I had and then to attract a new one. It worked very well, and we are very pleased with our new neighbor.

Do you have any interactions with Witches in the Salem, Massachusetts, area? What is your impression of the current interest in Witchcraft in Salem, centuries after the Witch hysteria of Puritan times?

I really do not have contact with folks in Salem. I see a lot of people, though, that seem to be attracted to it like a fad, which is both upsetting and understandable. Sometimes we have to try on different hats before we find the correct one.

Any other thoughts you care to add?

I think it's great that you're doing a book on us, and I hope that it inspires others to see us as just like anyone else. We're not scary, we don't worship Satan, and we don't eat babies. We love the Earth and want to save it and help others in the process. However, don't mess with us; we can take care of that shit!

GWION VRAN
Providence, Rhode Island

First, can you say a bit about who you are, where you live, and what you do for a living these days?

I am a lifetime New Yorker who happens to live in Providence, Rhode Island. I am the most Sagittarius person you will ever meet, flinging myself headlong and ever so fervently into my latest endeavors with a good amount of zest and gusto.

By trade, I am a graphic/design project manager. I graduated from Pratt Institute with a certificate in graphic design. I have spent most of my professional life in the investment banking industry, managing large print projects since 1996.

I moved to Rhode Island in 2012 in order to lend a hand to one of my dearest friends. The move took me out of the finance industry but allowed me to continue in many ways as a project manager and designer. My life in Rhode Island has the same focus as it had in New York and New Jersey in the mundane arena, except without the stress that is associated with New York suburbs.

Currently, I do much freelance design work, both print and digital. I am also the design director of *The Witches' Almanac*. My relationship with the *Almanac* began in 2000 as a writer of several features. I have taken an active role as an editor as well.

Well, enough about my mundane side . . . on the magickal side, I have had a long and winding path that I began traveling in 1972. My interest in the occult would not be sated easily. After so many years as a magician and a Witch, I pretty much consider myself a lifetime student.

I currently am the High Priest of Gardnerian, Minoan Brotherhood, and Alexandrian Covens as well as of the New England Covens of Traditionalist Witches (NECTW).

Gardnerian Witchcraft is based on the teaching that Gerald Gardner transmitted to his students, claiming that much of the practice was received via his initiation in the New Forest area. The Minoan Brotherhood is an all-male tradition based on the customs and calendar of Minoan and Aegean peoples. The NECTW takes its teachings from the familial practices of the late Gwen Thompson. Alexandrian Witchcraft is based on the teachings of Alex Sanders and is in many ways very similar to Gardnerian Witchcraft.

How and when did you decide you were a Witch?

I did not define myself as a Witch when I first forayed into the world of the occult. Rather, I identified as a magician, arriving at this conclusion at the tender age of eleven. I would scour the local library for anything that I could find on the occult arts. In the privacy of my room, while my family was sleeping, I could often be found surrounding myself in a ring of salt, invoking one spirit or another. Much to my surprise, the spirits would make themselves known in one way or another.

I would also peruse the shelves of the local bookstores. Of course, in 1972 the pickings were slim. Unlike today, most bookstores did not have an occult/New Age section. Be that as it may, I found a pocket book on Egyptian magic and began to execute the practices outlined in it. In short order, I had a white robe made from an old bedspread on which I meticulously painted the required symbols using berries from the woods. My altar was a simple flat stone, and my ritual space was the deep woods.

I found my way to the Magickal Childe bookstore in 1974, and it was there that I would truly learn what it was to be a Witch. It was under the watchful (and cranky) eye of Herman Slater that I would begin to hone the skills that would someday allow me to utter, "I am a Witch." Back then, a Witch by definition was someone who had received initiation into the "witch cult"; those of us who were in Herman's Pagan Way identified as Pagans. To call ourselves otherwise would bring a reprimand from Herman or his working partner.

In 1978, I finally could call myself a Witch. I left the cozy Pagan Way at the Magickal Childe, and I received initiation into Wicca two months before my seventeenth birthday, from the first known African-American Gardnerian High Priestess in the United States. I was one of the youngest initiates in the New York City area. In fact, my initiation caused quite an uproar. My initiating Priestess was known to a good many in the community, and while this did not affect her standing in the community, I was shunned out of fear. The situation fit rather well with my persona, as not only was I an outcast most of my life, I also had a love of shocking people.

How do you personally define Witchcraft?

Witchcraft is the magico-religious system that brings me into harmony with the world around me.

On the religious side, Witchcraft allows me to express divinity within myself as well as seeing it in my fellow humans and the natural world that surrounds me. I understand divinity to be both immanent and transcendent. Inasmuch as it is immanent, Witchcraft allows me to interact and assume divinity within myself via evocation. It allows me to see the sacred within others, animals, and minerals. I recognize the sacred within the world via the cycles that we live through. In my case, spring, summer, fall, and winter are times to remember the cycle of the divine as it manifests in the natural world.

It is through my understanding of divine as transcending that I am able to look beyond my world and aspire to divinity in the nonmaterial. The teaching and practices that I have honed over the years allow me to sit on the precipice of time and space to look into the eye of divinity. This encounter is one that is beyond words and beyond "practical understanding." The encounter of the transcendent is truly a kenning that integrates my being on all levels with the universe.

A quote from Aleister Crowley's *Magick, Book 4*:

> To "invoke" is to "call in", just as to "evoke" is to "call forth". This is the essential difference between the two branches of Magick. In invocation, the macrocosm floods the consciousness. In evocation, the magician, having become the macrocosm, creates a microcosm.*

Where there are dissonances in my life, I use magick to resolve the situation. This is where I believe that Witchcraft differs from other spiritual endeavors. My recourse for solving both mundane and spiritual incongruence is always magick. Eddie Buczynski drilled into my mind: "We are Witches; we don't pray, we do!"

Witchcraft is a way of life rather than a practice. It the prism through which I interpret meaning and participate in the world around me.

Which tradition of Witchcraft do you follow? How did you find that tradition?

I have been initiated and elevated through a number of traditions of Witchcraft. As I mentioned earlier, my initial training in Witchcraft was through Herman Slater's Pagan Way, which eventually grew to be his training Coven, also known as an outer court. The Coven that Herman ran for several years was a New York Welsh Tradition Coven (NYWT). I would say that in many ways I am very much grounded in that tradition.

Notwithstanding the above, the training that I received subsequent to my initiation was strictly Gardnerian. This was the tradition that I would call home for a number of years, including the more recent years. My foray into the world of Gardnerian Witchcraft began when my

---

*Aleister Crowley, *Magick, Book 4* (York Beach, Maine: Samuel Weiser, 2000), 147.

initiating High Priestess was invited by Herman Slater to give a lecture on Gardnerian Witchcraft to his training Coven. After the lecture was over, I decided to stay and talk with the lecturer, as I found her quite engaging. We spoke at length, and as I began to pack my notebook into my knapsack, she inquired as to how long I had been initiated. I advised that I was not an initiate but had been in the outer court for three years. She was shocked and offered me her phone number, which I happily accepted. After several calls and several face-to-face meetings, I asked for initiation. As I related in a previous question, I was underage; however, I was emancipated. She agreed to initiate and train me, and the rest is history.

Two years subsequent to my initiation and training as a Gardnerian, I was asked by Eddie Buczynski if I would be interested in forming the first coed Coven of the tripartite Minoan Witchcraft. I had known Eddie for a number of years as a mentor and then as a friend. I heartily agreed to take on the task. At the time, I was the High Priest of a Gardnerian Coven. Eddie and I decided that initially I would Circle with his Minoan Brother Coven (actually, Covens are called Groves in the Minoan system). Because of some very moving experiences, Eddie and I decided that my place in the Minoan system would best be served if I stayed in the Brotherhood. I stayed in Eddie's Grove beyond his departure and eventually struck out on my own to form a Grove when I moved to Florida. This was both a boon and a bane. The incipience of AIDs would decimate the Minoan Brotherhood. Eventually moving back to New York City, my Grove was the only Grove to survive the scourge of HIV. Out of my Grove came a number of leaders who would help to repopulate the Brotherhood. To this day, 99 percent of the Brotherhood takes their lineage from one of my initiates.

As the years went on, I eventually took initiations in the NYWT and later into the system out of which it sprang, the NECTW. It has been a long time since I ran an NYWT Coven, but I am still involved with the NECTW.

I also sought and took initiation into the Alexandrian Tradition.

The particular brand of Alexandrian Witchcraft that I practice is very much in line with my Gardnerian training.

What makes your approach or tradition unique from any others out there?

My approach to Witchcraft has always been one of wholeism. Each tradition that I practice fulfills a spiritual need that I have and allows me to bring perspective to the table. This is true whether I am working on a subject of interest for myself or for another. This is especially true in helping new seekers on a magical path. I have perspective and understand their needs, appropriately guiding them to a tradition that is best suited to their needs and journey.

My practice of Witchcraft has widened through the years to be more ceremonial as well as more "Witchcraft of the moment." I would consider myself integrative in my approach, inasmuch as there are times when I need to take myself out of a work environment in order to help a close friend or a Coven mate in a time of need. I no longer depend solely on the accoutrements of magic to accomplish an end to my means.

My stretching across many traditions also informs my personal practice. On any given night, you might find me invoking djinn, elementals, or gods in order to grow on a personal level. This has been a way of life for me for a goodly amount of my life.

While I might not suggest that this method is good for everyone taking their first steps on a magical path, I would say that every seeker should keep a keen eye toward integration and understanding of the many paths that exist.

Would you say that Witchcraft is a "craft" or a "religion"? And can you talk about the difference?

Well, there is Witchcraft with a capital *W*, and there is witchcraft all in lowercase.

The capitalized version of Witchcraft is a religious system that incorporates an understanding of magic as part of the process to change your environment as well as effecting change in the practitioner. At the core of many of the systems that classify themselves as Witchcraft is orthopraxis. It is by action rather than by thought/dogma that an understanding is gleaned of the interplay of ego, divinity, and the natural world. Ecstatic experience is reached through repetition of ritual in a specified manner. However, this is not exclusionary of contemplative modality, but in not having a scripture and dogma, each individual is engendered with responsibility of interpretation.

The lowercased version of witchcraft is used by many to mean a method of magic that is devoid of a religious structure and used to effect change. This can be for lofty ends as well as for some very banal needs of the practitioner. This type of witchcraft is more aligned with what many would consider "sorcery." Witchcraft of this type can be practiced by Pagan, Jew, Buddhist, and Christian alike. This practice might involve some sort of "God," but it is not requisite to invoke or believe in such a being.

Whom do Witches worship?

Since Witchcraft is such a broad term, I would like to first define my usage here. I will define Witchcraft in this instance as being a magico-religious, non-Christian system of European origin. I would include the Mediterranean origins as well.

Given the above, most traditions of Witchcraft worship a binary set of divine beings. For the most part the binary is a God(dess) and a consort who is of the opposite sex. It is through the interplay of the binary set that the cosmos and our world are brought into existence.

In all but one of the traditions that I practice, the binary consists of a male/female pair that are locked in a cycle of "fertility" and are associated with the Moon (female) and Sun (male). This is also translated into life (female) and death (male) and reincarnation (both). It is through the cycling of the agricultural and husbandry calendar that fertility, death, and rebirth are reenacted.

The exception to the above is in the Minoan Brotherhood (and Sisterhood for that matter). In this instance the binary is that of a "Great Mother" and her "Divine Son" and how the Witch is related to each. In the case of the Minoan Brotherhood there is a strong identification of the initiate with the Son and as a result the relationship of a child to the Great Mother. While I am not at liberty to really speak much on this, I can say that the Mother's cycles are related in a manner that significantly differs from the northern European model.

In all of the systems/traditions that I participate in, the emphasis is on the female segment of divinity, with the male being a complement rather than an opposite.

When Witches meet, what do they usually do?

Each meeting is an island unto itself. For the most part, meetings will involve a Circle, which is the primary method of worship in modern-day Witchcraft. In addition to worship within Circle, there may be other avenues that can be expressed at any given meeting.

During a typical Circle any member of the Coven may bring a need/want to the table to be worked on with magic as a group. When such an occasion arises, there usually will be a discussion as to whether it is appropriate for the group to undertake a specific working. If it is appropriate, the method in which to work the magic will be discussed and decided upon.

Often, a typical meeting would be a chance for Coven leaders to disseminate teaching that might be seasonal in nature or general teaching regarding the approach of a given tradition. While I can't give specifics beyond generality, I would also say that the nature of many meetings is to effect union with a deity and can be very ecstatic in nature.

Do Witches really do "spells" or can they do "magic"?

Many conflate spells and magic, with good reason. All spells are a form of magic; however, not all magic is done with spells.

My understanding is that the magic is defined as causing a change to occur in conformity with one's will or inner self. This can be high or low in nature. On a spectrum, we might consider magic to be "low" when we are casting a spell for needs in our mundane world, such as money, health, etc. Realize that labeling it as "low" magic does not mean it's insignificant. Rather, it is a statement that this type of magic is for some very mundane needs.

Now, magic that effects a change on the psyche and causes spiritual growth is very different from spell casting. In fact, I would actually change the spelling of the word to *Magick,* so that all understand that the undertaking is wholly different.

If you do any spells, can you give examples?

An example of spell casting might be healing. In this case, one might use a poppet to cause healing. The sorcerer/magician in this case would treat the poppet as the individual that they are trying to heal. In fact, in the mind, there is no distinction between the two. I won't go into the details because that would depend on the sickness, and also, this is best taught in person.

Are you a hereditary Witch?

I am not a hereditary Witch. That being said, I am an initiate and a High Priest of NECTW. This was originally a family tradition of the late Gwen Thompson. How far back into Gwen's family these practices go, we cannot be certain. However, we are sure that these family/hereditary practices go back a few generations and have been documented through interviews and genealogy by Andrew Theitic. Some the family lore is documented in his book *The Rede of the Wiccae,* which he coauthored with Robert Mathiesen. In being initiated into and working with this tradition, I can say without reservation that it has a very "family" feel to it.

Did your family carry stories about Witches or did you find out about it all recently?

My family did not relay any stories of Witchcraft.

Have you had relationships or friendships with other New England Witches? If so, with whom? And what were the most significant experiences or learnings you had from those encounters?

I have had deep relationships that go back decades with Witches in New

England. Specifically, I have known Andrew Theitic and many other members of NECTW for more than twenty-five years. In fact, in the early nineties I traveled to Rhode Island frequently to receive initiation and training in NECTW from Andrew Theitic and his High Priestess at the time, the late Lady Devon. I have continued this relationship and it is in good part the reason that I moved to Rhode Island. My learning and later leadership in NECTW have been extremely impactful on my life. I am sure that I would not be half the Priest that I am today had my studies not been enriched by the very fine Priests and Priestesses in NECTW.

I am also connected with individuals in the Salem area through lineage. Both my Minoan lineage and my Gardnerian lineage live on in Salem and the surrounding areas.

Do you have any interactions with Witches in the Salem, Massachusetts, area? What is your impression of the current interest in Witchcraft in Salem, centuries after the Witch hysteria of Puritan times?

Other than initiates who are down line from me, I have had very few contacts on a magical level with Witches in the Salem area. Unfortunately, Salem seems to be for the most part dominated by "pop" personalities and proprietors. While I would not characterize all the Witches in the Salem area to be pop Witches, I would say that the big personalities are the loudest in the crowd of Witches in Salem.

On the flip side of this coin, Salem has been instrumental in the third and fourth wave of Witches in the modern era. I would say that the first era in which Witchcraft became popular was generated by Ray and Rosemary Buckland in Long Island, New York. It was through them that many in the United States came to understand modern Witchcraft, and a multitude of communities can trace their way back to Long Island either directly as Gardnerians or secondarily because they owe much of their ritual structure to core principles that were taught by Ray and Rosemary or one of their students.

The second wave of Witches was promoted by the activities in New York City and in Chicago. Herman Slater was the driving force behind the New York City movement. It was his store the Magickal Childe that became the nexus for Witches from New York and outlying areas. Chicago was instrumental in the creation of the Pagan Way materials that would help to inform very large geographical areas, such as California.

The third and fourth waves in American Witchcraft were very much generated in New England and more specifically in Salem. In New England, we have the founding of one very big line of Alexandrian Witches through the efforts of Jim and Pat Baker. We also saw the phenomena of Salem coming to the fore in a more serious manner. This was fueled by some larger-than-life personalities who seemed to fill the airwaves around Halloween yearly. More recently, the bigger personalities are not teachers who happen to have a store; instead, the proprietors that seem to be the driving force. In some ways there is a constant buzz that is generated because of the history of Salem, but the concern seems to be fiscal rather than informative.

Have you experienced any difficulties—any problems, persecution, or prejudice—as a result of being a Witch? Can you describe a time or times when that happened?

In all my years of walking this path, I have only experienced one instance of prejudice. Working in the investment banking industry, I was quite out as Pagan. I always wore a pentagram that was quite visible. On one particular day, I was approached by a manager of a service area who stated that he saw my pentagram on my neck and knew me to be a "devil worshipper." I reflected on his statement and was conflicted as to whether I should escalate this matter to my management. In the end, I decided to confront the service area employee. I explained quietly but certainly resolutely that a discussion as to my religious leaning was inappropriate in a workplace environment. I told him that I had opted to advise him directly rather than doing so through his management. The employee was shaken by my aggressive stance and immediately apologized. From that moment onward, the individual went out of his way to avoid contact with me.

What are special holy days for Witches? Can you please describe what Witches do on their holy days? How do you celebrate?

There are eight ritual occasions that most traditions of Witchcraft observe: the equinoxes, solstices, and cross quarter days. In each instance, there is a celebration that is informed by the season as it relates to northern European agricultural and husbandry calendars. The exception to this is the Minoan Brotherhood, whose practices are based on an Aegean calendar as envisioned by Eddie Buczynski.

Most Witches see this as treading the wheel of life and death. Much of the practice in some way relates either through allegory or invocation of the cycle that it celebrates. While I can't relate details without breaking my oaths, I can talk in generalities.

The eight celebrations are seen as times of great joy, and as such, they would not be times in which the Coven would undertake works of magic unless an emergency situation presented itself. In addition to the commemorative ritual, there often is a feast that follows. The feast, like the ritual, will keep the season in mind. For example, the celebration that lands on August Eve is one that commemorates the first harvest, the harvest of the grains. In the feast that follows the ritual one is likely to find a meal that includes many grains and meals that focus on bread.

KIRK WHITE
Bethel, Vermont

First, can you say a bit about who you are, where you live, and what you do for a living these days?

I am a fifty-five-year-old native Vermonter. I've been a practicing Witch and magician since 1973, a psychotherapist for twenty years, and a licensed Oriental medical practitioner since 1994. I'm also a past co-president of the Covenant of the Goddess (North America's oldest and largest association of

Witches and Wiccans) and past director of the University of Vermont's parapsychology program, and I founded Cherry Hill Seminary, a professional Pagan ministry program with faculty and students worldwide (www.cherryhillseminary.org), and Standing Stone Academy, a Pagan healer training program. In 2006, wildhunt.org named me one of the "twenty-five most influential modern living Pagans today."

In addition to working as a consultant with Pagan seminaries nationwide such as the Aquarian Tabernacle Churches' Woolston-Steen Theological Seminary, I am a legal Pagan minister, a Freemason, and an adept in the Hermetic Order of the Golden Dawn. My skills and interests include traditional healing modalities, various magickal and spiritual traditions, and models of Pagan leadership and ministry.

To make a living, I work as a licensed acupuncturist and Chinese herbalist and also write books and give workshops around the country on healing and esoteric subjects. I have contributed to *Exploring the Pagan Path* and am the author of *Adept Circle Magick, Advanced Circle Magick, rEvolutions,* and *Masterful Magick.* I also own and operate a fifty-acre sacred retreat in the beautiful Green Mountains of Vermont (www.laurelinretreat.com), where we have been hosting Pagan gatherings since 1982. It is open to the public and also available for rental/reservation. We have groups come ranging in size from five or six people to over one thousand. We also host "Burner" events, LARP camps, weddings, Pagan festivals, camping retreats, and more.

Which religion were you raised in?

I grew up on a small farm in a small town with no nearby neighbor children, so I only played with my cousins and my brother. The day before I started kindergarten, my parents pulled me aside and told me that other kids might bring up religion or politics—ideas that they would have obviously gotten from their parents. But my parents had specifically not talked to me about either because they wanted me to figure those out for myself. So I spent large parts of my childhood and teens exploring various religions and philosophies to see what made them each unique.

How and when did you decide you were a Witch?

I always knew I was one; I was always interested in the occult and esoteric subjects. As a small child, we would visit my aunt Norma in Lebanon, New Hampshire, once a year. Each time we went there she should show my brother and me something—dowsing, pyramids, ESP, crystals. Just a quick introduction and let us try and that was it. No explanations. In 1973, when I was eleven, Aunt Norma sent me a copy of Paul Huson's *Mastering Witchcraft*, and I was off and running. I immediately set up an altar, started doing rituals, and tried to get my friends to join me (with very mixed results). Witchcraft, hormones, and occasional alcohol gives one lots of lessons on how *not* to do things.

When I got to college in 1980 I met a couple of other Witches, and we started a Coven. By 1987 it had become three Covens spread around Vermont, so we incorporated the Wiccan Church of Vermont as a legal church. We received IRS nonprofit status in 1987. By the early 1990s we had members and clergy throughout New England and elsewhere, many of whom were not Wiccan but instead other flavors of Paganism. So we changed the name to Church of the Sacred Earth: A Union of Pagan Congregations.

Over the years I have been exposed to, and occasionally initiated into, various types of Witchcraft: multiple British Traditional Witchcraft traditions, a no-name family tradition, "old Witchcraft," Neopagan eclectic traditions, and many others. I continue to learn and grow in my Witchcraft.

How do you personally define Witchcraft?

I define Witchcraft as any tradition that does spells. It is not necessarily a religion, and although there are many Witches who do have a Nature-based theology attached to their practice (such as Wicca and others), there are also Christian Witches, atheist Witches, and pretty much any-other-religion Witches. This is why all Wiccans are Witches but not all Witches are Wiccan.

Which tradition of Witchcraft do you follow? How did you find that tradition?

At this point I practice my own tradition. It is a mix of British Traditional influences, a family tradition, "old Craft," and various folk magic traditions. I've belonged to a number of groups, learned from various teachers and colleagues, and experimented with various approaches to see what works best for me. You pick up a lot in forty-plus years.

What makes your approach or tradition unique from any others out there?

It is my own mix based on my personal experiences. It draws on very folksy Witchcraft, root work, conjure, old Craft, cunning work, and Vermont folk traditions, mixes them with more transformative work such as initiatory ritual, shape-shifting, spirit and deity work, trance, and possession, adds a dash of "high magick," such as grimoire work, Enochian magic, renaissance astrological magic, or devotional work, puts it all in the context of "here and now" by digging in the dirt, talking to the trees, listening to the brook, and working with spirits of place, the weather and seasons, and plants and animals of place, and expresses itself through the fun, joy, occasional tears, creativity, and wonder of childhood.

Would you say that Witchcraft is a "craft" or a "religion"? And can you talk about the difference?

I would say that Witchcraft is a craft in that it involves certain skills and practices to do spells, divinations, etc. Wicca (and its offshoots) is a religion that practices Witchcraft.

Whom do Witches worship?

That is entirely up the Witch and her gods (or archetypes, the Tao, etc.). There are polytheist, pantheist, monotheist, nontheist, and even atheist Witches.

When Witches meet, what do they usually do?

Generally one or more things such as performing celebratory ritual, transformative ritual, and spell workings, studying and practicing various skills, working on personal improvement, healing, having fun, and gossiping. The mix of these things and the specific ways they are done vary based on tradition, season, and group and individual needs.

Do Witches really do "spells" or can they do "magic"?

Yes. But I generally teach that magick is a way of being. By being fully aware of the forces (nature, media, colors, smells, planets, etc.) that are around and operating on you and harmonizing yourself with the forces of Nature, your life becomes magickal and seemingly effortless. As awareness of a need arises, so does the answer for that need. When we are not paying attention and get out of sync with the forces of Nature, problems arise. And then spells are sometimes needed to get back on track. So in my experience and observation, as Witches mature in their practice, become more harmonized with the Divine, and become magickal "beings," they have to "do" magic in the form of spells much less.

If you do any spells, can you give examples?

I seldom do spells other than to teach other people about the principles of magick. At this point, they tend to fall on either end of the spectrum—either they are very simple folk spells such as are practiced in Appalachian hoodoo or they are very complex renaissance ceremonial magick operations.

Are you a hereditary Witch?

Not unless you count my Aunt Norma, which I don't.

Have you had relationships or friendships with other New England Witches? If so, with whom? And what were the most significant experiences or learnings you had from those encounters?

After forty years, I know many of the folks in the New England community, and I learn from them (usually informally) all the time. Many of the people I know are members of EarthSpirit, Covenant of the Goddess, Connecticut Wiccan & Pagan Network, and the Church of the Sacred Earth, but since I travel and teach at Pagan festivals and Pagan Pride Days, I literally know hundreds of people from every state of New England.

Do you have any interactions with Witches in the Salem, Massachusetts, area? What is your impression of the current interest in Witchcraft in Salem, centuries after the Witch hysteria of Puritan times?

Not on a regular basis. Salem has a complex relationship with Witchcraft, and the Witch community there reflects it.

Have you experienced any difficulties—any problems, persecution, or prejudice—as a result of being a Witch? Can you describe a time or times when that happened?

No. I believe in everyday interfaith work. If you make yourself a useful, highly valued, and fully integrated member of the community you live in, then people will tend to overlook your eccentricities. They know you as a person first, and they value you. So I've coached the elementary girls' basketball team, been president of the Rotary Club and the business associations, am leading our town's revitalization efforts, belong to the Masonic lodge, volunteer to help with community events, donate money, etc.

I am known and loved in my community. "Kirk is a great guy and a huge asset to our community. Oh yeah, and he's a witch."

What are special holy days for Witches? Can you please describe what Witches do on their holy days? How do you celebrate?

That depends on the tradition. One tradition I belong to celebrates specific seasonal/weather events such as the first snow, the first crocus bloom, etc. Another is very astrological and celebrates the exact astronomical solstices, equinoxes, and the midpoints between them. Then of course there are the British Traditional holy days: Winter Equinox/Yule,

Imbolc, the Vernal Equinox (I am from a time before it became trendy to give the solstices and equinoxes names to make them like the Irish-named holidays), Beltane, Midsummer, Lughnasadh, Autumnal Equinox, and Samhain. Generally these are celebrations and reenactments of mythic seasonal themes to help us recognize and honor the cycles of Nature and their correlation to the human life cycle. For me, there is also a significant recognition of the spirits of place and how their cycles change with the seasons, and the spirits of the ancestors. (My family has been in central Vermont since the 1740s, and our family cemetery plot adjoins our farm.)

Any other thoughts you care to add?

There are tons of things I could say, but I don't have the time to type them all out. I do better with in-person interviews, but then the interviewer has to do the typing. For more information about my work, visit www.revkirkwhite.com or https://en.wikipedia.org/wiki/Kirk_White.

LAURA WILDMAN-HANLON
Western Massachusetts

First, can you say a bit about who you are, where you live, and what you do for a living these days?

I am many things: wife, mother, daughter, sister, friend, worker, priestess, ritualist, teacher, writer, Morris dancer, hobbyist of many types of handwork, lover of learning, and movie addict, just to name a few. With over sixteen years of marriage, my husband and I have bucked the national trend of divorce. He is still my best friend. Plus the kids have threatened to tie us together if we ever do decide to part, so I guess we're stuck for life. As a parent of three active teens, we keep very busy bustling between school and family events. They bring us joy and challenges but mostly joy, every day. I'm blessed that my parents live close by so my children can experience the love of extended family. For work, I'm the office manager of a large department within a university.

I've authored three books: *What's Your Wicca I.Q.?*, *Wiccan*

Meditations, and *Celebrating the Pagan Soul.* I also researched and published an article on generational retentions within modern Paganism, which looked at whether children born within the movement were staying within it or leaving to join more traditional religions. (They are staying but following the general U.S. trend to become more spiritual in belief and forgo joining any specific practice.) A follow-up to this research is pending.

In the late 1980s I helped give birth to New Moon (NM), a Pagan community organization that offered monthly public classes, rituals, and Sabbat celebrations in Boston. We prided ourselves on the community's open nature and ability to work by consensus. When I moved to New York City, I helped establish New Moon New York (NMNY). NMNY's Beltane/May Day celebration in Central Park in the early 1990s featured five Maypoles with hundreds of participants. NM provided a place for Witches and Pagans to meet and learn from each other in a safe environment, to receive information on the numerous Pagan traditions, and to make connections with others who shared common beliefs. Through its events, NM helped bring people together, and from those interactions numerous other groups and Covens were formed.

In the late 1990s, working with Kirk White, who had the original vision, and Cat Chapin-Bishop, we founded and developed Cherry Hill Seminary, a virtual Pagan seminary offering distance education for Pagan ministry. While there, I held various positions including the dean of administration, dean of academics, and instructor. While I'm no longer affiliated with the seminary, it has gone on to complete the dream we had of a professional school offering a master of divinity degree and certificates.

Along with organizing and participating in an untold number of rituals and workshops, I have lectured and taught classes on Wicca and the Tarot for more than twenty years. I'm a recognized Wiccan clergy in my home state of Massachusetts and have officiated hundreds of wedding/handfastings and other rites of passage ceremonies. My Coven, Apple and Oak, was formed in 1995 and continues to meet regularly in Massachusetts.

We live in a very rural area surrounded by trees and fields. I share the land with a plethora of wild creatures including porcupines, fox, bear, coyotes, turkeys, raccoons, and ravens. Eagles occasionally can be seen overhead, and owls call to each other in the night. I love my home; a large bay window in my living room gives me a front-row view of the changing seasons. I can sit for hours, working on a project such as crocheting an afghan and watching the birds take turns at our bird feeder.

Which religion were you raised in?

I was raised Episcopalian, a branch of Christianity. My parents left the church just before I was to be confirmed. The confirmation ritual would have pledged me to the Christian faith and the church. It was during the early 1970s, and the Vietnam War was active. The preacher began discussing politics from the pulpit. My parents are firm believers in the separation of church and state, and these sermons concerned them, so they left the church. As I felt no deep tie to the church, I didn't care that we had stopped attending. With only a brief try at an evangelical "born again" phase in my later teens (there was this boy . . . he was really cute and deeply involved with a group), the faith or its practice never connected with my spirit. Christianity felt closed in and inflexible, while my spirit was expansive and diverse. To me "God" was not transcendent from creation but immanent, a connected part of it. With the exception of the stories of Jesus, the Bible made no sense to me at all. As an adult who takes vows very seriously, I am grateful to have been withdrawn from the faith before being asked to make the promise to adhere to it for life.

How and when did you decide you were a Witch?

As a child, my favorite stories were fairy tales and the myths of the gods and goddesses from around the world. As a preteen, I loved history, anthropology, and fantasy stories that contained magic and strong women characters. These books, and the rural environment in which I grew and watched the circle of life—the intricate pattern where one part relied on another—formed the cornerstone of my adult beliefs. The apple tree in my backyard produced flowers, which brought the bees and insects, which both fertilized the buds and fed the birds. The apples that were not eaten by hungry children fell to the ground to feed wild animals and to compost, becoming fertilizer that fed the tree, helping it grow to repeat the cycle next year. Remove one piece, and it would affect the whole. This was the microcosm, a physical representation of the macrocosm of life. I knew in my heart that the world was alive and all upon it were interconnected. I spent hours exploring the woods near my home and playing in the brook that ran through it. I believed there was a spirit who lived in the trees and in the waters, and I would create small rituals and leave offerings for Her.

One Christmas, when I was around the age of thirteen, I asked my parents for, and received, a Tarot deck (they thought it was a card game). I began offering divination card readings for friends and became quite accomplished at it. I don't remember how I heard about Tarot. Starhawk's *The Spiral Dance* and Margot Adler's *Drawing Down the Moon* were years away from being published. These were books that helped open the door for mainstream America to meet modern Paganism. I must have subconsciously tapped into what was already stirring across the country: the ideas of the 1960s, such as breaking through stereotypes, supporting women's rights, embracing diversity, and protecting the fragile ecosystem were all around. I did not yet call myself a Witch. At this time, the associations with the word were with devil worship, which I did not believe in and found both distasteful and appalling. I did, however, already believe in energy work and magic. I remember telling my friends that Witches didn't really need a cauldron, herbs, or other magical tools. All of these were just props to help them believe what they were doing would work. All they really needed was to work the energy and believe.

It wasn't until college, around 1977, during late-night discussions on religion with a dear friend, that the modern concept of Witchcraft and magical practice came into my consciousness. She shared my beliefs. I wasn't alone. Shortly afterward books on the subject, such as *The Spiral Dance*, became available in New Age bookstores. A small group of like-minded friends began meeting and creating rituals. At that point I embraced the word and was firmly a Witch.

How do you personally define Witchcraft?

First a statement. Modern Witchcraft, also called Wicca, is an experiential faith. It does not come from one book that must be adhered to. Because of this, every Witch has their own personal connection to the Divine and view of the world. Wicca is by nature diverse. Ask a Witch a question on belief and practice and you are probably going to get at least five different answers. It is not that we are confused. It is because we see the world as being multifaceted. There is no one definitive correct way to answer a question, and therefore all answers, and each Witch's personal view, are valid. For this reason, I can only speak of my personal beliefs and practices and not those of all Witches.

Witchcraft has moved from solely a magical practice into the spiritual and religious realm. It is a combination of old ideas and modern, of ancient mystic and occult traditions, folk customs, old Cunning magical practices, fragments of ancient Pagan celebrations, mythology, and modern ideas of ritual, energy, the sacredness of the Earth, polytheism, pantheism, animism, and diversity of spirit. A Witch, in the modern sense, is practicing a way of life. It is recognizing how each step, each word spoken, affects something beyond the self and how we must take responsibility for these actions. We hold no deity who removes the blemish of our wrongdoing. We own what we do and must make amends for our transgressions. Those who choose to walk this difficult path do so out of a true spiritual calling. Witchcraft, as it is practiced today, is an Earth-based spirituality that strives to work in balance and harmony with the cycles of nature.

Which tradition of Witchcraft do you follow? How did you find that tradition?

I am an Initiated Gardnerian Third-Degree High Priestess of the Liberal Gardnerian Protean line.

Gerald Brosseau Gardner (1884–1964) was the creator of the

modern practice of Witchcraft, also called Wicca. He had a lifelong interest in the occult and folklore. In 1939, he was introduced to members of and Initiated into the New Forest Coven in the New Forest area of England. After the repeal of the witchcraft laws in England in 1951, he began being public about his practices and published in 1954 *Witchcraft Today* and then in 1959 *The Meaning of Witchcraft*. This was the birth of what is called the Gardnerian Tradition. Most modern Wiccan traditions, whether recognized or not, come directly from the ideas put forth by Gardner.

I moved to New York City in 1990 and was introduced by a mutual friend to Judy Harrow. While I had been practicing Wicca for a number of years, up to that point I had chosen not to join a Coven. With years of experience, and having met a number of self-professed High Priests and Priestesses whose knowledge came only through books and who had little training or experience, I was hesitant about committing myself to any specific Coven or tradition. That changed when I met Judy. She was one of the most intelligent, caring women I had ever met. We found a deep connection through shared interests, and she invited me to attend one of her Coven's rituals. After a few repeat attendances, I was invited to join Proteus Coven and was soon after Initiated into the Tradition. While all members of a Coven are considered equal, Gardnerianism is hierarchical in its training. Each step takes the student deeper into the occult and the Tradition's Mysteries. Over the next few years, I was elevated to Second Degree and finally to Third Degree, the highest level within the Gardnerian Tradition.

In 1995 I moved from New York City to Massachusetts. On Samhain of that year my friend Geoff, another former member of Proteus, formed Apple and Oak Coven.

What makes your approach or tradition unique from any others out there?

The Gardnerian Tradition comes from the writings and practices of Gerald Gardner and his High Priestesses. It uses a specific form of practice. The Protean line of this tradition uses the bones, or structure, of the Gardnerian Tradition and overlays it with personal experiences and ideas. It is fluid and changing; we reject that which does not work for us and invent new forms in order to better fit individual and Coven needs. This is different from those who are stricter in their practice, and it is why we call ourselves a liberal branch of Gardnerian Witchcraft.

I love the history of my tradition. It has a traceable lineage. I am only six steps away from Gerald Gardner's original Coven. It is an initiatory religion, a mystery religion, with initiation being the gateway to the mysteries. The ritual used to initiate me into the Tradition was the same ritual used by Gardner and those who followed after him, and I use it when I initiate others into my Coven. When I'm a guest of another Gardnerian Coven, I know their practice will be similar to my own, as we share that commonality. While we are all independent in thought and practice, the Tradition links us together as an extended form of family.

As I said, Gardnerian Tradition training is hierarchical. It takes time to move from one level to another as the candidate integrates the experience and prepares for the next. It is not for those who are looking for a quick experience. I've had a number of people walk away before starting when they hear it takes a minimum of four to six years to obtain the level of Third Degree. I've had Coveners who took twelve to fifteen years before making the last step. A Coven is a small, committed group of people who have chosen to worship and work magic together, and this takes time. A new person must be integrated into the group, and if a person chooses to leave, it is devastating. For this reason, my Coven is very careful when deciding to extend an invitation to a potential candidate.

Would you say that Witchcraft is a "craft" or a "religion"? And can you talk about the difference?

It is both a craft and a religion. A craft is creating something using skill or expertise. Spell work is carefully crafting change, and Wicca is often called "the Craft of the Wise." A religion is a particular method or system to approach and worship the Divine. It has a form of organization, a format, and beliefs.

Witchcraft in ancient times was a method for controlling the environment and outcomes through spell work/magic. These concepts were based on folk tradition and magical principles, which did not necessarily need to be connected with any religious belief or system. However, modern Witchcraft, or Wicca, has moved this into the spiritual and religious realm. It has become an Earth-based religion that honors the sacredness of nature, often worshipping a god and goddess who are the personifications of the natural cycles of life.

In Wicca, there is no dogma, no authoritative doctrine that cannot be questioned. There is a recognition that nobody can have all the answers. There is no one grand leader; we are each our own Priest and Priestess. There is no standard creed, no official system of doctrines. There are, however, general trends in worldview concerning beliefs about the universe and the place of humans and others within it. These include belief in the following:

- ◄ Plurality and tolerance of diversity of opinion on the forms of the Divine and how to relate to them
- ◄ Polytheism (more than one form of the Divine)
- ◄ Divinity as immanent
- ◄ Wiccan Rede and magical ethics
- ◄ Magic
- ◄ Practices that center around the cycles found in nature and life

Whom do Witches worship?

This answer is as diverse as Witches themselves. It is a religion of personal experience, not of a book. For that reason, beliefs can vary between adherents. Every Witch is her or his own Priestess or Priest and does not require an intermediary between themselves and the Divine. We can each have our own revelation.

Some Witches are monotheistic in that they believe the gods and goddesses are all parts of one great deity. This All is worshipped in both the masculine and feminine forms, as a reflection of Nature. Some Wiccans are dualistic. This is the belief that all gods are aspects of one

God and all goddesses are one Goddess. Some worship the God in the forms of the Green Man and the Horned God of the Hunt and the Goddess as threefold—Maiden, Mother, Crone—whose manifestations correspond to the major phases of women's lives. Still others view a wide pantheon of deities in which every god and goddess is an individual entity, and they are all very real.

Some Witches do not believe in the gods at all but see them as archetypes, personalities, or a set of characteristics, which are shared throughout all cultures, giving form to myths and heroic stories that help express a culture's worldview—for example, the concept of the Mother Goddess or Liberty and Freedom.

When Witches meet, what do they usually do?

If we meet another Witch on the street, there is no secret handshake or code word; we just say, "Hello." It was years before the internet when I first became a Witch. It was hard to find others of like mind. When one did, you held on to those connections. I remember my brother, who was sharing an apartment with me at the time, came home saying he had met another Witch on the bus ride home. When I realized he hadn't gotten her number, I had him ride the bus at the same time for two weeks until he located her again and got the information for me. In the early years we were desperate for connection with others. Then the internet became easily available. This technology has greatly altered and changed our community. Individuals no longer need to search out open groups like New Moon in order to meet like-minded individuals. With a click, the world of Witchcraft and Wicca is available.

Today, when Witches gather together, whether it be in Covens or other groups, we socialize, we acknowledge the turning of the seasonal wheel and the cycles of nature and life, and we celebrate! The general format includes the honoring the God and Goddess as well as the energies of the elements that make up life: earth, air, fire, and water. Rituals need not include magic; however, if there is need, a magical working can be done.

Do Witches really do "spells" or can they do "magic"?

Witches see everyday life as magical, significant, and sacred. Magic is a form of science; it is a matter of knowing what to do and how to do it. Everyone has practiced a form of magic at one point in time or another. Making a wish and blowing out a birthday candle or wearing the lucky shirt on game day are two examples that come to mind. Both have intent, a focus, and the belief that if the ritual is done correctly, then a successful outcome will be achieved.

The Witches of the past who practiced the art of magic would have fallen into two categories: (1) village healers, herbalists, and Cunning men or women who provided spells to find lost articles, alleviate ailments, or provide protective magic and (2) ceremonial magicians whose complicated ritual forms were found among the educated and upper class. Modern Witchcraft, as practiced today, is a unique combination of the two.

Spells are created for the purpose of shaping and moving energy in order to facilitate change. For some Witches, magic is an integral practice of their religion used for personal growth, celebration, self-expression, helping others, and healing the planet. Others believe, because change begets change in ways often unanticipated, that magic should be used sparingly and only with great care. Many Wiccans take vows not to work magic for another without their express permission. Even healing without permission is considered unethical, as it uses magic to control the will of another. For example, a woman whose beloved aunt was extremely ill worked healing magic to help keep her alive. The woman received a distraught call from the aunt, asking if magic was being done toward her. The aunt told her that she felt it was her time to go, but something was keeping her here against her will. The woman thought she was doing good, but in actuality she was harming her aunt.

If you do any spells, can you give examples?

The most common request for workings my Coven receives is for healing. Next would be to locate a new job or home. I personally have a knack for parking magic. Even in the most congested of areas I usually can find a parking space right in front of or close by to whatever building I'm going to. When I'm officiating an outdoor wedding and a storm is brewing, I've been known to do a bit of weather work to ask the gods to hold the rain back until after the ceremony. I've done over three hundred weddings and have a great record of clear-sky ceremonies, although it could just be because the gods love a wedding. One thing an ethical Witch will not do is love magic, as that is working against someone's will. If attraction magic is really wanted, what can be done is magic to help bolster the confidence of the person and to help make the person be noticed by the other. If love is to occur, it will happen naturally.

Are you a hereditary Witch?

No.

Have you had relationships or friendships with other New England Witches? If so, with whom? And what were the most significant experiences or learnings you had from those encounters?

I live in New England, and most of my friendships are with local Witches. People with common interests tend to interact and build connections. Plus it is a small community. Due to vows, I'm not allowed to identify another Witch without their permission. This is to protect their identities from potential persecution and harassment. I know of people who, in the past, have had children removed from their custody solely because they identified as being a Witch. Others have lost their jobs and have been ridiculed. With the current political climate, where religious diversity is being called into question and hate crimes are on the rise, I do not want to put anyone at risk.

My entry into the greater Pagan community came in 1985 when I attended a Pagan retreat called "Rites of Spring." This gathering, held yearly in the Berkshires, is organized by the EarthSpirit Community.*

---

*From the EarthSpirit website (www.Earthspirit.org): "EarthSpirit is an organization dedicated to the preservation and development of Earth-centered spirituality, culture, and community. We particularly focus on the indigenous traditions of pre-Christian Europe, known collectively as Paganism, which have survived in varying degrees to the present day."

When I arrived, I was amazed to find well over one hundred Witches and Pagans. The number is considerably more today. The event offered classes on topics of interest to the community during the day and a drum circle with a large bonfire in the evening. Listening to the drumbeats, standing in a circle and singing as the Moon rose overhead, I felt my heart overflowing with joy. I felt I had come home. I was not alone. If you have never felt different, then it is hard to understand the emotions that come when you find a community with others who are like you. It is liberating and a great relief.

Do you have any interactions with Witches in the Salem, Massachusetts, area? What is your impression of the current interest in Witchcraft in Salem, centuries after the Witch hysteria of Puritan times?

When I lived in Boston, I met a few Witches who called Salem home, including the well-known Laurie Cabot. For many years I was a member of the Weavers, the local chapter of the Covenant of the Goddess, the oldest Wiccan "church" in the United States. We hosted the organization's annual conference in Salem in 2013.

There is a mystique to Salem for modern Witches, which I honestly do not understand. The twenty people who were executed in Salem during the hysteria were not Witches. They were innocent people who died with Christian prayers on their lips. It is the tantalizing word *Witchcraft* that has turned a place of tragedy into a tourist destination, and the possibility of Witchcraft has reverberated through the centuries and continues to draw people to the site. I find the commercializing of Salem, capitalizing on the deaths of these innocent people, distasteful and insulting to the dead and their families. That said, Salem has become a vibrant center for magic and magical people. It has provided a unique way to help reclaim the word *Witch,* connecting it from the past to the present and transforming it from dark and death to life, light, and possibilities. The streets are lined with occult shops and bookstores, and Witches hold public events that draw the curious as well as other Witches. The image of the Witch (albeit stereotyped as a hag on a broom) is everywhere, including on the police cars.

Have you experienced any difficulties—any problems, persecution, or prejudice—as a result of being a Witch? Can you describe a time or times when that happened?

Unfortunately, I have experienced prejudice. The most pointed and ironic comes from a time spent on an interfaith council. The newly formed group was debating on how, in the future, to begin the meetings. The general consensus was to start with a prayer. The discussion was on how to facilitate a rotation and what to do if the person whose turn it was couldn't make it. After a few minutes, one of the members raised his hand and said, "I don't know what the problem is. We are, after all, people of the Book." When I pointed out I was not, the conversation immediately stopped. A few members said that, despite the fact that I did not have a problem with their deity, they could not and would not be in the room if I offered a prayer to my goddess. The idea was removed and never brought up again. At another meeting discussing collection of data on religious affiliation, a member of this group voiced his belief that Wicca was not a "real" religion.

I also fought for a number of years to have an inclusive interfaith calendar available on campus for faculty, staff, and students. Today, the Pagan festival of Yule is included on holiday celebration posters along with Hindu, Jewish, Muslim, and others' holidays. We've come a long way.

What are special holy days for Witches? Can you please describe what Witches do on their holy days? How do you celebrate?

Wiccans celebrate eight main holidays, called Sabbats, which correspond with the seasonal and agricultural Wheel of the Year. Although most predate the Christian holidays, they correspond with the traditional English calendar. Four of these celebrations are solar, recognizing the solstices and equinoxes; therefore the dates move slightly yearly to reflect the transitional day of the Sun's apex. The other four are the cross quarter dates and come from the Celtic fire celebrations.

Wiccan rites, part of a Mystery Tradition, are not appropriate for children; however, the more Pagan celebrations are welcoming of all age groups and levels of experience.

Yule/Winter Solstice (12/21–12/23). The longest night, the shortest day. The word *Yule* comes directly from the Norse. It translates as "wheel." Many of the trappings of Christmas such as fir trees and red and green decorations come directly come from Pagan traditions. Mistletoe is sacred to, and has a long association with, the Druids. Even the story of the birth of Christ has its foundation in the myth of Mithras, a Roman god.

This is one of my favorite holidays. Friends and family gather to share the warmth of community. We make edible ornaments for the animals outside, and while singing to them a song, we hang the goodies on the trees around the house. Once back inside, we remember the personal events that occurred over the year and then, with all lights extinguished, allow ourselves to feel the dark of the season. It ends with a gleeful calling back of the Sun and the light. We leave, holding the warmth of the moment in our hearts with the hope that it will sustain us all through the winter months.

Imbolc/Candlemas (2/2). This is one of the four cross quarter fire rites. *Imbolc* is a Celtic word for lactation. In that part of the world, this is the time when the ewes would begin to show signs of pregnancy. It is the beginning of the end of winter. Even during the coldest and harshest of winters, the beginning of February is when the Earth begins to stir. Stand outside in February and listen to the birds. Wild creatures more sensitive to the increase in sunlight and the change of season than those of us who spend our time within heated buildings wake up and start to sing in preparation of spring. On the traditional calendar, it is Groundhog Day, when divination is done using a groundhog to predict how much longer the world has to wait for spring. It is a time of quiet reflection and patience. My Coven traditionally tries to spend time near a brook or other flowing waters, as this marks the cracking of the ice as the back of winter is broken.

Ostara/Spring Equinox (3/21–3/23). Day and night are in balance, and we move into the longer days. Eggs are being laid in nests, buds on the trees start to burst, and flowers poke their heads up from the muddy Earth. Ostara is the name of an ancient Germanic goddess whose symbols are spring flowers, eggs, and rabbits. These traditions remain today in the celebrations of Easter, to which She also loaned Her name. Similar to familiar secular traditions, we hunt for eggs. But ours are often decorated with divination symbols predicting for the finder her or his future in the next season. We plant our seed starts for our gardens, placing them on the windowsills or greenhouses to grow until the ground warms enough to transplant outside.

Beltane/May Day (5/1). As a Morris dancer, this is another of my favorite holidays. Morris dancing is a form of English folk dance with choreographed figures to be danced by groups of people often wearing bells and using sticks, swords, or handkerchiefs. The tradition of Morris dancing is extremely old. William Shakespeare mentioned Morris dancing in his writings, and they were considered silly old dances in his day. I start May Day by dancing up the Sun with my Morris team and others. This is not my Coven and not all Witches participate with this activity. What is more traditional for Pagans, and what I and my Coven, family, and friends do for Beltane, is to acknowledge it as the start of summer by dancing the Maypole. The Maypole is a tall pole with ribbons tied to the top that are long enough to reach the ground. Participants each take a ribbon, and usually with song, we weave the ribbons around the pole, completely covering it with the colorful strips. Among other things, it represents the drawing of the Sun's energy from above to the Earth below and of the fertility of the Earth around us. This is also another of the Celtic fire celebrations. Cattle were driven between two bonfires to bless them as they headed from the winter fields to the summer fields. Couples also leapt the flames, representing their own promises of facing the difficult future before them and blessing their union.

Litha/Summer Solstice (6/21–6/23). The longest day, the shortest night. For some Pagans this marks the battle between the Holly King and the Oak King, when the god of darker nights strikes a mortal blow to the old god of light, thus marking the decline of the daylight. The

Oak King sleeps until the Winter Solstice, at which point they meet again, but this time the Holly King will be defeated. For others this battle takes place at the equinoxes. Litha is a modern name for this holiday, coming from writings of the 1960s. My Coven tends to follow the Norse tradition for this holiday, drinking toasts in what is called a "blot," honoring our loved ones, the accomplishments we have made, and hopes for the future.

Lammas/Lughnasadh (8/01). Lammas is the name in the English tradition, while Lughnasadh is the name of the Celtic holiday marking the first harvest. It is celebrated with feasting and festivities. Named after the god Lugh, he of many talents, it often involved games and athletic competitions in what was once called the "Tailteann Games" (held in honor of Lugh's foster mother, the goddess Tailtiu). Today my Coven sometimes still holds friendly competitions with awards of chocolate and other treats to the victors. More often, we recognize the "spirit of the grain," which is harvested at this time, and give honor to his sacrifice. We also take a small lock of hair from our men and offer it to the goddess, requesting that She accept this small token and keep them safe from harm for another year.

Mabon/Fall Equinox (9/21–9/23). After this point, the night rules. Mabon, for my Coven, is a community celebration honoring the harvest and the beginning of preparation for winter. For the last dozen years or so, we have created the tradition of enacting the story of "Stone Soup." "Stone Soup" is the tale of a starving traveler who enters a village. The traveler goes door to door asking for food but is told at each one they have nothing to share, and hardly enough to feed themselves or their family. With empty pail, the traveler sets up camp in the center of town, fills the pail with water over a fire, and says is a voice loud enough for all to hear, "It doesn't matter because I have this yummy stone. I will make stone soup!" The stone is dropped into the hot water. The traveler tastes the "soup" and explains how wonderful it tastes, but that it seems to be missing something. At this point one of the villagers, who has been watching and listening, comes out and offers one vegetable. It is added to the pot. The traveler again goes through the motions of trying and exclaiming how good the soup is but that it is still missing something. Each time another villager comes forward to offer a vegetable. Eventually the entire town is enjoying what they call "the best stone soup they had ever eaten!" This tale, and the enacting of it, represents how together we can take care of each other and fill the needs of the whole. Each vegetable is a unique offering of what we contribute to our community.

Samhain (10/31). Some celebrate it on 11/1, and others hold their rite on whatever day represents the actual middle point between the Fall Equinox and Winter Solstice. My Coven tends to follow the latter. Samhain marks the last harvest of crops and the time to decide which animals will be food during the cold months and which will be kept and fed over the winter. With only the bones of the trees around us, the cold coming in, the blood and cries of the animals as they are slaughtered, and people wondering if they have enough food for the entire winter, it is not surprising that this holiday is associated with death. While children dress up in costumes and run around from house to house begging for candy, and people try to scare each other with their skeleton and ghost decorations, Wiccans celebrate this time as our most solemn of holidays. Much like the Mexican Day of the Dead, but coming from the Gaelic tradition, this is the day we recognize the passing of loved ones, those who influenced our lives and our ancestors. We believe the veil between the world of living and the world of spirit is very thin at this time, allowing us to speak to and be heard by those who have died. In my Coven we host a version of a "dumb supper," where meals are prepared in honor and remembrance of specific individuals. While we enjoy the food, we tell stories about them, sharing memories of who they were and what they meant to us. A portion of the feast is left as an offering outside, where it may compost, symbolizing that their bodies too are now a part of the Earth.

We also celebrate Full Moons and the New Moons as points for reconnecting with the energies of the Earth and the gods and to reaffirm our place within the cycle.

LYRION AₚTOWER
Wilton, New Hampshire

First, can you say a bit about who you are, where you live, and what you do for a living these days?

I'm Lyrion ApTower, and for over twenty-five years I've been the Priestess of the New Hampshire Granite Tower—a scion of the Tower Tradition in California, which has a long, rich and complex history. My husband and Priest, Raven ApTower, and I live at the Granite Tower Covenstead, Strawberry Meadow, in Wilton, New Hampshire, along with my current feline familiar, Twinkle—the most recent in a long line of magnificent children of Bast, deserving of an entire chapter.

I'm a long-retired Fortune 50 corporate communications writer who went on to run my own little PR and writing shop (WordWeaver) for about ten years or so—but, oh, the self-insurance premiums were killing me! But now that I'm older and able to write for the sheer joy of it, I do many handfastings, Sabbats/Esbats, life rituals of healing, aging, passing, parting, and community building as well as speaking in public and on interdenominational and civic panels throughout New Hampshire. I've been on WMUR's *Chronicle* talking about Witchcraft, sat in on a Keene community TV show several times, and was interviewed by three radio shows in Massachusetts.

I was enchanted to have various Muses perched on my shoulders whispering two chapbooks into my ear: *Passwords and Passages,* which described my experiences cycling through the Wiccan year, and *Musings & Miscellany*, which expanded on my feelings and understanding of loss and bereavement. I've also written many short stories and one steamy erotic poem, had several of my pieces selected for inclusion in *Witch Eye: A Zine of Feri Uprising,* the *We'Moon* calendars, the *In the Spirit of We'Moon: Celebrating 30 Years,* Crone magazine's *Women Coming of Age,* and *The War Crimes Times,* and was reviewed in *Mezlim:*

Practical Magick for the New Aeon. Then, one unbelievably magickal Full Moon night, I was doing a personal ritual under our Gathering Tree (a huge white pine named Theofila, for my great-grandmother) when I began to hear a song—softly, over and over, coming from somewhere up in the branches. I'll accept the fact that this sounds overly fanciful—but it really happened! The song kept running through my head until I started humming it out loud. Then, before I could forget it, I ran into the house, sat at the piano, and began to pick out the melody and scribble it down. It called itself "Chanson à la Lune" or "Song to the Moon." I realized after a while that it might be a good chant for the 2016 Full Moon Gathering of Women. I found a musical genius who transposed it to sheet music that the ladies could read (I have an odd unintelligible style). So when I stepped into the center of that 2016 Full Moon's closing Circle to release the fire lantern into the night while the women were singing, it was a terrifically powerful moment.

Which religion were you raised in?

If I wasn't at home, my folks always knew where I was: at the Tenafly, New Jersey, Presbyterian church up on the hill. I was a Sunday school teacher, sang in two choirs, was a disastrous first soloist (ouch!), and, during my teen years, was a frequent lector in the Grace Youth Chapel, originally called "the old stone chapel." I taught vacation Bible school and sock-hopped my feet off at the church-sponsored Teen Canteen (yes, that's right, kids—it was the *Tiger Town Teen Canteen!*). And because a voice in me hinted at something deeper, I took seminary classes where I learned from a guest Taoist priest that "all paths lead to the top of the mountain."

How and when did you decide you were a Witch?

Growing up, I had hints that I was a little different from most kids my age. My family first lived in Cotswold Manor, one of the most beautiful estates-cum-apartments in New Jersey, and the home of Glenn Miller and actor "Uncle" Dana Andrews. I used to play on the grounds, looking for fairies, which my grandmother told me lived under the topiary hedges. I hid in rhododendron thickets by the former stables and felt the Earth calling and holding me. I never told my parents where I was, because that place was "special," and my invisible friends played there. Although my parents did teach me that fairy queens slept in carnation flowers. It was an unbelievably magical childhood to which none of my friends could relate. Furthermore, once puberty hit and I learned about sex 'n' stuff, I started to have some serious questions about a virgin birth and a single male god creating the world. But above all, I wondered where, as a girl, my place was in this whole religion thing. However, times being as they were in the 1950s, the existence of a *real* Witch didn't even cross my mind, although I was already starting to wonder about "bigger things" and ask questions that my folks or the church didn't have the answers to.

My great-grandmother Theofila had "the sight" and foretold the death of one of her own sons, my great-uncle Leo. My grandmother Bun "knew things," and my mother, Claire, read palms and cards and could turn quartz crystals pale colors when she held them. One of her startling yet innocent questions to me was, "Honey, what does it mean when the crystal turns greenish?" This from a woman who was the first deaconess in the aforementioned Presbyterian church!

However, the event that I came to recognize as my "crisis of faith" or "wound that makes the Witch" occurred after a visit back to Tenafly as an adult in a last-minute visit to a Sunday sermon up on the hill. At that time, the Unites States and the world were in great psychic and emotional turmoil from the sudden onset of the Gulf War. The sermon, preached that Sunday, didn't address the urgent spiritual needs of the congregation. In fact, the young minister seemed oblivious to the horror that was occurring. He preached on some topic so irrelevant to that crucial time when the community needed hope to get by that I could not comprehend why in heaven's name he chose it! I was absolutely devastated. The core of my being was shaken—and my faith in the Christian doctrine to comfort deep anguish was shattered. I sobbed for seven hours during the drive back home to New Hampshire. Throughout that ride, I felt my soul sending an urgent prayer that my feet be put on a path where *I* could learn to offer emotional and spiritual help to those who were in pain. Why, I wondered, couldn't I become a minister at age forty, since I knew deep in my bones that I could do a better job? It wasn't more than two weeks later that I unknowingly met with a group of people who were Witches. Then I was truly "home."

How do you personally define Witchcraft?

From my personal point of view, Witches are frequently, but not exclusively, women, or gay men who have been wounded by the tenets of the Abrahamic patriarchy—by an unfeeling, perhaps unknowing society that demands conformity out of fear or ignorance of "other." Despite opposition and ostracism, these same people have been compelled to find a deep and close connection to Divinity and often weave an intensely individual, maverick spirituality that uplifts and ennobles their essence.

In fact, I discovered that most people don't even know they have the option to create their own spirituality. They are chained to the orthodox, expected, "approved" religions (or no religion at all), but once that "secret option" is uncovered, the beauty of the individual soul breaks through. I was overjoyed to discover that, yes indeed, as a woman, I had a very important connection with the feminine faces of Divinity—the goddesses—loads of them! Wicca showed me that Divinity wasn't reserved only for men. There were sacred goddesses everywhere—not "female figurines" as listed on the museum plaques, but representations of ancient revered goddesses! Wow! The figurines predated Christianity, and, admittedly, years do not confer authority—but women were revered as divine and equal to any male god earlier I had ever imagined.

The United States is undoubtedly a nation of teams. It's "us" versus "them"—the Sox versus the Yankees, the home team (us, the good guys) versus the away team (those bastards)—and cheerleaders whip the crowd into a frenzy. But far too often, a toxic masculinity pervades the games, and the fans of the other team can get emotionally and spiritually crushed. Now substitute the team names with the names of any of the three Abrahamic religions. When I look around, I find teams in every category everywhere, but no one is really "winning."

Witches are on the front line of ecological sanity—leading protests, writing, or visiting governmental agencies. Nature lovers are chaining themselves to, or living in, trees (thank you, Julia Butterfly) to raise awareness of the importance of Gaia. If nothing else, we are lovers of all the faces of Nature. We're animal rescuers, farmers, foresters, climatologists, herbalists, healers (yes, AMA board-certified physicians, too!), and wildcrafters (like myself). It's a partial list, to be sure. There's nothing as soothing as a silent experience alone in Nature. This is the legacy we've inherited from our ancestors—work with Nature, understand Her ways, then get off your butt to do something that contributes to Her healing. By the way, teach all this to your children—they're the ones who will carry on our legacy. The deeds they do should reflect respect for the Earth, honor for the ancestors, and self-discipline. I think that's how many of us feel: comfortable knowing we're connected in an honorable "family" with a worthy heritage.

In ancient days, folks weren't as distant from natural cycles as we are today. Back then an enclave of women all bled at the same time. Now, with more artificial lights and the invasion of seductive technologies, Nature's cycles have been hip-checked off the natural order of things. So I'm really grateful I have a calendar (OK, so it's on my computer!) that reminds me of the Equinoxes and Solstices, the Sabbats and Esbats—something the earliest farmers and country folk had to be mindful of if they wanted to survive and have food to live through the seasons.

I personally love these times when Covens in the area get together and celebrate the seasons. We party, hold workshops and classes, swap information (we call it cross-pollinating), see what's what with other groups, feast, and invite the gods and goddesses to bless the get-together. Rarely do attendees disdain individual differences; more often than not the differences are incorporated in other groups' activities.

Which tradition of Witchcraft do you follow? How did you find that tradition?

I met Raven, my husband and initiated Priest, while I was attending a formalized semiregimented, dues-paying kind of Wiccan "church." He was just in from California, where he'd been initiated into the New Reformed Orthodox Order of the Golden Dawn Tradition, which originated from a course project on Witchcraft at San Francisco State University in the late 1960s, and then the Tower Tradition—a small fam-trad with a long and complex lineage and history. At the time we met, I was also being taught by the Priest of the semiregimented "church," but the teachings there were superficial and not what I needed. I felt there was something more to be found in a deeper spirituality. Raven was gentle and knowledgeable—always encouraging me to ask why and look deeper. I could turn to him when theological, doctrinal, or personal ignorance arose. It was a happy day in September when he (and his Initiatrix Br----., my "grandmother in the Craft") initiated me into the Tower. We became the New Hampshire Granite Tower— to differentiate us from the folks back in California. I've never looked back. It has been a constant joy and has provided my ongoing identity as a Priestess, which I vow to hold until I die.

What makes your approach or tradition unique from any others out there?

The Granite Tower is not a Coven per se. We saw the damaged egos and personality issues caused in several formalized Covens we've known and opted not to follow suit, which isn't to say that we don't have a huge Pagan/Wiccan community that we work for and with. Furthermore, the Granite Tower is not a degreed tradition. No one holds a higher level of importance than anyone else. Some of us have been at it longer and can pass on a bit more knowledge—that's all. And there's a strong mandate for service to others. The Granite Tower is charged with helping any person of any—or no—religion find the path that meets the needs of *their* soul if they are discontented or are seeking a deeper connection to Divinity. We don't lean on them to become a Witch, Pagan, or heathen. When someone is so vulnerable, it's the equivalent of conversion at sword point, so we metaphorically clear the roads by day and light the towers at night in order that those who come after us can find their *own* path. I remember helping a young man find his way to comfort in a Christian community, and a woman find her path to Judaism. The former caused a somewhat convoluted yet oddly flattering situation (I suppose) because he was so overjoyed to have found *his* "place" and was so grateful for my listening to what his heart needed that he began to worry about me burning in hell because I was a Witch. The thought of me burning truly terrified him, and so we had many long-into-the-night reassuring discussions to dilute his anxiety. I was deeply touched that he cared so much.

Would you say that Witchcraft is a "craft" or a "religion"? And can you talk about the difference?

Personally, I don't feel Witchcraft is a religion. Religions are characterized by brick-and-mortar buildings, doctrines (you'll pardon the expression), litanies of proscriptions, bylaws, organized hierarchies, governing bodies, and fairly rigid rules and regulations. Money almost always plays a significant role, whether it's by tithing a percentage or putting money in the box or onto the passed plate. This is *in no way* a condemnation of the sincerity of religious belief, but I have found that Wicca/Witchcraft tends to avoid belief in "things unseen" and leans more heavily on *experiencing* them. There are very few brick-and-mortar Wiccan churches; most of us gather outdoors or in an occult cellar. When teaching, I cite Starhawk, who says one needn't believe in a rock; one can actually experience it by its heft and size. Furthermore, I don't need to believe in a sunset; I can experience it and in so doing, by the sheer glory of it, gasp at its beauty. In my opinion, that gasp is the instant that I touch Divinity. I don't need a book or someone else to interpret what that sunset means to me. It's my personal and very real experience, and obviously, I'm trying to increase the number of times that I can gasp in awe.

Then there are the seasonal celebratory aspects of Witchcraft. The various Pagan groups in our area that I know understand that the cycles of Nature, the world, and the cosmos reflect the birth-to-death spirals we ourselves travel through. Because Raven and I are now Sage and Crone, we no longer have the energy to host the eight holy days and Esbats. And besides, doing so prevents others from stepping up to the plate and growing in awareness of what's involved in assembling the necessities to present a meaningful seasonal celebration. Therefore, we're delighted to be invited to Circles all around the New England area for various Sabbats. I do host an annual Full Moon Gathering for Women, and we both have led the closing ritual at Celebrate Samhain organized for the past eleven years by the incomparable Kevin Sartoris of Muse Gifts & Books fame. The following weekend in October, we host our own Samhain at the Covenstead, and I'm involved in almost a dozen individual rites and rituals a year—so I keep my hand in.

On the other hand, the "craft" of Witchcraft appears as myriad expressions of innermost talent. Often, those inspirations appear when peacefully meditating. At other times that creativity blasts forth in a mad dash to the pen, forge, herb garden, charcoal, paint, fabric, loom, stones, gems, clay, camera, or stove. The resulting manifestation is most likely part of a personal connection to, and urgent expression of, a specific god or goddess. Sadly, however, I've learned that often those bursts of blazing and self-satisfying talent do not necessarily equate with financial profit—and so I must be content with the experience of the gods flowing through me. Of course, it's nice when the stuff sells!

Whom do Witches worship?

The word *worship* implies (at least to me) bowing down, groveling, self-abasement—perhaps kissing a ring—so I shy away from using it. I think "have reverence and deep respect for" is a bit closer to Wiccan practices. If we substitute a figure of Ishtar, the Morrígan, or Thor for that of Jesus and do nothing more than "worship," then it's SSDD (same stuff different day). It takes a bit more work to look through the physical idol/statue to see the highest qualities represented by that Divinity up there on my altar. I need to draw *those intangible traits* into myself—not get hung up on the statue. The physical thing can rot, be eaten by bugs, crack, and so on, but the principle it stands for will remain in the heart of a sincere and intelligent seeker. When I was called at 11 p.m. to pick up a friend at Logan Airport unexpectedly, I called Artemis/Diana into me. She represents light and protection of the vulnerable, and I felt her essence inform me when I drove like the wind (in the rain, by the way) to pick up my friend. That's the "drawing down" intent Margot Adler wrote about in her seminal book, *Drawing Down the Moon*.

When Witches meet, what do they usually do?

Celebrate seasonal and personal changes, hug, kiss, feast, dance. Some make love, play games, cross-pollinate ideas, and gossip. In other words, what just about any other group of friends would do—only we do it in handmade robes!

Do Witches really do "spells" or can they do "magic"?

Both. Often, after sunset at the right phase of the Moon, my daughter and I would get to work. We'd clear out a section of the kitchen, light candles and incense, get down herbs drying on the beams, open my herbal grimoire, put on a Loreena McKennitt or an Enya CD, then take a breath and soak up the mood. When we were under the influence of the scents, sights, and sounds, one of us would cast a Circle, and we'd begin to make magical or medicinal tinctures, decoctions, or incenses. Sometimes if there was a person in need present, I'd help them create a binding or show them how to protect their property or prepare themselves to attract an appropriate lover. I found the trick was not to do the magic *for* those requests, since the more the seeker puts into the working, the more committed and responsible they are for the outcome and the more potent its result will be. The results for that working will reside with the one who's doing it—not me. That's a responsibility I don't want to invoke.

The Wiccan Rede is one of the very few laws that exist in Witchcraft. In 1964, Doreen Valiente presented the Rede in simple language that lays out a moral system to guide Witches/Pagans. Though there have been many subsequent repharsings of it, the main tenet of the Rede is easily remembered thusly:

Eight words the Wiccan Rede fulfill, an it harm
none do what ye will.

The second portion of the Rede says:

Lest in thy self-defense it be, ever mind the Rule of
Three.

The Rule of Three states that what you give out, or do to others, comes back to you three times—it's akin to the Golden Rule.

And yes, I've led a cone of power that blew a stereo off a wall—but the husband, the crux of the problem, never bothered my friend again.

There's an old adage I am inclined to go along with that says you can't cure if you can't curse. There's the dark and the light to the Craft, and all must be kept in balance. Repercussions of *any* action must be understood and accepted. However, should I, or a child, or a dear friend, come under attack, I have the power to greatly curse the offender and know I will not experience retribution three times.

Are you a hereditary Witch?

No, though there are many instances where otherworldly experiences and manifestations have occurred thorough the matrilineal side of the family.

Have you experienced any difficulties—any problems, persecution, or prejudice—as a result of being a Witch? Can you describe a time or times when that happened?

My mother (the crystal-changing Presbyterian deaconess) was just thrilled when I told her I was a Witch becoming a Priestess. She was behind me 100 percent to the point that, I'm told, several of her close friends sighed when she rabbited on. On the other hand, my father would go into embarrassing rages when he discovered that my mother and her friends were reading the horoscopes, or "cards."

An ex-husband called my Pagan women friends "FemiNazis" (please note the title "*ex*-husband"). One of my sisters-in-law won't talk to me because I'm a Witch, though she has no idea whatsoever what that means, except what she has seen in gruesome Hieronymus Bosch paintings and German woodcuts!

There was a particularly discouraging instance when both Raven and I were invited by a dear Christian clergy friend to become part of an interdenominational advisory council at an extremely prominent religious site in southern New Hampshire. We were the only two Witches on it, but we worked quite happily with a Buddhist, a Muslim, at least two Christian ministers, clergy from the Tree of Life Church, an agnostic, and a Jew. We became quite close, realizing that the differences in our views of Divinity were fascinating to learn about but nothing that should divide us. However, somehow word got out to the Christian ministers in the region that "the Witches were taking over" the organization. This totally spurious information caused many scheduled weddings and services to be cancelled—not to mention causing a great deal of distress and anger on the part of the advisory council. Additionally, the "great experiment" of a true interdenominational group as counsel ended when the governing body of the organization refused to listen to any suggestions for improvements to the grounds and buildings and a new altar design that would represent *all* faiths that sought comfort there. So we resigned, and in solidarity, so did the entire advisory council.

Any other thoughts you care to add?

I feel the key to acceptance of anyone representing Wicca is personal integrity: the way I conduct myself and the values I represent have served me well in my dealings with the public and other groups. For example, the Granite Tower tapped friends inside and outside our community and gathered about seven hundred pounds of clothes for victims of Hurricane Sandy in New Jersey. In November 2016, we collected a huge load of warm winter clothes to go up to the Native Americans and supporters at Standing Rock, in the Dakotas. We've also collected/donated money for community members who are down on their luck or experiencing bad health.

There are occult actions we take as well—because it's not us who are the focus, it's the need of the "others." Recently we gave a presentation to our town, including the local police department, about Witchcraft—it was right before Samhain, when Witches are often dragged out of the closet to give a party some "panache" or "realism." Ha! But it was a well-attended event with lots of valid questions and positive comments. One town official said he could listen to us go on for another two hours because he was hearing fascinating information that he'd not been privy to all these years. I call that a successful night!

The Craft can be had by writing to me at sbmillett@tds.net.

MATOOKA MOONBEAR

Salem, New Hampshire

First, can you say a bit about who you are, where you live, and what you do for a living these days?

I am a self-identified Witch and have journeyed the Craft and other Earth-based spiritual practices for over twenty-five years. I am an accomplished Priestess in Feminine Mysteries, creating ritual, rites of passage, and shamanic initiation. My practices include multiple shamanic traditions that encompass working with animal allies and creating ritual tools such as sacred drums and rattles. I am the creator of Hoops of Life Divination, a shamanic reading system for guidance.

I am an ordained minister with the Temple of Witchcraft, where I served as lead minister for the Mother aspect (Ministry of Cancer), teaching and leading women's mystery circles for the temple. I have completed the Priestess path apprenticeship and am an initiated High Priestess with the Temple of Witchcraft and the Sisters of the Burning Branch (SOTBB). I am also a Reiki master teacher and Kriya massage therapist. I was a member of an Amma satsang for two years in New Mexico, and I continue to maintain annual visits with Amma. Because I am passionate about Divine Feminine Mysteries, up until now I believed my great work would be in the healing of the feminine principle in the psyche of humanity. Now I feel that it is in healing the Divine Masculine as well.

Presently I live in Manchester, New Hampshire, with my husband and pets. I continue to practice my vocation as a Witch and Priestess in the world, facilitating Full Moon rituals each month at the Temple of Witchcraft as well as offering workshops, rituals, sessions, and shamanic consultations through my Hoops of Life Divination readings. I also continue to practice massage therapy.

Which religion were you raised in?

My mother was raised Lutheran and my father Jewish. They parted when I was very young with the agreement to let me choose my path when I was old enough. I was not raised with any organized religion.

How and when did you decide you were a Witch?

When I was fourteen years of age, I proudly announced that I was a Witch to my mother and siblings! It just came over me! I looked for books, but there were none available at the time. It wasn't until the mid-1980s when the New Age was at its peak that I found books covering Earth-based spiritual practices. I used to frequent a New Age bookstore called the Expanded Mind and purchased shamanic books and Native American spirituality at first. When the store closed, I decided to open my own shop over my garage with a friend. We called it Morning Star Loft. It was more an Earth-based spirituality shop under the guise of the usual New Age metaphysics. One day, a woman in her sixties walked through the store and glanced over everything like she was on a mission. Then she walked up to me at the counter and asked if I was Wiccan. I responded with a no. She stared at me, and I saw the Crone . . . it sent an energy right through me! Her reply was, "Well, you should be!" Then she walked out. I was stunned, but then I remembered my proclamation at fourteen and knew this was my path.

We brought in books by Scott Cunningham, and after reading his books, a familiar feeling came over me like I was remembering, and I knew this was what I had been looking for as a teen.

How do you personally define Witchcraft?

My personal definition of Witchcraft is the practice of magick through the close relationship with nature and the elements earth, air, fire, and water. Practices include spell work, meditation, and journey skills and cultivating psychic powers such as communicating with nature.

Which tradition of Witchcraft do you follow?

The tradition of Witchcraft I presently follow is actually an eclectic blend of Divine Feminine through Dianic Traditions that I trained in with SOTBB and the Temple of Witchcraft. By this I continue to cultivate and integrate my practices of the Craft. For me they connect deeply because I first trained (online) in the Goddess School Tradition with SOTBB, where I found healing for my journey as a woman. It was that journey that prepared me to become the lead minister for Ministry of Cancer. Because this is a Divine Feminine ministry, I was uniquely qualified.

After a year of leading the Ministry of Cancer, I entered the Mystery School of the Temple of Witchcraft. I wanted to speak the same language as the other ministers and members of the Temple of Witchcraft Tradition. So, I made a five-year commitment to complete this journey and initiate as a High Priestess of the Temple of Witchcraft.

How did you find that tradition?

First of all, I want to share that for many years I was self-taught and practiced as a solitary Witch. I read books that were available to me at the time and practiced from what I read. I was also very drawn to writings from Sun Bear on Native American spirituality, which led me to my interest in shamanism. These personal studies cultivated my roots as a Witch.

Along the way I gathered with some women who were Dianic Witches. We held monthly circles for a short time, after which the circles faded, and I was on my own again. I met a Mohawk Elder who was willing to teach me his spiritual tradition if I studied with him for four years. Eventually I felt guided to return to the Goddess Mysteries, and this led to my quest for training in a tradition in 2005.

After my mother passed away in October 2005, I needed some sort of order. Some stability. I decided to search for training in an organized tradition and found the Goddess School. After reading about the school, I committed to my studies and initiated as a fourth-degree High Priestess of that tradition.

I met Christopher Penczak at a Witchy shop where he was teaching around 2004. He was friendly and warm to me, and I was touched by his presence. Occasionally I would show up at other workshops he was offering. One day, I had heard that he and his partners were officially starting the Temple of Witchcraft as an organized religion, and I approached him about it. We set up a meeting over dinner, where he shared his vision of how the Temple would be structured with the twelve zodiac ministries. Then he mentioned the Mother Ministry of Cancer, and I asked him straight out for the job! After some meetings within the Temple, I stepped into the position. After about a year, I decided to study the Temple traditions and signed up for their Mystery School. The rest is history.

What makes your approach or tradition unique from any others out there?

I think the fact that I use all the trainings that I have gathered in my life experience and integrate them into my expression of spirit as a Witch that is uniquely me. I am an expression of shamanism, which I cultivated through self-study, Goddess Mysteries, and the Temple of

Witchcraft. One of the ways this shows up in expression is through my Hoops of Life Divination reading system. I integrated all the traditions of Earth-based study as an honoring of the ancestors to dance upon the wheels of life and speak messages for shamanic consultations, to help others become aware of the rhythms and cycles they live, within the changes of the seasons and all stages of human life.

Would you say that Witchcraft is a "craft" or a "religion"? And can you talk about the difference?

I suppose one has to decide what it means to be in an organized religion. I believe a religion is responsible for growing one's spiritual evolution as a person. It is meant to be a guide for growth and a self-help aid as well. For me, Witchcraft is my spiritual journey and practice. All my expression of spirituality is through the Craft, using the timeless traditions of those who have come before us and given us what we know as Witchcraft today.

This is what Christopher Penczak accomplished, through his own spiritual journey in the Craft. He wove together all the proven spiritual workings of traditions that were upheld in each path into what is now our Temple of Witchcraft Tradition. This is not new; only the culmination of everything organized together is seemingly new. He did a fabulous job, and the process works well helping people not only practice Witchcraft but grow spiritually into ministerial-level High Priestesses and Priests.

Witchcraft can be practiced as a science without a focus on the spiritual components. There are Hermetic laws, such as "As above, so below," and Newton's law, which says, "What goes up must come down," as well as laws of attraction using the magnetic field of focused intention through spell work . . . this is what I mean by a science.

Whom do Witches worship?

Not all Witches worship; however, many of us are indeed Pagan and worship deities. For many it is a Goddess creation path. Often there are goddesses said to be the queens of Witches—Hecate, Diana, and

Aradia, to name a few. The worship of a god is usually as a goddess consort, like the Horned One or Green Man of primal nature.

When Witches meet, what do they usually do?

When we meet we celebrate the Witches' Wheel of the Year, starting with Halloween as our new year. We call it "Samhain." Then Yule, which is the Winter Solstice; Imbolc, the first stirrings of spring beneath the earth; Ostara, the return of the Maiden and outward signs of spring; Beltaine, also known a May Day; Litha, the Summer Solstice; Lammas, the first harvest of grain; Mabon, the second harvest of fruits; and back to Samhain, the third harvest of meat. We gather in these celebrations to do ritual, honor the season, and help turn the Wheel of the Year without and within us.

We also gather for Full Moons and Dark Moons, using the energies for magick and healing.

Do Witches really do "spells" or can they do "magic"?

Yes, we really do spells, and it is magick. I distinguish real magick, with a *k* at the end, versus the magic of illusionists done by magicians on TV.

If you do any spells, can you give examples?

My favorite go-to spells are improvised as needed in a moment. I often will use the four elements in whatever representations are available—perhaps by a stream for water and using a leaf for earth, a feather for air, and a match, lighter, candle, or the Sun for fire.

Petition spells are where you write your desire down and then burn it. But you can put your intention into an acorn or a stone and throw it into a body of water, too.

Are you a hereditary Witch?

I am not a hereditary Witch per se, but my mom was pretty magickal in her way. Also her great-grandmother on her mother's side was a psychic medium who used to help the police find missing people.

Did your family carry stories about Witches or did you find out about it all recently?

I just always felt magick, and the rest of it I have shared in writings above.

Have you had relationships or friendships with other New England Witches? If so, with whom? And what were the most significant experiences or learnings you had from those encounters?

I do have many friendships with New England Witches. I feel hesitant in naming my Witch friends, as I wish to honor their privacy. The list is long, as I am part of the Temple of Witchcraft community. I have had profound experiences in workshops and rituals held by the Temple for several years.

Do you have any interactions with Witches in the Salem, Massachusetts, area?

I do know a few Salem Witches. I do not have personal relationships with them. Some of them attend our Temple events.

What is your impression of the current interest in Witchcraft in Salem, centuries after the Witch hysteria of Puritan times?

Well, the town of Salem became well known, particularly because Laurie Cabot, the Official Witch of Salem, lives there. I personally am grateful to her for helping the area become more relaxed around the use of the word *Witch,* so much so that they capitalize on it. Now it is a big moneymaker.

Have you experienced any difficulties—any problems, persecution, or prejudice—as a result of being a Witch? Can you describe a time or times when that happened?

When I first came out of the broom closet, my then husband was furious about Witchcraft, so much so that he threatened our marriage! His anger shook me. I was so surprised by the response. Since then, I have had people back off getting to know me because of my religion. I have experienced coworkers treating me like the plague. I have not experienced public persecution.

What are special holy days for Witches?

Witches' holy days are called Sabbats. Everything about the holy days is about seasons—spring, summer, autumn, and winter—and the cycles of the solstices and equinoxes.

Witches believe that we help turn the Wheel of the Year by doing rituals for these sacred days. We surely align ourselves within by this work, deepening our spiritual process and connection to divinity in nature.

Samhain is the Witches' New Year, the ending of the cycle of life. Veils between the ancestors and our world are thin. The psychic connection is stronger because of it. Leaves have fallen. It is known as the third harvest of meat. In old times it was when livestock was slaughtered.

Yule is the Winter Solstice, the longest night and the rebirth of light. We begin to see the promise of light returning and celebrate the return of the solar gods.

Imbolc is in the early spring and the time of lambs being born. The light is growing stronger and the trees stir. We are in the middle of winter, yet there is hope.

Ostara is the Spring Equinox, when light and dark are equal. It is the return of the Maiden aspect of the Goddess. Spring is returning, and life is renewed. We consider our gardens and prepare for planting.

Beltane is also known as May Day. The dance of the Maypole is typical. We celebrate with joy that life has returned, and passions flow. The birds are building nests. It is mating season.

Litha is the Summer Solstice, the longest day. Though we are in the heat of summer, the days begin to grow shorter.

Lamas is the first harvest of grains, ground to make bread.

Mabon is the second harvest of fruits. Often grapes are made into wine.

Lunar days are called Esbats. Full Moon is ever celebrated for magick by Witches everywhere. The Moon has the power to move the tides of the sea. Spell work is often done on the Full Moon. The Dark

Moon is a powerful time to banish unwanted energies from our lives.

Can you please describe what Witches do on their holy days? How do you celebrate?

Witches embody the Sabbat day through honoring the essential energy of the meaning it brings. We do rituals in the day's name and call on the goddesses and gods of old. We have many ways of doing these rituals. What is pretty much constant is that we cast a magick circle of protection, creating a between-the-worlds space. We call on the four directions and elements, north for earth, east for air, south for fire, and west for water. Some Witches do east for fire and south for air.

We call on the powers of above, below, and between. We invite the Goddess and God. Once all this is in place we perform the rituals involving the power of that day. We offer cake and wine as the union of Goddess and God. This is done with a chalice and an athame (ritual knife). Putting the blade in a cup of wine three times represents the sacred rite of the Goddess and God's union. Once the magick is complete, we open all that we called in with hail and farewell, then open the magick circle.

Any other thoughts you care to add?

Only that I thank you for the opportunity to express myself here as a Witch.

Blessed be!

MORGAN DAIMLER

Connecticut

First, can you say a bit about who you are, where you live, and what you do for a living these days?

LAURA HINE-CERMAK

I live in southeast Connecticut with my husband and three children. At this point in my life I am an author, writing books on subjects relating to Irish Paganism, mythology, and fairy beliefs. I've previously held a diverse array of jobs including being an emergency medical technician and a school bus driver. My middle child has some complex medical issues that make working outside the home difficult, but writing is something I can do anytime on any schedule, so it's worked out well and allowed me to keep busy and keep some kind of income coming in.

Which religion were you raised in?

I was raised a secular agnostic, which basically means that I wasn't raised with any specific religion, but my family didn't discourage belief in a higher power, and we celebrated the generic secular holidays. Christmas was about Santa Claus and magic reindeer, Easter was about a magic bunny that brought candy, and so on. This was rather lucky for me, as I have always seen and related to spirits—having what the Irish call the "second sight" or "spirit sight"—and my family was pretty tolerant of me talking about seeing fairies and ghosts at a young age. I'm sure they put it down to a vivid imagination, but being in a position where it wasn't discouraged was good for me because I never repressed it or questioned my own sanity; it was just another aspect of reality to me.

How and when did you decide you were a Witch?

When I was eleven a friend introduced me to the idea of Wicca through Scott Cunningham's book. The concept of Paganism and Witchcraft fit in perfectly with the worldview I already had and made a lot more sense to me than what little I knew about monotheistic religions. I quickly went on to read other available books on Witchcraft, like those by Buckland and Leek, and within a short amount of time considered myself a practicing Witch, although later I would also start down a spiritual path that included Celtic Reconstruction. I see the two working together, as I view my Witchcraft more as a practice than a religion in itself, but that does get to be a gray area.

How do you personally define Witchcraft?

As I just mentioned, I see Witchcraft as a practice, although it does also cross over into my Pagan spirituality. For me Witchcraft is defined by the practice of folk magic, or low magic, and a strong connection to the land around you. It's about working with spirits and using the materials at hand, as opposed to high or ceremonial magic, which is more complex and requires harder-to-find, exotic materials. I think animism is a key aspect of my Witchcraft, and that becomes a segue into Witchcraft and Paganism for me and then into spirituality, which is why I say it's a gray area. I can, I think, be a Witch without any religion, but my spirituality is so caught up in my Witchcraft that it would be hard to sort them out.

Which tradition of Witchcraft do you follow? How did you find that tradition?

I have at this point developed my own approach to Witchcraft that I call "Fairy Witchcraft." It's based on the Celtic Fairy Faith* and on the practices of the old cunning folk and *bean feasa* (Wise Women) but also blends in the more solitary—some might say negative—aspects of Witchcraft, things that separated the old Witches from the more community-oriented cunning folk or Druids. To me, this is where the difference lies: Druidism is a service to the community, while Witchcraft is a personal practice. The actual spiritual beliefs are otherwise pretty similar.

What makes your approach or tradition unique from any others out there?

Since it's rooted in a Celtic Reconstructionist† methodology, it's a lot more historically based than many others, and it's focused a lot on the older forms of folk magic, spells, and charms that I've found in books, for example. It also focuses a lot more on dealing with spirits and creating alliances and working relationships there as well as protections and knowing how to banish things. I find that most modern forms of

---

*For more information on Fairy Faith, see the documentary by John Walker, *The Fairy Faith*.

†For more information on Celtic Reconstructionism, see "The CR FAQ: An Introduction to Celtic Reconstructionist Paganism" by Kathryn Price NicDhàna et al. at www .paganachd.com/faq.

Witchcraft don't deal as much with the spirits; they only focus on deities and don't do much with actual working magic, if you will, beyond things like prosperity spells or healing. This is more of a hands-in-the-dirt approach, I think. It's a bit more experiential as well and more focused on the idea that the Otherworld and its inhabitants are a reality that we need to acknowledge and deal with to succeed.

Would you say that Witchcraft is a "craft" or a "religion"? And can you talk about the difference?

I think it's both, although as I've mentioned I approach it more as a craft. I think any religion, particularly any Pagan religion, can be incorporated into a Witchcraft practice, but my own Witchcraft isn't necessarily about the religious end of it. The Paganism I practice is a spirituality that is based in honoring specific Irish deities, and several Germanic ones, and in connecting to and honoring the spirits around me, particularly the Good Neighbors—what most people would call fairies. I think I could be a Witch without being a Pagan, or religious at all, but I could also be a Pagan without practicing Witchcraft. So, to me, the two definitely cross over but are distinct.

Whom do Witches worship?

Most Witches I know worship a goddess and god paired together, or sometimes a goddess alone, usually from a known pantheon. In my own case the Witchcraft I practice acknowledges the deities associated with Fairy. I call them the liminal gods, and see them as kings and queens of Fairy, although also gods. It's kind of a fine line there even in the folklore. This is one of the aspects of my Witchcraft that is somewhat unique. It is something that has developed over a long period of time, and while I do also worship deities from the Irish pantheon as well as some Germanic ones, my Witchcraft tends to be very specific.

When Witches meet, what do they usually do?

Most Witches I know are pretty normal people who like to hang out and talk about the same things as non-Witches. But we can also get together and start talking about esoteric things, like herbs for magic, or making incense, or spell work. I enjoy spending time with other Witches just to get those different points of view and new ideas and ways of seeing things. I enjoy the conversations, even when we don't agree, and I like the way the community has such diversity in it.

Do Witches really do "spells" or can they do "magic"?

Witches do spells, certainly. As to whether the magic works or not, that's always going to be a matter of opinion. I believe magic is effective, which is why I practice several forms of it, but because it's like anything else that isn't tangible or easily measured and quantified, a die-hard skeptic will never have evidence solid enough to convince them. I would say, though, just from a psychological perspective that I think spells and magic still have real value because they make us feel empowered in our lives.

If you do any spells, can you give examples?

Much of the magic I personally practice is based on folk magic and on spells from older sources. I think the purpose of magic for the Witch is to make the Witch's life better, so I will do spells for health or protection and that sort of thing. I like to combine chanting with something physical like an object that can be kept as a talisman or charm, or burning a candle.

Are you a hereditary Witch?

I am not, no. I came to Witchcraft from a secular agnostic family with parents who had been Christian.

Did your family carry stories about Witches or did you find out about it all recently?

My family did not have stories about Witches, but there were stories about fairies, which did influence me. I think that aspect of my family heritage is interwoven through my own current practice to some degree.

Have you had relationships or friendships with other New England Witches? If so, with whom? And what were the most significant experiences or learnings you had from those encounters?

I am pretty active in my local New England Witchcraft community, so I have many friendships with local Witches. I cofounded a tradition called Crossroads Witchcraft with my friend Allison Joanne, who owns a store in Norwich, Connecticut, and that tradition is doing well and has many members now. It represents a combination of my own Fairy Witchcraft and her approach gained from her years of practice.

It would be hard beyond that to name specific individuals, but one thing I can say is that knowing so many people on such diverse paths who all consider themselves Witches has been a wonderful way to learn to appreciate diversity.

Do you have any interactions with Witches in the Salem, Massachusetts, area? What is your impression of the current interest in Witchcraft in Salem, centuries after the Witch hysteria of Puritan times?

I have been to Salem a couple of times as a tourist, and I admire the historical sites there. History is a big thing for me, and I think anyone who lives around here should visit Salem at least once to see where such an important event occurred. I don't know any Salem Witches very well, and the ones I met when I visited were mostly people running shops or doing tours.

I think that on one hand it's a bit odd for Witches to fixate on Salem when from a historical perspective we can say that almost certainly none of the people executed or accused were actually Witches, but on the other hand I can understand why Salem has become a symbol of freedom for Witches, and I think that's a good thing.

Have you experienced any difficulties—any problems, persecution, or prejudice—as a result of being a Witch? Can you describe a time or times when that happened?

I've been a Witch since the early 1990s, and I think things were definitely harder in my area back then. I once had an adult come up to me when I was maybe thirteen, in a bookstore while I was looking at occult books, and tell me I was going to hell in a very aggressive manner. I was laid off a job when I was in high school shortly after my employer found out I was Witch, and I had problems in school with people spreading rumors about me. When I was a sophomore, for example, a girl I didn't even know who sat behind me in a math class overheard me talking to another Pagan friend and then went around telling everyone I'd put a curse on her. That was especially difficult for me because I was actually a really shy person then and the rumor got back to my younger sister, who was mortified. I think things today are better than they used to be. Overall, though, I think I've been lucky because I know that it's worse for people in more religious areas.

What are special holy days for Witches? Can you please describe what Witches do on their holy days? How do you celebrate?

I celebrate the eight holy days that most Pagans acknowledge: the equinoxes and solstices as well as Imbolc, Bealtaine, Lughnasa, and Samhain. I also as a Witch acknowledge the Dark and Full Moons each month. For me holy days as a Witch are times to connect to the gods and spirits I honor and to work larger acts of magic. I celebrate by acknowledging my reason for being there, whatever the holy time is, making offerings to the gods and spirits, working magic, and doing divination. I also tend to sing a lot, which is just something I enjoy doing in ritual.

PENNY J. NOVACK
Berkshire Mountains, Massachusetts

First, can you say a bit about who you are, where you live, and what you do for a living these days?

I was trained in the Craft and initiated in 1968, though I already had a background in various religious and spiritual world practices. I live rurally in the northeastern Berkshire Mountains of Massachusetts on eighty-seven acres (or eighty-eight or eighty-nine, depending on my husband's memory) across a bridge that spans Clesson Brook—one of those brooks that doesn't run dry even with a drought and that can thunder with boulders being washed downstream in the spring melt.

As to my employment, I am retired. However, I still work for the local school system as a substitute teacher. For the rest, I join things, work for constructive change, and try to keep in touch with all my communities.

How and when did you decide you were a Witch?

I did not decide to be a Witch. I was advised by a Full Moon one night after a huge snowstorm that shut everything down and left me without a ride home. I was walking and complaining to it that I believed my spiritual growth had become stagnant. The Moon, astonishingly, answered. It told me that my problem was that even though I knew the Ultimate was genderless, I persisted in conceiving of it as male. And that was why I was so often in an antagonistic relationship with that essential Source. The Moon told me that until I could learn to conceive of the Prime Source as female as strongly as I did then as male, I could not progress. Then Witchcraft dropped into my life from several directions, much to my astonishment. I didn't even know about the Goddess having a place in the Craft. In fact, I knew nothing but that magic was a practice. The Goddess didn't leave much to chance there, I'd say.

How do you personally define Witchcraft?

Witchcraft with a capital *W* I define as being the magical and/or Priest/ess branch of the Old Religion in its various forms and regions of Europe. Some branches were quite shamanistic, and some much more ritualistic, based around the mythologies of the deities of their people. In the modern world there is a certain amount of mix-and-match going on since often people first find the Craft as a social and religious structure before they experience the gods/goddesses they belong to. This results in Witches having training in a particular tradition while perhaps their personal deity connection is from another pantheon or possibly from a drastically different part of the world. It can cause some confusion, but it also brings about syncretism, and that is one for the ages of humankind. It has always happened.

There is also the other kind of witchcraft, which is simply a practice of folk and ritual magic: magic for itself, magic for gain, magic to ease things. Such people may belong to a mainstream religion or may, in their process, have found Spiritualism. They practice the art of magic or the skills of herbalism, tarot, astrology, etc. They can be quite wise. Or foolish. But they are often not happy about being called Witches. They have a separate reality for their religious practices. And they don't want the label.

Which tradition of Witchcraft do you follow? How did you find that tradition?

I've come to see it as having been an eclectic mix of an unnamed traditional format dating back to at least the last years of the nineteenth century. The religious framework was strongly Goddess oriented, with some specific masculine deity relationships mostly around the seasons but primarily the artificer Manitou/God. I found many accretions—some Pennsy Dutch hexerei, for instance—and a very strong demand for rigor and research. While we were taught about ceremonial magic, we were not taught that magic was limited to any one tradition or that the deities we worked with were the only real ones.

What makes your approach or tradition unique from any others out there?

I don't know that our tradition is unique from any others. I don't know all the possible traditions in existence. What I found was that there was an insistence on looking for the power essence of the world around us, which superseded the use of formal ritual tools—though we did usually use formal ritual tools. The thing itself trumped the symbol of the thing at every turn. And we did not command the gods, the elements, or the Good Folk. We treated all with respect and circumspection. This was key to my understanding of what we were taught.

You were the first person to conduct a public Pagan ritual in the United States, as far as I am aware. Can you please talk about that? Did you encounter any difficulties from being a "public Pagan" in the 1960s?

I cannot say that I was the first person to do so. I'm not sure whether the Midwestern group Church of All Worlds had public rituals. They tended to think in terms of Groves, I believe, but I don't think they were very secretive. They called themselves Pagans, though in the beginning they had a really limited sense of historic Paganism. Then there was the Egyptian group out in California. I apologize for not remembering their name. Margot Adler wrote about them in her book, *Drawing Down the Moon*. And, of course, Feraferia was around for quite a while.

I know that Joe Wilson and Ed Sitch were doing something in the Chicago area, too. How public they were I don't know. I do know that we began the Philadelphia Pagan Way in 1971. There had been about a year of correspondence with Joe and Ed and a few other people here in the States and in Wales. For all I know it went further than that. Michael and John and Jeannette were much more active in creating the rituals than I was. Some of them were pretty awful, actually. Long windy invocations, lousy poetry. All the faults later Pagans were pleased to point out. For our particular use, we switched things around as it made sense, and I tried whenever possible to rewrite the invocations, etc. Long invocations are boring. I can't imagine the Goddess is fond of the bad poetry either.

Would you say that Witchcraft is a "craft" or a "religion"? And can you talk about the difference?

Hmmm. There is a magic craft element but a Witch can be a Witch with very little magic if they are a true Priest/ess of the gods. The gods come first, but it can also be the will of the gods that one serve as a healer, a teacher, a bard, or a Priest/ess at rituals for the community. The private practice of Witches ranges from solitary practitioners to Covens. Those who simply practice magic—whether formal or folk, energy healing or/ and herbalism—but without the mythic and cultural religious relationship have often been called witches. I have no problem with that. They are not practitioners of the Old Religion, so they are not Witches.

Whom do Witches worship?

The Old Gods.

When Witches meet, what do they usually do?

It depends on whether they're in the same tradition. And even then there's usually some circling the hall, so to speak. Come on, they're real people.

When Witches hang out socially they can relax because they share a paradigm. When Witches meet as a Coven they follow the practices of their tradition. In many traditions a Circle is cast, worship practices occur, and often at least some magic is performed. Often the magic is simply a general working for health and prosperity. Beyond that I would not try to explain because it would either take a book of great length and probably years of research and travel or it would be nonsense.

Do Witches really do "spells" or can they do "magic"?

Magic is a constant natural force, in my personal opinion. Many magical workings are done unconsciously, and doing spells is something even children try. Spells as formatted formulas—recipes, so to speak— are also common in every folk culture of all nationalities. Witches create frameworks that are essentially aimed to focus the mind and will toward accessing the magical force available within the world. Some use recipes/spells/formulas and find that works well; others create a framework anew each time something accessing magic must be done.

If you do any spells, can you give examples?

Weather songs are spells. There are small sayings to honor the earth and the seed when gardening. Your question doesn't give me scope to respond.

I do not tell people spells unless they are so simple and benign that I am sure they will not accidentally get into trouble or cause harm. People who have been trained are different, but I would hope they would not perceive a rote spell as some kind of end-all. It's only an example to take off from.

Are you a hereditary Witch?

No.

Have you had relationships or friendships with other New England Witches? If so, with whom? And what were the most significant experiences or learnings you had from those encounters?

Of course I have, and no I do not make public the names of people in my community. You know many of them. I was taught courtesy and confidentiality. Those who want to be named would say so. Do you want me to call everybody up and say Ellen wants to know who I hang with?

As to what I experienced/learned? Too much to tell. Ways of approaching healing, rituals that opened the energies of the Earth and brought tears to my eyes, laughter and sharing on levels as ordinary as a potluck and as deep as the soul itself. Every encounter is a new learning.

Do you have any interactions with Witches in the Salem, Massachusetts, area? What is your impression of the current interest in Witchcraft in Salem, centuries after the Witch hysteria of Puritan times?

I have had. They seemed like good people. But there were only a few and that was in 2013 when the Covenant of the Goddess had Merry Meet in Salem.

I'm not really conscious of it in a strong way. I think it's there, but it isn't part of my life. Some of the interest has always been there, of course. And Hollywood and television have used their idea of witches and Salem over the years. But it isn't in my personal life framework.

I know that you have been very politically active in the last year. Can you talk about how that intersects with your spiritual path?

I have personal politics relating to my concept of a better future within the structures of human society. These include finding ways to transform our society into one that is at least tolerant of others of differing faiths, ethnicities, races, and genders and finding social mechanisms to help transform institutions and, even more importantly, make it possible for everybody to be educated in terms of not only facts (scientific and otherwise) and skills but attitudes that allow greater success in life and economics. I think this is generally called "progressive" these days, though not so long ago it was "liberal." Language changes, and the realities chug right along, changing slowly, slowly.

However, in terms of my spirituality, anything that intersects with the health of earth, air, and water in the Gaian framework has deep spiritual meaning for me and always has. Whether or not our spiritual framework expresses itself by the gods of place, process, time, or transformation, Gaia remains the framework within which the truly sacred plays out. She may be a living ecosphere or a timeless goddess, but she is both to me. And we humans are trying to kill her stupidly and thoughtlessly while complaining all the while that we don't have any choice.

I believe our tragically organized economic system is at the core of much of which is destroying our Gaian and human future viability. I perceive its effect upon our living planet and the soul of Gaia as relevant to my spirituality. We humans must learn to behave ourselves in relation to each other, but that is our own evolutionary problem. To me it is not a spiritual problem. To others it is the only spiritual problem. It's a matter of focus.

You are quite an enthusiastic poet. I wonder if you could share some of your verse?

Touch Me

Goddess, you are all around me.
And I only awake enough
To know you a little—
But you move
And the hills are a glory

You speak and the trees are dancing
You touch me and I am real.

PENNY J. NOVACK, FROM *YOUR LUMINOUS SELF,*
HTTP://ASPHODELPRESS.COM/POETRY.HTML

Any other thoughts you care to add?

I struggle with this. I hope your other people are able to answer the questions in a more interesting way. You know I am her daughter, and I know you are her daughter, and we both honor the sacred, and that is what we meet within. But on many levels of being part of society we are different. When I was doing organizing of Pagan ritual and working on bringing the Old Religion as I knew it into the public sphere, I was doing it because there was no one else. You have worked for so long doing that kind of thing that I know it is your fate, your path. For me, the public sphere was taking on a task to honor what was sacred to me. I basically abandoned it when it became obvious that others were willing to take up the task. I was a poet and a metaphysician. Occasionally a scholar—though I make no great claims. I've met many people more charismatic in the resurgence of Paganism and Witchcraft, and I say, may the gods bless them. I am proud of much that I see in the way one is proud of family members who realize their talents and skills. I do not look for glamour and glitter. I look for the heart, the sacred core.

RAVEN GRIMASSI

Springfield, Massachusetts

First, can you say a bit about who you are, where you live, and what you do for a living these days?

I am a full-time author and teacher, with over twenty books in print. I have been a practitioner of Witchcraft for over forty-five years of adult life. I currently live in Massachusetts, where I love the distinct changing of the seasons. I teach classes and workshops on a variety of topics including Witchcraft, magic, and inner mystery traditions.

How and when did you decide you were a Witch?

I feel it was more decided for me than by me—that is, at least from the onset. My mother was born and raised in Italy, and when she emigrated to the United States, she brought with her what I call a peasant tradition of Witchcraft. It had been in her family lineage for several generations. I grew up with this enchanted worldview and formalized my place in it when I was thirteen. From that age forward I fully embraced the title and the ways of the Witch.

How do you personally define Witchcraft?

I feel that Witchcraft is a magical practice and a spiritual path. For me, it is rooted in pre-Christian European concepts and practices. I feel that Witchcraft is connected to the ancestral spirits and to spirits of the dead. Its magic is tied to the Spirit of the Land, the forces of Nature, and the mystical emanation of the Moon.

Which tradition of Witchcraft do you follow? How did you find that tradition?

For most of my life I practiced a form of Italian Witchcraft, which, as I mentioned, I inherited from my mother's lineage. However, I also practiced, and was initiated into, other systems such the Pictish-Gaelic, Brittic, and Traditionalist Celtic. In 2005 I created the system I now practice, which is called the Ash, Birch, and Willow Tradition. After several decades of practicing culturally based systems, I found myself exploring the commonalities of old European systems. I felt drawn to practicing the core elements of Witchcraft as opposed to how any singular culture expressed it. My system joins together ancient concepts with modern needs, and in this light the Ash, Birch, and Willow Tradition is ever ancient and ever new.

What makes your approach or tradition unique from any others out there?

We focus more on working with plant spirits of the Greenwood Realm. One important spirit we work with is the Mandrake, as this ally serves as a mediator with plant spirits and related chthonic entities. Outside of that we don't work with a formal Sun God figure, but instead we work with a terrestrial God, whom we call "He of the Deep-Wooded Places." He has a solar connection but it is secondary. We also work with a lunar Goddess whom we call "She of the White Round." Through them we touch the Divine within the celestial and the terrestrial.

Would you say that Witchcraft is a "craft" or a "religion"? And can you talk about the difference?

I see Witchcraft as a religion/spirituality that contains a magical system. Magic is the energy and process of creating desired manifestations; it is what a Witch does, whereas religion/spirituality is what a Witch is within. The religion is composed of an enchanted-world view in which there are spirits, entities, and deities who aid and support the Witch. Magic is the means and the tool a Witch uses to raise and direction energy as well as to interface with the forces of Nature.

Whom do Witches worship?

I would replace the word *worship* with the word *venerate*. I think that the simplest answer to this question is that Witches venerate the personification of celestial and terrestrial forces. These are commonly depicted as the Moon Goddess and the Horned God, or Antlered God. The Antlered God is most often associated with the Sun. There is also veneration of ancestors and of the Spirit of the Land. This may not be universal, but at least it is a marker of the older rooted traditions of Witchcraft.

When Witches meet, what do they usually do?

Formal meetings include performing rituals at the time of the Full Moon and during the Wheel of the Year, which is a collection of eight seasonal festivals. These are the solstice and equinox events along with four celebrations that fall between the equinoxes and solstices.

Full Moon rituals include the veneration of deities, works of healing, works of magic, and a celebratory feast. The Wheel of the Year rituals are about veneration of deities and the Spirit of the Land. They include singing, chanting, dancing, and merriment.

Do Witches really do "spells" or can they do "magic"?

Yes, I believe that the ability to perform magic is one of the things that defines being a Witch. A spell is simply a charted way to perform magic that manifests a personal desire. Magic is tapping into the source of power behind magic, as well as magic being the process through which energy is obtained, charged with an intention, and then directed off to manifest the desired outcome. The energy that becomes a work of magic emanates all around us. The art of magic teaches us how to gather this energy to us, make it cohesive for use, and then pass intent into the energy sphere. This becomes the vehicle through which magic is delivered.

If you do any spells, can you give examples?

Mortar and Pestle—The Calling. To perform the spell, begin by placing the mortar on its side. The pestle is inserted inside the mortar and rotated clockwise against the edge of the mortar. Begin moving slowly and then speed up the motion. Say the incantation (see below) and then pause to state your desire. Repeat the incantation for a total of three rounds:

> *Turn the Wheel*
> *Set the task*
> *Bring to me*
> *The thing I ask*
> *[State intent]*

Once the incantations have been completed, hold the mortar in one hand and the pestle in the other. Shake them off at each cardinal point (east, south, west, north) and say: "Go now to the four winds and return with my desire fulfilled."

Are you a hereditary Witch?

I prefer being called a "lineage bearer" as opposed to a hereditary, but yes, as I mentioned earlier, I cut my teeth, as they say, on an old system of Witchcraft from Italy. I call it a "peasant tradition" as it has many archaic elements rooted in the lore and magic of rural people. At its core is the veneration of ancestral spirits and the Spirit of the Land.

In the Italian language a female Witch is called a *Strega,* and a male Witch is a *Stregone.* In contemporary Italian language, Witchcraft is known as *Stregoneria.* I use the older form, which is *Stregheria.* The latter appears in eighteenth-century writings to denote a religious practice as opposed to just simple sorcery, which is what is denoted by *Stregoneria.*

Among Italian Witches who view Witchcraft as a religious practice, there are many different deities involved. Italy is comprised of many different regions with different dialects, customs, and lore. Therefore, there is no "one size fits all" when it comes to describing the Witchcraft of Old Italy. In the tradition that I practice we focus on a goddess named Tana and a god named Tanus, although there are other deities to call upon as well. That being said, the tradition itself was very much lunar based.

Many people associate the legendary figure Aradia with Italian Witchcraft. Folklorist Charles Leland wrote about her in the late nineteenth century in his book *Aradia: The Gospel of the Witches.* It depicted her as a goddess who came to Earth as a Witch to teach the arts to peasants who were suppressed by feudal lords. It should be noted that not all Italian Witches were, or are, connected to the story of Aradia. There are many Witches without a gospel.

Did your family carry stories about Witches or did you find out about it all recently?

I grew up with the old tales along with Italian folklore. It was something not spoken about to people outside the bloodline. It was empowering and isolating at the same time. In my adult life it became problematic and cost me many relationships that I greatly valued. It also brought skepticism, allegations, and disfavor. But one cannot truly stop being what one is in order to appease others. That does not last very long.

Have you had relationships or friendships with other New England Witches? If so, with whom? And what were the most significant experiences or learnings you had from those encounters?

Yes, I have had relationships with other Witches in New England. Some of them were business related and others were friendships of various depths and sorts. What I took away from these relationships was knowledge of the different types of personal character, integrity, and views of magic and ritual. The diversity of the Witch was quite significant to me.

Do you have any interactions with Witches in the Salem, Massachusetts, area? What is your impression of the current interest in Witchcraft in Salem, centuries after the Witch hysteria of Puritan times?

I rarely visit Salem anymore, but when I did it led me to meeting a variety of individuals. Among the most memorable are Christopher Penczak, Laurie Cabot, and Lori Bruno, to name but a few. I found in each person a passion and steadfastness in who they are and what they believe.

Any other thoughts you care to add?

One of the most valuable things to me about being in New England as a Witch is the area's changing of the seasons. I am from California, where the only way you know what season you're in is how the stores are decorated. New England brings to life the core of how and why the seasonal rites are formed, and the season calls for you to fully participate (as opposed to visualizing). This has enhanced my sense of the seasons as well as my appreciation for the lives of ancestors in days of old.

My books include *Italian Witchcraft, Cauldron of Memory, Spirit of the Witch, Old World Witchcraft, Grimoire of the Thorn-Blooded Witch*, and *Communing with the Ancestors*. For more information, you can visit me at http://houseofgrimassi.com.

RAVEN MORGAINE
Coventry, Rhode Island

First, can you say a bit about who you are, where you live, and what you do for a living these days?

I'm Raven Morgaine, owner and resident spiritual worker and artist at Familiar Spirits in Coventry, Rhode Island.

How and when did you decide you were a Witch?

I'm not sure people "decide" to be a Witch, any more than they decide to have green eyes. You certainly can choose to go out and study the Craft, find a Coven, and be initiated or even self-initiate, but you don't need to be initiated into any tradition to be a Witch. Witches are born, not made.

How do you personally define Witchcraft?

The purposeful manipulation of energies to affect a person, place, or thing, to be technical, but it is more; it's a way of life. For true Witches, the Craft permeates every aspect of their world, their homes, their art, and possibly (like me) their work.

Which tradition of Witchcraft do you follow? How did you find that tradition?

I personally do not follow any tradition of Witchcraft, though I do practice magic. I feel that so many of the new traditions that have popped up are watered-down copies of traditions that already existed. I'm a dinosaur in the Craft for sure. I learned in the 1970s and 1980s from people who learned in the 1940s and 1950s. What we learned wasn't Wicca; it was the Craft—undiluted, unreformed, un-dumbed down, unsterilized, live only in the light, do only "good" magic.

In my day we learned that Witchcraft had teeth and claws. We were taught to balance our light and dark, not abandon one for the other, which leaves you not only unbalanced but also, in the long run, ineffectual. Nothing in nature is either all good or all bad; what can cure can kill. I have always said that a Witch who can't hurt can't help.

What makes your approach or tradition unique from any others out there?

It's honest and involves personal accountability, which is something I find lacking in many, many, many traditions as well as in many modern Witches themselves. All the infighting and vendettas and personal agendas—it's all very disheartening and sad, frankly. And that is truly the reason I don't dedicate myself to any of the traditions. I don't practice the religion of Witchcraft; I practice the Craft, the art of magic.

Would you say that Witchcraft is a "craft" or a "religion"? And can you talk about the difference?

It can be either of those things or neither of them. Personally I view Witchcraft as an art and a science, and certainly a craft. For some Witches it certainly is a religion, but that isn't the craft part of it, the worship. You don't need religion to practice magic. These things are not mutually exclusive; it isn't that simple.

Whom do Witches worship?

Good question. I hear Hecate is becoming very popular these days. Witches who follow the religion typically worship the forces of nature personified as a Mother Goddess and a Father God. In my early encounters with that side of the Craft it was usually Pan, or a similarly horned god such as Herne, and Diana the Moon goddess or Gaea the Earth goddess. Many practitioners worship no specific deity at all, just God and Goddess in a general sense of the words. It really all comes down to the duality of nature, the equal and opposite forces that shape our world with their polarization.

When Witches meet, what do they usually do?

Mostly say hello. (Laughs.) I think what you're asking is what happens when a Coven of Witches meet? Depending on their customs or traditions, they do rituals to celebrate and give honor to the living Earth, worship their chosen deities, celebrate holidays, hold classes, or any number of things, really.

Do Witches really do "spells" or can they do "magic"?

Some do, some don't. Some can, many can't. Not because they lack the ability. We all have the ability to do magic. However, what we do not all share is the confidence or the trust in ourselves or belief that we can manipulate the physical world with candles, herbs, potions, and will, which is sad. I personally believe that the ability to do so is the birthright of every person on Earth. The few who have accepted that power, that gift—*they* (*we*) are the Witches of this world.

If you do any spells, can you give examples?

Personally I do many spells for my clients at Familiar Spirits, for healing, love, luck, protection—you name it, people want a spell for it. I'm always glad to be able to help the ones who come to me with honest open energy; those are the ones I cast for. The dishonest, evasive ones—those are the ones whose work I refuse. I have turned many people away, probably more than I've accepted, because their energy, motivation, reasons, and perceptions were not conducive or appropriate for what they were asking me to do, which of course would be counterintuitive, to say the least.

If you aren't going to be honest with me, then you probably will not be honest with yourself, which can greatly, *greatly* affect the spell in the worst possible ways and lead to failure rather than fruition.

Are you a hereditary Witch?

Not really. My adopted mom practiced a sort of Catholic Witchcraft; my adopted dad was an Irish Catholic Eucharistic minister. Talk about a mixed marriage. My life growing up was rather like an episode of *Bewitched* sometimes, but no, I don't come from some long line of Witches who passed the craft down through granny after granny, and to be honest, neither are most of the people who claim to be. It's always the same story: they were taught by some long-dead grandmother, never a father or uncle or cousin; it's always, always the dead grandmother. Of course, I'm not saying that it is never true, just that more often than not people feel it will give them some sort of position or unearned respect if they descend from some untraceable ancient bloodline, which frankly is sad. Respect should be earned through actions and accountability, not through who you are (or are not) related to.

Did your family carry stories about Witches or did you find out about it all recently?

Nope, not a one. I discovered the Craft when I was about twelve years old from a babysitter who was a legitimate High Priestess of a Coven that practiced on a neighbor's farm. My mom never called what she did magic, let alone Witchcraft. To her it was just, like, what you do, like burying saints and doing novenas and chanting the rosary. People she was unhappy with tended to have more problems than others, but she never claimed responsibility for that.

Have you had relationships or friendships with other New England Witches? If so, with whom? And what were the most significant experiences or learnings you had from those encounters?

As a person living in the public eye and owner of the only real Witchcraft/Voodoo shop in my town, I have met hundreds of Witches in New England. Vending at public Pagan events might up that estimate by quite a bit. There are many more of us than an outsider might think. Unfortunately, most of my most significant experiences have been with people who are untrustworthy, charlatans, users, and fakes pretending to be spiritual to make a quick buck and trick gullible clients out of their hard-earned cash. These also tend to be the ones who talk the loudest about how evolved, spiritual, or "powerful" they are.

Do you have any interactions with Witches in the Salem, Massachusetts, area? What is your impression of the current interest in Witchcraft in Salem, centuries after the Witch hysteria of Puritan times?

I have many friends in Salem and the surrounding area. It is important to realize that the Witchcraft craze did not begin or end with Salem; there were executions and trials in Rhode Island and Connecticut and as far away as Virginia. The persecution of witches lasted hundreds of years in Europe, not just the handful (by comparison) that it lasted in the New World. Salem got a lot of press, but it is not the be-all and end-all of the entire Witchcraft world.

I believe that the current interest in Witchcraft in that town comes in two different flavors: authentic and poser, plain and simple. I admire and respect the "authentics"; I know many of them, some better than others. The "posers," the ones who want to be Salem Witches because they think it's like some kind of merit badge, or it gives them some sort of status, make me sad. The chances that any real practitioners of Witchcraft were persecuted, tried, or executed in Salem are slim, and there is no factual information about any of the tried except for Tituba, but what she practiced came from the islands. She wouldn't have called it Witchcraft, nor would she have called herself a Witch. In fact, it was probably more like African magical traditions rather than anything else, so really what does it matter if you lived there or studied there?

The lineages of Witches in Salem are short lived and rather new. To act as if coming from a place where some of the worst displays of human ignorance and madness happened isn't really merit-badge worthy, in my opinion. I will say that many of the more famous modern Witches in Salem have done some wonderful pioneering, worked hard for their community, and opened many doors for those who come searching for the real magic, not the tourist tripe that overruns a good half of the town's many shops and venues.

I talk all the time about how important the very visual Witches were back in the beginning. The ones who made it easier for us to practice our craft without fear or even own shops like ours, because without them, we wouldn't be able to. So my opinion of Salem is very mixed . . . maybe obviously (laughs), but it's honest. The other fifty thousand witches in

New England get overlooked by media and authors, which is unfortunate because they have a wealth of stories and experiences that are just as important as those of our kin in other places.

Have you experienced any difficulties—any problems, persecution, or prejudice—as a result of being a Witch? Can you describe a time or times when that happened?

Of course. I think many of us, especially those of us who live in the public eye, deal with it almost daily, as I'm sure almost every other Witch has or does. Prejudice and discrimination are alive and well in America, as recent events have shown, and once again we all live under the thinly veiled threat of the revocation of religious freedom. My biggest, most disconcerting experience with this actually comes from the local Pagan community where I live.

Because my craft comes from a different place and a different worldview, Pagans often treat *it* the way Christians have historically treated *them*—with disbelief, mistrust, and discrimination. As they forget how they once cried out for tolerance and understanding, they have been less then reciprocal. I have heard more stories about myself than I can count. One half thinks I'm a saint, the other half says I'm an evil witch doctor. Before I opened Familiar Spirits, I lost jobs because of discrimination. I have lost friends, family members, and even contemporaries who refuse to believe that their Craft is *not* the only Craft, which shows the same single-mindedness they so despise in others.

The first month my shop was open, someone threw a piece of concrete through the glass doors. Shortly after that, paint was thrown on my front window, but we cleaned it up, prayed for protection, and made offerings, and we have remained in this town and building for four years. These acts of vandalism were done by other Witches, not Christians. Not religious right types, but other Witches, who wanted my business to fail. However, I refused to live under the boot heel of fear and rose above it. But then that's the shocking and alarming part, isn't it? That your own community, which should stand together, does more damage to each other and themselves than any outside force.

What are special holy days for Witches? Can you please describe what Witches do on their holy days? How do you celebrate?

Because the Craft that I practice is non-European, I don't really celebrate most of the Witches' holy days that people are familiar with. I do celebrate the Autumnal Equinox and Winter Solstice, most often privately, quietly, and in very personal ways and sometimes in a small family group. The rest are feast days dedicated to the spirits I work with directly, days that are considered to be the birthdays—for lack of better comparison—of these spirits and their special feast days. One example: New Year's Eve belongs to the spirit Yemaya. We call her the owner of the new year, and we celebrate by sending small rafts covered with flowers, fruit, sweets, strings of pears, mirrors, and combs, among other items prized by this Spirit of the Ocean, out into the sea to ask her to bless us and our work, families, children, etc., in the upcoming year.

The pilgrimage on this night in Brazil is a spectacular thing to behold as a river of people in white flow down the mountainside, onto the shores, and to the sea to praise the mother of all that live, the universal womb. For me there is no greater magic anywhere than to witness that and to be *part* of that.

Here is a simple charm for New Year's Eve: Find a beautiful shell, the kind with the opening on the side, not a hinged one. Write your wishes or petition on a small piece of paper and add holy herbs of Yemaya like bergamot, watercress, and white rose petals and perhaps even a small pearl or bit of silver. Seal the opening with wax from a white or blue candle, focus all of your psychic power—all your passion, desire, and will—on your goal, and toss the shell into the sea. Take seven steps backward before turning your back to the sea to go home.

Any other thoughts you'd like to share?

I am particularly disappointed in the state of affairs within our own community of Witches. There's something people like to call "Witch wars," which are basically very hypocritical; this one hates that one, so let's get all "Mean Girls" and try to sabotage their businesses or drag their names through the mud. We tear at each other like snarling wolves, instead of lifting each other up like *family* is meant to do. We are all children of this Earth, and we are better than this. To live in a place of such fear and scarcity is wasteful. There is enough for all. What we need to do is use our magic to heal each other and ourselves and get back to the wisdom we have so lost sight of.

ROXIE J. ZWICKER
Portsmouth, New Hampshire

First, can you say a bit about who you are, where you live, and what you do for a living these days?

The winding roads of New England have led me to the smallest seacoast in the country: Portsmouth, New Hampshire. The city dates back to 1623 and the old homes, cemeteries, and ocean beckoned me here and caused me to stay. Walking down the cobblestone sidewalks in the shadows of two-hundred-year-old buildings is like walking through a time machine, and there is something about it that feeds my deepest soul. There is no place I'd rather live, if given the choice, than in this "old town by the sea," as it's called by the locals.

I immediately connected on so many levels with the area, and I decided to learn as much as I could about the history, culture, and community. It wasn't long before I decided to volunteer on the board of directors for Portsmouth Harbor Lighthouse. When the first summer that I was on the board came to a close, I proposed a fund-raiser for the month of October. I thought it might be fun to do ghost walks in the local waterfront park to benefit the lighthouse. Back in the early 1990s I had taken a part-time job leading wagon rides of people into the woods for some Halloween storytelling, so I decided to build on the skills that I had gathered during those years. I spent some time researching the area and put a couple of walks on the schedule and sent out a few press releases. I was surprised by how quickly the walks took off; each walk sold out nearly immediately, and I had anywhere between fifty and sixty people on each tour. They lined up afterward to share their stories of the spirits that inhabited their homes or workplaces, or ones that had been passed down in their families.

I continued to do the walks for the lighthouse for the next several years and during that time I also began my own walking tour company, called New England Curiosities. I thought it would be something fun to do and would help connect me to the community. I didn't know what I had begun. What was planned as a few walks a couple times a month brought a lot of attention. Before I knew it, I was approached by a publisher to write a book about the haunted history of Portsmouth, which led to me authoring seven books on New England folklore. Once the first books were released, I was contacted by television stations, first some of the local New England channels and then the History Channel and Travel Channel. All the while I was working seventy hours a week in the finance department of a large international company. Echoing off my cubicle walls, my intuition told me that I would be making a change and to trust the process. All of my Tarot card readings signified a major change that would lead me into incredible creative opportunities. I trusted my intuition, and as scared as I was, I left my "day job," and I developed my own personal rituals to bring me the courage to move me forward.

I was lucky to have been approached by several businesses in the city who partnered with me for events and even served as a home base for my tours. Historical homes, organizations, and businesses welcomed me into their properties to share stories of spirits and history as well as to run an occasional spiritual workshop. Then came the day that one of the shops I partnered with, who knew well of my magickal leanings, asked if I would be interested in cohosting a workshop on love magick and divination. The workshop was a huge success and a lot of fun, with people from all spiritual paths in attendance. Behind the scenes I was still following up with my magickal work, and through meditation and reading signs from kindred spirits, I knew something big was about to break.

I'll never forget sitting in the back of the shop where I was working and hearing the words, "What would you think about being part of a pop-up Witchcraft and curiosity shop for the month of October?" My heart fluttered in my chest, and I couldn't believe what I was hearing. Finally, it was all coming together. Deadwick's Ethereal Emporium was conceived and work behind the scenes began. It was exciting to bring a Witchcraft shop back to Portsmouth, as there hadn't been one for a few years. The first shop in the city had flourished for a number of years, then another opened and seemed to do well for a time, but it eventually moved to a neighboring town. This was going to be a place where I could conduct Tarot and tea leaf readings as well as mix potions, create mojo bags, hold public circles, and teach workshops.

The month of October flew by like the shadow of a flying Witch over the Moon. People were coming to the store from everywhere in New England. What was going to happen after all the magick of the month passed at Samhain? The shop closed on November 1, as originally intended, yet people kept showing up at the door, and email and phone messages were received daily. The decision was made to reopen for December, but to close again until the following October. Once again the flurry of activity was amazing. The community, curiosity seekers, and practitioners were filling the store.

Discussions took place in the back room all month about the possibility of keeping the store open on a permanent basis, as there seemed to be an undeniable need. On Christmas Eve the announcement was made that the store would remain open to serve the community. I am pleased to be their business partner, resident magick maker, house reader, and local tour guide. Every morning my feet hit the floor with gratitude and my rituals are always filled with sincere thanks to the God and Goddess for their support and guidance. I choose to stay connected to the community outside the shop as well. I volunteer for several local organizations, particularly those that are involved with historical preservation, storytelling, and community media. My company New England Curiosities has evolved into a tour and event company, and I travel all over the Northeast to lecture on New England history, folklore, customs, and ghost stories.

I have also been called to open a sacred space called the Divinity Lounge in Portsmouth, New Hampshire—a classroom, peaceful retreat, and spiritual sanctuary to host community gatherings, which I am most proud of.

Which religion were you raised in?

My path is indeed the path of the Witch, and it has been a crooked one, since the day I was born in Boston, Massachusetts, in August 1970. I remained in the hospital for the first six months of my life due to a health condition that had to be closely monitored, and eventually I was adopted into a Jewish family that became less than welcoming over the years. I attended Passover dinners, bar mitzvahs, weddings, and all of the obligatory celebrations. No one really explained what the histories of the traditions were to me, but they never resonated with me anyway. The decision to move out of the city and into the countryside of Massachusetts is one that I am grateful for every day, and that's where I discovered my religion.

How and when did you decide you were a Witch?

I was able to grow up spending a lot of time outdoors as a child and that is where I started to connect with nature, fairies, trees, and spirits. I remember I used to sit in the grass and ask the flowers to move and bend against the wind, and I would place my hand over them to feel their energy. I probably wouldn't have described it as energy at the time, but somehow I knew that we were communicating in our own way. I recall late one summer afternoon, I was about eight or nine, and while on the playground, a light sun shower misted down from the sky. I reached out my hands for the refreshing feeling and closed my eyes. I saw and felt a warm golden glow around me and opened my eyes to see the raindrops turn to small white flowers falling from the sky.

There were no bushes of white flowers anywhere on or around the property I was standing on. The flowers tumbled around my feet and across my fingers, and they smelled so sweet. All of a sudden the flowers stopped falling from the sky and tiny silver specks, like a metallic glitter, fell instead. The ground was quickly covered in them. I couldn't believe my eyes. I picked them up along with some of the flowers and ran home. I found my favorite river stones in my room and took them, along with the flowers and silver glitter, and placed them in jar covers on my porch railing. I sat out on the porch for hours thinking about what had just happened, and I truly felt like I had been washed in magic. The next morning I went out to the porch and found that the little glitter flecks had gotten smaller, and the flowers had turned a light brown. Within a few days, the silver glitter had evaporated and the flowers had dried up. I wished and wished (and still wish) that someday it would happen again, as my heart felt so full and happy during that time. I thought about where they came from, and I knew in my soul it was a special gift for me.

It wasn't too long after the magick rain that I made a new friend on the playground. She seemed to be about my age, but I never asked her age, and oddly I never asked her name. She seemed to appear out of nowhere, but I was just happy to have a new little friend. I lived across the street from the playground, on the top floor of the apartment building, which was convenient for my mom, who would watch me from the window. I believe it was five or six times that I saw that little girl over a few weeks.

One day when I got home, my mother asked me who I was talking to out on the playground. I explained that there was a little girl on the playground with me. I was surprised to hear her say that there was no one on the playground but me. While I insisted that there was a little girl, I made sure to completely describe what she looked like to my mother. She explained that there had to be a reason as to why this little girl kept showing up and a reason why she didn't see her. Later that week she spoke to the property management and found out that there was a little girl matching my description who had drowned in the pond outside my bedroom window over thirty years before I saw her. I had to then contemplate what she was saying and what I had been seeing.

The next time I saw her out on the playground, she appeared to be smiling and happy. I know today that what happened next was a tremendous mistake on my part. I explained that I had told my mother about her. I then went on to tell her that she couldn't be talking to me, because I had found out that she had died in the pond, years before I was even born. Immediately, right before my eyes, she disappeared. She didn't turn and walk away. She was completely gone, and I never saw her again. I regret what I said to this day, and I've tried to make up for it in my spiritual work.

I think I was about eleven when I first started wearing a pentacle, and my motto has always been go big or go home, so the pentacle I had chosen was about the size of a half dollar and had a gold finish on a long chain. When I wore it to school, I remember the kids commenting and talking about it, completely misunderstanding its meaning. While I didn't speak as eloquently as I do today on the subject, I remember my response was to compare it to them wearing crosses, and to say that there was nothing evil about it, and that it represented the Earth and the elements. I enjoy looking back at some of my childhood pictures and seeing it displayed bold and bright. Somehow, everything I did seemed to stand out in the crowd. I never blended in and not much has changed today—and that's perfectly okay.

As I approached my teen years there were a couple more signposts on my path that connected me to the little Witch that was growing inside of me. My mother had two decks of Tarot cards in the house: the Rider Waite and an Egyptian Tarot deck that used to intrigue me. Of course, when I think of the availability of those tools to me at that time, it is important to note that you couldn't just go to your local bookstore to purchase Tarot cards; they were much more difficult to find.

So, I feel lucky that my mother mail-ordered these tools that I could explore.

I started doing little readings for myself and found that I was interested in my own interpretation of the cards as well as those in the accompanying books. I found myself reading my cards regularly and that the information I derived from them would come to pass.

It wasn't long after that I discovered tea leaf reading, and I bought a little china tea cup that had the zodiac and divination images on it. It seemed that I was totally hooked on fortune-telling, from its history to the application of interpretations, and I read and researched everything I could get my hands on. Whenever I went to the local library, I loved to peruse the old reference section of Witchcraft books. The reference section was located on the mezzanine, and the floors—constructed in 1894—were solid glass, which allowed the light to shine through from below and seemed to be magical in their own way. The books I was most interested in finding always seemed to be on the highest shelves all the way down the hallway. There was something about that that I really liked. I felt like a researcher from the past opening those dusty tomes and smelling the old pages, and when I sat with the books in the reference room, I always lost track of time, and I was usually the last one to leave. Something inside me just kept wanting to read more and learn as much as I could absorb. I found that I would skip reading my school homework assignments just so I could read another chapter in one of those old fascinating books. I still have an affinity and love for research libraries.

It's interesting to look back on those days, as the books that I piled on my reading desk leaned heavily toward the occult and Witchcraft, and there wasn't a New Age category at that time. Sometimes I would follow those books up with reading about legends and mythology from around the world. I had a particular affinity for unicorns, and my walls were covered in posters of medieval tapestries of them.

On the top of my stereo cabinet I placed a lace doily and some of my most treasured possessions: river stones, vintage pixie figurines, shells, candles, and unicorns, and that became my first altar. Sometimes I would put postcards of places I wanted to visit in the center of the altar, and I would sit there and silently think my wishes, while at other times I would just sit in front of the altar and write fantasy poetry. As the calendar pages turned, I knew that things on the altar had to be moved. In fact, some days I felt like my altar was speaking directly to me: "Take this figurine" or "Bring that candle holder"—I never questioned it; I just trusted what I was "hearing." I made the decision not to talk about it too much to kids in school or in the neighborhood.

Once in a while I would be inspired to walk through some of the local cemeteries, and I always found myself particularly excited if we were going to visit one on a school field trip. I could sense that there was movement around me, and sometimes I saw things out of the corner of my eye. There was a difference in my physical feelings, sometimes, standing at one particular grave as opposed to another. Strangely, when I look back, I never thought it was scary or bad; it was just an awareness that continued to develop—or tune in, so to speak.

We moved a lot when I was growing up, but I always seemed to tune in to the town that we lived in, so I could feel grounded in my own way. I went to three different junior high schools and two different high schools because we moved so much. Each time we moved into a new place, I made sure to greet the land within the first few days. I remember at one apartment in particular there were peppermint plants growing by the front door, so I went out and talked to them before I went to bed that night. I just felt that I had to because we were sharing the land together. Sometimes I would leave my favorite stones by the front door to connect with the space. I was always excited to find a place that had a lot of trees, and I would sit by the window and escape into the shapes of their branches and look for faces in their bark.

I've always been called to ancient tribal music, which seems to stir something deep inside me, and I've spent a lot of time looking into my past lives. Witchcraft has always seemed to me to be ancient, familiar, and intuitive all at the same time. Something tells me that somewhere along the way I'm picking up the threads from those in my bloodline who felt the same as I do.

I completely embraced the notion of being a Witch because it all seemed so natural to me. How could I be anything else? The religions that talked about divination being wrong and speaking to spirits as blasphemous were the furthest thing from me. In addition, there was a peacefulness that Witchcraft provided in my tumultuous upbringing that I couldn't find anywhere else. There was no way I was going to send my fairy spirit friends away because it was perceived as wrong or bad, and if all that meant I was a Witch, then I would be a Witch for life—and so it is.

How do you personally define Witchcraft?

To me, Witchcraft is a path where one seeks to call successfully upon magic energies and to follow their spiritual calling. That calling may include working with both feminine and masculine energies of the Goddess and God—both or either. And tuning in to the energies of astrology, the Sun, the Moon, the animals, and the elements, honoring the Wheel of the Year, the old holidays and traditions, and being in synchronization with the seasons and energies of Mother Earth and the cosmos. I am also a large believer in our ancestors being part of not only us but our path and legacy that we lend to future generations as well. Honoring and connecting people with ancestral spirits has been a large part of my personal practice, as I am adopted, and I feel that it is one of the reasons why I communicate with spirits and those seeking to connect with spirits. Witchcraft is all of that and more. I am a firm believer that you are a Witch 24/7—that it is not something that comes and goes, it is something that you become and are, and that there is magic in the everyday experience.

Which tradition of Witchcraft do you follow? How did you find that tradition?

While there are many traditions that speak to individuals depending upon the spirits or energies that they feel aligned with, I personally think that they are many paths leading to the same place. I also firmly believe that there is no "right" or "wrong" tradition of Witchcraft and that it is a very individual choice.

What makes your approach or tradition unique from any others out there?

I don't believe that my approach is unique for me; there are aspects of Witchcraft that I follow that are universal for many. What may be different are the twists and turns of my life path that cause me to call on particular energies or rituals at particular times. My goal is to help people feel comfortable with their spiritual choices and to offer up my experiences and gentle guidance on being empowered through Witchcraft to promote positive change and balance. One of the first things that I tell people in my circles and workshops is that the way I do things is not the right way; rather, the right way is *their* way and that they should tune in to what we are doing together and then take what supports them. Witchcraft doesn't have to be right or wrong, in my eyes. I've seen people get similar results in a situation, but they may have chosen to work with a different energy for the same conclusion.

Would you say that Witchcraft is a "craft" or a "religion"? And can you talk about the difference?

Whether we call Witchcraft a craft or religion is something that I can't completely solve, but here are my thoughts. If you look at the origins of the word *Witchcraft*, it is a religion. However, the Norse, Druids, and Celtic shamans among countless others practiced ancient Pagan traditions that were not labeled per se as Witchcraft. I believe the craft is the actual work that is done, whether it is done as spell work, herbalism, honoring God/Goddess/Diety, or working with energies or natural objects. There are many beliefs and just as many definitions, but I think each Witch brings the "craft" aspect to Witchcraft, weaving the web of magick, so to speak.

Whom do Witches worship?

Many Witches worship the masculine and feminine aspects of deity, also known as the God and Goddess. The God and Goddess are represented in the Sun and the Moon, so many Witches worship both of those aspects. However, some Witches also worship Mother Earth because they believe that without her, we would not survive. Many Witches worship various gods and goddesses of different traditions and mythology, while others may include working with a patron god or goddess that they feel called or aligned to on their spiritual path. I find that for myself, there are certain deities that you are called to at certain times, and there are some that stay with you on your lifelong path.

When Witches meet, what do they usually do?

When Witches have gatherings in my world, it's an opportunity for sitting in community for support and effecting positive change. When I conduct public circles, I always ask why people came and what they hope to take from the gathering. I spend time making sure we address the needs of people in the group. Some gatherings are focused on the Sabbats—the turns of the wheel—while others are focused on lunar cycles, or Esbats. We've gathered for healing circles and circles for working with gods or goddesses. I like to call quarters, cast a protective circle, and invite people to place sacred or personal objects on the altar for the gathering. Sometimes we will chant, dance, meditate, craft ritual items, or perform a combination of any of those things. Part of the circle is to raise energy collectively for those in circle and also for those in the community and the spirits of the Earth.

Some meetings are designed to be learned from through teaching, sharing, or storytelling. There always seems to be a lot to talk about when Witches meet up.

Do Witches really do "spells" or can they do "magic"?

Yes, I do spells, and I believe I can do magic. I've taught and spoken to many Witches who have great stories of spells that they have cast that have worked. I think sometimes that the results of spell work aren't anticipated—that people sometimes get what they need rather than what they want. I don't step into the arena of casting spells to hurt anyone, but it doesn't mean that I don't think those spells are effective as well. I think any concentration and alignment with corresponding energies can effect change. I believe that spells should be treated with great respect. Spells can affect much more than just the person casting the spell; as you move energy, it is creating a ripple that sometimes isn't immediately seen.

If you do any spells, can you give examples?

I've done spells to honor my ancestors and to help them move along on their path at Samhain. I have done spells for prosperity as well as for courage and releasing spiritual baggage. During one particular circle honoring the goddess Diana, I was seeking more joy and happiness on my path. I had been feeling overworked and quite burdened by day-to-day responsibilities. I created a recipe for a flaming cauldron wash, which was a combination of oils and resins designed to flame up out of the cauldron to aid in transformation. We sang in circle and focused on each of our intentions under the crescent of the Waxing Moon. Later that night, while on my way home, I was driving up my street and there in the center of the road was a beautiful white rabbit. I stopped the car and got out. He didn't move or try to run away as I approached him; he just sat there. Clearly he looked like a domesticated rabbit, as he was white and silver with beautiful blue eyes. Afraid that he might encounter a predatory animal in the neighborhood, I decided to bring him home and find out where he belonged the next day. Try as I might to find a home for that sweet rabbit, no one in the area claimed him. I noticed upon a closer look that he had a silver crescent Moon on the side of his head. Then I was surprised to find that, upon closer examination of the picture of the goddess Diana I had displayed on my altar, there was a little white rabbit at her feet. I knew it was meant to be.

I named the rabbit Hocus Pocus, and he offered me just what I was seeking: complete joy! You couldn't come home from work in a sad or bad mood, as he was always overjoyed in mannerism and expression every hour of every day. Anyone who encountered this rabbit found themselves feeling the magick that he brought with him. I have been lucky to have so many successful spells that I can't deny the power of intention and ritual. I've met some amazing fairies, gods and goddesses, spirits, and trees in my magickal travels.

Are you a hereditary Witch?

Not that I am aware of, but I think we all carry a bit of Paganism in our family tree. It just depends on how far back you want to go.

Did your family carry stories about Witches or did you find out about it all recently?

I was adopted, so this wasn't on their radar.

Have you had relationships or friendships with other New England Witches? If so, with whom? And what were the most significant experiences or learnings you had from those encounters?

I have many friendships with other New England Witches, and I find all of those connections to be supportive and uplifting. Some of the women are connected to me through the women's circle I facilitate in Portsmouth, New Hampshire. We oftentimes share wisdom and fellowship from our journey. I have attended many events with the Temple of Witchcraft based out of Salem, New Hampshire, and I've always felt welcome and comfortable. I've met a lot of people who have come up to me and said that they hadn't told anyone else that they practice Witchcraft, but that they were happy to know that there were more of us in the area.

Connection has often seemed to come up as an important thread for many people. I've sat in workshops with the Grimassis, and I've really enjoyed the way they present their teachings, particularly about working with trees, mandrake spirits, and the Tarot. I am inspired to listen to many points of view because there is always much to learn and discover. I've taken classes on herbalism and plant spirit communication with some amazing herbalists in New Hampshire, and I really respect the time and effort that these teachers put into learning their craft.

Do you have any interactions with Witches in the Salem, Massachusetts, area? What is your impression of the current interest in Witchcraft in Salem, centuries after the Witch hysteria of Puritan times?

Of course, being just about an hour north in New Hampshire, I do have interactions with Witches from Salem. There are many different opinions of what it means to be a Witch in Salem, and there are a variety of experiences that one can have in the Witch city. I think dialogue is good, since it's been hidden in the closet for so many years. Growing up in the 1970s and 1980s, watching Salem at the forefront of the current

Witchcraft movement in New England was wonderful. To be able to turn on the news and see rituals being done in the open in front of the community was very empowering. Hollywood and movies give the public varying degrees of what Witchcraft is and isn't, and theories and misconceptions abound.

What I think is great is that more and more people are seeking and asking questions, and now you can find Witches out of the broom closet not only in Salem, but everywhere. At Deadwick's we like to call ourselves the "Good Witches of the North." It's our tongue-in-cheek way of saying that Witches are everywhere. When we talk about Puritan times, which are covered at length in the Massachusetts school system, it's important to recall that the people who were put to death were not Witches. There are stories from Puritan times all over New England of people being accused and persecuted for being Witches that date back even earlier than the 1690s. If milk went sour, crops went bad, or there was disastrous weather, it could have been blamed on Witchcraft. Property disputes and personal vendettas kept the accusations of Witchcraft on everyone's tongue. Let's face it, people are curious about Witches, so we all have a responsibility in some way to tell people what Witches are and aren't.

Have you experienced any difficulties—any problems, persecution, or prejudice—as a result of being a Witch? Can you describe a time or times when that happened?

From time to time I will see someone glance at my pentacle and then give me a strange look, but that's been happening my entire life, so I just giggle to myself now when that happens. Sometimes when I walk down the street dressed in black, people will turn and say, "Oh, she's a Witch," and then whisper, to which I turn and smile and laughingly say, "That's right, I could put a spell on you," and then laugh. I believe there are many times when people don't know what to say. Sometimes people will walk into the shop, look around, and turn back and head out the door. Other people will come in and say, "Oh, it's like Harry Potter!"

What are special holy days for Witches? Can you please describe what Witches do on their holy days? How do you celebrate?

There are many holy days for Witches, but my personal favorites are Beltane, the Summer Solstice, the Autumnal Equinox, Samhain, and Yule. The Summer Solstice holds memories of many great rituals for me. Part of a ritual that I led included crystal divination and an invocation to the powerful solar energy that abounds to purify the mind, body, and emotions. Guests enjoyed a guided meditation that magically transported them to Stonehenge on the plain of Salisbury in England. The circle concluded with a colorful lantern walk through the city streets to the Portsmouth waterfront in celebration of the longest day of the year. We watched the Sun set over the river and at the same time enjoyed the full pink Moon rise over the ocean. The locals came out and took pictures of us as we walked the processional, and there were many people smiling as we sang on the waterfront docks.

Another Summer Solstice circle that I facilitated was on Star Island, just off the New Hampshire coastline. We looked to the west when the Sun was setting over the mainland, and the Full Moon was rising behind us in the east. The warmth of the rocks, which had been heating up in the June sunlight, was comforting and uplifting, and I was able to have a bonfire on the rocks that led out to an ocean cliff. When the tide started to come in after the ritual, it sounded like the ocean was singing to us. We looked at pictures of the bonfire the next morning, and we could see a beautiful fairy silhouette dancing in front of the flames.

One of my favorite Yule rituals that I attended was in the woods of northern New Hampshire. There was a beautiful little wooden house that was filled with music, incense, hot cider, and snacks as well as a roaring fireplace. Just outside the window was a beautiful labyrinth in the snow lit by luminary bags under a Waning Moon. The walk through the labyrinth was enchanting, listening to the crunching of the snow underfoot and looking at the light of the candles glowing in the snow. Pictures were taken as soon as I exited the circle, and there was a beautiful aura of energy around my body. It was truly a magickal turn of the wheel, and I didn't want the scent of the wood fire to leave my clothing.

Some Witches celebrate the holy days with ritual or feasting, while some may just step out into nature and meditate. Altars are oftentimes set as a focal point for the energies of the celebration. There is definitely a need for many to mark the passage of time and tune in to the energies of the Earth; it just seems natural. I don't think that there is any requirement for celebrating the holy days in a certain way; I believe it is whatever feels right to the individual. I love writing personal and group rituals and sometimes they come together so easily that I know that spirit is present, guiding my hand. I hope to someday publish my rituals and quarter calls in a book to share with others.

This is a direction call inspired by a Druid ritual. I wrote it for those who are looking to connect with the Earth's energies and find balance at the beginning of Winter Solstice/Yule.

Begin holding in hand rocks and crystals, with eyes closed, standing in the North quadrant of your space.

> We call to the North, Powers of Earth
> and the energy of Winter.

Imagine you are walking over scattered brown and gold leaves toward a copse of trees—hazel, elder, ash. Your boots are heavy with sticky mud as you pass beyond the brambles into this sliver of woodland. It is filled with winter silence, and the deep evergreen of pine and cedar trees welcome you. You kneel and touch the cold earth, which is covered in pine needles from winters past, in wonder . . .

> Sleeping roots and bones
> Cool shadows and cold stones
> Short days and long nights
> Pale skies and candle lights
> Hail Spirits of Earth!

Come to us,
Be with us in our sacred circle.

Then move to the East quadrant of your space, holding in hand incense and feather fan, with eyes closed.

We call to the East, Powers of Air
and the energy of Spring.

Imagine you are walking along a hill at dawn. The ground beneath your feet is frosty and hard as rock. You are walking east, and before you the sky is driven with the colors of dawn—reds, oranges, yellows, delicate pinks. The whole sky seems ablaze with color. You stand and feel the wind with its clear, cool touch. Your breath fogs in the icy air in front of you. Breathe in . . .

Cold wind blows,
Winter snows.
Ice flows.
Wings of birds
You have been stirred.
Hail Spirits of Air!
Come to us,
Be with us in our sacred circle.

Move to the South quadrant of your space and hold in hand a pillar candle in a cauldron, with eyes closed.

We call to the South, Powers of Fire
and the energy of Summer.

Imagine that you are sitting at a hearth fire in a shadowy building. The wind is high and it is cold outside. You warm your hands at the blaze. Look deep into the fire—what can you see? Beside you is a heap of dry brush and kindling. You heap wood on the fire and hear the rush of sparks and crackling flames as it catches. Feel its warmth on your face . . .

Blazing hearth
On winter earth;

Warmth of flame—
home again.
Hail Spirits of Fire!
Come to us,
Be with us in our sacred circle.

Move to the West quadrant of your space, holding in hand a chalice of ocean water collected beneath the moon, with eyes closed.

We call to the West, Powers of Water
and the energy of Fall.

Imagine that you are by a river in winter. It is surrounded by willow trees, and you notice their branches becoming yellow, covered in a cold moisture, as they get ready to sleep. The river is churning with rain water. It is washing the land clean. The water is silver gray, reflecting the chill rains that fall. You reach into the water and feel the bite of the cold . . .

Gray flood
Thickens mud.
River frost,
Frozen moss.
Winter chills,
Sleeping hills.
Hail Spirits of Water!
Come to us,
Be with us in our sacred circle.

•◆•

Any other thoughts you care to add?

One of my biggest focuses these days is working with spirits and ancestors. I have been amazed by the number of people I have spoken to from all spiritual paths who have had encounters with people on the other side of the veil. All too often people have told me that they think they are crazy because they heard their mother, uncle, or friend who had passed on talking to them, or they have even seen them or received a spiritual sign. There are so many people out there connecting with spirits, from my own personal experiences with everyone from police officers, Coast Guard service people, real estate agents, and attorneys. I know for certain that the spirit world is very real, and I'm a big believer in asking for signs and showing gratitude to those spirits that manifest enough energy to contact and connect with us. I've heard and experienced firsthand stories of spirits saving people's lives, removing obstacles from their lives, or helping them heal. We all have a spiritual support team of guides, spirits, and ancestors that are looking out for us on so many levels. The spirit world can share with us many of the reasons why we are here and what we can do to live a more fulfilled life. I encourage people to not be afraid of the spirit world; proceed with respect and you might be surprised by what you can discover. Slowing down and being present are just some of their messages, and I see that reflected over and over on my Witch's path.

SANCISTA BRUJO LUIS
Lowell, Massachusetts

First, can you say a bit about who you are, where you live, and what you do for a living these days?

I am Sancista Brujo Luis. I am the son of Puerto Rican immigrants who migrated to Massachusetts in the late 1960s. In my youth I would spend my summer vacations with my grandmother and other family members in Puerto Rico, but I was born, raised, and grew up in Lowell, Massachusetts.

I have worked all my life in the restaurant field, and early on, during my days off, I would consult and give readings to friends and family members using the Tarot. After a while I began to grow a small local clientele who would often ask me to prepare herbal baths and love potions and bless amulets and talismans for them. I then realized that I could make a comfortable living being the local *brujo* (male Witch) of my town, at least amongst the Hispanic community, and now I do this for a living.

Which religion were you raised in?

I was raised in both the Roman Catholic religion of my mother's side and the folk Spiritism of Puerto Rico, known as Espiritismo Criollo, from my father's side. Espiritismo Criollo is a blend of three spiritual belief systems and traditions: the remnants of the native indigenous Taino people of my island infused with European Spanish Christianity and West African traditional religions.

How and when did you decide you were a Witch?

I didn't decide; I was born this way. It's a part of my DNA, genes, chromosomes, makeup—it's just who I am. Even though my grandmother was a medium channeler, she was also a *bruja* (female Witch). I didn't have a concept of what a Witch was or what people perceived to be a Witch until I was around four or five years old and I saw *The Wizard of Oz* for the very first time. I remember that when I saw the Wicked Witch of the West, I felt a strong and familiar connection toward her. My love for the historical concept and figure of the Witch came from her. Later this was followed by Maleficent and Queen Grimhilde of the Disney of my youth. I notice that modern Witches shun those images of Witches. But I was raised with an elder who practiced, and as a child these Witches reminded me of many of the clients my grandmother consulted for. Some were beautiful businesswomen, some were teachers, others were ladies of the night or women who were abandoned by their husbands for another younger woman. Each was a bruja or believed in Witchcraft to some degree. One thing about the Hispanic culture and people: you either believe in Witchcraft or you don't, but everyone either fears it or respects it to some degree.

My grandmother, a spiritist medium herbalist and Witch, put it best: "I was born a Witch, and I shall die a Witch, and when I die may it be the Witches who dance around my corpse and bury me." This is the motto I use to this day.

How do you personally define Witchcraft?

Witchcraft is a state of being; it's something that you just are. It's hard to define in words. Something that you have been since you can remember. It's me respecting the Divine creation, nature, my surroundings, and the Earth and all its creation and interacting with the world of spirit.

Which tradition of Witchcraft do you follow? How did you find that tradition?

I practice Puerto Rican Espiritismo Criollo, traditional Hispanic Brujeria, which is unique to each island or country, and Puerto Rican Sanse, which is a branch of African Vodou and Taino shamanism mixed with European Spiritism.

Most Puerto Rican medium Witches practice from their homes, as they were brought up to do; it's a part of our culture. Some medium Witches are a part of a spiritual temple or spiritist center, both on the island and on the mainland. Many just practice for their family members and loved ones in the privacy of their homes.

What makes your approach or tradition unique from any others out there?

Well, in Puerto Rico most Witches are channelers. They can physically manifest a spirit guide or interact with spirit guides in some form. Every brujo or bruja has his or her own special *facultad* or *don* (faculty or gift) that they excel at or learn to develop under the apprenticeship of more advanced brujos and mediums, often of the family line. Some are stronger and others adept, but each has a gift. Wherever there is a botanica there are sure to be brujos in the vicinity. Many are not trusting of outsiders.

Would you say that Witchcraft is a "craft" or a "religion"? And can you talk about the difference?

I believe Witchcraft to be a craft of one's culture and upbringing, because many Witches I have met in my life practice or have practiced Witchcraft but also followed other religions such as Catholicism, Christianity, Santeria, Vodou, Spiritualism, Buddhism, Hinduism, and even a branch of Satanism.

It is an ancient craft passed down from one family member to the next, ever growing and assimilating into the culture around the individual. Some are shamanic in origin, but I would compare it to being a blacksmith: it was that particular person's craft. Now whether they practiced a religion besides their craft or not was left to the interpretation of each individual, depending on their culture or religious views.

Although Brujeria incorporates a lot of paraphernalia from various religious systems and/or cultures, we view it as a craft, not as a religion.

Whom do Witches worship?

I worship the Creator, the Cause of All Causes, that highly elevated entity we humans call God. I don't give God earthly feminine or masculine attributes or pretend to grasp the concept of God because that concept is incomprehensible to the human mind. I do also honor and venerate the spirits of Nature, the elements, spirit guides, and my bloodline ancestors.

When Witches meet, what do they usually do?

It depends on whom you ask. You could ask a Witch in Salem, and their answer would be different from a Coven of Witches in, let's say, Central or South America. In Hispanic countries Witches meet to work magic, remove a curse, or place a curse. Again, each Witch has their own agenda and code of what they will do or not do, and it's usually outlined by any religious dogmas and creeds that they may follow.

Some Witches in Hispanic countries join to remove earthbound entities or to conjure one up against an enemy. In my field or particular path, I am often called to channel spirits and to lead them into the light or help elevate lost souls. But I also read Tarot and bless amulets and talismans.

Do Witches really do "spells" or can they do "magic"?

Every Hispanic Witch I know practices some form of casting *hechizos* (spells), working magic, or doing *trabajo spiritual* (spiritual work).

Look in many Hispanic neighborhoods and you will often come across a botanica or enter into a Hispanic bodega shop where, if you look hard enough, you will find an assortment of candles with saints and elixirs and tonics for any Witchery need.

If you do any spells, can you give examples?

I could, yes. But they are different for each client.

Are you a hereditary Witch?

Yes. My grandmother was a Presidente de Mesa (President of the Altar) in a small spiritual center in Puerto Rico and was knowledgeable about Puerto Rican herbs and their healing and magical properties. She also consulted the Baraja Espanola (a Spanish deck of playing cards) for clients and often did spiritual and magical work.

Did your family carry stories about Witches or did you find out about it all recently?

Witchcraft, ghost stories, and many paranormal folk tales are a part of my culture, and many nights when I was a child we would sit around listening to our uncles' and aunts' stories of ghosts, demons, devils, and brujos and brujas of old.

Have you had relationships or friendships with other New England Witches? If so, with whom? And what were the most significant experiences or learnings you had from those encounters?

This question is tricky. I have experiences with both Hispanic brujos and American Wiccans and Witches.

When I was in my late teens and early twenties, I was part of a Wiccan Coven that lasted a few years. I remember I took my first trip to Salem, Massachusetts, with this Coven of young Witches. We were just exploring Wicca and at the time just learning about it. Now, mind you, my first book ever on Witchcraft was not about Wicca but more about traditional Witchcraft, and that was always the foundation on which I wanted to practice my craft. I don't want to discredit Wiccans or speak badly about them, but I never felt comfortable with Wicca. Anyway, as a Coven we would take trips to Salem until we had become friends with a local Witch shopkeeper on Pickering Wharf. This was in the early 1990s. This is when I was first exposed to the ego-filled Witches' wars that are such a part of Salem today. This is a story in itself.

Do you have any interactions with Witches in the Salem, Massachusetts, area? What is your impression of the current interest in Witchcraft in Salem, centuries after the Witch hysteria of Puritan times?

I rarely interact with Witches in Salem, with the exception of the public circle held on Halloween in Salem every year. I often go to these circles to meet other Witches from around the world who contact me and want to meet me.

Have you experienced any difficulties—any problems, persecution, or prejudice—as a result of being a Witch? Can you describe a time or times when that happened?

Funny, but no. I have faced prejudices for being Hispanic, but never for being a Witch. Most people I have met are tolerant, respectful, and many times very curious. Witches in Massachusetts are a part of the landscape, an important part of New England history—we have been a part of New England since the colonization. Each town and city has their local Witch.

What are special holy days for Witches? Can you please describe what Witches do on their holy days? How do you celebrate?

I practice Espiritismo usually with a group, and I honor some saint feast days, but most of the Sabbats with some exceptions I practice with a small group.

At Samhain, on or around Halloween, I try to go to Salem Massachusetts, and I am planning on future trips to New Orleans. I celebrate Día de los Santos, or All Saints' Day, which is November 2, by cleaning and organizing my altars, lighting candles, and placing fresh flowers and incense, and on El Día de los Muertos, or the Day of the Dead, I like to place a loaf of sweet bread, coffee, incense, and emergency candles outside in front of the house for the dead. I used to decorate sugar skulls, which is more of a Mexican tradition, but here in Massachusetts it would attract vermin. That's done on Halloween, or All Hallows' Eve, Día de los Santos, and Día de los Muertos.

For La Navidad, or the Nativity Christmas or Yule, I make a big meal for the family to come and gather, but traditionally January 6 was also honored as the day of the three mages. When my children were younger we used to leave a box of hay and water for the camel who brought the three Magi to the newborn babe. This is a Puerto Rican tradition that is slowly dying away. This is also the day I buy the year's bag of frankincense and myrrh.

February 2 is the feast of La Virgen de Candelaria, and we adorn the altars with flowers and candles.

On Pascua, or Easter, everyone gets new palm fronds and decorates the door by weaving crosses. The ones from the year before are given as gifts or placed away.

In May, we gather the water, the first rain of May. This water is especially good, as any first rain of May is believed to have curative and blessing properties. As a child I remember the old ladies leaving huge barrels outside in anticipation. The water was also saved because the Caribbean Islands would soon enter into the drought season, and of course this water was used for watering plants and washing. Today we use the first rain of May in spiritual herbal baths and for blessing.

The Summer Solstice is the feast of Saint John the Baptist, a very important feast that has become very commercialized. Big feasts, parades, and parties are held by the ocean in Puerto Rico and most Hispanic countries. Bonfires are built by the sea, and everyone has to jump over the fire at least once but no more than twelve times. Then before the stroke of midnight, everyone runs backward into the ocean and dunks in twelve times to wash away any sins that had built up throughout the year.

Fiesta de la Masa, or Loaf Mass, is not a huge feast any longer, but on August 1 or around that time we celebrate the three sisters, Mary Faith, Mary Hope, and Mary Charity by holding a special Spiritualist service for them. Also in the week of July 25 to August 1 many Afro-Puerto Ricans celebrate La Fiesta de Santiago Apostol, or the Feast of Saint James. It's usually celebrated with a huge Mardi Gras–like parade, music, festivities, and dancing. On the United States mainland, private parties are held for this saint.

We celebrate the Autumn Equinox by gathering apples and pumpkins. But Michaelmas is held as a really big time for those who honor Saint Michael, with elaborate parties full of drumming and festivities.

Any other thoughts you'd like to share?

For more information on me and my work, visit www.youtube.com /sancistabrujoluis or www.youtube.com/watch?v=Om6MCa6RazM. You can also find my book on the self-publishing site Lulu online: *Luz y Progreso, Light and Progress: A Handbook for Developing Mediums within the Puerto Rican Espiritismo Tradition* at www.lulu.com/shop /sancista-brujo-luis/luz-y-progreso-a-handbook-for-developing-mediums /paperback/product-22078390.html.

SPARROW
Northern Rhode Island

First, can you say a bit about who you are, where you live, and what you do for a living these days?

I grew up in the fifth largest city in Rhode Island (by population), but it always felt more like a suburb to me. In fact, when I was growing up in the '60s and '70s, Providence (our largest city) was more like a ghost town. It didn't feel much like a city at all. Although still small as cities go, Providence is beautiful and vibrant now, with pockets of colonial charm and some

truly magical places. However, I abandoned the city for the country in my thirteenth year as a Witch. I have no desire to go back. I live in a rural community in northern Rhode Island. My backyard, surrounded by woods, is my favorite sacred space. The music of the night is punctuated by a mated pair of barred owls, and the stars are innumerable when the sky is clear. Pitch-black darkness at the New Moon is followed by illumination almost bright enough to read by when She is full. The changing seasons are palpable here, yet Rhode Island being as small as it is, I can get to the nearest grocery store in just over ten minutes and to the heart of Providence in thirty.

Unfortunately, I work for corporate America. It gets harder every year. What started out as a career with a company that felt like a family has disintegrated. The decline was gradual, first becoming apparent post 9/11 as intense paranoia gripped the country and security increased in response to the attacks. Then came the Crash of 2008, or the economic crisis. Many of my colleagues share the opinion that it brought out the worst in corporate America. But one must make a living. Though I'd rather serve my Coven, my Tradition, and my spiritual path on a full-time basis, it does not pay the bills. In fact, it doesn't pay anything at all. So like most witches I know, I have two lives: one comprised of the role I play in the mundane world, and the life I live in my heart and my home.

How and when did you decide you were a Witch?

I have to start by disagreeing with my Portuguese grandmother, who shouted at my parents (referring to me and my two sisters), "They were born Catholic and they will die Catholic!" This outburst was brought about by my parents' conversion to born-again Christianity and subsequent membership in an independent Pentecostal church. Having a seriously spiritual bent since childhood, I joined them enthusiastically. All of my grandparents were Portuguese and none of them ever actually embraced our family's departure from the Catholic Church.

My first experiences with otherworldly power and energy were in the heart of that Pentecostal environment. Those folks take the descent of the Holy Spirit literally. They can raise some serious energy! Our song services lasted anywhere from twenty to forty minutes, always accompanied by clapping and often dancing. We spoke in tongues (glossolalia), shouted out divine revelations/prophecy in the middle of a service, and were sometimes "slain in the Spirit" at the altar. Having experienced that personally on two occasions, I dare anyone to remain standing when being hit by that force of energy—without ever being physically touched by the preacher.

Spirituality was important to me from an early age. My devotion to Christianity was based on a deep, personal relationship with whom I saw as God at that time in my life. I dreamed dreams and saw visions. I believed with every fiber of my being that I was called to the ministry. I ran up against some resistance. I was a girl. My second pastor told me that I would make a wonderful minister's wife some day.

After sage counsel from my parents and others, I banked on my brain instead of my heart. I went into the medical field, then married a sailor who got stationed in Hawaii. Being a sailor's wife is somewhat akin to being unwanted baggage. I couldn't find work due to my military address and an overprotective husband. So I enrolled in the University of Hawaii (UH) and signed up for a course called Major World Religions. My life was changed forever.

I learned that there were many sacred texts and that they held many of the same sacred truths. The one and only way to truth that I had been taught was a lie—or at least a very misguided interpretation. At first I felt betrayed. And then I felt lost. But once the blinders were removed, having glimpsed the larger picture, I could no longer embrace the smaller, narrow perspective.

I was surrounded by Buddhist temples in modern Hawaii, with its large Asian population, and Buddhism was my first attempt at a new path to enlightenment. However, I learned rather quickly that the East and the West are worlds apart. The language and the perspectives were alien. Try as I might, it felt foreign. Then I met a woman who called herself a Witch. My first reaction was to reject the concept. But I soon learned that the Pagan religion of my ancestors, with roots in a Western culture, was easier to understand—once I put my prejudice aside and listened.

This Witch had a Hawaiian friend who was a secret Pagan and honored the old ways. He brought us to some of the secret sacred places on Oahu. He showed us how to "tie" an offering in a freshly picked ti leaf so we could show our respect when we visited a *heiau* (an ancient Hawaiian temple or sacred site). Then the day came when I was led to the entrance of a cave and told that it belonged to Pele. Unbelievers were not welcome and only those who came in respect should dare to enter. I was afraid, but I so wanted to honor She who had made the islands. So I prepared my offering as I had been taught with trembling hands. I summoned up all the courage I could muster, and with arms outstretched before me, I carried the offering inside. It was cool and dark, but light enough to see that many offerings had been placed here before mine. I knelt to place my offering on the floor of the cave near the others. I decided that honesty was the best policy, so I whispered, "Pele, I am afraid. But I wanted to say thank you and that's more important than my fear." Suddenly She was there. A presence so strong that it nearly knocked me over. The energy was fiercely powerful, but somehow comforting at the same time. My heart nearly burst in my chest and my eyes filled with tears. The gods were real! She told me to go and to find the gods of my own people.

I decided that day that the path I should follow to find the gods of my own people was Witchcraft. That was twenty-nine years ago. I was initiated into the English Tradition shortly after Samhain in 1988. It was my first initiation into the first of three traditions before I found my home in NECTW (New England Covens of Traditional Witchcraft).

How do you personally define Witchcraft?

How to distill this answer to its essence is a challenge. I believe it is most aptly described as a way of life and a process of becoming. For some it is a religion, with all of the typical trappings. For others it is a philosophy—a metaphysical exploration with a set of ethics to guide you. For most I know well, it is a way of life or, more simply put, a way to get things done each and every day in a context that recognizes the connectedness and sacred in all things—including those that are not part of this physical realm perceived with the five basic senses.

Which tradition of Witchcraft do you follow? How did you find that tradition?

I am a member of the New England Covens of Traditionalist Witches (NECTW) founded by Lady Gwen Thompson, a hereditary witch from New Haven, Connecticut.

What makes your approach or tradition unique from any others out there?

Having been in two other traditions prior to NECTW, I can certainly identify uniqueness with regard to my own experiences. In general, there is a stronger emphasis on magic than on religion. Our Book of Shadows is approximately four hundred pages of hand-copied material, and more extensive than any I've seen. In comparison to other traditions I am familiar with, the training is more in-depth and intense. Since NECTW was derived from a family tradition, it retains much of that sense of family. If you imagine grandparents and grandchildren practicing together, it becomes obvious why we work robed, whereas some traditions practice skyclad (nude). We absolutely recognize the powerful exchange of energy between male and female and/or God and Goddess, but there is no Great Rite or simulation thereof between High Priestess and High Priest. There are myriad differences I am not at liberty to disclose without treading dangerously close to divulging oath-bound material.

Would you say that Witchcraft is a "craft" or a "religion"? And can you talk about the difference?

Language is fluid and modern definitions for "religion" have become more secular. However, most classic definitions of religion include a belief in a god/gods/superhuman. Those classic definitions typically elaborate by saying that religion includes a system of faith and/or worship. Most definitions for "craft" are entirely secular and mean an art, trade, or occupation requiring special skill.

For me personally, the answer would be that Witchcraft is both. However, that answer can vary widely depending upon whom you ask. Although there are witches who fall at both ends of the spectrum, I believe that the majority of differences would be measured by the degree of focus placed on religion versus craft by an individual, or a Coven, or a tradition. A unique aspect of Witchcraft is the underlying tenet that all witches are autonomous. By extension, all Covens are autonomous, even if they are members of the same tradition. So it would be entirely possible to find these two apparent opposites working harmoniously together within the same tradition: a devout Witch of Celtic persuasion who starts every day with a devotional ritual to Brigid and an atheist who believes that there are no gods but, instead, powerful thoughtforms that have become vast reservoirs of accessible energy.

Whom do Witches worship?

In NECTW, we have a god and goddess that are acknowledged by all members of the Tradition. They are mentioned by name in most of our rituals. In addition, each Coven has the option of choosing a Coven god and goddess. Whether the holy pair (matron and patron) is viewed symbolically or "worshipped" will depend largely on the High Priestess and High Priest of each Coven. It is important to keep in mind that it would be unlikely for a practitioner of Witchcraft to rely solely upon the generosity of a deity to achieve a desired outcome.

As for me, born in Aquarius with the moon in Cancer, my journey has been a lifelong struggle between logic and poetry, function and form, science and art . . . the list goes on. My intellect would not be truly satisfied without the metaphysical principles that bring some sense of order and provability. Yet my soul would yearn and wither without the poetry of prayer, the sight and scent of flower-strewn altars, the pageantry of ritual and the presence of the gods. So I connect with deities by learning their stories, studying the cultures where they thrived, and imagining as best I can what it would have been like to live in the times when their names were engraved upon the hearts of those who worshipped them. And for a select few, I honor them on their festival days with meditations, small offerings, and special meals prepared and then shared in memory of them.

When Witches meet, what do they usually do?

"Meet" is such a broad word. We gather together for rituals during each of the eight Sabbats (seasonal holidays) and thirteen Esbats (Full Moons). There are often additional rituals sprinkled throughout the year; not all of them include a formal "Circle." Examples would be a ritual called for a special purpose, such as a specific healing during a time of critical need, an initiation, or the celebration of a feast day or festival for a particular deity.

Most of our Covens have monthly meetings. The context of these meetings varies, but I believe most would agree that there's an administrative portion (what's coming next in the way of dates, times, and logistics), training or teaching, and sharing. There are private meetings between initiates and the Coven leaders. Also, each Witch is required to copy the Book of Shadows. Often this is done on an individual basis. At other times, several members of my Coven will come to my house on the same night and copy together. These sessions often lead to impromptu training or individual counseling as the need arises.

NECTW is like an extended family. We often create reasons to meet simply because we enjoy each other's company. We meet at local greenhouses to go plant shopping together and those versed in plant lore or herbalism share with all who are there. At least once a year my wife and I will host a bonfire in our backyard where we enjoy the fire and the sounds of the forest, revel in the stars, and identify the constellations overhead. We talk about the sacredness in all things and wonder aloud together at the beauty all around us—in the sights, the sounds, and the salamanders among the flames and the embers.

When we meet, we are genuinely happy to see each other. There are hugs and kisses all around. There are nicknames for most of us, favorite stories that are told and retold, songs that we sing, shared memories that bind us together, and feasting. Not only do we break bread together, we often prepare the food together. We try to eat seasonally as often as possible, to remember, to honor traditions, to be mindful of the turning of the Wheel. For indeed, we turn the Wheel in many ways in almost everything we do.

Do Witches really do "spells" or can they do "magic"?

Asking a Witch if he/she really does spells or magic is somewhat like asking if a bear sh**s in the woods.

Sarcastic humor aside, let me refer back to the Major World Religions class at UH that changed my life. My professor gave us an interesting definition of magic when teaching us about animism and shamanism. He said, "Think of magic as that which is employed to achieve a desired result when the available science and/or technology fails to do so." I love the way that definition strips away all the prejudice of any given culture and allows you to perceive magic as a technique or method for obtaining a desired outcome that can't be accomplished through ordinary or mechanical means. Of course, "doing magic" well and getting the desired results consistently requires training, discipline, and practice.

In my opinion, magic is very general, whereas a spell is a specific type of magic. I often think of a spell as a recipe. Both are a process whereby a number of ingredients, known to blend harmoniously, are combined to create a whole that is greater than the sum of its parts.

If you do any spells, can you give examples?

I can share the very first spell I learned. I remember fondly many occasions when my parents or my grandparents would excitedly encourage my sisters and I to look up into the evening sky to find the very first star. Upon finding it, we were taught to say:

> *Star light, star bright,*
> *first star I see tonight,*
> *I wish I may, I wish I might,*
> *have this wish I wish tonight.*

We would sometimes argue over who really saw it first, or who would get to make the wish. The adults would laugh and settle it by saying that the star was strong enough to grant all of our wishes, but only the very first star that we spied in the night sky could do so. More often than not, we would recite the magic words together.

I'm sure my Christian family would be horrified to learn that they are the ones who taught me my first ever magic spell, but all of the ingredients are there: the rhyming chant or words of power, the innate magical energy of the star itself, the singular clear intention, and the unswerving belief of a child (the will to make it so).

Are you a hereditary Witch?

If by hereditary you mean that I come from a biological family that practiced Witchcraft and I was initiated by a family member, then the answer is no.

Did your family carry stories about Witches or did you find out about it all recently?

There was no magical tradition in my family—witches were the stuff of fairy tales, and later, Hollywood. After nearly thirty years as a practicing Witch, I find it hard to think of my initial discovery as recent.

Have you had relationships with or friendships with other New England Witches? If so, with whom? And what were the most significant experiences or learnings you had from those encounters?

For centuries, it has been taboo to name another Witch. In honor of that tradition, I must refrain from answering this question.

Do you have any interactions with Witches in the Salem, Massachusetts area? What is your impression of the current interest in Witchcraft in Salem, centuries after the Witch hysteria of Puritan times?

Witches or not, the fact that so many people could have their reputations and lives destroyed at best, or actually be found guilty and put to death with so little evidence, is a tragedy. So we should remember the infamous Salem witch trials. That memory should stand as a warning against intolerance, mob mentality, and the presumption of guilt without concrete evidence. It should stand as an example of how important it is to insist on a separation of church and state. And it should be a constant reminder of how dangerous it is to view another human being as separate, other, or alien for any reason.

With all of this in mind, a visit to Salem should be a solemn experience, not unlike visiting the Vietnam Memorial, the Holocaust Museum, or the 9/11 Memorial Museum. I've been to Salem. Yes, there's a museum, and yes, there is a memorial (surprisingly, only since August 1992). Yet a visit to Salem is far from sobering in its overall effect. The entire town seems to promote the age-old, stereotypical witch: the cackling, green-skinned, broom-riding hag with a wart on her nose and a pointy black hat. Salem has turned Witchcraft into a commercial enterprise, capitalizing on the Hollywood witch (sexy siren or hideous monster—take your pick), the New Age movement, and even Goth subculture. Sadly, a naive seeker can innocently look for spiritual guidance in Salem and come away believing that a magic spell can be mass-produced, packaged with instructions, and purchased for $19.99. No understanding of metaphysical principles, no lessons on focused intent or controlling and directing energy, and no years of discipline and practice required.

I do know and respect a few Witches who live in the Salem area. Frankly, I've never understood the attraction.

Have you experienced any difficulties—any problems, persecution, or prejudice—as a result of being a Witch? Can you describe a time or times when that happened?

I do not hide the fact that I am a Witch, but I don't wear a banner or make a point of displaying my beliefs publicly either. It is simply neither appropriate nor necessary. However, one cannot help but be aware of the prejudice against Witchcraft that does indeed exist in our society. How often have you heard someone substitute the word "witch" for "bitch" in an effort to tone down the use of profanity in polite company? I have to admit that it causes me to pause and choose my words carefully when being asked to provide my religion on a medical form—especially if the form is being completed prior to a surgical procedure.

What are special holy days for Witches? Can you please describe what Witches do on their holy days? How do you celebrate?

I've mentioned the Sabbats and Esbats previously, yet this question generates a visceral reaction when contemplated. The idea of "special" or "holy" applied to only a subset of one's life highlights a paradox. As a Witch, I do indeed set aside fixed times to honor or focus on specific energies, events, or deities. Yet if one defines Witchcraft as I do—that is, "a way of life . . . in a context that recognizes the connectedness and sacred in all things"—then each and every day is a holy day. The trick is in remembering—which is not always an easy task.

Any other thoughts you care to add?

Sociology tells us that in order to function effectively as a group, there must be norms. I learned through experience that once you have two people in a relationship, both parties must invest time, energy, and compromise for that relationship to thrive. Add a third person, and you have the beginnings of politics . . . and those politics increase as the size of the group increases. It seems to me that there are too many people who get so distracted by the politics they miss the point of spiritual community entirely—and sometimes even spiritual practice in general. I find that sad. And when politics or power struggles lead true seekers astray—or worse, leave them disillusioned or hurt—I find that unforgivable.

NECTW is a small tradition. I know there are some who believe we are elitists. Perhaps that is partially true of all groups. After all, if we as individuals didn't feel in some way that we had found *THE BEST* community, why would we continue to practice within the context of our chosen traditions? One of the reasons I choose to stay in NECTW is because we are more like a family than a political body. Having been in two other traditions prior to finding my home in NECTW, I find it a relief to focus on my family, my betterment, and the spiritual development of myself and those in my Coven.

As a Witch, I feel obligated to tune in to the web of life around me. I don't always succeed since I, too, am susceptible to distractions. I get distracted by my job, the care and maintenance of my home, the irritating things that build up over the course of any average day. But throughout the day, I make a conscious effort to remember. And then I take a moment . . . to look out the window or step outside, to pet my dog and wonder at the depth of her soul within that small furry body, or simply to breathe and focus on that magical moment in between breaths wherein lies the potential for all possibilities. I've discovered through the years that balance is the key to just about everything. So I remind myself to seek that balance. I remind myself that as a Witch, I can create that balance.

TAMARIN LAUREL
The Hill Towns of Western Massachusetts

First, can you say a bit about who you are, where you live, and what you do for a living these days?

I have been a Coven-initiated Witch and Priestess since 1982. I have been co-owner—along with Adair Laurel—of AzureGreen.net, a large supplier of magical products for the past thirty years. I am openly known as a Witch in my rural community of Middlefield, in the Berkshire foothills of western Massachusetts.

Which religion were you raised in?

My childhood background in spiritual topics was as a Quaker and also as an explorer of occult and metaphysical subjects. I went to a Quaker high school, and my grandparents ran the Institute for the Study of Consciousness. The institute was an outgrowth of my grandfather, Arthur M. Young, exploring all subjects to see if they could be reasonably dismissed by science or not. He wished to further perfect his comprehensive theory about the nature of the universe. Throughout my childhood, there were many family tales from my grandparents of the psychics met and the mysterious phenomenon explored. Of these extraordinary people, I was most inspired by Arthur's friend Joan Grant, who was an author of many past-life-memory books and of current-life experiences with curing intractable psychological problems by exploring people's past lives.

How and when did you decide you were a Witch?

I never thought I needed to "find" a religion; I was quite sure that I would create my own path of spiritual exploration. But Witchcraft found me, and it leaves a lot of room for the individual creation of its practice. I was searching for a name, not a religion. I wanted a name that expressed my inner essence better than my birth name did. I started reading books on Witches because I had a vague impression that they used secret names, which I thought might be helpful, even though my other vague impressions of Witchcraft were those negative stigmas created by hundreds of years of the church's smear campaign against its Pagan predecessors and competitors. As I read, I felt at home with the Witches' way of seeing Nature as sacred and divinity as female as well as male. I appreciated the idea of using a Celtic tribal and shamanic practice, rather than something appropriated from Native Americans, and I liked the self-empowerment of working as a Priestess rather than being a follower.

How do you personally define Witchcraft?

I've heard that the word *Witch* links back to the base word related to *wick*, meaning the green and pliable shoots that indicate a plant is alive. Like wicker, or the willow withies when they are green, the Craft is a pliable practice that can bend and shape-shift to be many things, rather than only one. It is an ancient tradition, with roots stretching back into the mists of history. It is also a modern phenomenon, rising to public awareness only in the latter decades of the twentieth century, due to the efforts of a few British Traditional Witches who abandoned secrecy after the Witchcraft laws were repealed in 1951.

Witchcraft is a craft, but also a religion, and a way of life—or more exactly, a way of viewing the world and being in relation to it. When I was at the Parliament of the World's Religions, the practices and style that I found to be the most similar to Witchcraft were the ways of the Native American/First Nations people. Pagan, nature honoring, shamanically informed, and very diverse in individual and tribal practice—these are descriptions we share. In Witchcraft, the tribes are formed by the lineages of practice inherited through those from whom you have learned.

Which tradition of Witchcraft do you follow? How did you find that tradition?

Mingled in me, now, are the strands of many traditions I've learned from: Athanor, Alexandrian, Chalice Well, Reclaiming. I've also learned from teachers of esoteric lore—namely Dolores Ashcroft-Nowicki and R. J. Stewart—who were not specifically Wiccan but drew a lot of Witches to their workshops.

But I will start at the beginning. When I was eighteen, I bought from the Quaker conference bookstore the newly published book on Witchcraft by Starhawk called *The Spiral Dance*. And soon after that, I got Margot Adler's book *Drawing Down the Moon*. These were some of the first books available by modern American Witches. At that time, I lived in New York City, so I visited the flamboyant and somewhat creepy characters and space that made up the store called Magickal Childe. There I explained that I was interested in learning Witchcraft but would soon be moving to Boston, Massachusetts, to go to college. At that time, an organization called Pagan Way had an actual application for Seekers, which would get secretly forwarded to potential teachers in your area, who could then choose to contact you or not. So I moved to Boston and waited to see if contact came and also explored on my own.

Along with my roommates and some friends from Northeastern University's Women's Center, a group of us pursued a self-guided study circle—largely using books of a women's spirituality stripe. I liked the egalitarian nature of what we did but also recognized that a training path better informed by experience might be worth accepting and be worth the trade-off to a more hierarchal teacher-student structure.

My roommate had taken an evening adult education class on Witchcraft and was asked by the teacher if she wanted to continue classes privately with him. I asked if I could also come to those classes at his apartment. He met with me in a public location first, to interview me, and it turned out he was also a local teacher to whom my Pagan Way application had eventually been sent.

That teacher of Witchcraft at the Cambridge Center for Adult Education was Andras Corban.* The previous teacher had suggested him to the school when she'd wanted to quit. He had run the short semester series only three times by then. Each time, he would invite a few students from the class to continue training with him in a private teaching-Coven type of setting. The Alexandrian Coven he'd been part of previously had had a meltdown, and Andras was now building up a new Coven to work with and lead. Coven work involves personal growth that can raise unexpected challenges; it also involves the human dynamics within a group of people who are all exercising personal will and experiencing an uncanny bleed-through of emotions from psychic connections deeper than we are used to dealing with. This makes meltdown and reassembly a fairly common tale—both for Covens and for individuals engaged in raising and moving magical energies.

After some months of catching up on the teachings covered by the previous batches of students, Andras started to merge the several small

---

*For more details about Andras Corban (Arthen), please see my book *Being a Pagan*, in which there is an interview with him and more details about the EarthSpirit Community. —Ellen groups into one group functioning as a Coven more than a class. Among the first students snagged from the adult education course was Deirdre, whom Andras chose to become High Priestess for his new Coven, and later his wife and partner. Another of the prior students, whom I met and started to work with magically when the groups merged, was Adair, who later became my spouse and has been my partner ever since.

Adair, like me, had a strong sense of his own spiritual life and truth. He had not felt the need to seek out what others could teach . . . until he had a baby daughter, Buffie. Adair sensed she would want explanatory words and formal structure from him. He looked for these in many paths and eventually found the class on Witchcraft. It fit much closer to what expressed his wordless inner truth. Andras's newly formed Coven was named the Athanor Fellowship. Athanor is the tool of fire used in alchemists' experiments in transformation. Adair had been on a path of self-transformation, of making his soul a more precious material—like the alchemists turning lead into gold.

What makes your approach or tradition unique from any others out there?

From my experience in the Athanor Fellowship, I thought of the word *Coven* as being basically synonymous with "magical working group," with the only additional distinction being that *Coven* implied working from a Witchcraft context rather than a ceremonial magic or some other context. Although rituals for Sabbats and New and Full Moons were part of what our Coven did, they were not simply celebratory or reiterations of a certain traditional form. The magical influence of the seasons of the year and phases of the Moon were used as opportunities, as otherworldly doorways, for advancing one's magical work—both personal and group work.

For Adair and me, the main focus of magical work in the Athanor Fellowship was on experimental exploration of the spirit world and methods of personal growth. In addition to having that alchemist flavor of transformation by fire, another influence was the shamanic magic illuminated by Carlos Castaneda's books. These transformational and shamanic influences combined with learning from the practice of the traditional Witchcraft skills of psychic development, astral projection, directing healing energies, influencing circumstances through spell work, and journeying into Faerie.

This created many areas of magical work to focus on, and much of it was of such a highly personal nature that one would wish to share only within the close relationships of Coven mates and the protection of the traditional secrecy of Coven work. Andras's other goal for the Coven was to have it act as creator and host of public rituals and festivals. This created a good deal of tension between allocating time to pursuing the personal-focused magical work and organizing the public-focused events for others to attend. I preferred the personal work but found myself being fellow planner and organizer of the 1983 Rites of Spring festival, which was also the first festival I ever attended.

In that early to mid-1980s era of the history of Witchcraft and Paganism, festivals drew fellow practitioners from great distances. There was a shared sense of wanting to meet the extended family of Pagandom, which was rapidly emerging from secrecy. Adair and I, along with the kids, Buffie and Merlin, went to festivals in our home state of Massachusetts but also traveled as far as Wisconsin, Ohio, Maryland, and other nearer states. We typically attended two or three festivals each year, partly as vendors once we had started our Wiccan store. The kids actually went to even more festivals because they went with friends from this traveling gypsy network of festivalgoers.

I remember when you had a store in Easthampton, Massachusetts, called the Abyss. Can you talk a bit about your experiences there?

Both Adair and I felt drawn to live in the country as a more integrated way of living our Pagan values. In 1984 we moved from Boston into the more rural western part of Massachusetts, settling in Easthampton, since it was more affordable to our limited budget than the trendier Northampton. Adair fixed up the derelict house we could afford, staying home with the kids, while I went to work. The theory was that he would go back to working in paper mills after some transition time following his divorce from the kids' mother. But Buffie didn't like the idea of his going back to work. She was nine years old then. Adair meditated on the question of what to do instead and was quite surprised to get the answer that he should start a bookstore. Dubious at the prospect, he nonetheless bargained that if there turned out to be an available storefront near our home (and the kids' elementary school), he would try this course.

Serendipity and coincidence—and all those similar words used to describe when Fate has something in mind for you—led to opening a little main-street shop of alternative spirituality. It had shamanic, occult, Wiccan, Santeria, and Western mystery tradition flavors. (Eastern flavors of alternative spirituality seemed sufficiently covered by existing stores in Northampton.) We started the store with $2,000 to fix up the storefront, build shelves ourselves, and buy enough stock—picked by pendulum dowsing—to fill the four shelves by having all the book covers face out, rather than showing only spines. Adair put his magical intent into it, and the business has funded its own growth ever since. He'd only been going for a few weeks before needing more help, and I quit my regular job to come work in the store.

Ab Iss—ancient Egyptian words meaning "heart of wisdom"— were originally picked as the name for our small Coven that had been nameless but was trying to become formal enough to join the Covenant of the Goddess. When Adair opened the store, he borrowed this name for it. The name was soon anglicized into *Abyss*, which still means "profound depth" but loses the poetry of the unfathomable nature of the heart of wisdom. English is not a very poetic language for discussing spiritual concepts. After too many times of being remembered as "Abby's" by mainstream people who block out the unusual, we sought a new name when starting a mail-order catalog extension of the business. The new name was AzureGreen. Adair has always used cues to flag subtle shifts in reality, and a color shift from moss green to azure green was the cue that indicated shifting into the realm of Faerie. Since working with the energies of Faerie had always been part of the fabric of the business, AzureGreen was a name that would call out and enhance that quality.

We were helped along by other Witches in our area, particularly Lord Theo (Ted) Mills, whose Parker Coven was named after a long-dead relative persecuted for Witchcraft. Jeanine, the High Priestess of Parker Coven, had an incense business in Easthampton and helped us with shipping. Dick, whom we had met through an attempted self-starter Coven in Amherst, was very generous with his knowledge of running a bookstore. Lady Alexandria Foxmoore helped us from afar (her location was Maryland), including traveling with me to work a trade show.

But just because we knew Witches did not mean that we could share their names or Coven details with store customers. One of the recurring problems for a Witch store is that people ask how they can connect with a teaching Coven, or just other Witches individually. I never did come up with an excellent means of blind dating for pairing up possible teachers with possible students. Add to this that Covens are a delicate chemistry made up of the combination of people involved, and it is even harder to pair groups with new prospective members. Personally, I chose to cofound and work in a Coven of experienced peers (mainly Alexandrian), rather than being in a teaching Coven disrupted by successive waves of neophytes. This was named Turtle Coven and lasted for nine years.

I believe that one of the strengths of Witchcraft is the tradition of direct person-to-person transmittal of knowledge. At its best, this means that an experienced teacher is reckoning with the individual strengths and flaws of the neophyte, and on the other hand, the neophyte is aware of owing a personal debt to honor and pay forward this gift from the teacher. The act of learning therefore weaves in the concepts of personal responsibility and connection into a tribal group. Modern culture has made learning more of a personally acquired asset than a building of relationships.

But it is definitely easier for numerous Seekers to find a diverse bunch of how-to books than to be successfully matched with a training group in their area. During the decades since the 1970s, I have watched more books become available and have come across more people who are self-taught, and the expectation of what the "normal" path of becoming a Witch (or Wiccan or Pagan) is has shifted toward this common book-trained, solitary-practice, eclectic-tradition model.

In 2000 I wrote a book, which had begun as a personal diary of guided meditations to allow a conversation with my subconscious. The setting was a fictional school of magic, although many of the people, discussions, and events were drawn from my actual life. In 2002 it got published as *Initiation at Beltane*. It provides more of the ambiance of magical training rather than the recipe and study-workbook style prevalent in how-to books. I know that a magical working group offers an experience not gained by only working solo. But since this can be difficult to experience on the book-trained, solitary-practice path, I hoped the book could supply a taste of the way inner- and outer-world happenings start to interact as you embark on magical work. Someday I'd like Ezmereld—the fictional school of magic from the book—to have an outer-world, nonfictional counterpart.

Would you say that Witchcraft is a "craft" or a "religion"? And can you talk about the difference?

It is both. I wouldn't want to separate them. A craft not guided by spirit can too easily become nothing but a superficial hobby, while the absence of practical application and honing of skill, which practicing a craft demands, lets "religion" too easily drift into becoming merely a label for a style of worship service and doctrines. When I use the word *religion*, it is intended to keep the root meaning of "relinking" to spirit/ the sacred/the divine. I think that Witchcraft has actually suffered some collateral damage from the well-intentioned effort to make it a recognized religion. I value that effort because it brings the umbrella of constitutional protection and recognition of rights to folks practicing Witchcraft or Wicca. But I also feel that the emphasis on being a religion, since it plays out in a mainstream society with an existing definition about what religion means, begins to steer us away from our own truths.

Whom do Witches worship?

Worship is another of those problematic-definition words, like *religion*. It is defined very differently when a Witch uses it than when a Christian uses it or hears it. Using other words and phrases such as *honor, attune to, interact with,* and *look to for guidance* might be less confusing.

It seems more like hubris than wisdom for the limited perception of a human to dictate hard lines of distinction between spirit guides, revered heroes and tribal ancestors, demigods, angelic or enlightened beings, astral archetype forms, faerie spirits, devas, or gods and goddesses. I believe that we can be aided and informed by any of these, so it would not be out of place to show them some "worship"—if by that you mean bringing your attention into harmony with these spirits and opening to wisdom from them.

I believe that there are multiple planes of existence and more than one lifetime of learning the perfection of spirit within your plane. So it feels natural to believe that "gods" are simply further along in their evolutionary journey than humans but would have the same diversity of skills and interests as I know humans to have. I turn to a respected and accomplished human for help or inspiration either because they make themselves available as a role model or because their skills are particularly suited to the help I seek. Why would it be any different when turning to a spirit being? Therefore I expect each person to have different answers about which gods they interact with and even different answers at different times in their life or for different endeavors.

Witches have a diverse list of favorite gods and goddesses—be they from Celtic pantheons or Norse, Roman, Greek, Egyptian, or any other. But I suppose I have to mention one thing: only Christians tend to think of Satan as an object of worship. He is a strong part of the Christian mythos but absent from all those Pagan traditions I mentioned. Perhaps it is hard for some readers to imagine a worldview full of so many possibilities, yet without a scapegoat embodiment of all evil.

I can only suggest they try to imagine it. Witches may even view all deities as facets of a single divine force, turning polytheism into monotheism in a way. That's not my way. But our religion is not ruled by dogma that would exclude such a diversity of views.

When Witches meet, what do they usually do?

They usually talk about mutual friends and activities, plus books, TV shows, and movies—like other people do. But you probably mean: what are their formal actions of intent? The main intent is to live, perceive, and act from a state of being in greater accord with the unseen realms—in other words, being informed by the spirit world. Formal actions for that would include quieting the nattering of the conscious mind by using the tools of the subconscious mind—symbols and symbolic/ritualized actions. Next, you would let go of attachment to your veneer of a mortal-world identity in order to let your inner core truth shine out. (One traditional symbolic action for this is to divest yourself of your usual clothes and be "naked in your rites" or change into robes that speak to your mind of doing spiritual work.)

Traditions offer a couple of advantages: they provide patterns that worked for others, and they connect your actions to other people's. But fancy robes, or particular methods, aren't required. Witches should be focused on perceiving the energetic truth of something and remember that the important part of a ritual action is to achieve a certain state of being—in this case, taking an action that helps you let go of the trappings of your mundane self and continue in the guise of a more spiritually enlightened self.

Continuing the clearing of any impediments to a more spiritual and open state of being might include purification of yourself and the working space. You could smudge, cense, asperge, and literally sweep clear the space with a broom. Other states of being to be achieved in ritual are groundedness and centeredness and connection to deity. Often this is done in tandem with creating or acknowledging the circle and four directions around you. There is something about laying out the macrocosm of the world within the microcosm of your working space that centers you in both that place and the larger world. There is something about invoking the divine beings you intend to work with that calls your higher self forth to meet them as well.

Each of these stages of the ritual is meant to aid the shift of consciousness into a spiritual state of being. I've experienced it enough that my internal definition of the word *ritual* has come to mean that state of being spiritually quiet, centered, in union with the natural world, and having at-oneness with the divine. The literal details of ritual action do not mean "ritual" to me as much as the feeling that is achieved. Once you achieve that feeling—that shift to a spiritual consciousness— you can then do the intended work that the ritualized framework was meant to hold, support, and enhance.

When you are done, you must release the energy you have built up. Often this is done by unwinding your earlier trip into ritual, in reverse, by saying farewell to deities, directions, and circle. And then you are back to the starting point of groundedness, which also needs to be the ending point. It is even more important at the end because now you are doing the subtle task of reassimilating your spiritual experience into your everyday self. In the earlier shift to ritual consciousness, it is easy to notice the sense of relinking to the divine essence that is your soul's birthright. But in the shift back to the consciousness of your every-day life, the more difficult relinking is done, as you incorporate that spiritual experience in a manner that blesses your regular life experi-ence. If you do a lot of ritual, and it doesn't change your everyday life, you are not achieving this grounding of your soul's exploits into your regular life.

Do Witches really do "spells" or can they do "magic"?

A spell is simply an aid to focus the power of thought and direct, with purpose, the natural tendency for energy to move and to align into pat-terns. Our thoughts will have power whether or not we are consciously aware of it. I think being conscious of the way your thoughts are shaping your world is better than being unaware. A fear of seeming superstitious is a poor excuse for not taking responsibility for your thoughts and for the influence of your will. There are subtle powers that follow thought and will. It just makes the world full of bad spell casters because so many people deny that they are dealing in subtle forces and therefore don't take responsibility for their effects or work to change them.

A spell worker's approach is to consciously bring her positive intention to bear on life. This is done by using the tools that help focus intent—visualization, symbolism, and pattern association, which is usually called "correspondences" in the magical literature. Spell-casting techniques boil down to selecting and imbuing significance in the objects and actions we use, so that these, in turn, will set a pattern for our thoughts and energy.

Why choose to live in a world where objects and actions in your life are empty of significance? But if you are imbuing them with significance, then they might form a spell. Take a moment to notice where the pattern of associated thoughts leads when you consciously think about features of your daily life. Notice what intention feeds into it, and what actual subtle effect it has on your life. Cumulative subtle effects can become big effects, especially over time. *Magic* is just the word used to cover these subtle effects that are experienced but not fully understood in a manner that would give them a less murky description. But then *magic* becomes the word to describe the body of esoteric lore, tradition, superstition, and practices of people consciously interacting with the subtle forces in the physical and nonphysical worlds. "Doing magic" is directing and experiencing subtle energies. Yes, Witches do that. The concepts of the lore that is called *magic* (or *magick,* if you want to distinguish it from sleight of hand) gives one a lot more to work with in describing these subtle forces. So Witches study magic and use magical terminology and generally accept that Witchcraft involves a magical worldview.

If you do any spells, can you give examples?

One Witch I knew explained how she used the act of showering as a spell to cleanse all her energetic layers. I adopted that idea. We all accumulate mental, emotional, and physical crud, not to mention even subtler energetic nuances, so a spell of purification and cleansing should be used frequently. Don't wait until you feel really far out of sorts.

Since this spell is only using water from your household tap, you will need to work on creating a mental association of this water corresponding to the spiritual waters that replenish the world in a larger symbolic or metaphorical sense. Visualize the source waters you are tapping into in a way that is vivid and helpful to you. Everyone's mind associates things differently, so don't feel you must follow someone else's spell just because it works for their mind. Notice what associations you have and what works for you. Spell work is shaped by a wish for practical results, so don't trip yourself up by thinking of it as arcane and foreign instead of practical.

See if having physical objects, in addition to visualization, helps you. For example, you could make a cleansing-spell bag, a porous sachet of traditionally cleansing items like salt and lavender or other herbs, or crystals, and run that over yourself or just over some key chakra points. You could make and hang a waterproof amulet in your bathroom to use as a touchstone to signal starting or releasing this spell of cleansing. Often a formal ritual beforehand is used to create these spell objects, amulets, talismans, and touchstones, so that you can put a good amount of concentration into the aspects associated with the object. Later on, a bit of that ritually imbued intention is accessed each time you use, see, or touch the object.

Another example that is really common is for Witches to have some version of a protection spell on their cars. Additionally, there are innumerable ways of imparting a spell of blessing to a place or person. Simply keeping an altar of sacred items is a spell for blessing the place that the altar occupies and the people who see it.

I suggest that people start with spells for blessing, cleansing, and protection. It seems like you can stir up more associated hang-ups and difficulties than you ever wanted to unleash when you attempt spells for prosperity if you don't already have a good relationship with money. And any kind of spell coercing the behavior of others can raise conflict and unexpected consequences.

Are you a hereditary Witch?

No.

Did your family carry stories about Witches or did you find out about it all recently?

The family stories you could describe as being part of the wider Witchcraft wheelhouse. They were about psychics, mediums, past lives, astrology, mythology, paranormal phenomena, and nondogmatic exploration. On my own, I just had to find the rest of that wheelhouse: ritual, traditions, fellow Witches, shared culture, and a magical worldview.

Have you had relationships or friendships with other New England Witches? If so, with whom? And what were the most significant experiences or learnings you had from those encounters?

I feel very blessed by the many Witches I have had a chance to meet and get to know, and who have helped me grow. As I think back across the years, names surface like a line of poetry: Arachne, Janus, Vesto, Johanna, Shamash, Lakshmi, Morven, Raven, Runa, Anubis, Thoth, Morwynna, Michael, Vinnie. There are too many to make a complete list. Moreover, it can be a bad idea to name Witches, either by their Craft names, which they may only want to use in Craft settings, or by their mundane names. Given that there's still plenty of prejudice, it is not someone else's place to reveal another person's name in connection to Witchcraft.

Some of my nearer Witch neighbors I've seen recently, like Penny and Michael, who came to visit our Blossom Community Center's haunted house, and whose gift of a date palm tree reminds me of them regularly. Recently a retreat let me cross paths again with Laura. And an antifracking ritual was a reunion with longtime friends Mary Colleen and Ted, and also with Jennifer, whom I gratefully remember backed me up on the first time I was asked to perform a Wiccan funeral for someone I didn't know and to comfort all his Catholic relatives with my ritual (which seemed to work).

For other folks, I have to remember back to days now gone: memories of joining in enthusiastic harmonies at a chant workshop with Margot Adler, or discussing community with Isaac Bonewits during some lull at a festival, or hearing Judy Harrow's distinctive speaking style when she was at my house for a retreat. (Although I guess these beloved dead all came from New York, not New England.)

One of the things I greatly valued about my first Coven was being introduced to other Witches. We were members of the northeast local council of the Covenant of the Goddess (CoG), and I feel I've had deep connections to the other Witches I met through the CoG locally and nationally. CoG formalized the practice of introducing one Coven's members to other Witches by having an already-known Witch personally vouch for them. By this traditional form of introduction, Witches traveling through our area could visit as friends, not strangers—as did Oberon Zell (from California) when he came traveling with his unicorn long ago. Being connected originally through CoG meant New Mexico residents Amber K and Azrael knew they could visit Adair and me when in New England and when I traveled in California I could visit Don and Anna.

I got further connected to Boston Alexandrian Witches through the Turtle Coven Priest/ess exchanges and ritual visits and through the Society of Elder Faiths (SEF). In western Massachusetts, I circled and studied with Witches of Chalice Well Fellowship for the time when they were experimenting with a more open monthly ritual format and classes. I make a habit of attending the western Massachusetts Pagan Pride Day as a chance to see folks from the local area. And when time allows, I take online courses through Cherry Hill Seminary, which got its start in New England under Vermont founder Kirk White, although it is national and international now. Online, I'll also check out Witchvox.com, which is likewise international now, but founders Wren and Fritz had New England ties.

The sense of tribe and community created at festivals has always made me want to integrate community in my daily life. Now that I've put down roots in my country village, that sense of community is expressed more through the activities of the Blossom Center in Middlefield, for which members of the SEF helped perform a ground blessing ritual, with over 128 of the neighbors attending.

The only festival I have continued to attend in more recent years is the Vermont Witchcamp. Long ago, the Trillium Coven in Vermont approached the Reclaiming Tradition about starting a New England Witchcamp. Witchcamp is a week-long workshop and ritual intensive. After the many festivals I'd seen, I was impressed at how Vermont Witchcamp organizers were very conscious of shaping the energy throughout the event, creating a group greater than its parts, and making varied levels of connection between participants by a small affinity group, larger training path, coworkers in camp tasks, cabin mates, discussion groups, and independent workshop offerings. Witchcampers and other Reclaiming networks mainly stay connected online, so it is not specific to a geographic location. I've been somewhat surprised by how little mingling there is between Reclaiming folks and other trads in New England. I don't think the same is true where Reclaiming began, in the San Francisco Bay Area. But New England seems to have less habit of intermingling between different traditions.

Do you have any interactions with Witches in the Salem, Massachusetts, area? What is your impression of the current interest in Witchcraft in Salem, centuries after the Witch hysteria of Puritan times?

Because of the family business, we have lots of contact with Salem Witches. Adair and I and Buffie all still work at AzureGreen.net, along with eighteen other employees. AzureGreen sells to Witch stores, online shopping drop-shippers, and individuals. Personally, I don't end up traveling to Salem to see folks directly. But I know that an annual (or more frequent) trip to Salem was an enjoyed tradition for most of the Chalice Well Fellowship members, as it still is for lots of people. It's nice to have a destination place linked with your self-identity, and there are not many places that can fill that role. Salem is pretty unique because its name did get prominently linked with Witchcraft in America. Therefore it has that quality of association, of correspondence, which connects a visitor to Witchcraft as a subject. The original history may not be positive, but the contrast of new history versus old is quite hopeful. In Salem's recent history Witchcraft has played much more of a pillar-of-society role, since it holds a key place in the town's commerce and tourism.

I give the young Laurie Cabot a lot of credit for paving the way for this unique relationship between the subject of Witchcraft and a town. As I understand it, she made some positive press and impression by her psychic answers divining health problems. That good reputation may have aided acceptance of her association with the Salem chamber of commerce. The chamber asked her to represent and promote Witchcraft in Salem as a way to build tourism. Laurie went out of her way to be noticeable in appearance and activities as a way to attract attention to the Witch brand of Salem. And it worked. Where else would Google maps give you over fourteen vendors, within an approximately one-square-mile area, when you search for Witchcraft stores?

I give the current crop of Salem Witch store operators a lot of credit for keeping up the role of public interface. It is not an easy role. In any other town, the Witch store gets to focus on meeting the interests of being a community hub for Pagans. That's hard enough, as I recall from Abyss. In Salem, they must also be a hub for tourists. It's important to have these community hub locations, where notice boards can be read, questions asked, and readings and classes held. That's why we're happy to have AzureGreen supplies ordered through your local store, if your area is lucky enough to have one. In the age of internet buying it is more important than ever for customers to support the actual physical store locations as much as they can.

Have you experienced any difficulties—any problems, persecution, or prejudice—as a result of being a Witch? Can you describe a time or times when that happened?

We have been public Witches because of our business. But the store did get protests, by the Evangelical storefront church near it and the more secret spreading of negative gossip. More recently, that same spreading of negative gossip and innuendo, strident "righteous" verbal attacks, and encouraged opposition appeared in relation to a zoning permit the business was granted. In a town-wide vote, 73 percent of the voters approved permitting the expansion of our business. The local, old families in town supported the in-town jobs and the tax revenue. But a few newer residents were opposed to such a fanatic extent that they spent $50,000 in legal fees to temporarily obstruct the will of the voters over something that did not impact their lives. They were willing to accept and encourage the spread of negative stereotyping and ridiculous accusations, like animal sacrifice or the "Satanic sex orgy calendar of holidays" that was found on the internet somewhere and taped to the town hall door. We have no way of knowing how many ways and places the strident smear campaign has created prejudice against us. But it is hard to imagine that the merits of a business-sponsored blood drive would have been questioned and suspect, if done by another business, as it was when AzureGreen was the sponsor.

Most people are more susceptible than they realize to having their opinions shaped into negative impressions and then passing them on because they don't expect covert prejudice to have crept into what their friends have heard. People don't expect that they need to be wary of being co-opted into a mean-spirited agenda, so they aren't vigilant. One exasperated town selectman, who did know the extremist assertions and was tired of being asked specious questions about what would happen to our business's building in some possible future where we'd been driven out of town, finally snapped, "Then we'll just have to wash the goat's blood off the walls and put the building to a new use."

Overt attacks by fanatics can also bring out support. The only church in town, Middlefield Congregational Church, was pleased to offer its space to the monthly Wiccan rituals by Chalice Well Fellowship. They had wanted a chance to express support for us and to distinguish their Christian behavior as loving and generous, rather than fanatic, fearmongering, and divisive. Beyond the church itself, an overwhelming majority of townspeople have expressed their support for us. That is a big part of why we waited out the frivolous lawsuit.

What are special holy days for Witches? Can you please describe what Witches do on their holy days? How do you celebrate?

People who think of Witchcraft as foreign to them might be surprised that many of the celebratory holiday aspects will actually be familiar. That's because the Christian church appropriated many traditional Pagan holidays in Europe and the British Isles. But you can see the meaning of these aspects much better through the original Pagan lens. Christmas and Easter have very obvious Pagan underpinnings. The name *Easter* itself comes from that of a goddess of dawn (and of the East and of the fertility of the dawn of the year—namely spring). Her totem animal is the hare—famous for its frenzy of fertile activity in March. A classic ritual way of honoring her or invoking her help with fertility spells for the success of crops and herds was to use an egg—as symbolic of holding new life—and infuse it in red dye as symbolic of the power of the returning Sun bringing warmth and life back to Earth. The spell could be fancier by using many colors to make sigils and emblems on the egg to convey your specific hopes to the goddess of spring. I can't imagine how Christians explain Easter bunnies and colored eggs.

Even the timing of Easter is tied to the Full Moon and the Spring Equinox, in a holdover of the Pagan ways of marking time. Witches celebrate monthly Full Moons as well as the annual cycle of seasons created by Earth's relationship to the Sun. Four of the eight major Witch holidays are quarterly, on the Spring and Fall Equinoxes and Summer and Winter Solstices. The Winter Solstice—called Yule—is the time when all of the green of the "Greenwood" has contracted down to only showing in the evergreen trees, holly, and mistletoe, so these are the symbolic items used in ceremonially honoring the green of the growing season and calling for its return, along with the return of the Sun, symbolized by lights and candles.

The four greater Sabbats of the Witches' Wheel of the Year, or calendar of holidays, are at the cross quarter days beginning the months of November, February, May, and August. These offer the peak of energies begun at the quarters. They are from the Celtic tradition and marked the major turning points in the seasons experienced in a climate that is similar to New England's. The effective shift from summer to winter and back again came November 1 (Samhain) and May 1 (Beltaine). The Celts started their "day" with sunset, and that's why the folk tradition holdover puts the November 1 holiday on the evening of October 31— Halloween. The church glossed the old Pagan holiday as All Souls' Day and All Saints' Day (resulting in All Hallows' Eve). These still show the holy day's roots as a time of honoring the ancestors and spirits of the dead. Since this is the "sunset" time of the year, Samhain is often counted as the holiday that begins the New Year.

Personally, I like making a cycle beginning with the gateway of death. This may seem odd to our modern world concepts, which are so narrowed to a physical view of the world, where death is only an ending. In a spiritual view of the world, death is a doorway to spirit and to a wider horizon than that of mortal perception and concerns. Shedding your mortal identity corresponds to the divesting of your mundane garments that I mentioned as a good starting place for ritual activity. Having the long season of fallow darkness as the beginning of the year also corresponds better to the magical view that manifestation begins long before things emerge into a visible form on the physical plane. And starting your myth cycle with a time corresponding to the "descent into the Underworld" does provide the initiating journey experience that readies the hero self for meeting future challenges. It's a good practice, too, to begin a new adventure with touching base with your ancestors and spirit guides.

Even though the promise of the Sun's rebirth happens at Yule, it is not until February that winter is finally giving way to a new season of life with the lambing season. The February 1 holiday has old names such as Oimelc ("ewe's milk") and Imbolc ("in the belly") as well as Brigid's Day (Brigid is the Celtic goddess of childbirth and hearth fire) and Candlemas, as the church named it when taking over the Pagan holiday symbolism of celebrating and invoking the returning light with candles. It is also still celebrated as Groundhog Day (though a day later, on February 2), since that continues the Pagan tradition of this being a time to look to the strength of the Sun and seek an omen about the end of winter.

Opposite Brigid's Day is Lughnasad, Lugh's feast holiday, at the start of August. Lugh is a Celtic god of many skills, and this holiday begins the peak season of harvest. Despite this upbeat fact, Lughnasad can be a holiday that casts up surprising kernels of darkness because it is also a time when the Sun has begun its descent into death and darkness, the opposite of Candlemas as a time foretelling birth and light. I've noticed that groups holding open Lughnasad rituals sometimes trip on this fact that the energy at work can easily stray from being a simple celebration of summer bounty.

I think of the four cross quarter holidays as touching upon the key milestones in life: death (Samhain), birth (Imbolc or Brigid), the union of love (Beltaine), and harvest/inheritance and legacy (Lughnasad). A trio of these holidays speaks to the bindings that make a life. With birth comes the bond between parent and child and tribe and individual and the promise to be fulfilled to, and by, the next generation. With the union of love we create the mutual bond of marriage with another or "marriage" with the land we tend or ecstatic union with our deities. In our adulthood we, like Lugh, must come to terms with the varied claims, or bindings, of what we have inherited from our past, what we harvest from what we sowed, what we've gained as our many skills, how we meet our roles, and how we leave our mark upon the world. In complement to this trio of aspects that bind us to our world comes the unbinding of death to help us start afresh.

These are just a sampling of the many ways in which personal and mythic themes can weave through the energy nodes of the year represented by the holidays. Pagan and Witch orientation is toward having one symbol open up doorways to many answers and meanings rather than narrowing down to only one right answer or way of doing things.

Any other thoughts you care to add?

I'd like to have a community conversation about what our standards might be for deep integrity of practice and being a living witness for our values. I believe standards need to involve some amount of aspirational quality to encourage stretching ourselves to be more than we are now. But any reasonable standards must also be attainable and sustainable.

I noticed while narrating this interview about my life as a Witch that underneath I kept thinking I'd failed to make the time to create a tradition flavor of my own or to start and run a long-lasting teaching Coven that produces numerous competent teacher/leaders who hive into many daughter Covens, all while keeping a schedule of eight Sabbats and thirteen or twenty-four Moons, along with some inevitable other commitments. Of course, in addition, I should be exemplary at good spell work, healing work, psychic detection, and so on. Probably I'd need to be involved in several networking ventures outside of the trad family—perhaps an interfaith group or a community leaders' support group—participate in Covenant of the Goddess, maybe run a nonprofit organization, write books and articles, and be a political activist. All of these are the cumulative description of what doing a good job as a Witch looks like. It also sounds unsustainable, prone to burnout and overcommitment, which would undermine the value of maintaining grounded, centered attunement with the spirit world. There has to be a reasonable middle ground between a reader of a few Craft books and a Witch Queen Extraordinaire.

I'd also like better ways to interact with the wider Pagan community—ways that support one's personal practice without imposing overcommitment upon already-crowded schedules. I'd love to hear more brainstorming about ways to do this. Even many mainstream churches, with so much more infrastructure backing them, are finding it difficult to provide ample spiritual and community support, given the limitations of small congregations facing diverse needs and schedules. We need to be creative with low-overhead ways to nourish and connect with our community.

Lastly, I'd like to see Pagandom share its ecological platform with a wider public movement. Pagans express their strongly held value of stewardship for a sacred Earth, backed by a context of religious belief. I meet lots of other people who strongly believe that humans need to be good stewards of the Earth, but who wouldn't define their identity as Pagan. Rather than have Pagans working at a disadvantage from being few in number, and these other stewards working at a disadvantage from not having a larger philosophical context to their ecological values, I envision an overlap creating a shared cultural identity as "Earth stewards."

TERRY EIJI NAKAMURA-MEYERS
Lowell, Massachusetts

First, can you say a bit about who you are, where you live, and what you do for a living these days?

 I was born to a Japanese mother and a Cuban father in Japan. I was raised in Hawaii and Japan, moving between both countries every three or four years due to my father's employment. I speak Japanese and English fluently. I was a pediatric ER nurse for fourteen years but am currently aiming to find a new career and work as an Itako ("shamanic medium") when necessary.

Which religion were you raised in?

I was raised in a religion called Minzoku Shinto ("Folk Shintoisim"). It is a religion drawn from both the indigenous religion of Japan, Shinto, and Buddhism from China. Apart from being raised in this religion, my family has been practicing Itako shamanism for hundreds of years; I am currently the fifteenth head of our family's tradition.

How and when did you decide you were an Itako shaman?

Itako shamanism is not a tradition that can be picked. It is mostly hereditary, and one must show signs of Kamigakari or Miko-ke "shaman sickness," which sometimes comes in a form of sickness that doctors or modern medicine cannot cure or find the cause of, such as hysteria, insomnia, or a sudden onset of severe panic disorder, to name a few. For myself, I was born a stillborn and brought back to life. My grandmother, who is also an Itako, then knew the path that I would have to walk in this lifetime.

How do you personally define Witchcraft?

I understand Witchcraft as a way of life, an art that is learned by working with nature and higher elevated spirits as well as lower spirits, and a practice that is ever changing and nonorganized. I see Witches as healers, psychopomps, and people who can understand reality outside the rational mind, "the box," and become one with both the material world and unseen forces.

Can you talk about the tradition you follow?

An Itako is more shaman than a Witch, but in Japan they both would be considered the same since we do not have a word for Witch. The closest word will be Itako/miko, roughly translated as "shaman woman" or "god child," both used for either sex.

What makes your approach or tradition unique from any others out there?

Itako shamanism is unique in that it is only practiced in northern Japan, and it is an oral tradition. It is also unique in that it is not known outside of Japan. It is a dying tradition and practiced by only six or seven, including myself, in the world. And I am the only Itako outside of Japan.

Would you say that Itako is a "craft" or a "religion"? And can you talk about the difference?

Itako shamanism is a craft that is learned by the individual. There is no doctrine or unified practice as in organized religion. We are taught the basics from our elders, and we make each practice unique to ourselves. It is a craft that is not written in stone but knowledge that is ever changing.

Whom do you worship?

We do not necessarily worship; we honor multitudes of deities, Shinto and Buddhist, as well as our ancestors as elevated spirits.

When practitioners of Itako shamanism meet, what do they usually do?

Twice a year the rituals typically take place on Mount Osore, or Osorezan, in northern Japan, which is locally associated with "traditional" shamans. But we have our own practices in our own homes with our own shrines. We are mostly solitary practitioners and only get together on certain days of the year. We are also received in clients' homes to do spiritual consultation.

Do Itako do "spells" or can they do "magic"?

Yes, we do practice spellcraft.

If you do any spells, can you give examples?

Majinai ("spellcraft magic") is used for bringing down fevers, attracting luck, exorcisms etc., *uranai* is fortune-telling, and *kami-oroshi* ("bringing down the gods") and *hotoke-oroshi* ("bringing down the dead") are both done in a mediumistic manner.

Are you a hereditary practitioner?

Yes, I am currently the fifteenth head of our family's hereditary tradition. The stories I was taught make up some of my earliest memories. Daily life was enriched with tradition: what to do and what was taboo, what mantra and sutra to use, which spell to say for issues that concern anything from missing homework to a first heartbreak. Almost everything we did had a ritual behind it.

Have you had relationships or friendships with New England Witches? If so, with whom? And what were the most significant experiences or learnings you had from those encounters?

I have had only one encounter with another Witch here in Massachusetts. I have found that our practices are very similar despite the Eastern/Western cultural differences.

Do you have any interactions with Witches in the Salem, Massachusetts, area? What is your impression of the current interest in Witchcraft in Salem, centuries after the Witch hysteria of Puritan times?

I do not have any association with any Witches in Salem or their practices. I am new to the state, so I am still ignorant of my surroundings. However, I do in fact appreciate the openness and freedom to practice one's beliefs that I have seen during my few visits to Salem.

Have you experienced any difficulties—any problems, persecution, or prejudice—as a result of being a traditional shaman? Can you describe a time or times when that happened?

I personally have not experienced any difficulties as a result of being a shaman. Most, if not all, do not know that I am a Witch/shaman, since I practice privately.

What are special holy days in your tradition? Can you please describe what Itako do on their holy days? How do you celebrate?

We have many holy days. On the Chinese New Year in February we make offerings and hold a ceremony to refresh our house/hearth deities. In July we hold an *obon*, a three-day ceremony to pray for our ancestors and celebrate their return, much like Samhain in the West. In August we have a ceremony called *yokabi* where we cleanse our home and being from spirits and send them to where they need to go. In December we prepare to send our hearth deity to the heavens to intercede for our good fortune in the upcoming year.

Anything else you care to add?

Early on in my life I showed strange signs of being a little different from the other children, seeing things other children didn't see, hear, or smell. When I was eleven, my grandmother trained me in our family's "craft." The training was for 108 days, when I was handed over by my mother to stay at my grandmother's home in Japan. The training mostly consisted of water austerities or water purification, which we call *mizugori*. It was done three times a day—morning, noon, and night. Thirty-three buckets of ice water, drawn from the well in the backyard, were poured over my head, and I had to memorize multiple sutras, *norito* ("Shinto prayers"), majinai ("folk spells"), and *wasan* ("songs") and learn how to properly use the tools of an Itako, including the *irataka-juzu*, a long rosary made of soapberry nuts and old Japanese brass coins, fox jawbones, bear claws, antlers, etc. This rosary is used by rubbing the beads together and speaking or singing specific prayers or for communicating with the other side—deities, ancestor spirits, exorcisms of negative spirits' entities, energies, etc.

A second tool was what we call an *Odaiji* ("the precious object"). It is a bamboo tube filled with objects of power and protection, which every miko family has. Only the owner and/or the one who created it—in my case, me and my grandmother—are allowed to open it. If it's opened by anyone else, the power is lost, and a new one must be created. We wear this Odaiji on our backs. It is held by a rope on either side of the bamboo tube that we sling over our right shoulder and under our left arm.

The third item is a pair of house deities called *oshirasama* ("the white gods"), both carved from sticks of mulberry, one with a woman's face, the other with a man's face, or most times a horse's face. They are covered with a new piece of cloth every February 15 on *ko-shogatsu* ("old calendar new year.") Some families keep stacking new cloths over the old ones from the year before, so sometimes you will know how old the oshirasama are by counting the layers of cloth on them. Our family tradition is to stack strips of cloth for only twelve years and then start over again from the beginning. We give out the old cloth as amulets to the public for good luck, and we call this cloth the *osendaku*. Every year after refreshing their spirits by adding a new cloth, we sing a long prayer song called *oshira-asobi* "the playing of the white gods." Almost every household had a pair of these hearth deities, but the practice, just like the Itako, has waned. The Itako was hired by each house to perform the oshira ritual every year. My grandmother said she had to perform this ritual at about forty to fifty houses when she was younger, but in 2010 she performed this service at only eight houses. These people were all from the older generation that still revered the old folk deities; the younger generation mostly do not know what oshirasama are.

The fourth tool was the catalpa bow, which my grandmother had used in her time when she received it from her aunt, who was her teacher. I have not received one nor trained in using one. The one my grandmother was to pass down to me was destroyed during the war time, and she never received a new one to use. I was just told of how it was used. It was a curved bow made of catalpa wood and to use it you had to tap on the bow string with a bamboo stick about twelve inches in length while reciting prayers. It was used mainly for hotoke-oroshi. The tapping sound on the bow string helped induce a trance that allowed the Itako to receive the spirit in their mouth so it could speak.

TIANA MIRAPAE, A.K.A. LADY TIANA SOPHIA
Temple of Sophia, Goddess Mountain Sanctuary, Montague, Massachusetts

First, can you say a bit about who you are, where you live, and what you do for a living these days?

I am the founder, director, and High Priestess of the Temple of Sophia and the Wisdom School of SOPHIA on Goddess Mountain. We celebrate the eight Sabbats with ritual high magick as well as many Hebrew holy days, integrating tribal Judaism and the spiritual, magickal, and medicinal wisdom of many sacred traditions.

I was ordained as a Priestess of the Witches of Avalon Church in 2006 and ordained as a Kohenet Hebrew Priestess by the Kohenet Institute in 2013. I am Ma'ayan Ahavat Shehkinah, the Wellspring of Shehkinah's Love! I am a passionate JeWitch extraordinaire.

I was born out of the ashes of Auschwitz.

Both of my parents were Holocaust survivors.

I was raised in the "Holy Land" of Crown Heights, Brooklyn, with Chasidic-Orthodox parents who were deeply grieving, raging, and traumatized by the devastating loss of their families, identities, and an entire civilization. I yearned to heal or at least soothe my family's traumatic wounds. I yearned for a loving, joyous, protecting God. I yearned for a loving Divine Feminine. I yearned for a way to express my love for God, Spirit, and Nature. But growing up in that post-war New York *shtetl* (Jewish village) of Holocaust survivors, there was just darkness, pain, grief, rage, and sorrow.

It was unimaginable for a girl to become a rabbi or to even see a woman on the *bimah* (pulpit). There was no joy or Ruach (spirit) there for me.

This patriarchal religion with its long history of oppression and suffering was confusing for me. I turned my interests to cultural anthropology, mythology, philosophy, and psychology and dove into studying various spiritual wisdom traditions. I became a HindJew, a BuddJew, then kinda DruIsh, and now a JeWitch. I was a student of Ram Dass. I received *shahkti-pat* (psychic transference) from my guru Swami Muktananda, which awakened a part of my mind. I studied Buddhist psychology and meditation with Chogyam Trungpa Rinpoche at Naropa Institute and opened the first yoga *satsang* meditation studio in Brooklyn in 1974.

It seemed that, one minute, I was a seventeen-year-old hippie protesting the war in Vietnam at the City College of New York, and then quite suddenly, I moved to Israel to study theater and psychology at Tel Aviv University. This is where my past life/ancestral memories awakened. Wherever I went in this Holy Land, "flashbacks" occurred. A detailed vision of a mosaic appeared in my mind one day as I was exploring Haifa. As I turned onto a side street, there was an archaeological dig going on. They were dusting off the floor of an ancient temple from 2000 BC, and there, on the floor, was the picture of the mosaic I'd seen. Another time, I was at the Western Wall and walking into the Arab *shuk* (market) on the Via Dolorosa (I didn't know what that meant at the time) and "experienced" being in the crowd when

Jesus carried the cross. This was disturbing to me and not something I could relate to. I went to my psychology professor and told him what was happening to me. He had a colleague hypnotize me. I spoke ancient Aramaic and named places on ancient maps of the Middle East that dated back to 6000 BC. I awoke with the weight of carrying the water pitcher, still on my head, and the memory of talking to my friends at the desert well about my beloved coming to visit.

I became an avid student of meditation, hypnosis, astral projection, ESP, mind and psychic development, yoga, Jungian dream work, and divination. I traveled the world to find the best teachers. Memories of being a medicine woman in many lifetimes became stronger and clearer. I studied herbal medicine: Western, Mayan, Inca, Native American, and Chinese traditions, homeopathy, and ayurveda, as well as qigong. All that led to plant spirit medicine, animal spirit allies, and working with the archangels, star beings/celestials, and crystals. The ReUnification of the Three Mother Worlds—humans with plant/tree spirits, humans with animal spirits, and humans with the Earth spirits (elementals and faeries)—became my passion and quest.

I came to realize, pretty early on, that one cannot heal trauma at the level of the mind and not even at the level of emotion and body. One must heal at the level of soul and spirit to truly release the past and become our true and authentic self. Becoming a shamanic healer changed everything! Now I could journey beyond fear, violence, and death, through time and space, to heal the roots and origins of the "problem" and its patterns from the past seven generations, on behalf of those who came before us and for our descendants for the next seven generations from now. We are the ancestors who are creating a new legacy to pass forward—one of partnership, compassion, freedom, and JOY!

As a modern-day medicine woman, I am trained in a wide variety of modalities. I'm a licensed integrative psychotherapist, certified somatic EMDR consultant and therapist, TAT: Tapas Acupressure practitioner, hypnotherapist, Reiki master, classical homeopath, clinical master herbalist, holistic nutritionist, shamanic healer, Wisdom Keeper of the Munay Ki Rites, and a *mesa* carrier. I have been the integrative psychotherapist and holistic practitioner in a gynecology practice for thirty-plus years. I specialize in healing trauma, depression, anxiety, and women's health issues, as well as working with individuals and couples specializing in communication, sacred intimacy, and sex therapy. I practice and teach holistic medicine, integrating and healing mind, body, emotions, sexuality, spirit, and soul.

Best of all, I am mother to my two brilliant, beautiful daughters, grandmother (Zaftah), Faerie Goddess Mama, and sister to my spirit heart family. I live on Goddess Mountain with my two temple puppies, Shalomo (Peace) and Ohevet (Love), my cat, Charlie Dandelion, and the Earth spirits and faeries of this beautiful sacred land that I am blessed to steward.

How and when did you decide you were a Witch?

Ha! When I could no longer deny it and as soon as I met other Witches. I didn't even know, for sure, that there were others of "us" left, so solitary and isolated we have been. Throughout my life I sought out Witches, but they were in secret Covens, kind of creepy, and not open to community (and way before the internet). One spring May Day, I made it my mission to find a Beltaine ritual. I was inspired, like so many of us, by the book *The Mists of Avalon*. I tracked down a group of Pagans having a Beltaine ritual in western Massachusetts. That day, I felt like I had stepped through the veil and found my people. There were Druids and Witches of various traditions: Faerie, Strega, Gardnerian, Alexandrian, Celtic, Dianic, etc. I felt myself, my heart, connected with those familiar souls. I deeply prayed my gratitude and intentions on the woven Maypole, and as I released my offering to her, I knew that I have always been in joyous service to Goddess, our Lady, to the Divine Feminine. The gateways of memories flooded through me as a priestess, shaman, healer, and Witch.

As I mentioned, one of my gifts is that I've always remembered many of my past lives. I remembered many of the sacred wisdom traditions I'd come from including the lore, the medicine, and the rituals. My ancestral lineage terrified and traumatized me on so many levels that I became a spiritual seeker and student of other cultures and ancient teachings. Synchronistic pilgrimages to sacred sites in foreign lands would awaken many memories in me. I had been Native American, Japanese, Hawaiian, Russian, Chinese, Scottish, English, Italian, Greek, German, French, Mayan, Incan . . . and I was able to learn and speak many of these languages easily. What was especially amazing to me was to remember my relationship with the plants, trees, rivers, and ocean, and to remember the goddesses of the land and to remember how to use their medicine and magick. Mother Nature attuned me to myself, over and over. She was my Source, my Mother, my healer.

Around the turn of the last century, in 1999, I met the Witches who would become my Coven mates at a Samhain ritual facilitated by the EarthSpirit Community in Northampton, Massachusetts. We recognized each other's souls and began working together magickally, immediately. A few months later, I was invited to attend a gathering of the Witches of the Well of Avalon. I joked that it was my letter from Hogwarts. I was so excited that I wept with joy! I felt so honored to find peers amongst the Witches of various traditions that I so admired and respected.

How do you personally define Witchcraft?

Witchcraft is working in partnership with the Divine and the forces of Nature for the greatest good of all concerned. Living life mindfully with magick, mysticism, and Nature medicine, in partnership with our benevolent and wise Spirit guides, aligned with the Moon, Sun, and stars. Witchcraft is being awake and connected to the Goddess.

What tradition of Witchcraft do you follow? How did you find that tradition?

I was blessed to know and study with many fine teachers and Witches of many magickal traditions, such as Strega and Dianic. I loved aspects of them all, but my true resonance comes from Sophia.

I founded the Sophia Tradition, well, because the Goddess told me to, and all I could say was, "Thank you." She said, "Build me a temple and a sacred, holy site for community to enjoy." For a moment, I thought, "How can I do this, I'm a single parent?" Blah, blah, blah, but argue with Goddess, really? So, I responded, "Thank you, my Lady, I am truly blessed to serve you." And she has given me back ten thousand-fold!

The goddess of wisdom and love, Sophia, claimed my ass! Originally, SOPHIA was an acronym for Sisterhood of Priestesses, Healers, Intuitives, and Alchemists. But very soon, she told me that it was important to train men as well, to serve Goddess and community as Priests and Shamans. The acronym for the Wisdom School of SOPHIA now stands for Shamans, Oracles, Priests/Priestesses, Healers, Intuitives, and Alchemists.

In the Sophia Tradition, we explore and embrace the Sacred Feminine and the Sacred Masculine and the relationship they have together, within us and between us. We are the embodiment of the Tree of Life. The Wisdom School of SOPHIA helps students explore and heal their ancestral and past life roots, utilizing shamanic healing medicine from many ancient wisdom traditions.

Would you say that Witchcraft is a "craft" or a "religion"? And can you talk about the difference?

Honestly, I was a bit shocked to realize that when I was ordained as a Priestess of the Well of Avalon, I was actually clergy and therefore now part of a "religion." I thought I had run away from religion, especially the patriarchal nightmare. When I became ordained as a Kohenet Hebrew Priestess, I was then clergy in two world religions. Whoa, how did that happen? Goddess has a great sense of humor!

As High Priestess of the Temple of Sophia, I facilitate ritual high magick celebrations for all eight Sabbats, the Dark, New, and Full Moon rituals, and rites of passage ceremonies. As a Kohenet Hebrew Priestess, I facilitate ritual magick ceremonies as well for Jewish holy days and blessing ways. So, for me, being a Witch has actually become a religion, yet it's more of a way of life. I am turning the Wheel of the Seasons, living in Nature mindfully, with all that is sacred, with gratitude and love. More and more, I live, work, play, dance, and pray with Spirit in all that I do. There is no separation, just grace.

Anyone can practice the Craft of Witchcraft as a solitary or as a spiritual, magickal practice without it having any "religious" overtones. One can practice the Craft while simultaneously practicing a different religion and coming from many religious belief systems and backgrounds.

Whom do Witches worship?

In the Sophia Tradition, we don't so much "worship" as we honor, respect, and work in partnership with the Goddess; the Divine Feminine and Sacred Masculine; Mother Nature and the forces of Nature (air, fire, water, and earth); the Earth spirits, elementals, and Fey; plants, trees, and animals spirits; stones and crystals; celestials, benevolent ancestors, ascended masters, and archangels of various traditions; love, joy, peace, compassion, wisdom, medicine, and magick; the love of wisdom and the wisdom of love; and the beauty way.

We believe that all life is sacred.

When Witches meet, what do they usually do?

We usually meet at a particular time of the year (equinox, solstice) or Sun or Moon phase to turn the Wheel and utilize the forces of Nature to work with and manifest our intentions, desires, wishes, and dreams for ourselves and others, for our community, and for our world. We do spell work, ritual high magick, chanting, drumming, laughing, breathing, grounding, and connecting. We create sacred space, cast circle, and invoke our spirit guides and allies. We work from mindful, clear, positive intention with consensus. We join forces with all that is sacred and we make magick!

Do Witches really do "spells" or can they do "magic"?

Yes, part of our magick is that we do magick spells.

If you do any spells, can you give examples?

The only rule is "Harm no one." With that said, one can do a binding spell by putting a person's troublesome behavior into a freezer so they will "chill out." Or we can do a "spell with a shell" to send your blessed wishes out to flow. We also make poppets that represent those who need a healing, and we engrave candles with symbols and then light them for a particular intention.

Are you a hereditary Witch?

I have been a Witch, medicine woman, Healer, shaman, and priestess through innumerable past lives. Ancestrally, my mother, who survived the Warsaw ghetto and Auschwitz, taught me to trust my intuition and my dreams. At the end of WWII, as the Allies approached the concentration camp, the Jewish prisoners were brought on a death march. In the middle of the night, my mother awoke from a dream. Her father had come to her and said, "Save yourself." She didn't know what to do, but she got up, tied her scarf around her to cover the Star of David on her back, and started walking away from the encampment. Every moment, she expected to hear the Nazi shouts, the dogs, and the gunshots. But they didn't come. She escaped that night, and everyone else was shot to death the next morning. My mother didn't "practice" Witchcraft, but there were many superstitions and *bubbe meises* (grandmother stories) that she told and observed as part of the Jewish culture of eastern Europe: tying a red *bindle* (bow) on a baby carriage to keep away the "evil eye," turning a glass upside down to find a lost object, making an amulet for a safe trip, lighting a candle to help heal from surgery or to pass an exam, listening to the voices of the ancestors as we lit the Shabbat candles and chanted the Sh'ma. There were also prayers to protect us from lightning and thunder and a holiday, Tu B'Shvat, to celebrate the birthday of the trees.

Did your family carry stories about Witches or did you find out about it all recently?

I was studying with a shaman in South America who said to me, "You are never going to be a Guatemalan shaman, ya know. Look to your own culture for your medicine and mysticism." I was devastated. Surely he didn't understand that I was from a Jewish culture of pain, guilt, and suffering—there was no magick there, just grief, trauma, and loss. But then I looked! I was blissfully amazed at the rich lineage of magick, medicine, and mysticism that are the deep roots and wide branches of my ancestry! Whodathunk?

It turns out that there have been "Witches," enchantresses, sorceresses, diviners, magic workers, and shamanic healers documented throughout the Old Testament, the Babylonian Bible, the Talmud, and the Kabbalah. The great rabbi and mage, the Baal Shem Tov, founder of the Chasidic movement, was "trained" by the "Witches," the women of the forest. There are innumerable stores of the miracles and healings he performed such as depossessions, house clearings, astral projection and bilocality, divination, spell work, shape-shifting, and spontaneous healings.

Every town, from Babylonian villages to eastern European shtetles, had their "Witch/enchantress," just as they had a matchmaker, a butcher, and a tailor. She was an esteemed and respected part of the culture. She might have been called upon to heal little Yitzhak's nightmares, create a prayer for newlyweds' fertility, or make a talisman for a travelers' safety.

And then there are the *shtretelech,* the Jewish faerie folk. Over fifty thousand Jewish folk and faerie tales were recorded prior to WWII. Along with the annihilation of the great Jewish civilization that thrived in Europe for thousands of years, the faerie folklore was buried too. After the Holocaust, people were too traumatized to tell the stories. Those who had emigrated to the United States prior to the war often didn't want to be identified as Jewish and rejected their religion and the culture they had left behind. I thought I had to be of Celtic origin to have a close connection with the faerie folk. How delightful to know that they are everywhere.

As a Kohenet Hebrew Priestess, I dove deeply into—and am still unpacking—all the rich, amazing, powerful magick and mysticism that are an integral part of my Hebrew ancestral lineage. Every Hebrew holy day and Hebrew letter is filled with symbolism, *gematria* (numerology), and prayers for working in partnership with Nature. The Kabbalah is a brilliant blueprint and foundation for living life in a mindful, magickal, and spiritual way. The Hebrew calendar is a thirteen-Moon calendar, and all the holy days fall either on a New or Full Moon. Judaism was originally an Earth-based, tribal, God/Goddess spirituality, and that is the resonance I dance, sing, and pray with today. As a Kohenet, I embody Shekhinah, She who dwells within to provide the wellspring of Her love and healing power.

Have you had relationships or friendships with other New England Witches? If so, with whom? And what were the most significant experiences or learnings you had with these encounters?

I honor and respect all of my sister and brother Witches of the Craft, regardless of their tradition. I enjoy and celebrate our similarities and differences. I truly believe in living the concept of "perfect love and perfect trust," from our highest self. All Witches are welcome to all our ritual gatherings at Goddess Mountain Sanctuary Temple of Sophia. In fact, all people of all traditions and backgrounds are welcome, as long as they come in love and trust and respect sacred space.

Do you have any interactions with Witches in the Salem, Massachusetts, area? What is your impression of the current interest in Witches of Salem, centuries after the Witch hysteria in Puritan times?

It appears to me that Harry Potter has brought Witchcraft to the mainstream. There is more information about the Craft out there in books and media than ever before. I think that Arthur Miller's *Crucible* made Salem famous again in the twentieth century, and the town has been a huge tourist attraction at Halloween time for decades. I rarely have any direct interactions with Salem Witches as I live in western Massachusetts, and we are usually holding rituals at the same time.

What are special holy days for Witches? Can you please describe what Witches do on their holy days? How do you celebrate?

The Temple of Sophia is a Goddess temple and the sacred land is our Goddess (GoddUs) Mountain temple sanctuary. We facilitate ritual magick celebrations for all eight Earth-based spiritual holy days: Winter and Summer Solstices; Spring and Autumn Equinoxes; and the cross quarters of Beltaine/Mayfest, Lughnassadh/first harvest, Samhain/Halloween, and Imbolc/Brigid.

The students of the Wisdom School of SOPHIA co-create, collaborate, and facilitate community rituals as part of their training as Priests and Priestesses. There is a lot of chanting, dancing, drumming, praying, raising cones of energy, and laughing going on. Our ritual magick celebrations involve full community participation. They are not spectator sports, theatrical performances, or parties. Each person weaves their magick for the "greatest good of all," individually and collectively. We invite all who come to have the intention of "perfect love and perfect trust" and to be responsible for holding sacred space with loving-kindness and a welcome friendliness. Goddess willing, a beautiful, powerful, joy-filled, transformational, magickal experience is had by all.

We also hold rituals on the Dark Moon, the New Moon, and the Full Moon. I/we facilitate all the rites of passage rituals, each one unique, co-creative, and meaningful, from birth to death and beyond: life, reincarnation, rebirth—ancestral healing back seven generations, on behalf of our descendants for the next seven generations from now. We are the ancestors creating a new legacy, a new healthy, loving, partnership paradigm, now and for our children's children and for Mother Earth.

I/we facilitate blessing ways before a birth or wedding, rituals after a loss (divorce, hysterectomy, miscarriage) or for a new beginning (home, job, relationship), coming-of-age ceremonies for young people, house and land clearings, and weddings/memorial services. I/we also facilitate as a SOPHIA Shaman-Priest/ess during end-of-life transitions, further enhancing the hospice experience with shamanic healing rites. I also hold private magickal healing retreats for individuals, couples, and groups.

We respect and honor the ancient wisdom of many sacred traditions and all interfaith beliefs, and we fully support our LGBTQ community. We are the sacred Tree of Life! At Sukkot, an ancient Hebrew harvest festival, we combine the *lulavk,* leaves of three species of trees, with an *etrog* (citron) and shake them in the seven sacred directions to pray for water and sustenance for all. We facilitate sacred flower bath ceremonies, *mikvahs,* to cleanse, prepare, and purify us before or after a rite of passage or significant experience. I often integrate Chanukah, the Festival of Miracles and Light, with the Winter Solstice; Tu B'Shvat, the holy day of the trees, with Imbolc; the Spring Equinox with Purim or Passover; and on and on. Clearly, I am a ritual junkie!

We are weaving, spiraling, and embodying our magick, our highest intentions, our greatest desires, and our soul's purpose on this sacred Earth Walk! And we do so in partnership with all our beloved spirit guides and allies, extraordinary assistants in all we do. We are casting a spell of such magnitude, exponentially connecting with the matrix of light and all crystal beings. And we do so with the power, wisdom, beauty, and strength of the Goddess, the Feminine Divine. She brings us balance of loving-kindness, intuition, assertiveness, and the pleasure of chocolate. We explore and embrace the Sacred Masculine to heal the wounds of the patriarchal nightmare. We partner with his qualities of support, loving-kindness, protection, and even home repair!

You can find more information on the following websites: www.schoolofsophia.com, www.templeofsophia.com, www.tianamirapae.com, www.gyngroup.com.

YSSION ASTRAEOS
Rhode Island

First, can you say a bit about who you are, where you live, and what you do for a living these days?

I was born in 1972 and my Sun sign is Capricorn. I live in an old house with my beloved wife, family, animal friends, and trees on a hill near the ocean. I primarily do solution development related to business intelligence, efficiency, and automation. I've been into role playing (Dungeons & Dragons) since age ten and picked up an interest in theater as I got older. The visualization and transformation skills that began developing when I was young served as a foundation for the endeavors I pursue today, such as guided meditations and invocations. The hats I wear describe me well: husband, father, Priest, Mystic, Witch, scientist, tree hugger, gamer. I am a child, consort, and Priest of The Goddess, and I am a Priest and vessel for The God.

Which religion were you raised in?

I was raised and confirmed Roman Catholic. Given my current beliefs and practices, I find it amusing to reflect on the fact that at age sixteen I was asked to play Jesus in the Passion play. I had already decided that I would not find fulfillment within Christianity but was excited to be in a play of any sort. I even grew out a sparse "beard" for it. In retrospect, that event was essentially my last real interaction with the Church as a member. The experience of standing in a church during a mass, honestly attempting to portray Jesus, was quite valuable, and I will surely not have the chance to receive it again.

How and when did you decide you were a Witch?

It was more like the result of self-discovery than a decision. I gradually acquired a context and opinion of what the word *Witch* means, specifically to me. Over time I came to find myself to be of that nature. It was somewhat of a self-fulfilling prophesy sort of process, actually.

How do you personally define Witchcraft?

As we all know, the term *Witchcraft* is applied to a broad range of activities, time periods, and cultures, and though I've tried, I don't have a simple catch-all definition. I generally distinguish between a contemporary concept of Witchcraft and the Witchcraft of antiquity. I view today's as having a more predominant cult nature, whereas the Witchcraft of the past seems to have been more of a solitary practice. In my conception, the cultists of the past, such as those in the mystery cults of ancient Greece and Rome, weren't necessarily considered the same people as the Witches.

Which tradition of Witchcraft do you follow? How did you find that tradition?

I was first initiated into the Alexandrian Tradition (Alex Sanders) and have since also become involved in the New England Coven of Traditionalist Witches (Gwen Thompson). In my opinion it is often less about finding the tradition than it is about finding the people. I found my people by attending a workshop on candle magick in an herb shop where I noticed a flyer regarding a Craft study group. I contacted the person holding the group, and the rest fell into place over the next couple of years.

What makes your approach or tradition unique from any others out there?

My personal approach tends to lean toward the Kabbalah, mysticism, and ritual. Overall it is about the pursuit of self-betterment through exploration and discovery. For example, astrology and birth charts are used to establish a concept and basis for understanding and anticipating our own behavior—"Know thyself," as was written at the Temple of Apollo at Delphi.

Would you say that Witchcraft is a "craft" or a "religion"? And can you talk about the difference?

Within the framework of Witchcraft today, this varies widely between individuals and groups. Personally, though I accept the responsibilities of Priesthood, I view neither of my Craft paths as a religion. The Craft is my practice and my passion. I practice religiously, but it's not a religion. I practice devotion, but I am not a devotee.

Whom do Witches worship?

I'll answer the question, "Do Witches worship and if so whom?" I do not worship anything external or separate from myself, for at the end of the day I disregard any fundamental separation between the two. That being said, it is certainly not correct to suggest that this attitude is a standard for practitioners. We agree upon what we are doing and how we do it, but we don't need to agree on why we do it; the answer to why we do our work is personal.

In terms of deity forms that are acknowledged by contemporary Witches, regardless of whether they are worshipped per se, there are most commonly The Goddess and The God. When nameless, they represent archetypes of masculinity and femininity. When named, such as Diana or Cernunnos, they are aspects of the Divine Feminine and Masculine. Pantheons vary widely as well. I lean toward the Greek, Celtic, and Egyptian mythologies.

When Witches meet, what do they usually do?

We hold regular meetings of various sorts. We meet to Circle, we meet to celebrate, we meet to discuss or make plans. We tend not to meet solely for the sake of socializing, as we choose to distinguish our mundane selves from our magickal selves.

Do Witches really do "spells" or can they do "magic"?

Absolutely, both. The way I define it, magick is natural, and we all do it all the time. The difference lies in being aware of this fact. Being aware allows one to develop and refine techniques. It's similar to those who refine their prayer habits through dedication and repetition. Belief opens the door to miracles in both cases.

Spells are a subset of magick. A friend who has passed, Christine Jones, once pointed out to me that a spell is a period of time. To cast a spell is to change the course of events, through direction of will, for a period of time. Any magick I do that has a defined start and end is essentially a spell.

If you do any spells, can you give examples?

I make a wish every time I blow out birthday candles or see a shooting star. I light candles with purpose, often. I use symbols and notes to condense my intentions and by fire release them to the universe to manifest as The Goddess allows. I write rhymes, I chant, and I dance.

Are you a hereditary Witch?

To my knowledge I have no elders within my extended family who have openly admitted magickal practice of any sort.

Did your family carry stories about Witches or did you find out about it all recently?

There was no discussion of that sort at all within my family or upbringing. Around age twenty I discovered that there were people in the world who actually believed magick was real. Prior to that I had only been aware of those who believed in the power of prayer.

Have you had relationships or friendships with other New England Witches? If so, with whom? And what were the most significant experiences or learnings you had from those encounters?

Absolutely. My traditions have members residing around the country and the globe. There are also several sister traditions with relatively similar members and practices. Every once in a while there is an event where several or many Covens gather for Sabbats or workshops. Significant experiences occur each and every time I meet new Witches. As a result of the practice, Witches tend to have a refined energy about them. Simply gathering and meeting and talking and feeling a new Witch's energy is a significant encounter. At times, when revealing a deep or personal aspect of one's own beliefs or experiences, sparks of serendipity rain down on discussions, and reflections have hints of destiny. Often times such interactions result in unforeseen spiritual growth spurts.

Do you have any interactions with Witches in the Salem, Massachusetts, area? What is your impression of the current interest in Witchcraft in Salem, centuries after the Witch hysteria of Puritan times?

The Witches I am friendly with in Salem tend to be shop owners, readers, and the like. In general I view Salem as one of many great, quaint New England villages, one of which we live in. I associate the Burning Times with fear, hysteria, and the falsely accused. I expect that most, if not all, of those burned there were not "Witches" at all. When I visit today it almost feels like being there serves to heal the land, just a little bit, of the fear that encompassed those times.

Have you experienced any difficulties—any problems, persecution, or prejudice—as a result of being a Witch? Can you describe a time or times when that happened?

I am ever aware of the risk of causing fear in others due to their preconceived notions of what I do and how it could affect them. I have not personally experienced any persecution or prejudice, but I stay predominantly underground and acknowledge Murphy's Law.

What are special holy days for Witches? Can you please describe what Witches do on their holy days? How do you celebrate?

We follow both the solar Wheel of the Year and the cycles of the moon. We Circle thirteen times each year on Full Moons for lunar cycle acknowledgment (Esbats), and eight times each year for solar cycle acknowledgment (Sabbats). The eight Sabbats consist of two solstices and two equinoxes, plus the four halfway points in between. The

Sabbats tend to be festivals and more celebratory, and the Esbats tend to emphasize magickal work. We Circle, we dance, and we feast.

Any other thoughts you care to add?

One topic that hasn't been raised yet is Love. Our practice is fundamentally based on Love with a capital *L*. It's Love in the context of embracing the interconnectedness of all things in nature. It is an appreciation for all spirits, their unique purpose in this life, and their essential contribution to the evolution of humanity and the Earth. It is a Love for Divinity, and an understanding that it springs forth from within each of us. Essentially all Witches whom I have met have shared this desire, capacity, and inclination to Love. The strategic projection of Love is what best defines my practice. Here's a spell: "With this entry I do cast, a Spell that forever and a day shall last, to remind: we unite in Blessed Bliss, drawn together and bound with one Starry kiss." Blessed be those who bring us and hold us together through turbulent times.

Sources and Resources

The following sources are arranged by the chapter in which they appear.

HISTORY OF WITCH PERSECUTIONS

Becker, Marshall J. "An American Witch Bottle: Evidence for the Practice of 'White Witchcraft' in Colonial Pennsylvania." *Archaeology Magazine* archive 2009, http://archive.archaeology.org/online/features/halloween/witch_bottle.html.

Brooks, Rebecca Beatrice. "Tituba: The Slave of Salem." *History of Massachusetts* (blog). Accessed 9/2/2016. http://historyofmassachusetts.org/tituba-the-slave-of-salem.

Brooks, Rebecca Beatrice, and Susannah Martin. "Accused Witch from Salisbury." *History of Massachusetts* (blog). February 14, 2012. http://historyofmassachusetts.org/susannah-martin-accused-witch-from-salisbury.

Castelow, Ellen. "Witches in Britain." Historic UK. Accessed 9/27/2016. www.historic-uk.com/CultureUK/Witches-in-Britain.

Gates Jr., Henry Louis. "The 'Black' Witch of Salem?" The Root. April 14, 2014. www.theroot.com/articles/history/2014/04/who_was_tituba_the_black_witch_of_salem.

Johnson, Bonnie. "Susanna North Martin." RootsWeb. Accessed 3/1/2017. www.rootsweb.ancestry.com/~nwa/sm.html.

Kors, Alan Charles, and Edward Peters. *Witchcraft in Europe, 400–1700: A Documentary History.* 2nd ed. Philadelphia: University of Pennsylvania Press, 2000.

K-Z, Anna. "Ergot Theory Could Clear Accused Witches." The Salem Journal: The Aftermath; Witches' Remise (on the website for the University of Chicago). Accessed 9/10/2016. http://people.ucls.uchicago.edu/~snekros /Salem%20Journal/Aftermath/AnnaK.html.

Lewis, Jone Johnson. "Tituba and the Salem Witch Trials." ThoughtCo. Updated May 29, 2017. www.thoughtco.com/tituba-salem-witch-trials-3530572.

Linder, Douglas. "A Brief History of Witchcraft Persecutions before Salem (2005)." www.olma.org/ourpages/auto/2014/9/29/50854287/Text%201 %20-%20Witchcraft%20Before%20Salem.pdf.

McAffee, Michelle. "Susannah (North) Martin, Salem Witch Trials." Geni. Updated October 24, 2017. www.geni.com/people/Susannah-North-Martin -Salem-Witch-Trials/6000000003615754555.

Pioneer Valley History Network's Remarkable Women of the Pioneer Valley. "Mary Parsons of Springfield." Accessed 10/1/2016. https://pvhn2.word press.com/1600-2/mary-parsons-of-springfield.

Roberts, Jeanie. "Hugh and Mary Parsons: Witches of Springfield." The Family Connection. September 5, 2016. www.jeaniesgenealogy.com/2016/09 /hugh-and-mary-parsons-witches-of.html.

Schiff, Stacy. "Unraveling the Many Mysteries of Tituba, the Star Witness of the Salem Witch Trials." *Smithsonian Magazine*, November 2015. www.smithsonianmag.com/history/unraveling-mysteries-tituba-salem -witch-trials-180956960/?no-ist.

"Tituba." Salem Witchcraft Trials, Famous Trials (1692). Accessed 9/2/2017. http://law2.umkc.edu/faculty/projects/ftrials/salem/ASA_TIT.HTM.

Tracy, Stephanie. "Witchcraft in 16th & 17th Century England." The Tudor Enthusiast. October 31, 2012. http://thetudorenthusiast.weebly.com /my-tudor-blog/witchcraft-in-16th-17th-century-england.

ACCUSED WITCHES IN NEW ENGLAND AND INTERVIEWS WITH THEIR DESCENDANTS

Arn and Jody. "Welthian Loring (Richards) 1599–1679." *Stagge-Parker Histories* (blog with various quotes from ancestry.com). Accessed 8/12/2016. http:// stagge-parker.blogspot.com/2011/08/welthian-loring-1599-1679.html.

Austin, Anne Taite. "Important Persons in the Salem Court Records: Mary Easty." Salem Witch Trials: Documentary Archive and Transcriptions

Project. Spring 2001. http://salem.lib.virginia.edu/people?group
.num=&mbio.num=mb9.

Behling, Sam. "Mary Bliss Parsons." RootsWeb. Accessed 7/18/2016. http://
homepages.rootsweb.ancestry.com/~sam/bliss/mary.html.

Beran, Evelyn. "Sanford-Shulsen Family." RootsWeb. Accessed 8/12/2016.
https://wc.rootsweb.ancestry.com/cgi-bin/igm.cgi?op=GET&db=sanford
-shulsen&id=I6162.

Boltwood, Lucius M., and Sylvester Judd. Transcribed by K. T. "Witchcraft
in Hadley, MA." Northampton: 1863. Genealogy Trails History Group.
http://genealogytrails.com/mass/hampshire/history_chap21.html.

Davis, Heather G. "Excerpts from the Biographical Sketch about Thomas
Richards in the Outstanding Historical Series, 'The Great Migration
Begins,' by Robert Charles Anderson." Family Search. Accessed 8/12/2016.
https://familysearch.org/photos/artifacts/4343148.

Durston, Chris. "The Puritan War on Christmas." *History Today* 35, no. 12
(December 1985). www.historytoday.com/chris-durston/puritan-war-christmas.

Genealogy.com. "My Genealogy Home Page: Information about Rebecca
Towne." Accessed 8/27/2016. www.genealogy.com/ftm/n/u/r/Mervin
-Nurss-PA/WEBSITE-0001/UHP-0133.html.

Jennings, Margery. "Our Founding Mother." On Seger Mountain. Accessed
8/20/2016. www.onsegermountain.org/witchcraft.html.

Marshall, Bridget M. "Mary (Reeve) Webster, the 'Witch' of Hadley" (talk).
May 2003. http://faculty.uml.edu/bmarshall/Mary%20Webster.htm.

Marshall, Bridget M., Victoria Getis, and Matthew Mattingly. The website
for the University of Massachusetts, Amherst. "The Mary (Bliss) Parsons
Story." https://ccbit.cs.umass.edu/parsons/hnmockup/story.html. "The
Witchcraft Trial." https://ccbit.cs.umass.edu/parsons/hnmockup/witch
crafttrial.html. "Slander." https://ccbit.cs.umass.edu/parsons/hnmockup
/slander.html. All accessed 7/18/2016.

Sajdak, Ken. "A Witch in the Family?" Accessed 8/12/2016. http://sportsage
.net/familyhistory/?p=803.

Starkey, Marion L. *The Devil in Massachusetts: A Modern Enquiry into the
Salem Witch Trials.* New York: Anchor Books, 1989.

Stuhler, Linda S. "My 8th Great-Grandmother: The Witch of Hartford,
Connecticut." Inmates of Willard. Accessed 8/14/2016. https://inmates
ofwillard.com/2012/07/19/my-8th-great-grandmother-the-witch-of
-hartford-connecticut.

Taylor, John M. "Connecticut Witch Trials: The Witchcraft Delusion in Colonial Connecticut (1647–1697)." *Turn the Hearts* (blog). Accessed 8/14/2016. http://larkturnthehearts.blogspot.com/2010/02/conneticut-witch-trials.html.

Tuller, Roberta. "Mary Town Estey." An American Family History. 2017. www.anamericanfamilyhistory.com/Towne%20Family/TowneMaryEstey.html.

———. "Rebecca Towne Nurse." An American Family History. Accessed 8/27/2016. www.anamericanfamilyhistory.com/Towne%20Family/TowneRebeccaNurse.html.

We Relate. "Wealthian Loring." Accessed 8/12/2016. www.werelate.org/wiki/Person:Welthian_Loring_(2).

Wikipedia. "Mary (Bliss) Parsons." Accessed 7/18/2016. https://en.wikipedia.org/wiki/Mary_(Bliss)_Parsons.

WikiTree. "Mary (Reeve) Webster (abt. 1624–1698)." Accessed 7/18/2016. www.wikitree.com/wiki/Reeve-483.

———. "Rebecca (Steele) Greensmith (1629–aft.1662)." Accessed 8/14/2016. www.wikitree.com/wiki/Steele-1811.

Ziegler, Bethany. "Honoring the Accused: Lineage Society Honors Ancestors Tried for Witchcraft." *The Star Democrat*. October 27, 2013. www.stardem.com/life/article_d11cf5a8-4f88-54ac-be54-a880c6e6c67d.html.

WITCHCRAFT NEVER DIED

The following are sources for the material included in Peter Muise's introduction to the "Modern Witches of New England" chapter. Brackets at the end of the source indicate the subject matter in the essay that the source applies to.

Bayliss, Clara Kern. "Witchcraft." *The Journal of American Folklore* 21, no. 82 (Oct.–Dec. 1908). [Nineteenth-century belief in magic and witchcraft]

Bergen, Fanny. "Some Bits of Plant-Lore." *The Journal of American Folklore* 5, no. 16 (Jan.–Mar. 1892). [Nineteenth-century belief in magic and witchcraft]

Citro, Joseph. *Weird New England*. New York: Sterling Publishing, 2005. [Mary Nasson's ghost]

Cothren, William. *History of Ancient Woodbury, Connecticut: From the First Indian Deed in 1659 to 1854*. Vol. 2. Waterbury, Conn.: Bronson Brothers, 1872. [Moll Cramer's ghost]

Crow, Lorien. "The Witch of Woodbury." One New England. October 13, 2011. www.onenewengland.com/article.php?id=406. [Moll Cramer's ghost]

Currier, John McNab. "Contributions to New England Folklore." *The Journal of American Folklore* 2, no. 7 (Oct.–Dec. 1889). [Nineteenth-century belief in magic and witchcraft]

———. "Contributions to New England Folklore." *The Journal of American Folklore* 4, no. 14 (Jul.–Sep. 1891). [Nineteenth-century belief in magic and witchcraft]

Davies, Owen. *America Bewitched: The Story of Witchcraft after Salem*. Oxford: Oxford University Press, 2013. [Elizabeth Estes Slander case and Salem's christian science trial]

De Camp, L. Sprague. *Lovecraft: A Biography*. London: New English Library, 1975. [A. O. Spare, S. Jackson, and H. P. Lovecraft]

Dorson, Richard. *Jonathan Draws the Long Bow*. Cambridge, Mass.: Harvard University Press, 1946. [Simeon Smith]

Emery, George Alexander. *Ancient City of Gorgeana and Modern Town of York (Maine): From Its Earliest Settlement to the Present Time; Also Its Beaches and Summer Resorts*. Boston: Boston Stereotype Foundry, 1894. [Mary Nasson's ghost]

Franklin, Ruth. *Shirley Jackson: A Rather Haunted Life*. New York: Liveright Publishing, 2016. [A. O. Spare, S. Jackson, and H. P. Lovecraft]

Godbeer, Richard. *The Devil's Dominion: Magic and Religion in Early New England*. New York: Cambridge University Press, 1992. [Puritan folk magic and defensive magic]

Grant, Kenneth. *The Magical Revival*. London: Muller, 1972. [A. O. Spare, S. Jackson, and H. P. Lovecraft]

Kenyon, Theda. "Witches Still Live." *The North American Review* 228, no. 5 (Nov. 1929): 620–26. [Twentieth-century Witchcraft]

Muise, Peter. *Legends and Lore of the North Shore*. Charleston, S.C.: History Press, 2014. [Giles Corey's ghost; Elizabeth Estes Slander case and Salem's christian science trial; and Dogtown Witches, Edward Dimond, and Moll Pitcher]

Philips, David E. *Legendary Connecticut*. Hartford, Conn.: Spoonwood Press, 1984. [Hannah Cranna's funeral]

Plummer, George. *History of Wentworth*. Concord, N.H.: Rumford Press, 1930. [Simeon Smith]

Quinn, D. Michael. *Early Mormonism and the Magic World View*. Salt Lake City, Utah: Signature Books, 1998. [Magic among the Puritan elite]

Simmons, William S. *Spirit of the New England Tribes: Indian History and Folklore.* Hanover, N.H.: University Press of New England, 1986. [Native American shamanism]

Simpson, Dorothy. *The Maine Islands in Story and Legend.* Philadelphia: Lippincott, 1960. [Judith Howard's funeral]

Skinner, Charles. *Myths and Legends of Our Own Land.* Philadelphia: Lippincott, 1896. [Aunt Rachel's curse]

Speare, Eva A. *New Hampshire Folk Tales.* Plymouth, N.H.: New Hampshire Federation of Women's Clubs, 1932. [Twentieth-century Witchcraft]

Wikipedia. "Laurie Cabot." https://en.wikipedia.org/wiki/Laurie_Cabot. [Laurie Cabot]

Woodward, Walter W. *Prospero's America: John Winthrop, Jr., Alchemy, and the Creation of New England Culture, 1606–1676.* Chapel Hill, N.C.: University of North Carolina Press, 2013. [Magic among the Puritan elite]

FURTHER READING ON WITCHES
AND WITCHCRAFT

Here are a few titles that have been recommended by practicing Witches. These volumes will give you a good overview of what Witches believe, the obstacles they face in the modern world, and how they practice day to day.

Eilers, Dana. *Pagans and the Law: Understand Your Rights.* Franklin Lakes, N.J.: New Page Books, the Career Press, 2009.

Farrar, Stewart. *What Witches Do: A Modern Coven Revealed.* London: Robert Hale, 2010.

Hopman, Ellen Evert. *Being a Pagan: Druids, Wiccans, and Witches Today.* Rochester, Vt.: Destiny Books, 2001.

Huson, Paul. *Mastering Witchcraft: A Practical Guide for Witches, Warlocks and Covens.* New York: Perigee Trade, 1980.

Hutton, Ronald. *The Triumph of the Moon: A History of Modern Pagan Witchcraft.* New York: Oxford University, 2001.

Leland, Charles. *Aradia: The Gospel of the Witches.* Blaine, Wash.: Phoenix Publishing, 1990.

Roderick, Timothy. *Wicca: A Year and a Day, 366 Days of Spiritual Practice in the Craft of the Wise.* Woodbury, Minn.: Llewellyn Publications, 2005.
Valiente, Doreen. *Where Witchcraft Lives,* 4th ed. Brighton, U.K.: Centre for Pagan Studies Ltd, 2014.

PUBLIC RESOURCES FOR FURTHER EDUCATION ABOUT WITCHES, PAGANS, DRUIDS, AND HEATHENS IN NEW ENGLAND

I cannot personally vouch for all of these groups, so as always, buyer beware. Please note: this is not an exhaustive list of all New England groups. For a more comprehensive list of public groups and services, please see www.witchvox.com.

Connecticut

Mithras Oasis O.T.O., www.mithras-oto.org
Society of Witchcraft and Old Magick, www.societyofwitchcraft.com
Temple of Witchcraft, templeofwitchcraft.org/CT
Twilight Fire Circle, ww.twilightfirecircle.org

Maine

Forest Sanctuary, www.forestsanctuarymaine.org
Maine Pagan Clergy Association, www.mainepaganclergy.org
Temple of the Feminine Divine, www.templeofthefemininedivine.org

Massachusetts

Central Mass Wiccan Meetup, wiccan.meetup.com/169/?a=mu_wuh8wxiyia
Chthonioi-Alexandrian Tradition, www.chthonioi.org
Church of Ildanach, www.churchofildanach.org
Circle of the Silver Willow, www.thesilverwillow.com
Cornucopia Collective, cornucopiacollective.com
Druid Tribe of the Oak, www.tribeoftheoak.com
EarthSpirit Community, www.earthspirit.com
Heathen/Asatru Jardarmen Kindred, www.jardarmenkindred.com

Phoenix Song, http://gleewood.org/phoenixsong

Radical Fairies (Boston), http://groups.yahoo.com/group/BostonRadicalFaeries

Rowanberry Coven, http://rowanberry.org

Shaman Circle of Cape Cod, http://spiritwalkministry.com/shaman_circle

Society of Elder Faiths, www.elderfaiths.org

Starlight Coven, http://starlightcoven.org

Temenos Stemmaphaede, www.minoan-brotherhood.org

Temple of Sophia, www.templeofsophia.com

New Hampshire

Concord UU Earth-Centered Spirituality Group, http://concorduu.org
/worship/ecsg

Foundation Wicca, www.foundationwicca.org

Frithstead Anglo-Saxon Heathen Fellowship, www.frithsteadfellowship.org

Granite State Heathen Meetup, www.meetup.com/Granite-State-Heathens

Nine Roses Coven New England, http://9rosesne.wix.com/ninerosescoven

Pagan in Recovery, www.thepaganinrecovery.com

Per Weben Benu: House of Phoenix Rising, www.perwebenbenu.org

Temple of Witchcraft, www.templeofwitchcraft.org

White Winds, www.witchvox.com/vn/vn_detail/dt_gr.html?a=usnh&id=40535

Rhode Island

Coven of Astraeos, http://astraeos.weebly.com

Horn and Cauldron, Church of the Earth, www.hornandcauldron.com

Key, Candle & Crossroads, Church of the Earth, www.keycandleandcrossroads
.com

Kunisu Grove, http://kunisu.org

New England Covens of Traditionalist Witches, www.nectw.org/Providence
Coven, http://providencecoven.org

Society of the Evening Star, www.sotes.org

Spiral Tree Grove, Church of the Earth, www.spiraltreegrove.com

The Witches' Almanac, thewitchesalmanac.com

Vermont

Laurelin Retreat, www.laurelinretreat.com

Pagan Alliance Church, www.paganalliancechurch.org

Vermont Witchcamp, www.vermontwitchcamp.net

Index